Practical DV Filmmaking

Practical DV Filmmaking
A step-by-step guide for beginners

Russell Evans

Focal Press

OXFORD AMSTERDAM BOSTON LONDON NEW YORK PARIS
SAN DIEGO SAN FRANCISCO SINGAPORE SYDNEY TOKYO

Focal Press
An imprint of Elsevier Science
Linacre House, Jordan Hill, Oxford OX2 8DP
225 Wildwood Avenue, Woburn, MA 01801–2041

First published 2002

British Library Cataloguing in Publication Data
Evans, Russell
   Practical DV filmmaking: a step-by-step guide for
   beginners
   1. Digital video – Amateurs' manuals
   I. Title
   778.5'9'0285

Library of Congress Cataloguing in Publication Data
A catalogue record for this book is available from the Library of Congress

ISBN 0 240 51657 5

For information on all Focal Press publications visit our website at:
www.focalpress.com

Composition by Genesis Typesetting, Rochester, Kent
Printed and bound in Great Britain

Contents

Preface

This book promises a lot. But it only does so because, apart from your camcorder, you probably already have the most important tools to put into action what it asks: imagination, commitment and the need to think for yourself.

This book has been designed to give you a complete introduction to filmmaking. To achieve this, we don't look at just the technical stuff. Technical knowledge is crucial and we will look in detail at all the skills you need to know about, but if we left it there the book would only be half useful. We are going to go further by taking the steps you can follow to become a filmmaker, as opposed to a filmmaker's assistant; someone who comes up with ideas and puts them into action rather than someone who puts other people's ideas into action.

Throughout the book, there are projects which take you through the exploration of different kinds of films and lead you to find out what sort of filmmaker you are. Any book that doesn't talk about filmmaking *art* as well as *process* is keeping something from you. It's like giving you matches and sticks but not telling you how to light a fire. So, we have matches and we have sticks – technical ins and outs – but we have the hot stuff too: the means of helping you advance towards becoming an individual and original filmmaker.

There are 14 projects throughout the book, each one covering different aspects of the filmmaking process and each one developing different skills. Ideally, you will go through all of them, but feel free to try the projects in any order. The projects at the start are relatively straightforward, dealing with individual skills, while those towards the end of the book ask you to start juggling different skills in one film. But as you go through the book, each chapter covers the information you need and helps signpost the way towards completing the project successfully.

The main text has lots of diversions. These are designed to let you decide how deeply you go into each area. Additional detailed information is sometimes given, or you may be told about a film that may help clarify a point. Or you might be directed to another part of the book to get more help with a particular point. In order to keep you right up-to-date with news relating to each topic, relevant websites are given on most pages, or you can check into the site relating specifically to this book. The aim of all these side-routes is to let you take the book any way you want: skim over the surface and investigate several projects on a need-to-know basis, or go further, getting more technical or artistic information about a topic. At the end of each chapter, a summary has been compiled which offers a 'crunched-down' version of the main points in the chapter. If you want to be reminded of what a particular chapter covers, or want to check it out before going further, look at 'The Crunch'.

Towards the end of the book is a section on understanding films. This section helps to put your own activity as a filmmaker into some context so that you become aware of the kinds of questions levelled at filmmakers today and build opinions on today's main questions and debates.

The accompanying CD-ROM contains software to help get you started in DV editing and further information connected with parts of this book, including stuff we had to take out to keep the book reasonably portable.

Don't let anyone tell you that filmmaking is just for the few. There really is no mystery to the process, no secret language spoken by those in the know. There are skills to learn and certain ways of working that will get you where you want to go quicker, but you can do it yourself. It is true that some types of film will present more obstacles than others and can be more time-consuming, and it's also true that you need to work harder than you ever thought to get the sort of film you imagined. But the main thought to keep in mind, repeated like a mantra, is 'there is no reason why I can't do this'.

Acknowledgements

This book would not have been possible without help from lots of people. Many thanks are due to Jenny Welham and Christina Donaldson at Focal Press, who have been ever-patient, committed and encouraging. Thanks also to Nick Wright for many helpful suggestions; to Jess Search at Shooting People for useful contacts; to Piotr Skopiak for lending stills and background material; and to Kate Stanworth at the BFI for picture research. Thanks also to Kate Gower-Smith for suggestions and encouragement.

Many filmmakers added comments and/or film stills: thanks to Amber Mosdell, Sarah Norman, Sid Goto of RESFEST, Debra Watson, Kevin Lapper, Mark Innocenti, Lydio Wysocki, Paul Cowling, Carlo Ortu, Emily Corcoran, Jon Price, Ed Spencer, Hannah Chamberlain, James Kendall and Vera Herchenbach.

But particular thanks go to Wendy Klein for relentless support, contributions and inspiration, and to Esme and Zoe for diversions.

1 An overview of filmmaking

1. Think big

'Four years ago, if you had a video and you wanted people to see it, you had to invite them all over to your house for a beer. With the web, it's possible to produce a movie with almost no budget and get a million people to watch it.'

David Trescot, group product manager at Adobe, giving his view about the ease with which you can now go out and make movies.

There is no doubt that with a camcorder and an Internet connection you have one of the most powerful tools for communicating. If you have the energy and the will you can shoot a short movie on any subject, in your own unique style, show it to a global audience, and promote and advertise it yourself. This doesn't mean setting up street-corner makeshift cinemas or photocopied posters glued on the walls around town. With what is now called desktop editing, you are more in control of the filmmaking process than any previous generation, and furthermore have less need for the established industry than ever before. Changes to the film industry as entertainment and as an art form are here to stay and simply by possessing an Internet connection, a camcorder and basic edit software you are a part of it.

Interview

'I think technology has always been relative, you know. I think yeah, there's a hell of a lot more you can do technically now than you could ever do before. It's never been cheaper to make a movie and get more people to see your film than ever before. You can get a digital camera for a couple of thousand dollars and your own desktop editing system for a couple of grand, and you're making movies.'

Dan Myrick, co-director, The Blair Witch Project

Since those comments the price of both shooting and editing equipment has more than halved, twice.

This is a great opportunity but you may now be getting a sense of the problem that goes with it. Although inspiring, for many this is daunting. As the spotlight moves your way the need to have developed yourself as a filmmaker is profound; you need to find out what kind of films you make, how to come up with ideas good enough to film and how to get the knowledge that makes other people take you seriously. Your only obligation is to stand out from the crowd, do your own thing, don't emulate what everyone else is doing when the whole world starts making movies. Take advantage of this moment and start getting to know what it is that a movie by you looks like.

This isn't a new phenomenon, even if the technology is in its infancy. Some of the finest directors have started their careers making films on no budgets, with no help from big studios. David Lynch made the classic film, *Eraserhead* (1976), at weekends over a number of years while holding down a day job; within 5 years of its release he was being offered the chance to direct *Return of the Jedi*. George Romero made his seminal zombie film *Night of the Living Dead* (1969) with almost no funds, relying on the commitment of friends willing to be part-time zombies, but without being paid. Robert Rodriguez went from making a film with a borrowed camera – *El Mariachi* (1992) – to making hit films such as *From Dusk Till Dawn* (1995) and *Spy Kids* (2001).

The difference for today's filmmakers is that you can go further. Not only can you get hold of good cameras capable of broadcast quality images, but you can edit these films at home without having to endure the budget-crippling prices of the rent-by-the-hour edit unit. When it's finished you can show it on one of the many web cinemas, short film festivals or TV access slots. The potential is there to place your short movies in millions of homes around the world.

Digital video has affected the independent, low-budget filmmaker more than any other part of the film industry. These self-financing, ever-resourceful people would make movies whatever it cost them and however long it takes. But it is now a realistic aim to say that you want to make movies and do so without mortgaging your soul. All you need is a camcorder, a computer, a limitless imagination and the desire to tell it your way.

2. The filmmaking process

To begin with, it would be useful to get to grips with the process of making a film as a whole. What actually do these people do? Why does it take so long between thinking of the film and getting down to shooting it?

The whole project starts life as an idea, in your imagination. You may have a story you wish to tell, or a theme you want to work with. Whatever it is, it starts in darkness, probably a collection of images you see appearing in the film, played out in no real order in your mind's eye. Most directors favour getting as much material on paper as you can at this stage to establish the detail of an idea. Others suggest more idiosyncratic approaches. Robert Rodriguez recommends you 'stare at a blank projection screen. See your film, watch it from start to finish.' Whatever your initial idea, it is crucial to get to know it at this early stage as clearly as possible, even though you have only a broad outline of the project in mind you do have the initial spark: the images, atmosphere or look of the film. It is this that you should try to pin down and keep as it will become the main creative thrust of the project, seeing you through the obstacles and possible wrong turns to come.

Did you know?
Robert Rodriguez famously delivered a lecture on how to become a filmmaker at London's National Film School in 1996 in just 10 minutes.

Stage 1: Planning

The first stage of making a movie is centred on getting the film developed as much as possible before you start shooting. Substantial changes during shooting are expensive and disrupt continuity, or worse can result in a discordant and messy film. Good planning means that when you get to start shooting you go through a smoother process than without. You will encounter surprises and have to make changes here and there, but planning means you encounter more of the right sort of surprises and know how to solve the less welcome ones. The aim is to let your ideas grow and develop to a point at which you know every aspect of the project better than anyone else. You know the relative significance of each part of the story, the kinds of motifs and ideas that are running through it, and the kind of atmosphere that is to dominate. In a sense, when you commit your ideas to paper you are taking them out of the comforting darkness of the imagination, where you don't notice the loose ends and rough structure of a film, and exposing them to light. Some aspects of your ideas survive, some don't, but it is better that the project changes now than later. Work on paper is cheap; work on film is expensive, what with crew, food for everyone, lights, power and so on. An hour of scriptwriting can equal a day of shooting and a week of editing.

Visual blueprints

In planning your film you will make detailed written and visual blueprints of how the film will look and sound from the first to the last moment. Step 1 involves a written outline in the form of a short story. Even if your film does not rely on plot at all you need to basically and simply write down all the scenes that you envisage in the order that you think they may occur. Getting to that stage may involve noting down all the elements of the film and producing several different versions of an outline. This rough draft we can call a treatment. Following that you will produce a range of material which will trace the steps you take as you develop and grow the film.

Early visualizations

If you have ever found yourself doodling with a pen and paper then you will have some idea of what this stage of work involves. To some people what you draw when doodling is a true reflection of the natural inclinations of your mind; some people draw closed-in little boxes, tightly stuck together, others draw blossoming spirals or crystal-like structures. It doesn't take a certificate in psychology to work out the meanings of the things we find ourselves drawing; what you are doing is reflecting the current inner architecture of your thoughts, not the thoughts themselves as such but the shape they take. Whatever your doodles look like – dark and angular, bold and bright – these can be viewed as potential design notes for a film. Of course, this is only relevant if you are determined to find and display your own personal world view, as opposed to following the needs of a client or audience focus group.

In a practical sense, what you are doing when drawing visualizations is a long set of small sketches, perhaps each the size of a cigarette packet. Each one is a quick outline of a possible scene from the film. These are drawn in no particular order, but the order you draw them does say something about the relative importance of each to you. Each sketch should be quick and uncomplicated, showing the main elements in the shot and hinting at the kind of light in the frame. The aim is not to correct them or judge them in any way until you've gone through the whole exercise, with as many frames as possible on paper. Following this, you can then start to group your sketches together and compare the overall style of each frame.

Storyboard

The storyboard is used to explain the detail of the visual side of the film to a crew and allow those people working on a film to plan props, camera lenses and work schedules effectively. Working on a low budget with just yourself and a few friends does not excuse you from this process; it offers a chance to refine both the look and structure of your film and pare it down, stripping it of elements that divert from the idea, making it a project which fulfils the specific aims you had in mind right at the start.

In preparing a storyboard, you will draw frames on one vertical column of the paper with corresponding dialogue, notes or sound written next to it. This document is the most detailed visual and written description of the whole film, the single blueprint which you try to stick to throughout the shooting process. Although storyboarding was rigidly adhered to by directors such as Alfred Hitchcock, for the most part it is simply the most accurate plan you have at this point, ready to be challenged and altered during filming.

Script

In films where you have a story, a script is going to be the only way to prepare it and iron out the inconsistencies. Even in films where there are no speaking roles you may find it useful to prepare a script showing only directors notes, as it gives yet another opportunity to hone your idea, add to it or subtract.

The importance of each stage of planning is relative to the sort of film you are making. Abstract, theme-based movies will demand more consideration of visual aspects while character studies with intense dialogue will need more attention paid to the script. All films, however, need to go through the learning curve of planning and emerge fully formed before a camera starts showing up the faults. Know your film.

Did you know?
An abstract movie is not something you usually see in the multiplex. It's got more in common with music video than feature films in that it is based on a theme and has sequences that develop this throughout the film.

Stage 2: Shooting

Shooting is, to some, a time where the film takes on a whole life of its own, to others a simple regurgitation of a paper storyboard. In practical terms, it seems simple enough: plan out a series of shots, go and shoot them just like it shows here on paper, tick off the scenes one by one and go home. In an ideal situation this is more or less what happens, but since it is an art form it is natural to assume that the creative process continues throughout the project, through planning, shooting and editing (even through to marketing, but more of that in Chapter 8). So, you should expect to encounter obstacles and temptations along the way. Obstacles in the form of challenges to your plans, temptations in the sense of other, seemingly better, ideas that come up possibly deviating from the original one. Great planning for a film is about giving you confidence from knowing your idea inside out, giving you the commitment to get round problems and the confidence to know the good from the bad when new ideas come up.

Another important point to realize about filming is how nothing ever works out the way you imagine it will. Every good filmmaker needs to have plan B available constantly, followed by C, D, E and so on. When working on a low budget this is more likely in that you have to rely more on goodwill, people helping you out, lending you equipment. But you also find that a shot that looks perfect on paper just isn't possible for real. You may want the bank to be seen from the telephone box and it may be really crucial for the scene, but when you get there it becomes obvious that that tree in full leaf is going to get in the way. The answer is improvisation: the ability to think fast and clearly on set so that you stay in line with your plans, coming up with ideas that can solve a problem. If you don't do this, your crew and actors will quickly realize there is a power vacuum and start arguing about the best way forward. So, plan to improvise.

Stage 3: Editing

Priorities

In editing a film you will add a further layer of development to the whole creative act as your footage – all those tapes accrued over days or weeks of filming – is cut together in a way which best resembles your plans. Editing brings your film out of the uncertainty that is the initial idea and out of the scramble that is filming. It is about order, priorities, structure, pace, timing, accuracy. Knowing how to place your clips in the right order is perhaps a triumph of instinct over technology and, given the range of technical trickery on offer even in mid-level editing software, knowing when to stop editing is important. If you know what you want you are less likely to get side-tracked by the powerful influence of all that wonderful technology.

Skills you need

When you look back over the process of making your first production, you may find that the skills you thought were essential to filmmaking – those centring on the technical aspects of the medium – were secondary to the more esoteric. Some filmmakers talk about the ability to remain both in control and open to new ideas; to negotiate your way through problems; to see all aspects of the process, however mundane, as having some creative contribution to the project, that nothing is purely technical; to think of a low budget as less a hindrance to realizing your imagination than a way towards doing so more artfully, more ingeniously.

The Crunch

- Know what it is you want to make clearly.
- Planning the film will save you time and money later.
- Enjoy surprises.
- Handle the pressure – it's worth it to have your name at the end of the film.
- Improvise to get you out of trouble.
- Be prepared, your footage will always disappoint you straight after filming because you are tired and it's late and you just want to go home.
- Postpone any rash decisions made after viewing your rushes – footage improves with time.
- Look forward to editing – you are in charge again.

3. Low-budget filmmaking

Big money vs small money

In industry terms, there is a specific level below which you are considered to be a low-budget production. A standard budget in Hollywood terms can be somewhere in the region of £25 million to £30 million; low budget is seen as anything operating on less than £6 million. But these figures are losing their relevance now that digital video (DV) has brought the general cost of shooting and editing a movie down to something most people can afford. Consider, for instance, a book recently quite popular with aspiring filmmakers which stated that you could make a movie for under $10 000 (about £6000). Once, this would have seemed like a tall order, but with broadcast quality cameras now well within the mid-range of the domestic market, and edit software, at a basic level, downloadable for free on the Internet, the picture has changed. A more likely heading now could be something like 'make a movie for under $1000'. Or, more attractive still, make a short film and show it on the web, all for under $100. Expressed like this, it's easy to see how the term low-budget filmmaker has had to be re-evaluated.

Cheaper movies

Increasingly, as the cost of filmmaking goes down, more and more directors will find that they, by default, are low-budget people. The medium-budget movies of yesterday are today's low budget. But while medium-sized productions will see their money go further than before, many will simply aim higher, trying previously expensive genres like science fiction and period costume drama. At the lower end of the scale, the effect is more dramatic, opening the door for many more filmmakers to get their work seen.

Micro-budget: even smaller

Below even this there has now emerged the so-called micro-budget filmmaker and the no-budget filmmaker, though it has to be said that the latter has been part of the landscape of the industry since movies began. The micro-budget filmmaker is operating without outside funding, relying on private income or small state grants, loans, and the investment of friends and relatives.

On the positive side, however, they have no floor to their budgets, almost no absolute minimum amount of money needed to begin a movie. A film shot on DV and edited at home on a PC will have costs primarily in front of the camera, in the form of props, actors, locations and so on. The traditionally high cost of filmmaking has usually been based on behind-the-camera items such as film stock, expensive cameras and edit units. You can wipe away other parts of the standard film budget if you write, direct and produce the film yourself, deferring your fee until, or if, someone buys the film and you make a profit.

Low budget means 'different'

For many people working in the micro- and low/no-budget sector, these categories represent more than a total on a budget sheet. They mark a film as being innovative, different, challenging the system. Low/no budget means you are prepared to make a movie with a different sort of commitment to those people getting percentage points from a blockbuster. It means you are prepared to put in unpaid time, your own money, and rely on networking and dealing within the filmmaking community to get your film made.

Interview
'I think that is the beauty of a lower budget and these kind of formats that you really can do something different and tell your own story in a different way. You can experiment where you can't on a bigger budget. In a way, I was doing that on "*Slacker*" 10 years ago, narratively speaking. I think that's why that caught on, because it was sort of its own animal. It wasn't a genre film trying to get bought into Hollywood; it just sort of existed on its own terms. I think people admire that because it didn't seem like it was trying to be anything. It wasn't a calling card to Hollywood.'

Richard Linklater, director of the influential Slacker (1991)

DV technology

In terms of technology, too, you are challenging the industry. For those determined to make a film but without funds, the appeal of DV is now widespread. Among cinematographers, digital video is not believed to have the same quality as celluloid film and there is a conviction that it cannot match the subtlety of celluloid in terms of the way it records light. But manufacturers are continually pushing these distinctions, producing DV cameras which challenge the viewer to tell the difference between the two methods.

> **Tip**   If you want the effect of using celluloid film while still using video, you can try a plug-in which changes the movie once you have edited it. These basically roughen the appearance of the movie and imitate the colours and light you see in film. But filmmakers debate whether they benefit the movie or just downgrade its picture quality. Try CineLook, available from www.polar-graphics.com.

New techniques of transferring tape to 35 mm film for projection have convinced filmmakers that they are not precluding the possibility of selling a film to a distributor by using digital, as was the case. With many new cinemas converting to digital projection, using digital copies of films or showing movies beamed digitally by satellite, the door is opening for DV filmmakers to get their work seen in theatres. This is being fostered both by the low- and high-budget sectors: Pixar and Disney favour digital projection for their CGI animated movies, while at the other end of the scale the influential Dogme group of filmmakers, who advocate an effects-free, naturalistic method of filmmaking, have produced the first film shot on DV – Thomas Vinterberg's *Festen* – and saw it go on to win coveted prizes at the Cannes and Berlin Film Festivals. These events help to remove the stigma of digital as being a format not suitable for the serious filmmaker, as a mere stepping stone to using celluloid. An even more significant blow in favour of digital has been the proliferation of the online cinema and preference of these sites for digital movies.

Short films

Another major change to the low- and micro-budget sector is the re-emergence of the short film. In the UK, since the abolition of a levy which supported short films and enabled them to be seen at cinemas, the short film has been without a home. Although the short film has always enjoyed a place at the heart of the independent movement, it has always been seen as the filmmaker's introduction to a career, the on-the-job film school where you move quickly from one short project to the next, picking up skills and knowledge along the way. Due to the way the industry is structured, geared in favour of feature films by theatres and distributors, it has always had to accept that it is a form held in low esteem by those at the top. The Internet is quickly changing this view, as successful filmmakers including David Lynch, Bernardo Bertolucci and Spike Jonze submit short films for Internet broadcasting. On the negative side, online cinemas have found that lack of high bandwith restricts the length of movies on the web; someone downloading a movie doesn't expect to sit for 30 minutes before it can be viewed. They want the movie now and the only way online cinemas can deliver is by squeezing the film right down and keeping films around 5 minutes in length, or less. By default, the short film has become the film of choice for the Internet viewer, but due to the relatively slow pace of the hardware that connects the Internet, in reality it's the only kind available. And a short is a cheap film, thereby favouring those at the bottom of the budgetary scale.

Did you know?
Bandwidth refers to the speed at which data can be sent across the Internet. High bandwidth is good for filmmakers and film sites, but is much more expensive for the user as it involves a certain level of connection and speed of modem.

Go to: See Chapter 7:2 for more details about how movie data are reduced, known as video compression.

Television

Television has proved to be a good proving ground for new directors to get short, self-financed films seen. Although at odds with the high production values demanded by television, low-budget shorts fulfil an important role for the programmer: they are short (easy to programme), they reflect new trends, they tend to be sharp and provocative. They are like the movie versions of garage bands – rough but remarkable. Most national broadcasters offer access slots for new filmmakers to air their films, allowing the untried and untested to find an audience and sink or float. Such slots, like Channel Four's *Shooting Gallery*, have helped many people move on to bigger productions, sometimes providing completion costs (covering post-production work) for their submitted film. With cinemas rarely showing new short films, television is becoming one of the main benefactors of the aspiring filmmaker.

So what?

What does all this mean for the small, aspiring filmmaker? Low- and micro-budget is no longer a place to escape from, but the place where opportunities exist on a greater scale than before. It is not without obstacles and struggle, and to this extent is just like it always was and there are no greater financial rewards than there were. But this sector is perhaps less dependent than ever before on those higher up in the industry. The tools of filmmaking are accessible even without large budgets and filmmakers can increasingly bypass the distribution machine that keeps so many films out of view.

The net effect of this is that the filmmaker with radical ideas, who wants to try new ways of telling a story, or of showing us the world, or simply wants to place before us issues that those at the top would rather ignore – these people have a greater chance than ever to take their ideas directly to the audience. In such a profit-driven industry as filmmaking, this is dangerous territory as it threatens to let new trends float straight to the surface without first being intercepted (and marketed) by the middlemen (studio bosses, film distributors, television programmers). But what is easily forgotten is that the history of cinema tells us that radical ideas are what it needs to thrive, that independent directors – independent in means and spirit – enable filmmaking to grow and evolve. Join that club.

The Crunch

- You have a valuable skill: the ability to make cheap films.
- DV technology is helping low-budget filmmakers more than anyone else.
- Break down the gates: do something new, make films your way.

2 | Choosing what to make

1. Forms and genres

The aim of these sections is to start thinking about what will characterize your films. What are your preferences? Do you want to make films with straight stories, or are non-narrative films going to inspire you more? Does the music video allow you to be more imaginative than, say, a drama? And how can you get underneath other filmmakers' work to see what motivates their films.

Part of your task is to move as quickly as you can towards a position where you know what is out there and how you fit into it – or perhaps how you break into it. Understanding what other people make does not restrict you to emulating them; it allows you to get to grips with the territory called film you are entering and to assess whether you want, metaphorically, to borrow someone else's house on that territory or build your own. Better still, take apart what you see and build your own according to your needs, avoiding their mistakes.

To begin with we will take a look at the kinds of work being done with film and video today.

More than just movies

Over the last 20 years, the use of the moving image has grown beyond the traditional feature film, beyond genre movies. Now, video is everywhere, breaking out of conventional cinema and television and giving rise to many other ways of using the medium. Broadcast media, in particular satellite television, have helped foster these new forms as they provide a contemporary and dynamic edge to a station. MTV, for example, uses slots between its programmes consisting of unusual and experimental animations and micro-shorts. Usually non-narrative, this use of video is exciting for new filmmakers, who see it as a chance to develop new ideas and get them seen by a wide audience.

> **Did you know?**
> Genre refers to a type of movie, such as the thriller, the western or the war movie. Movies within a certain genre tend to have similar characteristics, such as style, structure, story and so on. Sub-genres exist within these, such as the prison camp escape sub-genre, part of the war movie genre.

Narrative film

A narrative movie uses a story as its main motivation. Since the birth of cinema, narrative has been the driving force of the film industry, to the extent that other forms are described by how much or how little they address narrative. It evolved largely from the dominance of literary media in culture and borrows hugely from literature in the way stories are told, even down to the use of cutaways in editing. But as a primarily visual medium, film has other possibilities and many filmmakers have tempered the dominance of plot and increased the use of visual signs and symbols to develop the themes and meanings of a film, including some of the great directors, such as Stanley Kubrick and Andrei Tarkovsky.

Figure 2.1 *Clear Conscience* (2000) by Shane Jones, a narrative movie detailing a burglary.

Within narrative film, there have arisen many conventions about how you tell a story. Largely due to the need to agree a common code with the viewing public which can be applied to each and every film, there are certain ways of shooting and editing which will disguise the actual process of filmmaking and draw attention only to the plot and the characters within it. Thus, film becomes a true escapist experience.

If you work with stories now, however, you need to possess some detailed knowledge of these conventions, as if they are a set of signs which an increasingly knowing audience are going to decipher. This means that you can subvert conventions and can mix signs from different forms (for instance, by including parts of other genres, as in Tarantino's *Pulp Fiction*), but all the time you have to be aware of where you stand within the wider framework of narrative film. Audiences develop their awareness of these signs in narrative film simply by seeing lots of films, so as a filmmaker you are equally able to read the signs and make up your own.

Go to: Chapter 4:4 for more details about conventions of scriptwriting. Also, look at Chapter 9:2 for an outline of how filmmakers subvert these rules and give us a new take on narrative film.

Narrative film may be the established dominant mode, but entering this area doesn't mean you have to follow film trends, making cliché-ridden films that only emulate other directors. Certainly, this may be true within the profit-driven industry of Hollywood, but there are numerous directors who follow their own path by turning narrative into something that is their own.

The short movie

Short movies (average 10 minutes in length or less) are the filmmaker's school. Almost all filmmakers have made several before going on to make successful features, the shorts serving as a place to try out ideas, road-test stories, and develop style and exercise conventions. The quick pace of short movie production also helps build confidence, as you can make one with very few resources or time. For many years the short was on the fringes of cinema, but video has brought about a resurgence, lowering production costs to just tens or hundreds of pounds. But there has also been an increase in the outlets for showing this kind of movie. Many television stations, mostly cable or satellite, offer slots for unknown filmmakers to show short films, helping them to advance towards other, larger productions. Film festivals now exist especially for short movies, while almost all the larger ones represent shorts at particular slots. It's not as easy a medium to work within as it appears; it requires a keen sense of the essentials of storytelling in a dense and compressed way, without any superfluous areas. But it remains a vital starting point for a filmmaker's career.[1]

The micro-short

This development of the narrative movie is relatively new, resulting from the need for shorter-than-short movies that download fast over the Internet. The particular constraints of movies lasting less than a minute are invigorating, helping you to develop faster as a filmmaker. The micro-short is mainly seen in websites where you are more likely to get a showing than with standard short movies, although the use of it for filling the gaps in satellite stations is growing. Straight narrative sits as easily as abstract movies in this form, although many narrative versions tend to be more successful because of the startling way they compress conventional storytelling into small spaces. Many of the projects in this book are suited to this format.[2]

[1] www.aussieshortfilms.com.au/   Australian short film agency.
www.atomfilms.com/   Major Internet short film provider.
www.ifilm.com/   Highly rated film provider.
[2] www.in-movies.co.uk/films/search.php   Good venue for online micro-short movies.

Non-fiction

Documentary has a long and honourable tradition of seeking the truth, of dragging it out from under a rock, and to this extent it is an exciting and provocative place for a filmmaker to work. But as the ways of big business and government have become more wily and shrewd, engaging spin and marketing to protect interests, so filmmakers have started to employ new means of cutting through it. What is now called the non-fiction film is as creative and interesting a field as narrative film, and is a fascinating place for the independent filmmaker to start a career. It allows the chance to put together a narrative and employ the tricks you would like to use in narrative film, but without the cost of actors or sets. There is a fine line to tread between non-fiction and semi-fiction, and yet this need to work within a straight, factual form, while mixing it with aspects that make the film more creative, is what makes it such a fruitful training ground.[3]

Figure 2.2 *Manifesto* (2000) by Rachel Creed, Jon Price, Ed Spencer and Jeremy Stephens. This non-fiction movie uses strong lighting as a continuity device to connect interviews from a wide range of people regarding their beliefs.

Film View

Filmmakers such as Errol Morris (*The Thin Blue Line*, 1988), Michael Moore (*Roger and Me*, 1989) and Nick Broomfield (*Kurt and Courtney*, 1999) made radical changes to the documentary form. They redirected the idea of the factual film towards something more like a mix of fact with the kind of dramatic, narrative techniques they saw watching feature films.

[3] www.idfa.nl/ International Documentary Festival, Amsterdam.

Non-narrative

This encompasses a whole range of work where other elements of the film are dominant, rather than plot. Visual meaning is the dominant factor and rather than tell stories, the film develops a theme. There are varying levels of feature film that fall into this category, including the abstract movie and the semi-narrative, in which plot is pushed down the scale of importance in favour of images and signs.

Music video

The idea of a short film which accompanies a piece of music grew out of films such as *A Hard Day's Night* (Richard Lester, 1964). This form has always been a primarily commercial one, as it is explicitly linked to the promotion of an artist for increased sales. But as with the advertising commercial, the number of film directors who have found this form a place to define and develop their approach and style indicates that it offers a lot more than it possibly should. Being free of the constraints of telling a story is very liberating. Its educative value is in the way it forces the director to focus on visual aspects of the film, on how the camera moves or is placed, how colours and imagery can affect the film, how symbols can convey ideas. For the aspiring filmmaker, the music video asks you to deal with the medium in a visual way and devise ever new creative and innovative ways of grabbing attention. As we shall see in later chapters, being comfortable with non-narrative film gives your narrative films greater depth of meaning.[4]

Advertising commercial

Similar to the music video, this form is also a training ground for young filmmakers. The fast output of commercials and the need to say as much as possible in the shortest space of time means that the practitioner has to master non-verbal signs and symbols, all of which later help with your more conventional movies, by giving them more references to the wider world and therefore connecting with the audience more fully. As a form to practice with, the commercial asks you to work within a narrow brief, but it is this very constraint which often encourages creativity and the development of new solutions.

Insert/infill

The growth of satellite stations catering for a specifically youth or arts oriented or speciality audience such as MTV has led to the birth of a new form of shorter-than-short movie. Mixed in with music videos or sandwiched between arts programmes, the broadcaster has sought some way of grabbing audiences of decreasing attention span by showing brief programmes, often less than a minute in length. These are stylish, unusual pieces of work, often displaying new ways of combining animation, live action, text or still images and pushing the creative possibilities of the medium to the limit. Meaning and content are less important than the visually arresting or

---

[4] www.mvpa.com/   Organization helping video music producers. Lots of information.

innovative image. While you probably may get frustrated by its limitations after a while, it is a great way of trying out new ideas and expanding your horizons quickly. If you want to make fast progress with investigating the artistic potential of the medium and try an area that has no discernible rules yet, then this is for you.[5]

Multimedia/projections

Many live rock concerts now include large-scale video projections behind the band, utilizing everything that the medium can offer, from shaped projection screens (for example, the 1996 USA tour of Pink Floyd), to multiple, text-layered, spinning screens (such as the Chemical Brothers 1997 tour, Europe). Related to the music video but free from its commercial constraints, these projections are a return to the idea of the moving image as a spectacle, like the earliest short films in the 1890s. The aim is to produce a series of images that can reflect the band's kind of music, fitting in to just about anywhere in the concert and can be looped to play throughout the evening. This form is closest in style to music mixing by dance-club DJs, where several records are selected for a session, with the DJ mixing and layering them to build a certain mood. But instead of sounds, you work with images, developing a theme that reflects the band's persona.[6]

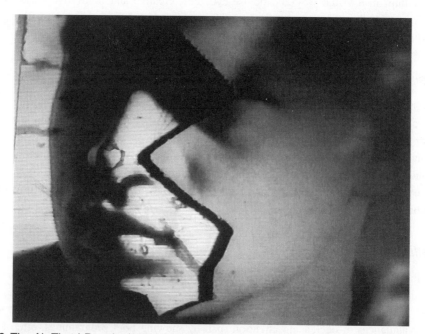

Figure 2.3 *The Air That I Breathe* (2001) by Alayne Latham. An example of video art, this movie uses unusual methods of video layering to achieve a rich and textured look.

[5] www.mtv.com/   Information about MTV.
[6] www.tomato.co.uk/   Excellent group of multimedia artists.

Did you know?
Investigate these further by looking at videos of live concert footage for relevant bands. Try also live concerts by U2, Manic Street Preachers and almost any live club/dance act.

The Crunch

- Get to know what area of filmmaking you prefer. Maybe it's several areas.
- Feature films are just the tip of the film industry iceberg – other types of filmmaking are just as popular and far more achievable.
- Short productions help you develop more quickly
- Try anything once – most forms are going to help you in whatever kind of film you prefer making.
- The more mistakes you make the more you improve. Exercise your right to fail; at least will you do it your way.
- Invent, experiment, imitate, re-invent, do anything.

Project 1. In-camera edit

In this project, we are going to use the camera alone to construct a film, without the need to edit. The purpose is to show in a very short space of time what you can achieve on camera and get through some initial skills fast. Before you can visualize how your ideas will look on the screen, we need to find out how the camera sees the world. It is better to work this out now than when you are starting to shoot a larger production. This project enables you to learn quickly about camera use, taking short steps quickly.

Shoot and edit in-camera

The in-cam edit is a simple idea: it involves shooting each scene of a film, in the order in which they occur. If it goes well, then at the end of shooting you can take out the tape and play it as a finished film. This is the most basic method of making a film, but is an unexpectedly instructive way to learn about filmmaking and in a compressed way it takes you through the whole process of making a film, illustrating how the various elements interact. For example, while shooting this project you quickly realize that every movement of the camera counts, that you have to arrive at decisions fast and that there is little room for mistakes. One of the problems about video as a format is that it discourages decision making by allowing the filmmaker to shoot just about everything and decide later what to use. The in-cam edit film asks that you work in a quick, concise way.

It also introduces a vital concept in a film: the sequencing of shots. This is an idea so central to the whole filmmaking process that it is sometimes ignored. The way in which you decide to order a sequence of scenes and the effect on the rest of the film when you change this order is best experienced for real, rather than as a paper exercise. A film is like an anagram; even changes of just one letter can radically alter the meaning of a word, just as one scene moved elsewhere in a film can alter the whole.

Finally, this method is a great morale booster; it takes you out of the still waters of paper development and into the fast lanes, where you can discover quickly whether your ideas will work as you had intended. It also means that you can use this method for other films; an idea for a movie can be tried on for size before you go ahead and make it for real.

Stage 1: Find an idea

Although this film has a basic kind of narrative, it is simple enough to not lumber you with too much detailed storytelling. As with every project, simpler stories allow you much greater opportunities to focus on the way you are shooting the film, with less information to be conveyed.

As starting ideas, the following are examples of the mini-narratives you could choose:

- Making a cup of coffee.
- Preparing a meal.
- Escaping down a flight of stairs.
- A short journey.

They each involve a direct progression in physical terms from A to B. First, there was no coffee, now there is; first she is at home, now she is at the airport. These ideas may be simple but don't dismiss them just yet. By keeping the story to a minimum they enable you to focus attention on the way you tell the narrative; the fun (the difficulty) comes in how and where you point the camera, what scenes you choose to show and how much you show. The multitude of choices is what makes filming stimulating.

To develop the idea a little more, make a list of the shots you think you will need to convey the action.

Stage 2: Visualizing

Follow the guidelines above about sketching ideas for shots. List the shots you think you would like to shoot down one side of a sheet of paper, and then draw images that could represent these adjacent to them.

Stage 3: Shooting

With an in-cam edit movie, you will take the first scene on your list and shoot it. It may be useful to do a couple of rehearsals if there is action or dialogue. During a rehearsal, remain looking at the scene through the camera; this encourages you to stay on the lookout for new, better ways of shooting it. If the scene goes wrong, just rewind and tape over with a better version, but do so as accurately as you can, hitching the new clip seamlessly onto the last one. Carry on like this until you have completed the whole film.

Technical glitches

Cameras have their quirks and one of these is the tendency for some to rewind a couple of seconds once you stop filming. Manufacturers have good intentions with this as it is designed to prevent 'snow' caused by the blank tape showing through between shots. So it rewinds slightly to overlap each piece of film onto the next. If yours does this, simply work out how much it is rewinding and build this into the length of the shot. If your shot is going to last 10 seconds, make it last 10 plus the extra, so it rewinds back where you wanted it.

Evaluation

This is the first project and it is worth going over a few points to see what has been gained. First, don't worry if the final film differs often from the initial plans. A good film is not judged by how closely you have followed a pre-set path; if you have found better ways to shoot a scene while filming, use them. This is a good indication of the way your ideas are evolving about how to convey a scene, even during production.

1 Did you convey the brief plot adequately using the most economical shots? If you compress information to a smaller number of shots the overall effect is more professional.
2 Did you manage to show more than one aspect, or view, of the action in a shot or did you find yourself having to constantly cut to close-ups to show what was going on? Maybe you moved the camera to new angles now and then to make the movie more interesting to watch.
3 Have you found it relatively easy to consider a number of different elements of filming simultaneously? Did you, for instance, find that you could think about the framing of the camera, the light on the subject and convey the right information, at the same time?
4 The sequence of the shots is also important. Were you able to show the progression of events in order so it looked smooth and realistic?
5 You may also have noticed, when watching your movie later, that the length of each shot makes a difference about how the film works. It is very difficult to cut a shot correctly when using this sledgehammer approach to filmmaking, but you may have noticed how some of the more successful shots were the shorter ones. This is why cutting away to different views of the action is a useful technique.

In general, success for this first film, however, is to be judged simply by whether you enjoyed making the film and found yourself with a short film which says what you wanted it to say. In a very short space of time, you have picked up some valuable skills in using the camera, telling a narrative and sequencing shots. And by planning on paper at the start you help ensure that these areas work well before you pick up the camera.

2. Preferences and style

Your first interview

This is going to be your first interview, a way of working out what sort of filmmaker you are or are going to be. Self-knowledge is what makes you different, enabling you to make your movies look distinctively your own, stopping you from becoming a carbon copy of every other filmmaker. Most of the projects in this book leave a large area of the production open to individual preference. In most of these, you are given certain leads or certain restrictions, but are free to take the movie your own way. This means that you may make movies a certain way, light them, shoot them and edit them to your own ideas about what makes a good movie.

The following questions are a summary of the kind of self-inquiry you should get into before, during and after each production. Look at them and devise some of your own every time you make something new. Also try keeping a journal, recording ideas that could develop into films, observations about other people's films and notes about your own working method.

Pre-production

- What type of film have you chosen to make?
- If using narrative, have you tended to use particular plots, such as character- or action-based stories?
- How do you work with other people? Is a collaborative process better for you or do you prefer to recruit for a project which you have evolved?
- How do you use storyboards? Are they a near-exact blueprint of the film-to-be or do they act only as a trigger to encourage ideas to occur on set?
- Is using your own script important to you? Or can you work with material other people have written?
- Do you find that your own experiences play a part in the film?
- Are there literary or artistic forms that you like, such as surrealism?
- How long does it take you to settle on an idea for a film? Do you scrap plans repeatedly?
- If you use narrative, what kinds of stories do you prefer?
- Within a story, do you prefer focusing on the character or the action?
- What part of the script of your next movie are you most looking forward to making? Look at what attracts you to these scenes, whether it is the use of lighting, the possibility of doing unusual tricks with the camera or the action within the scene.
- Are you confident about your plans? (A: don't worry, no one is at the early stages.)

Production

- How exact are you about keeping to your initial plans? How important is improvisation and spontaneity?
- How are your sets lit? Do you prefer lighting for realism or for dramatic effect?

- What makes you work more effectively on set? Music playing, other people challenging you, coffee?
- How do you use the camera? Is it often moving, often stationary?
- Are there certain kinds of composition you prefer: wide shots, low angle shots, close-ups, symmetrical arrangements, or is it dependent on the movie?
- Is the use of colour important to you? Is colour simply a design solution or a chance to get more meaning into the film?
- How did you deal with obstacles to a film's progress? Did you tend to negotiate and work around it, or did the whole project come close to collapse?
- Do you like actors? Are they cardboard shapes to make your compositions look good or do you thrive on the ideas and experience they bring to the production?
- When shooting, how do you deal with challenges from your crew?
- If you ran into problems from the public, or from people who have the power to obstruct you in your work (tube station won't let you film), how do you respond? Did you use diplomacy and sweet talk or expletives and a loud hailer?
- Was your sound clearly recorded?
- Do you deal with a dozen technical issues at the same time: good sound, lighting, camera in the right place, pizzas ordered?

Post-production

- Look at your footage, fast forwarding through them. Describe the most common kind of shot you have.
- How long, in your opinion, is too long for a cut? Maybe you prefer long cuts or fast, punchy ones.
- Does a long cut make you feel uncomfortable or is it appropriate now and then?
- Do you use certain filters in your edit software to alter the look of the movie?
- How do you use sound? Do you like natural sound or that which is constructed by you from layers of tracks?
- Is music important?
- Look at the structure of the film. Look at how you have sought to convey the story or themes you chose; is it a simple, classic structure, or one that plays around with other methods?

Did you know?
A cut is an edited piece of footage, a continuous run between one edit and the next.

Promoting the film

- If you had to compare your movie with others, which ones would they be?
- What do you think audiences would most like and dislike about your movie?
- Describe the sort of person who you think would most want to watch your movie – their musical tastes, age, interests.

- Do you see this film as something that you could actively promote or is it more of a stepping stone to other projects?
- Think about the budget of the movie and consider a sum which you feel is appropriate to spend on promoting the movie, whether this involves sending it websites or entering it in festivals.
- Imagine what you think would be the most extreme reactions to your movie. Look at how it differs from the mainstream movies in theatres.
- Imagine what people would most like about the movie. In what ways does it sit comfortably with mainstream audiences?

Movie style

Every film you make, including all aborted and half-finished projects, is giving information about you. As you make more films you may notice certain kinds of film you prefer, certain themes and ideas that recur, a certain preference for one way of lighting a set or pointing the camera. This all adds up to your own personal stamp, the signature that you leave on everything you make.

Don't put style first

Style is a central part of your movie, but before we get too caught up with finding a style that no one else has and keeping it, we need to have some caution. There is a hierarchy about the way style should evolve: if you put what you think is your style into the fabric of a film *before* it has had a chance to develop, you risk seriously hampering its development – and your own. But if instead you concentrate on the solutions and methods that work best for you and which you prefer, then style naturally arises. Style evolves from the way you respond to each problem, but once you start becoming self-conscious about this and impose a style – reversing the hierarchy involved – over your methods, then you may lose your way as a filmmaker.

Style choices

When considering style, think about how you have used these elements in your film:

- Type of theme.
- Type of story (if any).
- Images.
- Composition.
- Lighting.
- Setting and location.
- Use of artificial light or preference for natural.
- Use of camera support (tripods).
- Use of soundtrack including music.
- Use of colour.
- Use of symbols or motifs (if any).
- Structure and pace.

The way you reveal your style is through the individual choices you make throughout the movie, from planning to editing, and these stem from the kind of choice you made about the overall theme in it.

It's also worth noting the way that subject matter affects style. Horror movies possess few characteristics of comedies and so we expect a certain style when we see a horror movie, another when we see a comedy. However, as we shall see later in Chapter 9:2 ('Key ideas in films'), cultural changes – in particular, what is called post-modernism – have led filmmakers to mix and match styles.

The Crunch

- Ask yourself many questions about what you do and how you do it.
- Get a journal or diary. Keep a record of how you respond to these questions after each movie you make.
- Sort out what you like before anything else; style comes later and is based on these decisions.
- The individual way *you* make a movie is a valuable commodity. Get to know what your films look like.

Project 2. In-camera edit: music and image

We have had a look at the in-camera edit in Project 1 and perhaps you can see the uses of it for constructing fast, easy-to-assemble movies, enabling you to move quickly through the various types of movie out there. That project was focused on the narrative movie which emphasizes the continuity of action in a straight line, from event A to event B and so on. But that way of using video is only half of the story. We need to have a look at what happens when we gather images for the sole reason that they look good and they add up to something interesting. It is also much easier to experiment with the camera when you are free of the restrictions of plot and can instead playfully investigate what the world looks like through the lens. It sounds easy but, as many filmmakers find, the lens is a new way of looking at the world.

Stage 1

To give us some starting point for the movie, we will need to take some inspiration from elsewhere. Choose a piece of music which you can listen to throughout filming and which can provide the focus for the kind of image you get. To put it in practical terms: make a music video consisting of a collection of shots that fit the music.

As we will see in the later music video project, there are in-depth ways of developing this kind of film, but for now we need only to provide a backdrop to the music, an excuse to play with the camera.

Stage 2

When you have a piece of music selected, take the camera and start looking for possible shots. On this first foray don't expect to do any filming yet; just make lots of notes of what you have seen and what it looked like through the camera. Look through the camera lens almost continually so that you don't miss anything useful. For example, you may walk past a waiting row of traffic. But what does it look like if you place the camera on the floor (on the pavement, not the road) looking directly across the vast rows of tyres. The shapes you see take this simple event out of context and therefore make us – the audience – see it afresh, which is your ultimate aim.

Stage 3

The process of having to edit in-camera, or rather make it up as you go along, ensures a certain spontaneity in the film. Don't be tempted to erase shots that don't seem to fit and replace them with more acceptable ones. The aim of this project is to make immediate decisions about what looks interesting. If it looks good, use it. Think later. The net result of this is that it lets you move fast, gathering images from a wide array of sources, but all related to the same starting point of inspiration: the music track. Let's take as an example a piece of dance music, slightly trance-like and with a strong rhythm. When you listen to this track while searching for images to film you may be drawn to images of crowds, of fast-moving traffic, or the architectural shapes and patterns of streets from high above. It does not matter what your interpretation is of the music, only that you see it reflected in the images.

Evaluation

The images you gathered should relate strongly to the music, but bear in mind that this is a personal view, so don't worry if no one else shares your ideas.

Success for this movie depends squarely on whether you managed to freely play with the camera, regardless of whether this is reflected in the shots themselves. It is the process you went through in experimenting and trying out shots that matters. But if your film does possess a constant running theme, reflecting the images you 'see' when you listen to the music, then you have made a coherent piece of work. More importantly, you have managed to keep in control of what the camera can do, using it for your own ends.

As an afterthought, take time to go through the shots you gathered and look for similarities in the types of shot. Do you use the camera more on close-ups, for instance, or use lots of camera movement? Get to know what you like and put this knowledge into action later.

3. Investigating other filmmakers

Where do you fit in?

Part of the process of defining your own approach is to see how you fit into the broader context of film and video today. Merely by existing in the same shared culture as other filmmakers – within and without national boundaries – you automatically have a stake in it. Even if you cut yourself off from all developments in the medium, you still cannot escape the fact that you are part of the whole form that is film and the best option is to notice where you fit into this.

To do this, it is useful to look at other filmmakers working around you, to see how they work, what they do, how it differs from or is similar to your own. Simply by being aware of new developments and trends you gain valuable knowledge about how your films relate to the outside world. This is not a particularly arduous task: you need only see lots of movies, especially those you have never heard of, outside your usual sphere of interest, and try to understand what the filmmaker is trying to achieve. It is not important to like a film, only that you understand its motives, its purpose and its methods. To help with this, look at film journals, or read respected film columns. If you can attend film festivals you get to see all undercurrents and emerging trends as they occur, and often have access to the filmmakers themselves following screenings.[7]

Tip   For good film columns, try reading the UK *Guardian* and the *New York Times*, both of which are available online.

Go to: Go to Chapter 8:3 for details of international film festivals. See CD-ROM for complete listings of festivals.

Local filmmakers and groups

Investigating filmmakers does not have to focus solely on those at the upper or middle strata of the industry. If there are filmmakers' groups locally, you can gain valuable insights into how other people work who are at the same stage of development as yourself. You can help (and learn) on their shoots, and they can help crew your own. You can gain valuable shooting experience, see others working from the inside, share equipment – and maybe even find a collaborator. If there are no groups locally, set one up with the help of your local public arts network. Or advertise in a filmmaker's journal or online to attract members also interested in meeting to discuss each other's work and offer mutual support. Trying to make films without contact from other filmmakers can be like working in a vacuum: nothing gets in and nothing gets out.

Tip   For details of whether there are filmmakers' groups near you, try contacting government-sponsored arts funding agencies in your area.

---

[7] http://film.guardian.co.uk/   Online reviews and news.
www.nytimes.com/pages/arts/index.html   *New York Times* reviews.

Work experience

For first-hand experience of seeing how other people make movies, find work on a film set. In the low-budget, independent sector, you can get unpaid work helping on a set; place a notice on an online filmmakers' notice-board or take up one of the many pleas from filmmakers needing help, some offering board and food in return for a few days work. The experience you gain is in practical knowledge of technical issues, working methods and good practice, and you will make valuable contacts for your own future productions.

> **Tip**   Place a notice on an online filmmakers' bulletin-board such as Indiewire.com or Shooting People.org.uk. to find work experience on a set.

The Crunch

- Other filmmakers can help you develop, get out there and meet people.
- Try film-set work experience. Filmmakers will often help each other, especially at the lower end of the industry.
- Phone people you have maybe never met and ask to help on their film.
- Get involved locally. Enquire at local public or community arts agencies for ways of contacting other people making films.

3 | Inside video

1. What is digital technology?

Digital video (DV) has come a long way in a very short space of time. In a few years it has affected both the top and bottom of the television and film industries. In broadcasting, DV has ousted Betacam SP, the expensive technology used in nearly all programme making, while at the consumer level it has vastly improved quality and enabled this group to get involved in movie making. The winners, unexpectedly, are the people at the bottom, who can now access broadcast picture quality and can edit films with high-quality software to match the best in the industry. But before we run off with our winnings, it is worth looking inside this gift and trying to understand why it works so well and how it offers us what it does. Perhaps then we can get more of a feel for the kind of technology we are using.

> **Did you know?**
> Betacam is an analog format which has been the industry's backbone prior to the digital age. It offers a significant increase in quality above other analog formats like S-VHS, by using what is called a 'time multiplex method'. Signals carrying luminance and colour are transmitted and recorded in a staggered process.

Digital vs analog

There are two formats currently used in video – analog and digital – but a comparison between the two is slightly unfair as analog cannot be said to have any advantage over DV. You may get some more interesting results if you were to compare celluloid film with DV, but even there the move is towards digital editing of a film print.[1]

Analog

The difference lies in the way that the image that the camera sees is captured. Analog stores information about the images by way of variable waves, recorded as electrical signals. These are

---

[1] www.dvcentral.org/   Wide range of digital video information.

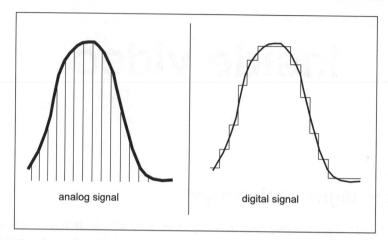

analog signal   digital signal

Figure 3.1 The digital signal on the right works by attaching a quantity to the wave. Each step of the curve is recorded as a number and this can then be reproduced more accurately than the analog signal on the left.

represented as up or down movements in a wave and look like peaks and valleys (see Figure 3.1). The degree to which these waves peak or trough means that the range of variables possible is almost infinite. These are rather like waves on the ocean responding to the fluctuating strength of wind or tide; sometimes there is a great distance between top and base within the wave, sometimes it is calm. But the problem lies in the fact that once you start recording these waves, copying them onto another tape, some of this information gets lost. The vast range of these wave variations demands a great deal of the equipment reading or scanning it. Peaks get lower and troughs get shallower, affecting the way the signal reads when you watch it. It is called analog because the signal is a copy to begin with: it is, literally, analogous to the source. Like the term 'analogy', it is a likeness and likenesses are not, by their nature, perfect copies. To a certain extent, the downfall of analog is to do with the range of variables each wave can offer; it is easy to vary the signal further, resulting in loss of information.[2]

Digital

Digital, on the other hand, is a different story. It is called digital because it records information by the use of numbers: ones and zeros, which correspond to 'on' or 'off' commands. It has no variables as does the wave of analog; a signal is either one or the other, black or white, yes or no. This means that when the tape signal degrades after copying or playing, which happens however hard you try to avoid it, it alters only the strength of the yes or no, the on or off, the one or zero. It still gets read as one or the other, regardless of the strength of the signal. This is why digital is a better method of storing and reproducing information.

[2] http://desktopvideo.about.com/cs/analogcamcorders/   Information on analog camcorders.

It is the reproduction of it that is crucial, since the ability to edit without loss of quality and to transmit those pictures out to the world without loss of quality is to remain true to a director's original intentions.

To explain why analog is a less than perfect answer, you could compare it to photocopying an image. If you take a picture and photocopy it you produce a version of the original. If you want to alter the picture and then re-copy it, you lose some information and the resulting copy is less clear than the original. Repeat this process several times and you end up with a muddy, useless image. With digital, you are approaching the picture wholly differently: imagine breaking the tonal values and colours of that photo down into numerical values, in turn represented by ones and zeros. You have then got a set of instructions for the make-up of that picture and can send these instructions anywhere. All that it requires is that the receiver has the same information as the sender in order to be able to reassemble the image from the numbers it is given. With the right decoding knowledge it will reconstruct the image. Furthermore, because it exists in terms of numbers, it can be manipulated more easily, so that a picture can be turned black and white by exchanging one set of numbers for another, while keeping the rest unchanged.

Advantages of DV over analog

Picture resolution

In general, the resolution of a picture on DV is about 25 per cent better than a comparable image on S-VHS – the best consumer-level tape for analog – and has about twice the horizontal resolution of a VHS recording. However, DV offers about the same quality as Betacam, previously the highest-level analog format, which is a remarkable leap forward for the low-budget filmmaker.

Colour rendition

This refers to how well the format reproduces colour accurately. Analog is prone to vision 'noise', or interference, which smears and blurs colours. With DV, colour rendition is more true to what a digital camera first recorded. Edges are sharper, shapes more defined. But, as with analog, a lack of adequate light in DV filming quickly reduces quality.

Copying

DV offers greater quality control when copying. Since digital loses virtually no information each time it is copied, images can be transmitted or stored and the image that is read by the player is as good as the one on the master copy. The image is limited only by the quality of the playing instrument. Storing a film on any digital format guarantees greater longevity too. Magnetic tape is vulnerable to all sorts of environmental change, including heat, humidity and other magnetic fields.

Did you know?
With analog editing, the final movie was at least four or five generations old, meaning that it had degraded significantly since the first camera recording. Digital copies are no such thing; to be exact they are reproductions built from the same set of instructions.

Compatibility

In addition, digital is 'backwards compatible', meaning that digital movies can be stored on analog VHS tapes, but analog cannot be stored digitally, until it has been translated into digital signals.

Countries using PAL	Countries using NTSC	Countries using SECAM
Argentina	Carribean islands	Albania
Algeria	Canada	Bulgaria
Andorra	Chile	Colombia
Australia	El Salvador	Czech Republic
Austria	Guatemala	Egypt
Belgium	Japan	Former USSR
Brazil	South Korea	France
China	Mexico	Iran
Denmark	Peru	Poland
Germany	Puerto Rico	Romania
Greece	USA	Zaire
Finland	Venezuela	
Hong Kong		
Iceland		
India		
Indonesia		
Ireland		
Israel		
Italy		
Kenya		
Malaysia		
Netherlands		
New Zealand		
Norway		
Portugal		
South Africa		
Spain		
Sweden		
Switzerland		
Turkey		
United Kingdom		
Zimbabwe		

Figure 3.2 Table of international TV standards.

Broadcast standards

Most countries have very specific guidelines about what kind of picture quality is acceptable for broadcast. Pictures have to measure up to a set of standards and failure to meet these consistently may lead to the license to broadcast being revoked. Broadcasters would reject material from filmmakers which didn't meet these technical standards. Some digital camcorders meet these specifications, but at the lower end there is a slight, but important, difference. This difference between a movie shot on a DV camera and the same shot on Betacam SP format would go unnoticed by 95 per cent of the population. Qualitatively, they look the same, but in terms of quantity of information, they are slightly apart. Further down the scale, VHS, or even S-VHS, falls far short of the quality threshold.

This becomes an issue if you start making films that you would like to sell to television companies. Most consumer DV cameras work on a slightly poorer resolution to DV cameras in the upper price range, and are known as YUV 4:1:1 – they slightly undershoot the necessary specifications. The more expensive cameras, such as the Sony DSR200, use a resolution of YUV 4:2:2, equal to Betacam and easily meeting broadcast specifications. However, it is useful to note that most cable television stations will accept 4:1:1. The Y stands for intensity and the U and V are for different colour signals. This way of encoding a signal is used in broadcasting by processing intensity separately from colours.[3]

Did you know?
4:1:1 and other similar figures are simply a way of marking how well a camcorder records what it sees. It is a way of measuring the ratio between brightness signal and colour signal.

Tip The term 'broadcast quality' has changed considerably since DV became a consumer item; in terms of the consumer it has become a loose term and often simply refers to a quality far above that offered by analog, but not necessarily meeting broadcast technical quality guidelines. Whatever the publicity blurb says, check with an independent advisor first (don't even trust direct contact with a manufacturer) before committing yourself to an expensive camera that claims to be broadcast standard but stops your programmes being accepted by television companies.

Audio comparison

The CD format in music offers superior quality to analog (though many musicians doubt it beats old-style valve amplifiers in playback quality) and almost 'lossless' copying. As you would expect, then,

[3] www.3dresearch.com/video/Countries2.html   News and updates on international broadcasting standards.

audio channels on DV are comparable to CD and, when recorded on 16-bit stereo, offer unparalleled quality.

Go to: Chapter 6:4, 'Sound in editing', for information on interference on DV audio.

A brief history of digital technology

The revolution in digital technology in moving pictures is the result of a triangle of factors meeting at the same time and growing simultaneously:

- The demand from consumers to make movies.
- More efficient manufacturing of products, making them more affordable.
- Advances in technology.

Editors familiar with the old system of analog editing don't need any reminding of the drawbacks of this process. Certainly, editing took longer, was more costly and was accomplished in very different surroundings. This last point is more significant than it seems; editing was limited by the bulk of the equipment needed and its expense meant that you normally had to go to a studio to do it.

Digital editing on PCs has changed all that and has had an impact not only on the way that editing is performed, but also what can be achieved. Put it this way: if a young unknown director has to rent an editing unit, eating up large portions of his or her budget on a daily basis, editing becomes a direct, straight-to-the-point business. There is no time to play, nor to evolve some shots and let the film evolve in an organic way. But if that director's son or daughter makes a film today, chances are they will edit when they want, where they want, for as long as they want. With a PC – larger than the domestic sort – they now have the luxury of being able to make several versions of a scene, of trying out radical ways of ordering sequences. The kind of flexibility available during shooting, of being able to experiment (within the constraints of a budget) and try out several takes, now expands into the editing stage, with creative benefits for filmmaker and film.

Apple and Windows

But to start further back, in the early 1980s, it is the arrival of the Apple Computer in 1984 that heralded the start of the multimedia age 'for the rest of us', as the company logo read. The big leap forward was the graphical user interface, in other words, a more user-friendly way of dealing with computers, by having windows instead of glowing green letters on a black screen. This windows layout is the only feasible way for creative programs to work, where lateral thinking is central and you need to be able to look at several different kinds of commands at once. The use of Microsoft Windows on the vast majority of the world's computers is directly a result of the pioneering work done by Apple's founders and by companies such as Lotus, Adobe and Digital Research Inc.

Perhaps even more significant was the view by Apple that computers could be creative tools, as the first Macintoshs came equipped with painting packages as well as spreadsheets. Rather than adopt a passive, consumer ethos for its products, Apple foresaw the Mac as something owned by makers, users, creators.[4]

DVC and FireWire

1994 would be as good a time as any to say that the march of progress turned into a dash with the arrival of a standard recording format, the agreement between manufacturers of the DVC (Digital Video Cassette) and the patent of Apple's FireWire cable, able to transfer data at an improved rate.

Go to: Chapter 6:3, 'Starting to work in digital editing'.

CD-ROM and DVD

The audio CD was a milestone for music distribution, but the major problem with video is the sheer size of the data. The size of a television screen is measured in pixels – small dots arranged in neat rows. In America, the NTSC system is based on using 640×480 pixels, while in territories using another system, PAL, the number is higher, at 720×560. To convey the information needed to show simply a black and white image, we would need 38 400 bytes of information. But don't forget, that is just one frame, a single still image. You are going to need 25 of those (or 30 in NTSC) to make a second of video.

Compression

Already we are far outside the boundaries of the standard floppy disc, and even the comparatively gargantuan CD-ROM will quake under the strain of squeezing the average short movie onto one disc. The next leap forward, therefore, looked at ways of condensing data down into manageable amounts; manageable, that is, for the small PCs used by most people, not the vast models steaming away at film studios. Compression is the saviour of DV filmmaking and has led to the development of DVD as a consumer solution to watching digitally stored movies on disc. Compression has since leapt forward with the help of an international standard, devised by the Motion Picture Experts Group, or MPEG for short.

Go to: Chapter 7:2, 'Video compression'.

DV vs Digital 8

Due to the separate growth of camcorder manufacturing in different companies, two digital formats exist. However, most companies are making DV rather than Digital 8.

Digital 8

- Can play Hi8 and Super8 tapes.
- Costs less than DV, but this is expected to become less significant.

[4] www.apple-history.com/history.html   History of Apple Inc.

- Is made only by Sony.
- All Digital 8 camcorders have FireWire ports.[5]

DV

- Higher resolution video.
- Better tape design – lighter and quieter.
- All other manufacturers make it, including Sony.
- Tapes have longer recording time.
- Cameras have longer battery life.

The Crunch

- Become technical: most artists have to work at this bit, but it is worth it because you are in control.
- Get to know about broadcast standards for your country or the place you might want to show your work.
- Analog is long gone – digital is going to give you better results.
- FireWire is good – you need it.
- DV cassettes are good.
- DVD is going to help you, CD-ROMs less so. Maybe get a DVD writer.

2. How does the camcorder work?

Before we look at the inner workings of the video camera, we need first to define what we are looking at. Not all cameras can record images; some simply pass them on to another device which commits them to tape. In television, for example, cameras in the studio relay images elsewhere and so are not, technically, camcorders, just cameras. For simplicity, then, we will talk throughout this section about the camera that records images as well as seeing them, from entry-level consumer models through to those in the upper range used in filmmaking.

How images get onto tape

To understand how the image gets onto the digital tape, we could start at the beginning and follow the whole process. It basically runs like this:

- image through the lens;
- image is sensed by a CCD chip;
- gets translated into ones and zeros;
- and gets transferred to tape.

[5] www.sony.com/   Link to Digital 8 information.

Surrounding this process are a range of features that help modify the image, making it clearer or more stable, if needed. Audio signals recorded simultaneously go straight from the microphone, getting translated into digital information, and on the tape, are matched with the images accompanying them.

Lens

The lens is the point at which the image crosses into the camcorder, using an iris which functions much the same as the human eye. Lens quality is crucial since the camcorder may have a perfect method of recording what it sees, but must see perfectly to begin with. Lower-priced camcorders will not have lens quality of those in the upper levels; some camcorders offer a variety of lenses, enabling you to increase quality, while others are fixed.

Lens and the iris

The iris on the lens controls the amount of light entering the camcorder and will quickly shrink if too much is entering or dilate if there is too little. The reason it must do this is to satisfy the amount of information required by the CCD chip situated near the lens. If there is too little light and the required pixels do not each receive instructions, then the chip steps in and starts adding its own default information. This is known as 'noise' and is read as tiny white dots all over the screen, which is why you get a grainy image if you shoot in low light conditions.

Zoom

A further function of the lens is zoom. Digital camcorders zoom in one of two ways: optical or digital zoom. Optical zoom is by far the better option, as it magnifies the image using two glass lenses; in other words, it reads the image far away more correctly. Digital zoom, however, is almost without merit, as it simply enlarges the image it saw, drastically reducing resolution. It's rather like asking for a bigger portion at a restaurant and the waiter simply spreads your existing one more thinly around the plate; you gain nothing by using digital zoom, only a blow-up using the same small amount of information.

CCD

CCD refers to the Charge-Coupled Device, a set of sensors near the lens which collect what the lens sees and convert the image into digital signals. There are two sorts, again determined by which end of the price range you look at:

- *Single-chip*. These dominate the lower, more domestic end of the market. It collects over 300 000 pixel bits of information, which sounds a lot but is considerably less than the three-chip.
- *Three-chip*. This one is found in any of the better camcorders in the mid and upper ranges. The big difference here is that there are three chips, each gathering 300 000 bits of information, but this time each chip gathers just one colour each: red, green or blue. The one-chip gathers all colours together and so has to squeeze all three groups of information into one chip. The additional quality of the three-chip is worth about an extra 20 per cent in terms of picture and colour resolution.

If you want to make programmes for broadcast then you need to get a three-chip. Most people will not notice the difference between one-chip and three-chip, but broadcasters will notice and do not accept certain quality of pictures. But if you intend to show only on the web, this difference is going to be reduced later, so it may not be useful.

From chip to tape

Digital tape is much more rugged than that used for analog S-VHS or VHS video. It is made of an advanced form of metal evaporated (ME) tape. It consists of a double-coated magnetic layer, which is in turn coated in tough carbon, to prevent the tape wearing out. This enables stored digital information to be played back without any loss of quality, with the overall construction of the tape preventing picture noise, or interference. 'Bleeding' from the audio track to the video tracks is also unlikely, further reducing interference.

Recording standards

There are several other factors which are worth mentioning in relation to recording. If you intend to make movies or programmes for selling in other countries, you need to know about the differences in broadcast standards around the world. Ultimately, this affects anyone who makes films because few people can afford to ignore the potentially lucrative returns in foreign markets. None of these problems are insurmountable, but being aware of them before you start a project can increase your chances of selling your work to a wide range of markets.

PAL, NTSC and SECAM

Each country has its own specification for how many lines a television signal must produce and how many frames per second it should have. In Europe and Australia, the standard is PAL (Phase Alternating Line), which operates on a high level of quality in terms of pixels on screen but slightly lower frame rate. In America, the standard is called NTSC (National Television Systems Committee) and has a lower number of pixels on the screen but operates on a faster frame rate, of 29.9 (often rounded up to 30). A different system called SECAM ('sequential couleur avec memoire', or sequential colour with memory) is used in parts of eastern Europe, some African countries, parts of South America and the former states of the USSR (see Figure 3.2). SECAM is closer to PAL than NTSC, using the same bandwidth as PAL but transmitting colour information sequentially. Countries using SECAM can play PAL videos or DVDs more easily than NTSC.

To complicate matters, there is also a version of PAL known as PAL 60, leaving the old PAL to be known as PAL 50. The new version is intended to help address the problems of NTSC users viewing PAL movies. NTSC uses a frame rate of 30 frames per second while PAL uses 25, but the new PAL also uses 30.

Pixels

The number of pixels, or dots on the screen, is determined by how many vertical and horizontal lines the signal has. The NTSC ratio of 640 × 480 has roughly 307 000 pixels, whereas PAL has 720 × 560, giving it the edge with over 400 000. This will lead to greater clarity and sharpness in PAL, but it suffers when it comes to frame rate.

Frame rate

Frame rate (the number of individual pictures that have to make up a single second of tape) affects smoothness of movement. A film shot on fewer frames per second (fps) will look more jerky than one on higher fps. To illustrate this, some animation companies such as Disney have tried to achieve immaculate smoothness of action by animating at 40 fps. Realistically, the difference of five frames between PAL (25 fps) and NTSC (29.9 fps) is not going to affect quality a great deal, but it is important to edit in the right frame rate for the market you wish to sell to.

Film View

For a glimpse at what high-frame-rate animation looks like, watch *The Nightmare Before Christmas* (Henry Selick, 1993).

Timecode

A further, more complicated factor in frame rate is timecode. In terms of frame rate, timecode is more of a headache with NTSC than with PAL. PAL, with its nice, easily divisible numbers (25 goes into 100 neatly) presents no problem for accurate timecode. The 29.9 fps of NTSC, however, needs to operate with something called 'drop-frame timecode', in which certain frame numbers – not your actual hard-won frames themselves from the footage – are dropped out to keep everything in round numbers. It gets rid of two frames every minute but skips every tenth minute. Thankfully, you no longer have to worry about drop-frame timecode as many edit programs offer you the chance to work in this method. But it is essential if you intend to work in productions of 60 minutes or more as you would end up with an error rate of 3.6 seconds every hour. If you are intending to sell broadcast material to zones with other broadcast standards, check what they use and edit the movie with this in mind.

Go to: Chapter 6:6 for more details about what timecode is and how it works with the camera.

The Crunch

- You need manual override on your camera.
- Get a three-CCD-chip camera if you can.
- Understand the way cameras record so you can use them creatively.
- OK, maybe you don't want to know all this technical stuff, but make sure someone in your next crew does.

3. Choosing the right camcorder

If you are making movies, the purchase of a camcorder is probably the most crucial decision you will make. Digital video is better than any other kind of camera but still there are differences between models, not just in price or the range of extra features, but in the ways your camera could hold you back once your career gets going, if you buy the wrong one for your needs. So this means working out what you intend to use your camera for and on what kind of format they will eventually be shown, whether it's cinema, television, the web or an art gallery.

Your ideal camera

Let's start with some questions to find out what kind you need to buy. At this stage try not to consider price; think of what you would ideally like to do and who will see your movies.

Do you want to make movies that could be sold for broadcast?

- *Yes*: you need a camera that works with at least 4:2:2 DV, enabling you to produce quality that meets broadcast requirements.
- *No*: you can use any camera working with 4:1:1 format. They are cheaper than those above.

Go to: Chapter 8:1 for more help with deciding where and how you want to show your movies.

Do you want to show your work on the web?

- *Yes*: you can go for lower price-band camcorders. There is no gain in buying more expensive models. The eventual quality of the picture you show on the web will not benefit from broadcast quality cameras.
- *No*: if quality is an issue for you then aim for professional models as opposed to consumer.

  Go to: Chapter 7:1 for details of what web movies are and where you can show them.

Do you want to make movies that could reasonably be blown up to 35 mm (or played on a DV projector at a cinema) and used for theatrical release?

- *Yes*: you will need a mid- to high-band camera with audio XLR input or the ability to plug in a mixing board, allowing you to record the highest quality 16-bit stereo sound. You need a camera with three CCD chips because the scale of projection will reveal the quality differences with single-chip models.
- *No*: any camera will be sufficient if you intend to bypass television or theatrical showings. However, audio XLR is still a good investment but not essential for you.

Go to: Chapter 5:7 for what this kind of input can offer you when recording sound.

Do you want to sell movies to cable channels?

- *Yes*: You are safer with three-chip cameras with 4:4:2 DV, but many cable channels, especially those offering access lots for new filmmakers, will accept lower quality.
- *No*: any standard camera if you are not intending any broadcast or other release.

Do you want to make movies just for the web, or for distributing on DVD or CD-ROM without any other release?

- *Yes*: in this case, you don't need to worry about picture quality too much as the web and CD-ROM will need to take away some quality in order to compress the movie, so a single-chip, less expensive model will be fine. DVD, however, compresses films without losing quality, so if you intend to sell your work on DVD then you should aim for the better models.
- *No*: lower-priced models will produce very good results, but getting a better camera built to higher standards means you can get into other markets later if you have bigger plans for your films.

Go to: Chapter 7:2. You need to know about 'video compression' and the kinds of restrictions this places on your movie.

As you can see, the higher band cameras are preferable for use when you intend to push your movie towards theatrical or broadcast release. Lower band is sufficient for (most) cable television and ideal for use if showing work on the web or on CD-ROM.

Whatever your plans, the main features you need are not quite the ones the manufacturer sells the model on. All those incentives to buy a camera because it offers a number of special effects should be ignored in favour of the camera which does very little but what it does, it does brilliantly.[6]

Camera features

Lens ✓

All lenses are not built equally. Manufacturers rarely boast about the kind of lens on a model, and information is hard to get hold of, for the simple reason that most users are more interested in additional effects features than lenses. Look at trade magazine reports for insights into lens quality. Some manufacturers are now taking lens quality more seriously; Panasonic, for example, teamed up with quality lens specialist Leica, while Sony uses Carl Ziess on some models.

---

[6] www.panasonic.com/consumer_electronics/camcorder/default.asp   Panasonic camcorders.
www.reviewfinder.com/0/180.asp   Reviews of most camcorders.
www.jvc.com/   JVC camcorders.
www.sony.co.jp/en/Products/DSR-PD150/   Sony camcorder information.
www.canondv.com/gl1/   Canon camcorder information.

CCD ✓

If you can stretch your budget, you must get a three-chip model. These will give you clearer colour resolution and yet are not necessarily at the top of the price band. The Panasonic NV-DX110, for example, is a three-chip model at the affordable lower end of the mid-range.

Manual focus ✓

All automatic features are one day going to work against your filmmaking and are only occasionally useful, and yet all cameras include them. An absolutely essential feature is a manual override, so that you can set focal length yourself. Good compositions in camerawork won't be possible without this override.

Go to: Chapter 5:2. The problem with auto focus is that it determines for you what is and is not in focus, and if you are interested in good composition this will probably give you the wrong bits in focus.

Manual exposure ✓

As with focus, automatic exposure is going to upset all your best-laid plans when it comes to lighting your set. Override is essential.

Colour viewfinder ✖

Many camcorders incorporate a colour LCD viewfinder, but you can hook up to an external monitor if necessary or play back rushes on a monitor to test their suitability. These small, 3.5-inch screens can be useful tools and forming a composition is much easier through one of these, as they enable you to see more clearly how you are arranging a shot. But it remains an inessential feature that you can live without and they wear down the battery twice as fast as when you use the eyepiece.

Date/time labelling ✖

You don't really have a choice here as almost all cameras include this.

Editing in camera ✖

There is nothing to be gained in having the ability to edit your movies in camera. In its most basic forms, editing software is available free to download for some programs.

Go to: Chapter 6:3 for an overview of editing software.

Fade out ✖

As an edit function, this is not needed. Avoid using this when shooting.

Image stabilization ✓

There are two types on cameras, both designed to counter the wobbling that results from these cameras now weighing less than children's toy replica versions. Electronic stabilizers are not as good as optical stabilizers, but they do cost less. As a general function, however, stabilizers are no substitute for a tripod.

Audio inputs ✓

You will already have a microphone input socket, but it would be useful to have a type of socket mentioned earlier, the XLR, which minimizes 'noise' or interference within the mic and from the mic affecting the camera body.

Remote control ✖

Not needed unless you intend to do some remote filming without a camera operator.

Manual shutter speed ✓

This refers to the amount of time light is allowed to hit the lens. Faster shutter speeds are useful for recording fast movement or coping with particular lighting conditions, such as excessive brightness. It is essential that you can override this auto function, and try to get as wide a range of manual speeds as possible.

Title generator ✖

This allows you to insert your own titles on your movie. Editing is the best place to put credits, so you don't need this feature.

Manual white balance ✓

This feature is on all camcorders and is designed to ensure that white objects remain white regardless of the colour of the light: daylight, tungsten, sunset and so on. You may also want to override this facility in order to achieve creative effects, so make sure that this is possible.

Widescreen (aspect ratio settings) ✓

Some camcorders allow you to film in different aspect ratios. Aspect ratio refers to the relative length of the horizontal and vertical sides of the screen. Television has mostly used a nearly square ratio of 4:3, while cinema has preferred a much wider, letterbox shape. The trend is more and more towards rectangular aspect ratios and Europe has adopted a standard of 16:9 for television. If your camera can film in different aspect ratios, it could save you some headaches when editing. Changing aspect ratio during post-production is less satisfactory than if the film starts life as a particular shape. If you try to lose a piece at the top and bottom of the screen *during* editing, some of your original compositions will be compromised, or vital picture information lost. Sometimes, this function is called 'cinema' rather than widescreen, but in any case, check what precise aspect ratio is offered. Note, also, that some television companies won't buy a film if it is shot in a certain aspect ratio and films are better if they are shot on the right aspect ratio rather than edited into it during post-production.[7]

Zoom optical ✓/zoom digital ✖

This refers to the camcorder's ability to get closer to a subject without being physically close. Any kind of *digital* zoom is unnecessary since it only reduces picture quality and you should opt for *optical* zoom if you have the choice. Optical zoom differs from digital because it moves two glass lenses apart to zoom in on an object. But think about whether you will actually use this feature very often; zoom, in general, is not as satisfactory as tracking towards a subject, due to the unnatural effect of most zooming.

Timecode ✓

It is essential while filming that you make full use of timecode. Your films will look just as good without it, but timecode was invented to help professionals edit quickly and efficiently. You need a camcorder which enables you to maintain continuous timecode throughout a tape, by searching for the last timecode point on the tape (the last bit of filming you did) and hitching the new clip right after it. The reason for this is that when you edit with your tape, the computer needs to know the precise start and end point of each clip, so that it can locate them on the tape. There are ways to get around this, so if you already have footage which has timecode interruptions, you can still edit with them. Cameras in the mid to upper price range deal with timecode more fully, while consumer models rarely mention it; some cameras refer to this only as 'search for end of recorded part on a cassette' or 'blank search'. But remember that you don't need any special features for timecode except an ability to record it on your tape; timecoding your tapes in advance means you don't need to use these features. Check also how your camera records timecode onto the tape. Some record onto an audio track (not advisable as it can bleed into the video track), some don't.

Go to: Chapter 6:6 for a detailed look at what timecode is and how to use it well.

Additional features

As well as deciding which of the above you need and which you don't, you may also need to consider the following.

Handling ✓

Check how easy each camcorder is to handle. Where are the most useful features situated and are they easily accessible? How easy is it to change tapes (some insist you take the camcorder off a tripod before getting at the tape)?

---

[7] www.geocities.com/SiliconValley/Bay/2933/favaspectratio.html   Comprehensive information on aspect ratios.

Size of the camcorder

Try out different models to see which you prefer. Some people like heavier, bigger camcorders as they are slightly steadier and easier to use when shooting hand-held.

Long battery life ✓

Power is one of the most important issues when buying a camcorder. Check how long the battery lasts and how expensive extra ones are (sometimes cheaper if bought with the initial purchase of the camcorder). You need a display on the viewfinder which tells you when your battery is running low.

Inputs

Some, though very few, camcorders allow you to record from analog sources direct onto the camera. Because of the implications for piracy, this feature is uncommon, but manufacturers are working on ways of preventing pre-recorded video films from being captured. As far as DV inputs are concerned, you certainly need the ability to record back onto tape from your PC after editing. An S-Video output will help in viewing your footage on a television monitor.

FireWire (also known as IEEE 1394, or iLink) ✓

This is a crucial addition to your camera. You need to have the ability to take footage out from your camcorder using this cable. Some camcorders use a six-pin and some a four-pin, but adapters are available; whatever inputs you have on a camcorder, this is a necessity. Images downloaded from other cables, such as USB, will lose quality and will be frustratingly slow.

Sturdiness ✓

Some camcorders are designed for the traveller and are more hard-wearing than others. A model with an aluminium body will be more resilient than plastic and is an issue if you intend to work in difficult situations, such as documentary and travel work.

Multimedia card ✖

This is a useful extra feature which enables you to take still pictures using the camcorder and store them on a multimedia card, a small 8 MB card about a third of the size of a credit card. You don't need to buy a digital stills camera if you have this feature. Cards typically store between 50 and 100 still pictures depending on the quality you choose and replacement cards with bigger memory can be bought. You can also copy stills from the cassette onto this. This feature allows you to record possible locations or try set-ups of scenes and incorporate the pictures as part of a rough storyboard. It is not going to have any decisive effect on your films and is really just an extra selling point.

Extras and accessories

There are a number of items that you may need in addition to the camcorder.

Spare batteries ✓

Two extras should enable you to have one in use, one ready to use and one on charge. You really cannot get away with having just one battery unless you intend to shoot everything using mains supply. However, some camcorders use new lithium ion batteries, which can offer up to 7 hours or more of battery capacity, and will keep you updated, minute by minute, about how much power is left.

Carry case ✓

A hard case is going to keep your equipment from possible damage.

The Crunch

- Get the best camera you can, at the top of the range, with no frills (big LCD monitor you can live without and so on).
- The best camera will let you make films for television or cinema. Don't sell yourself short.
- Everything must have manual override.
- Get the best lens you can.
- Learn to enjoy being with your camera.

4. Camcorder guide

This section introduces you to the most user-friendly camcorders for the filmmaker on a low budget. There are three sections: basic, mid-range and upper range. Beyond that you start to get into the broadcasting range which demands far higher prices. For now, though, these cameras will all let you make movies and it is not necessarily true that price is the best indication of quality. In each category there are camcorders which are outperformed by other, less expensive models.

Basic DV camcorders

They do what they should and while they are far better than any analog camera you may have used, they won't record with sufficient quality to get you into television slots. Choose these if you just want to make movies because you want to. They won't make you a star – yet. In 2001, these were priced below £1000.

Panasonic NV-DS15

Optical and digital zoom, manual focus dial, 11 recording digital effects, takes digital photos, zoom microphone, night vision mode, super image stabilizer. LCD monitor, FireWire out, external microphone input and headphones.

JVC GR-DVL20, DVL–30 and DVL–40

Three levels of camcorder with large LCD monitors, optical zoom, high picture quality, snap shot mode. On the negative side, there are no external headphone or mic sockets. The camera body is also not the best quality for rugged filming work.

Samsung VP-D55/65

Two levels of camcorder, slightly different in features. Optical and digital zoom. Average, 2.5-inch LCD monitor. DV output socket, while the D65 has output and input.

JVC GR-DVL100

A consumer-level camcorder with optical and digital zoom, 800 000-pixel CCD, digital snapshot mode, built-in lamp, EasyEdit editing program bundled with it, digital effects, DV out socket, no DV in.

JVC GR-DVL107

Slightly better than JVC's DVL100, it has almost identical functions but includes a DV input socket. Also has good manual control. On the negative side, it has no input for external mics or headphones, while the built-in mic is poor (as most tend to be at this level).

Panasonic NV-DS150 ✓

A step up from Panasonic's entry-level DS–15, it has similar features but offers better value for money with the inclusion of a DV input socket.

Mid-range basic camcorders

In this range, the camcorder may still not provide broadcast quality recording, but will offer a better deal on what entry-level camcorders do. Picture quality may be higher and the camera may be more compact. You may not notice much difference between these and the previous category unless you look carefully at picture resolution. In 2001, these were priced between £1000 and £1500.

Canon DM-MV300/MV3001

A very compact camcorder, with optical and digital zoom, manual focus and full manual options, seven digital effects, image stabilizer. LCD monitor, FireWire out.

Sharp VL-SD20

A larger-than-average LCD monitor (3-inch), high picture quality, full manual control, digital effects. However, there is no viewfinder, so battery life can be shorter than expected. Motor noise is unusually present.

Canon DM-MV20

Even more compact than Canon's other entry at this level, this model has a lightweight body, optical zoom, 2.5-inch LCD screen, FireWire out socket and great looking design. However, external mic and headphone sockets are located on an optional unit that clicks onto the main body. Sound quality is poor. Expensive compared to cheaper, similar-level camcorders.

Sony DCR-PC4/5

One of the most compact at this level, it has optical and digital zoom, very stylish, good CCD (1/4-inch), full manual controls, 2.5-inch LCD monitor with touch-screen controls, night vision, FireWire out socket, image stabilizer, 20-scene edit controller.

Sharp VL-PD3

A compact and light body, optical zoom, 2.5-inch LCD monitor, good picture and sound quality, good image manipulation software bundled with it, still photo option. But there is no DV in socket, which might be expected at this price range. And there are no external mic or headphone sockets.

Sony DCR-TRV6

A basic camera were it not for the Carl Zeiss lens, leading to better picture quality. Optical and digital zoom, advanced CCD, 2.5-inch LCD monitor, full manual focus control, 20-shot in-camera edit facility, night vision, FireWire out socket.

Canon DM-MV30/MV30i ✓

A good camcorder with all-round performance and many features, making the MV30i the preferred buy in this category. Picture and sound quality is high, FireWire in and out sockets, full manual control, good image stabilizer. Huge LCD monitor (3.5-inch).

JVC GR-DVX4

Easy to use with one hand, very small and compact. Good picture and sound quality, FireWire out socket, 2.5-inch monitor, still photo facility with auto-flash and red-eye reduction. But there is no DV in socket. Not the best option at this price range.

JVC DVL–9800

The same price as the previous JVC model, but this one includes DV in and out sockets. Full manual control, image stabilizer, light body, compact. Sound quality can be poor, however.

Sharp VL-PD6H

Full manual features and good picture quality, but this camera lacks external mic and headphones inputs. The LCD monitor is detachable, but cables that connect it are prone to wear and tear.

Sony DCR TRV11

Optical and digital zoom plus manual override and night vision, but most attractive features are the Carl Zeiss lens, and the FireWire in and out sockets.

Panasonic NV-DS35B

A camcorder that performs also as a high-quality stills camera. Includes manual controls and is very compact and lightweight. This model is excellent value for the price; the only drawback for some people could be the absence of a DV in socket. Priced at the lower end of this category.

Sony DCR-PC2 and PC3

Until recently this was the smallest camcorder in the world but did not compromise on quality, with a Zeiss lens, 2.5-inch monitor with touch-sensitive panel, extended life battery (3 hours maximum) and a manual focus ring. The only negative comment from some users is the operating noise.

Sony DCR-PC100 ✓

The mega-pixel model enables superior picture quality, and sound quality is equally high. Manual focus and other manual override, DV link in and out, optical zoom. This model is exceptionally good value and follow-up versions will undoubtedly build on this success.

Sony DCR-TRV8 and TRV10

Both versions have 3.5-inch LCD monitors and colour viewfinders, DV out socket (no DV in socket), optical zoom, long battery life, high picture and audio quality. On the down side, there is no override on the shutter speed, while the larger monitor is grainy, so hardly worth the extra inch. Sony's DCR-PC100 is a better option, and cheaper.

JVC GR-DVL9700

For the price, this camera is not good value. On the plus side, there is a large (1/3-inch) CCD, flash for stills photography, manual override, optical zoom, 3.5-inch LCD monitor, image stabilizer. But there is no DV in socket.

Panasonic NV-EX3

Creeping up to the highest price in this category, this is at present the world's smallest camcorder. It is lightweight, but the manual controls are awkward to operate due to its size. It has a DV out socket but no DV input, full manual control, optical zoom, a fast-charge battery and an S-Video out socket.

Upper range camcorders

These cameras are going to offer better picture quality, mostly due to better lens technology and triple CCD chips. Mega-pixel technology also provides a clearer, denser screen. At the top end of this section there is no reason why you can't make great-looking feature films. At the time this was written, these prices ranged from £1600 to £2700.

Panasonic NV-DX100 and DX110 ✓

For what are designed as consumer models (with correspondingly low price) these two models are excellent value, offering three-chip CCDs, full manual control, optical zoom, 2.5-inch LCD monitor and DV in socket (DX110 only). The DX100 was voted 1998 Camcorder of the Year by *Camcorder User* magazine.

JVC GR-DVL9500 and DVL9600

A great value camcorder offering high-speed recording, slow motion recording (the first to do so), photo mode, DV in and out sockets, good edit software bundled with it, digital stereo sound, 3.8-inch LCD monitor and a colour viewfinder.

Sony DCR-TRV890 and TRV900

The TRV900 offers better value, with more features for roughly the same price: DV and analog VCR inputs, optical image stabilizer, triple CCD image quality, 3.5-inch LCD monitor.

Canon XM1

Probably the cheapest camcorder to offer near-professional quality, it is the first to use fluorite lens technology within camcorders, which enables it to focus colours more precisely and avoid colour differences within the frame. It has full manual controls, a 2.5-inch LCD monitor, DV input and output sockets, stereo sound and a sturdy body casing. It is hard to beat this camera for quality or price.

Sony DCR-VX1000

This was the first DV camcorder and is used widely by many broadcasters for outside work due to its sturdy body and creative, manual controls. It has optical zoom and image stabilizer, three-CCD chip and colour viewfinder. However, its battery life is relatively short and it has no DV output socket.

Sony DCR-VX2000

The updated version of the above model, this has three-chip quality, a manual zoom ring, excellent LCD and viewfinder clarity, DV input and output sockets, and it includes analog input for transferring old footage to DV. The only downside is that you have to recharge the battery on the camera itself.

Sony DCR-VX9000

Designed to be used by professionals, this camera offers triple CCD chip quality, optical zoom lens, 3 hours tape recording time, overexposure warning. But the full-size DV tapes are expensive and there is no DV input socket.

Canon DM-XL1 ✓

The top of the range camera in this section. Optical zoom, interchangeable lenses, full manual override, lightweight body for its size, audio line in, macro lens facility, high-quality three-CCD chip and DV link in and out. Unbeatable for the low-end professional.

The Crunch

- Regardless of the camera, it is down to you and your imagination and skill to make great films.
- However, the cameras in the upper ranges are (usually) better value. A little more money can buy you a lot more quality.
- Shop around, and try the Internet.
- Beware of second-hand cameras unless you know what faults to look for.
- Make deals with your retailer: can they throw in a carry case? A spare battery? A three-movie Hollywood deal?

5. Operating a camcorder

Every model of camcorder is different, but there are certain ways of handling camcorders that make the best of what you've got. From the point of view of the filmmaker, as opposed to the tourist or home-movie maker, some features need to be looked at a little closer.

Camera support

Digital cameras are so lightweight that the problem of camera shake is more pronounced than with previous models and the need to support the camera in some way is crucial. Even hand-held work is going to be vastly different for digital cameras than for film, so whatever your preference in films you will need to make some plans for reducing camera shake. Check that your camera has a universal tripod fitting on its base. Many tripods offer a quick release plate which locks the camera onto the tripod without having to screw the camera onto the tripod each time.

Zoom control

Using zoom on a subject does not always produce good results; zoom controls tend to move at a constant rate and this can look quite unnatural. It is considered to be a slightly redundant way of recording, except in non-fiction work, unless used as a self-conscious device. Use zoom only when a tracking shot towards the subject is not an option.

Film View
Watch *Cape Fear* (Martin Scorsese, 1991) for a good demonstration of how to use these kinds of odd camera movements positively. In several shots, an extremely fast zoom-in takes the viewer to the centre of the action, effective because of the menacing subject matter but also because of the dislocating effect of such zooms.

Focusing

Automatic focusing is useful for tourist movies, but in productions where artistic considerations are high, this is going to stop you from getting good compositions. Be prepared to use the manual override option to use your own focus on certain shots. Automatic focus works by the camera sensing the distance between itself and the nearest object, through the use of infrared beams bounced off its target. The problem with this is that it can't focus on everything within the frame, so it chooses only that which is in the middle of the viewfinder. This renders any slightly adventurous compositions out of focus. When interviewing a subject, for example, it may look more interesting to place the head to one side of the screen, improving depth. You will need to focus manually if you are to avoid getting the wall next to the figure in focus and the head blurred. To do this, use automatic focus on the subject but place it in the middle of the screen, let the auto focus find its optimum point after a few seconds and then switch to manual mode, freezing the focus at this. Then pan the camera to the right composition. Moving the camera closer or nearer to the subject will again render it out of focus and you must go through the process again. Deal with moving, unpredictable subjects like flames and running water in a similar way, but pan the camera to the side first so that you let the auto focus settle on a solid object the same distance from the camera.

Aperture and depth of field

Aperture refers to the opening or iris which allows varied amounts of light through the lens. Aperture affects both the light entering the camera and the range of the frame that is in focus, known as depth of field. Lenses also affect the range of your focus. For example, wide angle lenses allow for a far greater range of focus, from objects far away to those near the camera, while telephoto lenses have very little depth of field, resulting in blurring behind the main subject.

Altering the iris

The iris can be altered for creative uses, using manual controls:

- *Closing the iris* so that it is very small will let less light in and also enable objects in the foreground and background to be in focus – something that may look unnatural or could be just the effect you want.

- *Closing the iris* can also result in well-lit sets appearing to have extreme contrast; the dark areas are unreadable and the white are strong and bright.
- *Opening up the iris* will result in a narrow band of focus, so that objects or people moving towards or away from the camera are easily thrown out of focus.
- *Opening up the iris* will also make normal lighting conditions seem over-lit; even an average lamp will seem to glow unnaturally.

If you manually operate the iris, beware of distortion at the edges of the frame.

Light and the camera

Beware of the way the iris treats light; the camcorder thinks it is doing you a favour by removing some of the light on a bright set or opening itself up to lighten a dark interior. This automatic light meter causes problems as it is going to stop you from using creative lighting effects. Video, in general, does not like to be deprived of light and will react badly if you try to work in conditions that differ from the norm. Just about all filmmaking involves using lighting in some way that the camera's automatic functions may not respond best to. In this case, check that your automatic functions are switched off, but also that you have sufficient light for just part of the frame. You need to get to know how your camera reacts to different lighting set-ups and how far you can push it in terms of overly dark or bright lighting.

You also need to avoid any fluctuation of the aperture during recording. For example, a tracking shot of a figure in movement between a desk with a bright lamp to a darker corner of the room will present problems because of changes in level of light available. Moving between these two places, the camera is designed to step in and open up the iris as it gets to the darker corner. But that loses the whole effect as the two places will appear to the viewer to be lit equally, with the uncomfortable moment in between the two places as the iris shudders around to get the aperture right.

White balance

White balance is a tool – usually automatic in most cameras – which assesses the temperature of light entering the lens and compensates to alter any inaccuracies in colour, to something approaching the mid-range in degrees kelvin. Colours seen in natural daylight are more true than colours seen under artificial light, due to the effect the different colour temperature has on natural colours.

Go to: Chapter 5:8 for a table on colour temperature and the result of using different light sources.

The automatic white balance feature filters out some of these colours to arrive at a more realistic light and should be used for each new take. As with other functions, you can alter it manually and use it as a creative tool so that, for instance, daylight looks bluer and colder than it should – by setting the white balance for indoor, household light it would assume there is too much orange and remove some from the picture. Get to know how your camera functions when you set the colour balance incorrectly.[8]

Power

Batteries are expensive and don't last long, but cables are a hindrance. Think about how you can spread the use of your batteries, or hitch up to the mains as often as possible. Loss of power creeps up on you and almost always happens when you are about to shoot a crucial scene that can't wait. Some cameras in the upper range tell you when you are low on power or have a power meter to keep you informed constantly. Check whether your camera warns you when your battery is running low. If you are on location and have no access to mains supply, conserve power by restricting the amount you rehearse on camera or play with different camera set-ups and do not use the LCD display if your camera has one fitted. Try using a dummy lens, such as a still camera, to try out different compositions or framing, so that when you use the video camera you use less power looking for shots. If you do get stuck without power suddenly, hold the weak battery under your armpit for a short time; sometimes body warmth is all it needs to give you that last bit of power to finish the shoot.

Audio inputs

These will allow you to use external microphones for recording, or the use of mixing boards (on some models). Using external mics is strongly recommended.

Listening to audio

Most cameras have built-in speakers so that you can hear what is being recorded. These are no substitute for padded earphones, however, and sometimes cause feedback.

Timecode

Most consumer-level models do not refer to timecode as such, but do have functions to allow you to start recording right after the last frame of the last take you shot, thereby ensuring that you don't break timecode. Models above this level will all allow you to record with timecode.

The Crunch

- Be in control of the camera.
- Use timecode.
- Learn how to move with it.
- Get a tripod but don't overuse it.
- Zooming in or out does not look great.
- Always get the image in focus.
- Always use an external mic.

---

[8] www.stld.org.uk/Colour_Temperature.htm   Good explanation of colour temperature.

Project 3. In-camera edit: hand-made movie

The aim of this film is to encourage you to use the camera with complete control over every aspect of what it is doing. Cameras are easy: they do what you want, when you want, but they let you down when it comes to helping you be creative. Don't forget, the aim of every camera manufacturer is to make life easier for you. But you don't want an easy life, that's why you are trying to make films, so we need to practice telling the camera to listen and do it your way.

To achieve this, we will make a short film that is made with the camera on *manual settings throughout*. If you have to resort to using automatic settings, it is so that you can deceive the camera, but more on this later. As with other films in this book, we need to make it short, lasting less than 4 minutes. The film is going to made in camera, so you will, as with the last project, be shooting each shot as you need them in the order they appear.

Stage 1

In this film, the subject matter is not the most critical element; it is no more than a vehicle for the actions and movement of the camera. The theme running through this film (it is too open-ended to call it a story) is titled '*A Day in the Life*'.

The film is going to follow you as you go through a typical day, encountering various situations and people. Since you have to keep the movie short, it might be useful to divide the film into sections, looking at different parts of your day. Before we go any further, try to put out of your mind any thoughts about this being in any way a dull premise for a film (just in case). Consider Kevin Smith's stunning debut feature, *Clerks* (1993), which was filmed entirely in the New Jersey shop where he worked. Smith manages to make one location and very little else go a long way, turning in a film which catapulted him into the big time.

Stage 2

Spend some time getting to know what the manual features on your camera are there for. Look at the guide to camera features elsewhere in this chapter and look to see what yours has. Check:

- Where is the manual and auto button (if yours has manual override)?
- Have you got a manual focus ring (unlikely, unless you have a camera from the upper price range)?
- Have you got manual iris control (aperture)?
- Have you got manual white balance?
- How about manual shutter speed?

This project works regardless of how many features you do or don't have, as it looks at how to exercise control over the camera, whatever model that may be.

Stage 3

Choose a day and start filming. Shoot some shots of, for instance, what your house looks like in the morning, about who eats breakfast in your kitchen, where you have to go to work or study, who you meet along the way, where you eat for lunch, who you meet in the evening and where you go, what it's like at night in your town. In all these situations, you will have to encounter environments which are very different to each other in terms of what the camera sees. Conditions will vary from place to place and from day to night, providing you with opportunities to encounter a wide range of situations.

Before we go further, let's take a look at how to handle sound. This project can operate on two levels: a basic level that looks only at what the camera sees, and a more advanced level for those who want to start using an external mic. Take the basic for now, if you prefer, and then come back to this project later when you have got to grips with sound recording in Chapter 5:7. If you choose to use an external mic (you probably guessed by now that the camera's own, built-in mic is not going to fit this project), then you would do well to read the later chapter on sound to help you experiment with the way sound records. But if you want a short cut for now, try using a directional mic and pointing it at whatever or whoever you want to record. Try the built-in mic at least once so that you know what you are not missing.

The aim of this film is not particularly to produce a great-looking film at the end, but rather to encounter problems. You won't be able to solve all of them and you may need to get some help from the automatic button on the camera, but at least you will know the limits of what you can achieve manually and what you need some help for.

Some of the areas you may encounter are considered below.

Light

Usually, you expect your camera to take care of exposure when you enter a new lighting situation. Exposure refers to the amount of light which enters the lens: too much and it is too bright to see anything clearly, too little and it is too dim to see clearly. Let's suppose you start filming in your kitchen in the early morning. You may have a couple of fluorescent lights in the room and some semblance of daylight entering from the window. You have two problems to deal with here: the first involving the intensity of the light within the room and the second concerning the colour temperature of the light. A lack of intensity of light is easy to deal with on set simply by adding more light, but at home you are going to have to get the iris control and try various settings until you have what looks like a good image on the LCD monitor. Open the iris up a little if the image looks too dark, or close it down slightly if it is too bright. Go through all the manual options it gives you until you are satisfied with the image, then start filming.

Colour temperature (measured in degrees kelvin) affects the colour of the light we see. For example, a candle gives off a very orange, warm cast of colour, while daylight on a late afternoon in winter would give off a blueish cast. If you have standard household lights in the kitchen, they may give an orange tint to the film, but none of this would be picked up by the camera as it would remove some of the extra colour. But what happens if you want extra orange? How does the picture look? For this, you may have to resort to the automatic white balance if no other option is available, but at this point run through the manual options it gives you (if any). Some cameras suggest a few settings for the most common lighting situations: indoor, outdoor, bright day, cloudy day and so on. Try out some of these settings incorrectly. If you try, for instance, cloudy outdoor settings for shooting in your kitchen it will assume that there is a dominance of blue in the scene, which would occur in this kind of light, and balance it with taking away some of the blue. The net effect is a kitchen more orange than usual, as what little blue there was is turned down even further.

Go to: Chapter 5:8 for more details on colour temperature and its effect on the camera.

Shutter speed

If your camera has options for changing the shutter speed you can alter these to take into account different situations. Shutter speed refers to the amount of time it takes the camera to open and close the shutter. It opens at a rate of 1/50 for PAL and 1/60 for NTSC, but may increase this if recording fast movement. A fast car, for example, at close range, will appear blurred unless a higher, or faster, shutter speed is used (for example, from 1/125 to 1/400). However, faster shutter speed needs higher light levels, so altering these settings can produce some effects. Try shooting a fast car on a slow shutter speed and perhaps you might enjoy the blurring of the image, particularly if a stationary figure is in the foreground to contrast against it. Then you might want to play around with how a fast shutter speed – requiring more light – records in a low-light environment.

Go to: These terms refer to national broadcast standards and differ from country to country. Go to Chapter 3:1 for a complete guide to which format is found where.

Focus

Focus rings (a ring around the lens which you turn to alter the focus manually) is rare on most camcorders. Without any manual means to alter focus you will have to rely on using (or abusing) the automatic focus feature. Auto focus works by projecting an infrared beam at the nearest object *in the middle of the frame* and assessing from the speed of its return how far away it is. So far so good. But if you want to stop the camera from doing this constantly you will have to let it find one particular setting and stay there. For example, if you meet a few friends and decide to put them in this film, you can shoot straight at them by putting them in the middle of the frame, which is going to look dull, or you can get a more interesting shot. Home movies and tourist movies put people in the middle, but filmmakers want more in their shots and so may move these people slightly to the side so that we see a few other elements of the scene. So, set up your friends so that the arrangement looks less predictable, then set the focus automatically, then turn it off and see what happens.

The result is that your friends are going to be in focus most of the time. If they move a great deal within the frame that's fine, as long as they move across the frame rather than close to or further away from you. But if you had left the auto focus switched on continually your friends would be switching in and out of focus every time they vacated the very middle of the screen. So, in this case, you use auto to get what you want, then get rid of it. Now *you* are in control of the camera.

Evaluation

This project is unusual compared to the others in this book in that it relies very much on improvisation and on making mistakes. At each step of the way, you are wresting control from the automatic settings of the camera and seeing what happens when you shoot against the way it suggests. After all, the settings it gives are simply designed to give you what is considered to be the closest representation of reality. But in most filming you are trying to create illusions, to improve reality in some way, and so it becomes crucial to defeat these realist tendencies in the camera. You know where they are if you need them. They are, for instance, very useful in determining the right amount of light for a given scene, to ensure that we can see what is happening. But even here it is better that you learn about adding more light on set than opening up the camera iris to compensate.

The editing of this film is almost a side-issue and we can overlook any sudden jumps or parts that don't seem to fit, but if you have managed to produce a film that does have some sense of flow to it and compresses the day very neatly into a few minutes, then you have scored well. If you are less pleased with the editing, use it to practice on when we start to look at DV editing in later projects.

6. Video safety and good practice

Treat your camcorder well

Water

A camcorder can be irreparable if damaged with water. Protect it from rain and wipe off moisture from the casing. Salt water is especially harmful, and can do damage to the outer casing as well as the inner workings.

Condensation

Some camcorders warn you if condensation is building up inside the camera and many will switch off automatically. To remedy this, take out the cassette, if the camera will let you. If it is not possible, switch off and wait 2 or 3 hours. Once you have removed the cassette, leave the cassette compartment open for 2 or 3 hours, to dry, in a non-dusty room at average temperature. Condensation is particularly problematic if you film in extremely cold places and the water freezes. If this happens, let the camera thaw naturally at room temperature and then go through the same process as for condensation.

Magnetized equipment

Any magnetic field can adversely affect recording. Television monitors, video games and loudspeakers generate fields which distort picture quality. No lasting damage is done to the camera itself, but your footage could be ruined. Test how the camera performs if you are in any doubt and play back the results on a monitor. Occasionally, the actual mechanism of the camera can be affected, temporarily, but this is often solved by unplugging your power supply or removing the battery and then reconnecting.

Sunlight

Pointing the viewfinder at sunlight can do great damage to inner working parts. Worse, it can permanently damage your eyesight too.

Radio transmitters and power lines

If you have ever listened to radio near an overhead power line you will have heard an amount of interference. This noise badly affects your video recording, so avoid shooting near pylons or other high-voltage lines. Radio transmitters will have a similar effect on the sound and image. Mobile phones also cause problems with sound interference while recording.

Excessive use

Many camcorders are not designed to be used for excessively long periods, as for example in surveillance filming; the inside temperature of the camera can cause malfunctions.

Dust and sand

Take care when inserting the cassette that no fine dust or sand enters the camera. If you are using the camera in a potentially dusty environment, use a protective cover. If you don't have a cover, you can improvise with a black bin-liner, wrapped around the casing. But beware that the camera could overheat over a period of time.

Cleaning

Some camcorders react badly to being cleaned with benzine or thinners. The body casing can be deformed as a result. Use a soft cloth with mild, dilute detergent mixed with water. Wring out the cloth until nearly dry before use. Never clean the camera while the battery or mains supply is attached.

Clean lenses rarely, and with great care. Avoid getting the lens dirty. Try fitting a protective clear UV filter (semi) permanently to the front of the lens if the camera has a filter thread fitted. You can always buy another cheap filter when it gets damaged.

Cleaning the video recording heads is advised, but with care. Sometimes, after a lot of use, dirt and tape particles build up on the video heads, obstructing perfect quality recording. Some cameras tell you when this is happening, with a display on the monitor. To clean the heads, get hold of a cleaning cassette, which cleans as it plays. But don't do this too often; the cleaning cassette is an abrasive cleaner.

Power – AC adapter

- When you charge your battery, make sure that the temperature of the battery is not excessively high or low. Charging when the battery is outside the right temperature will not adversely affect the charger; it will simply not charge. Some camcorder adapters will start to charge automatically once the right temperature is reached.
- When the battery is warm, charging can take longer.
- The AC adapter may affect radio reception, so don't charge near your radio antennae. One metre away from the charger is sufficient.
- Keep the terminals of the charger and the battery clean to enable maximum charging power.

Battery care

- Batteries for many camcorders work by generating electricity through a chemical reaction, using lithium. The reaction is easily affected by temperature and humidity, and impedes the amount of power you get from it. At very cold temperatures, a battery may have its life-span cut down to just 5 minutes, while high temperatures may cause the battery to switch off for some time.
- Protect the battery terminals from moisture, as this can cause rust to develop.
- If metal objects touch both battery terminals at the same time they may cause it to short-circuit and generate serious amounts of heat, even starting a fire. If you pick up a battery that is short-circuiting, you may receive burns.
- Do not leave the battery attached to the camera for long periods when it is not in use, as this can damage the voltage level of the battery and affect its ability to recharge.[9]

Using the LCD monitor

- Temperature will affect picture quality on an LCD monitor. When cold, the picture is darker then usual, even in reasonable climates. After a while the ambient heat of the camera is enough to rectify this, but bear it in mind if you use the monitor in cold environments. Over 100 000 pixels are used on these monitors but less than 1 per cent will be inactive, sometimes affecting picture quality. Don't worry about this as it does not affect recorded picture quality.
- Remember that using the LCD monitor will run down the power in the battery much faster than if you use only the viewfinder; a 1-hour life-span is reduced to 30 minutes when using the monitor.

Videotape care

Even though DV tapes are much more sturdy than VHS or S-VHS, they are still prone to problems from poor handling.

---

[9] www.eurobatteries.com/sitepages/batteryglossary.htm   Vast amount of detail on all battery types and how to handle them safely.

Storage

- Always store tape vertically, with the tape rewound, in its case.
- Store away from magnetic fields, direct sunlight, or excessive moisture or dust.
- Avoid touching the tape.
- Avoid dropping the tape, or causing any other shock or impact to it.
- Cars are very bad for tapes; the temperature inside the vehicle rises and falls dramatically when not in use.
- If cassettes are excessively cold, let them warm up to average room temperature for a couple of hours.
- Do not leave the cassette in the camcorder for long periods.
- Rewind the tapes after use; tape stretching can occur.
- Always label your tapes, the moment you take them out of the camera, before you reach for the next tape. Every filmmaker has stories of having to trawl through numerous tapes looking for a particular lost piece of footage.[10]

The Crunch

- Don't skip this bit – you might get sued if something goes wrong.
- Films about people getting sued don't end happily.

---

[10] http://aic.stanford.edu/treasure/video.html   Excellent in-depth article on tape care.

4 | Pre-production

1. Working out a budget

DV is less expensive

The size of your budget should be part of the decision-making process from the start of the development process. How much or how little you have will play a key role in deciding what kind of film you make.

A DV film is going to cost far less than its conventional forerunner. Moreover, getting high quality, or even broadcast quality, images is now within reach of most micro-budget filmmakers, throwing up the possibility that a first movie by an unknown director will be of sufficient technical quality to find a buyer, leading to distribution. Until now, the best a low-budget director could hope for was to work on 16 mm film, which could be blown up to academy 35 mm at great expense should the film find its way into theatres. Soon, however, the debut DV director could be showing a film on digital projectors, beamed from satellite to theatres, saving huge costs previously spent on printing copies of the movie on celluloid.[1]

Film View
The low-budget hit feature *The Last Broadcast* (Steven Avalos and Lance Weiler, 1998), and reputed precursor to *Blair Witch*, did just this in 2000, all for a movie which cost just $900. Peter Broderick, founder of Next Wave Films which supported the movie, said: 'When people ask me how much they need to make a feature, I ask them how much they have, because that will be enough.'

---

[1] www.nextwavefilms.com/ulbp/index.html   Helpful resource for ultra-low-budget filmmakers with big ambitions.
www.cybergecko.com/no-budge.htm   Detailed database with international members and good forum for low-budget filmmakers.

Equipment

Getting hold of equipment also used to take some ingenuity. Expensive film cameras, rolls of film, lights and editing units were all guaranteed to take up a large slice of a budget, but digital camcorders are now getting cheaper with each new model and arriving with added features. Edit software is likely to have been bundled free onto your PC, while others still can be downloaded free from the Internet.

Developing a budget

Once you have your basic equipment you can start to divide costs into the two main areas used in feature film budgeting: above-the-line and below-the-line.

Go to: the CD-ROM accompanying this book for a template of a typical film budget; build your own from this model.

Above-the-line

Above-the-line refers to those people in a production who contribute to the main artistic aspects of the film. Therefore, the director, producer, writer and cast will be allocated a certain amount of the budget, often taking up one third of the total above-the-line.

Below-the-line

Other areas such as design, props, lighting, consumables and all other production costs are entered separately, 'below-the-line'. In big-budget productions it is more likely that above-the-line takes up a disproportionate amount of the budget.

Tip   Most features allow 5 per cent of the budget to the director and producer, 5 per cent for the script, 20 per cent for the actors, 20 per cent to the studio (independent movies don't have this overhead), 35 per cent for equipment, tapes and crew, 5 per cent for taxes, and 10 per cent for all the costs you haven't thought of yet. DV filmmakers will find equipment costs far below this figure.

In low-budget productions, however, it's likely that since you as director will occupy several, if not all, of the positions above-the-line and are probably giving up your spare time to get this together (in other words, you are not getting paid), you could find yourself with a budget sheet that has almost no above-the-line costs. In this case, it is the below-the-line costs that will be disproportionate, since these are almost immovable, such as transport expenses, videotape, props and so on.

Budgets influence stories

If you fall into the category of filmmaker who has little or no disposable income to invest in a film and wish to simply get what you can for as little as possible, then it would be useful to let your available budget affect the kind of film you are going to make. It's not too cynical to suggest that you centre a story around the props, locations and people you already have access to for free; in other words, objects you already own, places you can use as settings for the story and actors who will act for free or non-actors who may not expect to be paid.

Certain types of film are going to cost more than others. If you take a look at the synopses of films currently doing the rounds at film festivals or online cinemas, it is common to find certain genres represented more than others. Epic genre movies are rare but plots centring on relationships, road movies or crime all figure highly as they involve few post-production effects or extravagant locations and props.

Go to: Chapter 4:4 for advice about how to work out good stories for a low-budget movie.

Perhaps even more noticeable is the originality of these films. An unusual story, an unfamiliar or quirky take on a subject all result from a need to grab the audience's attention by means other than expensive special effects. In a sense, ingenious and creative ideas for films excuse you from the need to raise large budgets; the value of the film is in the way you have used the medium itself rather than what you have spent on it.[2]

Reducing costs

The least expensive kind of film varies, then, according to what you have access to, but there are a number of other points that can help in reducing the budget of any movie. If we now look at the kinds of sub-headings found in a typical budget, we can start to look at ways that costs could be kept to a minimum.[3]

Above-the-line

1 *Screenplay.* Write the film yourself, from your own original material.
2 *Producer.* On a larger production, a producer acts as business manager and administrator, pulling the various financial, legal and logistical threads together. Getting involved in these aspects of a small production yourself gives you an essential schooling in the business side of the industry.
3 *Director.* Direct the movie yourself. You can still collaborate with other people on a movie as long as you all forego payment.

[2] www.malamute.cc/company/pages/filmbudget.htm   Useful template for low-budget movies.
[3] www.budgetcheetah.com/   Tools for filmmakers to devise budgets.
   www.chicagomediaworks.com/2instructworks/3editing_doc/3docedit_budgetmpl/3editing_docsbudgetem
   plate.html   Long-winded address but helpful templates for documentary filmmakers.

4 *Cast*. If your story requires actors there are a number of ways of involving a cast while keeping costs low. Acting on film can be good experience, adding to an actor's résumé, and many are willing to work on small productions for free provided they have no other commitments but may, entirely reasonably, leave your production in mid-shoot if a paid job comes up. Deferred payment is another route, in which you say that you will pay everyone if the movie makes a profit. If your cast and crew believe strongly in the project's merits they will see this as equivalent to holding shares in the movie. But try to be as open as possible with people about the possibility that any money will be forthcoming; most independent movies, including successful ones, see little profit.

'I knew there would not be any profits. To offer deferments would have been dishonest. With "*Demonsoul*" everybody worked on a voluntary basis. It was quite clear that there wasn't going to be any money for anyone at a later date so there was no point offering it.'

Simon Onwurah, producer, Demonsoul

Below-the-line

1 *Sets*. Use locations rather than sets. If you need, for instance, an interior set of an office, find a suitable real location rather than building the set yourself in a studio. Compromise in your aims so that you can use real settings; if a room is not quite right, it is still saving you much money.
2 *Props*. Build your story around props you have access to or can acquire cheaply.
3 *Costumes*. Again, follow the same ideas as for locations; set the film in the here and now, avoiding period costumes.
4 *Laboratory*. In films shot on celluloid this is one of the largest expenses, together with film stock, while DV filmmaking removes this whole item from the budget.
5 *Stock*. Following on from the last item, however, the amount of videotape you need is greater than that used on similar-length movies shot on celluloid. Buy the highest quality you can afford and expect to shoot more than you will use. You should try to use tapes a limited number of times – once if analog VHS, three or four if S-VHS – in order to keep the quality high and consistent throughout shooting. DV tapes, however, are built very differently to analog tapes and will last considerably longer, enabling you to re-record over them many more times.

When shooting you should try to keep all the takes you film, regardless of the amount of space this may occupy, and avoid the temptation to rewind and record over the bad take. In early projects, you may need up to an hour of blank tape for every minute that you will edit, but as you become more experienced in making movies this will fall dramatically. The ratio of 'total film shot' to 'film used in final film' is known as the 'shooting ratio'.

6 *Editing*. Provided you have the hardware and software necessary to get your tapes onto your PC, edit them and put the finished film back onto tape or whatever format you need, you are making a huge saving compared to the budgets used in non-digital films. A typical film in the late 1990s costing less than $500 000 – classified as low budget – saw editing costs take up 10 per cent of the overall budget. If you edit the movie yourself and do so using your own desktop edit unit, you are making big savings.

7 *Sound and music*. Use original material, avoiding complicated and expensive copyright fees. Basic software is available for creating your own sounds, enabling adequate music to be placed on your film with little or no musical knowledge and, as it is originated digitally, can be used in an editing software program with no loss of quality.

Go to: Chapter 6:4 for more details of using music, creating your own or obtaining free soundtracks from the Internet.

8 *Insurance*. In larger productions insurance is a non-negotiable item. It is essential to protect the production company against claims from injuries or worse incurred by cast or crew during filming. It can also cover loss of tape or stock, delays in production caused by damage or illness to sets or people and damage to others' property due to production. In small productions where many of the roles are unpaid or filled by the director/writer/producer, it may not be necessary to set up such packages of insurance. Your own household insurance is unlikely to pay for equipment lost or damaged on location, so it may be useful to set up an extension to your existing cover. Actors receiving payment will expect some cover in the event of injury on set. It does not follow, however, that unpaid cast will exclude you from blame if injuries stop them from taking a paid job right after your production. If insurance cannot be arranged, try to come to some written agreement with crew and cast prior to filming.

9 *Additional costs*. Just about every micro/low-budget film comes in over budget. It is almost a rule that the smaller the budget the more likely you are to need to be flexible. This is mainly because of the notorious 'additional costs'. Notorious because they creep up on you and end up devouring half the film's budget on items such as extra gaffer tape, photocopying, petrol, parking tickets, mobile phone calls. One particular budget from a filmmaker who was aiming to bring in a 10-minute film for under £120 went far beyond this when the line 'additional costs' was added. End-of-shoot drinks and food alone added 50 per cent to the budget, while unforeseen petrol to ferry around unpaid actors and crew added 20 per cent.

How much money is needed?

As we have seen, at a certain low level of budget it is desirable to work out what funds are available and then look at what kind of film is possible. This is part of the creative process and to a certain extent plays a part in most directors' minds at whatever level they operate. Even on larger budget films it is common to find the story compromised by a lack of funds. It is no different to van Gogh deciding that he would paint a small picture today rather than a large one if that's all the canvas he had.

If you have managed to involve crew and cast without payment and follow the ideas listed above for reducing costs, the main immovable costs are videotapes and items seen in front of the camera; in other words, sets, dressing and locations. To be safe, add 20 per cent onto the cost to allow for unforeseen extras, but even then the cost of a short, self-made film can be less than a small family's weekly food bill (but with a greater life-span).

Getting investment

Raising money for larger productions as a completely unknown filmmaker is complicated but not impossible. Producer Simon Onwurah helped put together the finance for *Welcome II the Terrordome* (1994). 'It was an elaborate thing. Friends and family at first, and then we decided to come up with a private investors' scheme which tapped small investors and individuals. Some money came from sponsorship by companies as well.'

Even unknown filmmakers can, and do, raise money from companies, charitable agencies, family friends and state arts agencies. If you go for this option, approach it as a business proposition. This means putting together a business plan, résumés, showreel, budget and screenplay. You can never be too professional about this, so think about devising a company name and get some headed paper and even a website domain name to demonstrate that you see this as a serious venture, reflecting your own commitment to it. Become professional: get yourself a suit, turn up to meetings on time and be well prepared, projecting the image of someone they can invest money in. Getting together a business package is going to need some investment itself, but many banks are very keen for the custom of the small business and will send free of charge a range of material showing how to put together a good-looking package, and some may offer discount vouchers from local companies for costs such as printing.[4]

Compiling an investment package

The following should be included.

Résumés (curriculum vitae)

These should reflect the talent you have managed to coax into your project. Ask for detailed résumés from your crew and include any references that suggest that these people know what they are doing, or have studied somewhere to be able to do this, or have raised finance previously. Keep these short, summarizing the important information, and include photos where possible. If you or anyone in your team have received any publicity from any source, include it to suggest that you are, as a group, on the way up and are worth investing in.

Showreel

This is a selection of clips of the projects you have worked on so far, usually on VHS tape. Include those of your team as well. It is an extension of the résumé and is your chance to show that you do, indeed, know what you are doing and have picked up a camera before, that you have all the skills needed to finish the movie.

---

[4] www.dcita.gov.au/nsapi-graphics/?MIval=dca_dispdoc&ID=3453   Australian resource for investment in film but useful information for all filmmakers.
http://investcan.ic.gc.ca/en_film.htm   Canadian government information on film investment.

> **Tip**   On a note of caution, you may see postings on independent filmmaker websites offering to make you a showreel, including some interviews with yourself. These are generally regarded as something to be avoided, exploiting the desire of filmmakers to get themselves marketed.

If neither you nor your team have made any movies yet, then don't be shy about it. Include it if you have the material, even if it consists of half-finished drafts for movies and experiments, but don't worry if you have none.

Background material

A range of development material will help convince the potential investor that you have planned the film and have a hard-working and realistic approach to your work. Include a screenplay if you have one, a short synopsis describing the film in only a few paragraphs, artwork, sketches, storyboards, even possible advertisement designs for the film. Also include some indication of the assets you have which help in making the movie, such as editing software, mics or cameras.

Budget

Make your budget as detailed as you can, giving estimates at the conservative, upper end of the scale to be on the safe side. Investors will be more impressed by a realistic budget than a cheaper one with no hope of success. You should not have to seek extra funding halfway through production, even if much of Hollywood does exactly that.

Getting private backers for your film is not easy, but there are enough anecdotes about well-established directors who have gone to great lengths to get cash for a first film to convince that it's worth a try. The young Sam Raimi, unable to secure funding for his first feature, sent investment packages to all the doctors and dentists in Michigan, eventually raising enough money to make *Evil Dead* (1982).

Copyright

But be careful if you are sending out material that you feel could easily be imitated or copied by someone else. Your movie belongs to you even though you haven't shot it yet, so copyright the story or treatment and any other information or material you want to safeguard, including company name. Simply state at the foot of each sheet that copyright is owned by you and that this material cannot be reproduced in any way, including electronically. Doing this makes you look more professional, and therefore good value to a potential investor.

Beware investment firms

You may also hear about companies that specialize in getting funds for new businesses. Such companies will invest in high-risk projects for gain, but even they often draw the line at getting involved in the notoriously unpredictable film business. There are, however, some who only work in entertainment and will advertise their services on Internet filmmaker sites, offering to raise finance for your film. Beware about committing yourself to deals if you are unfamiliar with this territory. It is common for you to lose 50 per cent of your profits – should there be any – to your backer, but this may be no more than what you would pay out to other private backers. To be on the safe side, don't take part in such a scheme unless you fully understand what you are signing and can repay any loans with or without your movie making a profit. And certainly avoid signing anything that puts your property or other collateral on the line if you can't repay. If you are keen to take this route, it may be safer to seek out someone from a law background rather than a credit/loans background. Many law firms have specialists in finding investment for entertainment projects, but this is more common in cities where the film industry is prominent.

Funding a movie on credit cards

It is now common to hear of films made at the low end of the scale which have been financed entirely on credit cards. But it is becoming more common still to hear of filmmakers saddled with insurmountable debt as they struggle to repay borrowed money and rising interest. The temptation is great: fill in a few forms and you get sent cheques for all the money to make your movie. But try to think of the long term; think of how you will finance your next project if you are having to work day and night to fend off the debt collector. Before you commit yourself to using credit, think first about the absolute worst case scenario; consider what should happen if your film does not recoup any of its costs and you end up borrowing more than you first thought. If the figures you come up with look manageable then proceed, but exercise caution.

The Crunch

- Make use of what you have free.
- Some genres and stories are expensive.
- Don't spend beyond your budget.
- Avoid credit card movie-making.
- Cover many filmmaking roles yourself.
- If you want investment, plan well and make a package (see Chapter 8 for more help with promotion).

2. Using the Internet to build a project

The Internet is a huge resource for you as a filmmaker and there are many sites that will address your needs, at whatever level you are working at in the industry. You can get in touch with other people in the same position, perhaps looking to get involved in a production, wanting to recruit people, needing advice about technical aspects of the process or to buy, borrow or sell equipment.

The fast-moving nature of the web is an ideal place for an industry as reliant on change and innovation as that of the filmmaker. For Grant Millar, of BT online cinema Getoutthere.com, the Internet 'offers filmmakers new and exciting ways of communicating and making your mark'. Ben Reneker, meanwhile, who manages a successful Internet information site for filmmakers, RealMind.com, believes that 'the Internet will revolutionize the distribution of independent media. It has opened the doors for thousands of filmmakers.'[5]

These, and the hundreds of other sites, display the underbelly of the film industry, populated by enthusiastic, dynamically driven filmmakers, most of whom are disarmingly realistic about the amount of work needed and their chances of success. It is this ability to communicate more widely across the Internet that has pushed up the morale of this kind of filmmaker. Medium- and big-budget filmmakers have found that networking and participating in the filmmaking community is more straightforward once the doors are open, when you have a well-received production or a lucky break and you have a calling card to help you move on to the next project.

Operating far outside of the established film industry, and even beyond the thriving independent scene, they are now able to support each far more than ever before. While small-scale filmmakers have perhaps managed to build self-nurturing communities within particular cities or towns, now these are expanding in national and global terms.

What's available

The following kinds of questions can be addressed using Internet sites:

- I want to know how to contact other people to make a film with.
- I want information and advice on how to make my film.
- I want to know how professionals rate cameras, software, festivals, competitions, funding agencies, training opportunities.
- What opportunities are there to get money to make my film?
- I want to read about how current filmmakers are managing to make films.
- I want to show my film, get feedback and maybe sell it.

There are many online independent filmmaking magazine sites. Although the Internet is global, many sites address a particular territory and therefore are restricted in what they offer in terms of recruiting fellow workers, but on the plus side these do offer a way into working in other countries that was previously difficult.[6]

---

[5] www.getoutthere.bt.com/   British Telecom movie and music showcase.
www.realmind.com   UK-based Internet information site.

[6] www.filmmaking.net/   Filmmakers online resource.
www.cyberfilmschool.com/   Filmmakers online school and resources.
www.filmmaking.net   Articles and FAQs on filmmaking.
www.indiewire.com/   US-based forum for filmmakers to exchange job news and opinions.
www.shootingpeople.org   Highly rated, fast-moving filmmakers exchange for news, jobs and views.

As with all aspects of the Internet, it is easier if you know exactly what you are looking for. Inputting the word 'filmmakers' can produce thousands of possibilities, but starting from a site well established among filmmakers can produce links to sites of similar quality. You can't rely on sites to be accurate, but if what you want is communication rather than information, then this is not a factor; some of the most successful sites are aware that interacting with visitors or visitors interacting with each other is vital to sustaining a site and most filmmakers want to participate rather than simply receive information. As such, many include classified ads and discussion lines within a site and rely on a constant traffic of filmmakers seeking help.[7]

Equipment

For equipment, you can get as much information as you need, short of actually road-testing a product. Most manufacturers offer details about their products online (but if you buy direct from them are rarely the most competitive) and many edit software packages can be downloaded for a trial period or in some cases as freeware. Sound and music are available, sometimes for free, and there is even a growing number offering free footage from which you could compile a movie soundtrack.[8]

Did you know?
Freeware is a term given to software which you can download legally on the Internet for no charge.

Filmmakers talking to each other

But it is the ability to put people in touch with each other that is having the most impact. Sites such as Shooting People in the UK and Indiewire in the USA operate fast-moving, responsive classified ads. Their growing popularity has become part of the digital revolution in filmmaking, and are watched by those higher up in the industry, eager to identify trends.

Interview
'There are excellent writing resources, like wordplay.com or moviebytes.com, and producers and directors will find creativeplanet.com interesting.'

Mark Innocenti, filmmaker, screenwriter, USA

---

[7] www.dvfilmmaker.com/   Resources and message board for digital filmmaking.
www.dvcafe.com   Tips, news and views on DV filmmaking.
www.dscoop.com   Broadcast site with news and information on DV filmmaking.
www.dvfilmmaker.com   News and views on DV filmmaking.
[8] www.stonewashed.net/sfx.html   Free sound effects for downloading.
www.sounddogs.com/start.asp   Largest online sound library.
www.trackline.com/   Royalty-free music library.

Looking for people to work with

As you become more interested in making movies, you will have reached a point where either you want to be part of a group making a film or you have a clear idea of a film you would like to make and need crew to help you. The second option offers more possibilities but requires more thought. In order to recruit the right people for your project you need to plan and develop the film as far as you are able, allowing others to get a clear, well-defined idea of what you are trying to do. Building up a team will require you to be very specific about your aims for the project and how far you are prepared to go in terms of distribution and sale.

Interview

'I recruited all my crew and production team from shootingpeople.org.uk. From my personal point of view I was looking for people with enthusiasm for my project rather than tons of experience.'

Amber Mosdell, filmmaker, UK

How to post a message

If you choose to post a message on a site, check first whether it will appear for one day only or whether it stays indefinitely until you remove it. Follow the points below in preparing a message.

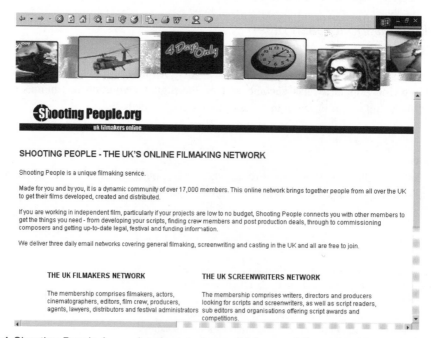

Figure 4.1 Shooting People (www.shootingpeople.org.uk) is one of the most popular filmmakers' bulletin-boards for recruiting film crews, getting advice or posting messages.

Figure 4.2 The Indiewire (www.indiewire.com) bulletin-board focuses on filmmakers in the USA.

Be specific

How many people do you need? Do they need skills in certain areas or is this a collaborative film where each member needs general filmmaking skills? Give a clear outline of the film, a 'pitch', but don't be tempted to make the project sound bigger or more grand than it is.

Be honest

If you are new to filmmaking, say so. Similarly, be blunt about whether you can pay anyone, about how much time you can commit and what equipment you actually have right now. And don't worry if your posting starts to sound too particular; just about any set-up will attract some response.

Timing

Give exact details of dates you provisionally intend to work on and whether any follow-up dates would be needed.

Distribution

Don't give false hope of where your film will end up. Avoid aiming too high or appearing to be unrealistic about your chances of success. Some ads tell you that merely participating in this particular film is reward enough and will make a great addition to your résumé.

Contacting you

In asking for replies, try where possible to use email addresses rather than land addresses or phone numbers. It is useful to set up an address specifically for a particular project, and this is terminated when you end the production. You could make this a remote access address, such as hotmail or similar. If you receive replies it would be advisable, on a note of personal safety, to agree to meet in busy public places rather than at your home address, taking the same kind of precautions you might expect in lonely hearts ads.

Budget

Giving details of a budget is no longer an indication of the level on which you are working. Ambitious short films can be cheap, as can even feature films. Since DV has taken hold of the low-budget film world, budget sheets have smaller figures and more 'nil cost' entries than ever, without compromising too much on quality. Don't be worried about going further and describing yourself as a low- or no-budget filmmaker. Rather than put people off, this term now has come to denote a certain underground, maverick approach to the craft and with it the suggestion of something innovative and challenging.

Who are you looking for?

Ask yourself what skills you have and then look at what you don't. Go about recruiting people who are going to add to the production rather than those who are simply going to double up on what you yourself can already handle. If you are confident in more than one area, you may feel that placing yourself in one particular role is a better use of your time than trying to cover all bases.

Look at the roles outlined in the chapter on working with other people and identify which you want to work in and which you can hand out to others. In terms of numbers, as a broad guide, a crew of four would be sufficient for a small-scale, low-budget short film, not including actors.

This would consist of:

- a camera operator;
- a director;
- an editor;
- a sound operator.

Not all of these people will be necessary throughout the project, but you may find people who want to be involved in all aspects of the project and who don't limit their time to their role. This sort of blurring of a job description is rarely seen higher up in the industry, as the inclusion of a pay cheque in the equation formalizes a person's relationship with a project. Your film can only benefit from involving people who want to be kept involved on a larger scale, but some may be uncomfortable spreading out artistic input among the whole crew.

The Internet can help you find the right people to work with and is an effective short cut to entering the industry at grass roots level. Once you are working on a project you will find it useful to be able to seek advice on the logistical and technical aspects of filmmaking, reaching practitioners from all parts of the process. The Internet is going to become a powerful ally in overcoming problems at all stages of a film; with the absence of a big budget to get what you want, the online community of independent, low-budget filmmakers is working out its own way to get films made and seen.

The Crunch

- Use the Internet to talk to other filmmakers.
- Ask for advice; people are willing to help.
- Use the Internet for getting information about equipment.
- Get crew for a film by recruiting on the Internet.

3. Working with a crew

Billy Wilder's famous aphorism that making a film is 'a collection of creative people, in a profit-driven system' is apt; to many filmmakers theirs is a collaborative art form, involving a balancing act between the various creative people involved and the commercial needs of the industry. Although our culture has grown to expect one person to author a film it is, in reality, a group effort.

Whatever the size of your production, working with other people is invariably going to help your development as a filmmaker, clarifying what you do and giving you more confidence in your ability.

Choosing to work alone or as part of a group is determined as often by practicalities as by creative concerns. In practice, it is entirely feasible to make a short film alone and with no other production staff apart from actors. Furthermore, if you work in certain kinds of film you can see the whole production through from start to finish without involving other people. Certainly, documentary and some forms of music video can be accomplished alone, as can many forms of documentary. This may become restrictive, however, and as the ambition of your plans grows so too does the need to draw in other people who share your enthusiasm for a project.

Working solo

If you choose to work alone you are in total control of the production. You call the shots and dictate how the project progresses; if you wish to change direction you do so without discussion.

On the other hand, you may feel less confident about remaining on target and following through the plans you set out at the beginning of a project. Filming has a notorious ability to steer you from your intended route with the result that you end up with drafts for two or three films rather than finished footage for one. Like-minded people can be a steadying influence, restraining the more extravagant changes of plan and acting as a sounding board for the testing of new ideas.

A small crew

Deciding how many people to work with can be an important factor in the success or otherwise of your plans. A large crew can be cumbersome and unresponsive to changing situations, while working with a small number of people can lead to a healthy degree of flexibility, as much as does a solo effort. When filming on a low budget it pays to be opportunistic, noticing chances for borrowed props, equipment or locations which could either cut costs or benefit the overall production.

Film View
Director George Lucas noted the beneficial nature of working with a small crew, having had straightforward and enjoyable shoots on the small-scale *American Graffiti* (1973) and *THX 1138* (1970), in contrast to the problematic and cumbersome process on the larger-scale *Star Wars* (1977).

Co-operation

In a production where the costs start to exceed your monthly disposable income, sharing the costs can be a necessity. Working with other people does not mean adding to your costs, particularly if you adopt an approach where you see yourself as collaborating with other filmmakers rather than employing them. In a co-production – a small number of people working towards a shared goal with equal control – costs are spread. While it may be more straightforward to have one person in overall artistic control of a film, this is by no means the only model. The low-budget strata of the film industry is more dependent on mutual co-operation than any other, and to a large extent has succeeded in producing a constant stream of new talent precisely because its participants are ready and willing to help each other make movies.

Being candid about your lack of funding and payment is better than promising cash that never turns up. At the lower end of the industry people will work for you for free or, more likely, with you, provided you can convince them that your film is going to be of the quality that will help them get noticed, and look good on a showreel or résumé. This doesn't mean you can presume non-payment. In fact, to offer something goes some way to making your production look professional. One posting on an Internet recruitment site for filmmakers was open about what was on offer: 'editor needed, familiar with Premiere, for short film. This is a great looking film and although I can't offer payment you will be blown away by the footage. It'll look great on your CV (résumé).' An editor was found and the film completed and, it appears, all parties were happy with the experience.

Paying your crew does, however, make it easier to expect 'performance' from the people you pay, easier to ask them to work long hours during bad weather and turn up on time, and easier to make sure that actors don't leave your production for a paid job midway through filming (and who could blame them?). Also, be careful about paying some members of the crew and not others, tempting if you have some experienced people and some first-timers. It can split a crew apart when it is discovered that some are being paid for what others do for nothing. Your production could end unceremoniously.

Sharing power on set

Working without payment does suggest certain rights in terms of how much one is allowed to contribute to the artistic route the film takes. Sharing power in a production, in other words including the opinions and ideas of those you work with, may increase their sense of involvement in, and therefore commitment to, a production, supplanting payment with shared artistic input to retain the services of those you need to help complete your project. The net result for you is greater quality of work from your crew and a commitment to see the project through to the end. With so many potential films, especially shorts, abandoning shooting because one or more members of the crew have moved on to more attractive projects, you need to keep people on board.

Interview
'In terms of the hierarchy, with the director at the top, I prefer a more collaborative approach. I think it is good to get everyone's feedback whilst on the shoot . . .but you have to be careful as everybody can interpret the script differently.'

Mark Smith, filmmaker, Neon Films, UK

Other people are good for your movie

If you work with even a small number of people on a production it is likely that your ideas will be tested and questioned. This sort of experience is crucial in pushing your idea to its most highly developed point and ensuring that the eventual film itself is the best you can possibly make. Some filmmakers prefer to be resolutely in charge of a film, but others recognize that almost no member of the crew found on a film set is purely a technician; most come with some creative ideas about each stage of production.

The idea of pushing a project as far as possible is best done in a competitive atmosphere. Three or four people, each enthusiastic about a project and determined to prove themselves in an ultimately supportive group, can raise standards and lead to some highly original works, often to the surprise of each member.

Filmmaking can be a meeting of creative minds, but you don't have to lose control over the direction of your film when you start to involve other people; they can be as committed to the original idea as you.

While it is possible to make films alone, the nature of low-budget filmmaking is such that you need all the help you can get and can only benefit from extending artistic input to include other people with other skills and experiences. Your crew need to agree on the basic aims of a project and the integrity of the initial ideas, but beyond that they may help push the movie higher than you could alone.

What kinds of roles are needed?

Hollywood method

Throughout the film industry a certain number of clearly defined roles have evolved within a film production. To a certain extent these have developed in line with the demands of the medium to emulate business, with a hierarchy of roles.[9]

Tip   Being part of a union may help to get you further within the industry. The crew you work with may be unionized, but the short film and independent sector in general tends to use non-union labour, usually to avoid (by mutual consent) the standard fees required by union crews. In the UK this is BECTU (Broadcasting, Entertainment and Cinematography Technicians Union); in the USA the main union is referred to as the IA, a shortened form of the International Alliance for Theatrical Stage and Moving Picture Employees.

- *Director.* Acts as artistic controller, holding the project together with a single vision of the style and tone of the movie.
- *Producer.* Runs the production as business manager.
- *Production manager.* Responsible for the organization of the production under the producer.
- *Director of cinematography.* One of the most important roles on set, this person is responsible for lighting the set and the operating of the camera. However, in practice, the DP rarely operates the camera, but is responsible for every photographic aspect of the film, and for managing the camera crew.
- *Continuity.* Person responsible for the perfect matching of all elements in a scene, so that when edited the different takes work seamlessly together.
- *Sound mixer/boom handler.* These jobs cover, respectively, the correct mixing of sounds during filming and the adequate placing of the camera on set.

Low-budget groups

In large productions managing sums greater than the turnover of many businesses, this hierarchy of roles is an essential way of remaining on target and within budget. But in the low-budget sector there

---

[9] www.bectu.org.uk/   British media union.
   www.iatse.lm.com/   North American territories union.

are opportunities and benefits from doing it differently. Although this hierarchical structure remains the default method for many, it belies the reality where roles merge and responsibilities change. Many low-budget films work on a pared-down model that places the director (who has often written the script), the producer (who shares artistic commitment to the film and is rarely a simple business manager) and the director of cinematography on a more or less equal footing. One person may well have instigated the project, but each of this team must feel central to the decision-making process. Once a project is established, other members of the crew may be recruited.

At this level it is common for the director to have written the film, to have an abiding interest in shooting or editing or both, and in many cases may fulfil all roles. More often, a number of people initially brought into a project for a specific skill will also contribute to a range of other areas. It may, in fact, be difficult to find skilled people who have no interest in any other part of a production than their own specialism. They may have a range of skills in other areas resulting from time spent making films where two or three people cover every skill area.

A basic crew, by skill not job description

At its most basic, a small crew needs to consist of:

- someone who understands cameras and lighting;
- someone who understands sound;
- someone who edits;
- someone who makes sure everyone is pulling in the same direction;
- someone who others trust to make the final artistic decisions.

You as a filmmaker can adopt some or all of these roles, and can include other people to cover some or all of these roles. It doesn't automatically follow that you as a group have to stick to the roles you adopt; you can share and merge these to reflect the breadth of experience brought by each member.

The kind of people you need

The need to operate without pay cheques and contracts requires filmmakers to renegotiate the power structure within a production. Without money greasing the wheels of production, you need to rely more on consulting and bargaining. Low-budget film crews have fewer members working as a crew and are therefore more flexible and responsive to new methods of working. They can devise new methods without having to worry too much about contractual implications and can encourage the spread of creative input across the film crew.

In terms of the basic crew needed, it is useful to have:

- One person who understands the idea behind the film better than anyone else, and this is usually the person who first devised it.

- Several people who each understand and contribute to the overall creative drive of the film.
- These people must be able to cover each of the technical and artistic roles outlined in the more traditional model above, but it is likely that they will overlap in skills.
- Rather than placing the director at the top of a vertical hierarchy, this person may be placed at the centre of the group, having equal contact with each person and acting as conduit for the suggestions and contributions of each member.
- If there is a hierarchy in this model, it places the ideas and aims of the project as paramount, and insists that all members agree at the outset what the aims are for the movie and abide by them; members are subordinate only to the general blueprint of the film rather than to an individual.

Groups that work well

In observing many groups of filmmakers where members worked well towards an outcome, there are some roles that recur, aside from the technical or traditional roles that are seen in the conventional model. These could be termed personality types, at the risk of treading into pop-psychology waters, and imply that the artistic process of making a film is reliant on the combination of various characters as much as on skills. If you are trying to find people to work with on a project, this list may help in devising a group that works well and pitches in together.

Successful filmmaking groups have included:

- *The artistic warden.* Someone who is committed to keeping the film as close to the original plans and ideas of the film as possible. This person acts as a kind of earth wire, channelling all new ideas back to the main aims and checking that deviations from the film are consistent with the agreed plan.
- *The creative driver.* A person who thrives on generating new ideas and while sticking to the plans for the film is adept at devising new and better ways of fulfilling them. A creative livewire, this person is often one jump ahead of the other members, but does need reigning in from time to time.
- *The sceptic.* This member sees the film from an audience's point of view, questioning whether elements of the film will work and applying a cooler, business-oriented view to the proceedings.
- *The technical perfectionist.* Although each member may possess more than adequate technical skills, this person acts as a technical quality controller and may have more understanding than most about equipment or software used in production.

The characters listed above are not exhaustive but do suggest certain key types who seem to work well towards a successful outcome. If nothing else, observations of this sort tell us that dividing a crew by skill roles alone is only half the story, that other factors contribute to the 'good group'.

Make ground rules for everyone

Aside from whether a filmmaker takes the traditional model or works in other ways there are, again from observations of groups that successfully work together, certain ground rules that may ensure that

Figure 4.3 *Journey Through Life* (2001) by Sarah Kelland used a small crew of friends, each taking a variety of roles, to shoot this music video.

the group remains on good terms throughout production and which seem to bring out the most in each member. In 'good groups' these have included:

- *Everyone has an input.* Everyone involved in the production is part of the artistic process. No one's role is purely technical; everyone has something to contribute in terms of experience and technique.
- *Everyone is here to learn.* If it goes wrong in places, don't attribute blame. Don't exclude anyone from the opportunity to make mistakes and learn.
- *Only the best will do.* A belief that the production is going to be absolutely the best that can be achieved right now, given budget size.
- *The integrity of the initial idea.* Throughout production it is the ideas and plans drawn up at the start which were agreed on by all involved that are deferred to. When changes or problems arise, all members refer back to the original plans.

The Crunch

- Working solo can be tough.
- Short and low-budget films use smaller groups; large budgets need large crews.
- Treat everyone with respect.
- Try to pay people you work with; if you can't then be straight about this.
- Crew working for free need to be consulted and included: share power on set.

- Find people who work well together, not just technical skills.
- Get written agreements for public showing from everyone.
- Get insurance.

4. Script and structure

Interview

'There is no substitute for a great story. Any script or film that seeks to go deeper than mere formula and throws some light on the human condition is going to get noticed because audiences are hungry for great stories. Especially in low-budget independent film, where there are no special effects budgets or major stars to hide behind, story must be king.'

Mark Innocenti, filmmaker, USA

The aim of this section is to look at ways of working more effectively with narrative. We are going to see what holds a film together and what makes up the bones of it, onto which you add the body of plot, character and theme. We can call this skeleton 'film structure' and it is the most crucial part of a film's development.

Even loose narratives, where the plot just seems to meander around, need to have a structure that holds the whole film together. This doesn't mean you have to stick with this; if you are aware of the way your film works as a whole you can then proceed to let this structure drop now and then, if you want. Filmmaking has been likened to a drive in a car. If you let yourself get taken over by the experience you risk running into a wall, but if you can navigate and keep your sights on the view ahead and behind at all times you may well end up where you wanted to go. You therefore need to have a good all-round view of what you've done, what is coming up and any potential obstacles in your way as you film.

Film View

Bodies, Rest and Motion (Michael Steinberg, 1993) successfully holds down a rambling story focusing on the interaction of several characters in a small town. Without major events to push the film forward, it needs a firm structure to keep it on track.

Good script structure also keeps your movie coherent, looking like you have an overall vision and control over it. The aim is to make a film that stands as one piece, rather than one which appears to have been made by several people, each with different aims and ideas about the direction it's going in.[10]

---

[10] www.teleport.com/~cdeemer/scrwriter.html   Professional tips and news for screenwriters.

Interview
'The short film I made recently was part of an MA course at Goldsmiths [University College in London]. The short film is called *Simon Says* and is a comedy about two people who get set up on a date as part of a bet, the date goes embarrassingly wrong, but the guy who set them up is the loser in the end. It's about image, personality, confidence and playing with people's emotions and lives.'

Amber Mosdell, filmmaker, UK

Write your own script

Writing the story and screenplay yourself is going to relieve you of a large item on the budget sheet and is, after all, probably why you started making films in the first place – the opportunity to express yourself. The ideas below apply equally to the standard 90-minute feature as to the short film.

1 Complete a brief paragraph outlining the story from start to finish. This avoids details and simply lists the events of the plot and your vision of the kind of film it will be.
2 Write a treatment. This is a short story of the film, and would last for about 30 pages in a 90-minute feature. For short films 5–10 pages is fine.
3 Draft screenplay. Using the treatment as the basis, write the screenplay with director's notes, dialogue and any other information which helps to describe the scene.
4 The final screenplay may not necessarily be the second draft; it is likely you will go into several more drafts before you are satisfied. In any case, the last draft will always be shorter than the previous. Each sheet on your screenplay will correspond to 1 minute of film time. In shorts, however, there is less pressure to cost out the whole film, so the 1 minute = 1 page rule is rarely observed.

There is not the space to discuss the finer points of screenwriting, but this is one of the most useful skills you can acquire as a filmmaker and puts you more in control of the medium than any other role. If you find that scriptwriting is not what you want to be doing, or if you find that you get more inspired by other people's stories then you may want to consider how to get hold of that material, but more on that later.[11]

Classic script structure

Classic structure, seen in mainstream, popular narrative movies, is a good place to start in understanding this idea. But let's make it plain from the start: this is only one way of structuring a film.

[11] www.screenwritersutopia.com/ Screenwriters tips and news.
www.screentalk.org/ Screenwriter's magazine.
www.insidefilm.com/screenwriting.html Screenwriting articles and interviews.
www.writerscomputer.com/ Books and software for screenwriters.

As we will see at the end of this book (see Chapter 9, 'Understanding film'), there are undeniable financial reasons why certain ways of telling a story have flourished and others have not. Classic Hollywood approaches to film structure are based on the need to deliver a story that resembles what we grew up thinking of as a proper story, something with a beginning, a middle and an end, which safely delivers us a happy outcome. Some of the most powerful films reject this in favour of something which is more provocative, and end up getting huge box office receipts, against expectation. But the people who wrote those – Stanley Kubrick, Terrence Malick and Martin Scorsese, for example – have all been schooled in classic screenwriting forms and are then more confident to blow them out of the water. So, let's get down to it. Classic structure operates more or less along a three-act formula like this:

- somebody is somewhere and everything's normal;
- something happens to this somebody, and normality is disrupted;
- the somebody has to cope with it and do something about the something that happened, returning back to normality.

Film View

As examples, try watching Malick's *Thin Red Line* (1999), which takes a refreshing detour from the usual Vietnam movie, while Kubrick's *The Killing* (1956) uses complex flashback to tell a simple heist story.

It consists of three events: the first and last are circumstances or situations while the middle consists of action. So, a person is in one set of (fine) circumstances at the start of the movie and through a stream of action is taken into a new set of circumstances at the last section of the movie – also fine but different. This is often referred to as 'state–action–new state'.

Classic structure in big-budget movies

The ultimate aim of this structure is to return the situation to the way it was before the event that changed everything. We can try to apply this structure to many films. In *Independence Day* (Roland Emmerich, 1996):

- we see the world on a normal day and focus on a particular character;
- the aliens invade;
- then we see how the main character (played by Will Smith) copes with this and tries to return the situation to the way it was before the invasion.

In *Die Hard* (John McTiernan, 1988):

- visiting cop McClane (Bruce Willis) goes to see his estranged wife;
- soon, the building is hijacked by a group of international terrorists, taking his wife hostage;
- McClane tries to defeat the terrorists and release the hostages.

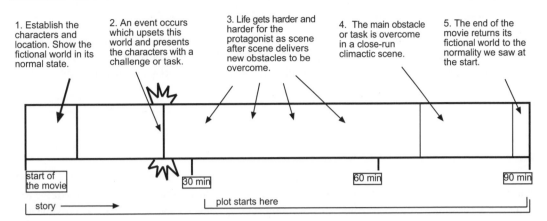

1. Establish the characters and location. Show the fictional world in its normal state.

2. An event occurs which upsets this world and presents the characters with a challenge or task.

3. Life gets harder and harder for the protagonist as scene after scene delivers new obstacles to be overcome.

4. The main obstacle or task is overcome in a close-run climactic scene.

5. The end of the movie returns its fictional world to the normality we saw at the start.

start of the movie

30 min

60 min

90 min

story

plot starts here

Figure 4.4 Classic film structure.

In this film, the narrative structure is very strong, with few diversions from the straight-line development of the action-based plot. We are taken from a quiet start, through endless near misses and cliffhangers, towards an upbeat conclusion in which all is resolved. There are clear stages in the action and we are accustomed to this kind of structure in this genre of movie.

In these films, good storytelling is about what methods you use to combine these stages of the story together and whether you can do so without the audience being too aware of it. This way of telling stories appeals to us because it takes us for a ride; we go from normality, through to struggle and difficulty, through to resolution and back to normality again, but we are meant to be changed somehow by the process. Like a good fairground ride, we are returned to the place we paid our money and took our seats. So, Will Smith in *Independence Day* learns family commitment, while Bruce Willis, in *Die Hard*, enjoys a reunion with his estranged wife.

Script structure

Use 'the three acts'

To a certain extent, we have to look at psychology to see why we desire stories to run a certain way. We could define the classic structure we have just looked at as one influenced by fairy tales and folk myths. As you have noticed, it tends to run in three acts.

Act I

In these simple stories it was important to relate the sometimes fantastical events of the story to the real lives of the audience and that meant beginning in normality, in the natural state of the world with which the listener could relate. This Act I would typically involve the introduction of the main characters, the setting, the period in history and so on, but may give some hint of the events to come. This state of normality can be a pleasant or unpleasant state, but it must be represented as normality. If this state can be presented as everyday and ordinary *for these inhabitants*, then the impact of the challenge in Act II is greater.

> **Tip**   If you are interested in the kinds of tales that inspired other scriptwriters, including George Lucas (*Star Wars* script), look at the archetypal characters and situations in Snow White, Sleeping Beauty, Hansel and Gretel and your own culture's folk tales.

Act II

In Act II, the main protagonist encounters an event which challenges the normal state of their world. This must involve some hardship such as an invasion, the breakdown of a marriage, the loss of the loot or a false accusation. As far as possible, this event must be as hopeless and devastating as possible and, to quote scriptwriting guru Robert McKee's advice: 'Thou shalt not make life easy for the protagonist.' Nothing in drama is going to advance without conflict; it is the fuel on which the story travels. This act is the most difficult, most challenging, full of cliffhangers, near misses and false hopes.[12]

> **Tip**   McKee's top ten is: **1**. Don't take the crisis/climax out of the protagonist's hands. **2**. Don't make life easy for the protagonist. **3**. Dramatize what you want to say, don't just get a character to say it. **4**. Let the audience know what the protagonist knows. **5**. Respect the audience. **6**. Do much research. **7**. Don't over-complicate the plot. **8**. Take characters to the farthest reaches of conflict. **9**. Use sub-text everywhere. **10**. Rewrite.

Act III

Once the protagonist has encountered this life-changing event, it is then up to him or her to overcome it and triumph. This, the final act, becomes the quest and motivation of the movie's main character. In depicting this, it is important to show the audience what is happening rather than tell it. Exposition is cheap – important events can be described between two characters over a glass of beer – but to *show* is to truly make the most of what cinema can offer. In the slightly moralistic Hollywood tradition, the protagonist will have gained something by this conflict, whereby the struggle and the triumph over it brings with it some reward in the form of heightened humanity or insight into the human condition, in short, a better person. In the closing act of Hitchcock's *The Birds*, for example, we notice how the bickering between the characters gives way to family closeness as they survive wave after wave of bird attacks.[13]

---

[12] www.mckeestory.com/   Robert McKee's seminars in USA and Japan.
[13] http://members.tripod.com/~afronord/analysis.html   Excellent detail on script structure.

Did you know?
Exposition refers to the way you establish the world of the film at the start. It explains in what period in history the film is set, who is involved in the story and generally describes the normal state of the characters' world.

Film View
In terms of structure, *The Birds* is a good example of a director deciding to terminate the story, or the 'fairground ride', before it is resolved. At the end we are given no final answers about the destination, success or failure of the main characters. On its release in theatres in 1963, audiences demanded to know whether the final reel was missing.

How the acts work together

The three acts are related in different ways. Act I does not cause Act II, but Act II causes Act III, through a series of choices and surprises. If Act II is the one with the most setbacks and surprises, the final act is often the one with the most action, and may alter the style of editing established throughout the movie. This act also possesses the most ups and downs in terms of crises. Early in Act III the protagonist may often encounter a crisis which threatens the entire plan. In *North by Northwest* (Alfred Hitchcock, 1959), for example, the main character, Thornhill, sees that Eve, whom he cares about, is in mortal danger. Thornhill has to rescue her, possibly jeopardizing his freedom.

At the end of Act III, there is often a climactic resolution to the conflicts of the film, often referring right back to the initial aims of the film raised in the opening scenes. Script devices may be used to signal a link between the start and end of the movie, so that the audience feel that they have been returned back 'home' to the start of the narrative, back to normality. For example, in *The Birds* again, a pair of lovebirds are bought as a gift at the start of the film and act as a device to kick-start the plot. When the birds are brought out to the escape car at the end of the film we sense that some sort of closure is going on, that the end is near, even though other aspects of the plot are unresolved; it's a clever way of drawing the film to a close without concluding it fully.

Lengths of each act

It is hard to be precise about how much time should be given to each act, but a rough guide can be found if we take a look at the standard 90-minute Hollywood film. Within the first 20 minutes or thereabouts, the main character needs to encounter the event that leads to Act II. Roughly midway through the film the situation for the protagonist must be about as bad as it gets and does not need to improve until we get within the last 15 minutes. This is a very rough guide and applies to a very overused formula, but it does give some idea of the relative lengths of each act.

Pinch points

A further indicator of strong structuring is to notice what are called 'pinch points' in the story. A pinch point is a scriptwriter's term for a part of the story which pushes the action a little further. These are not huge leaps or changes in the action but a nudge and push towards the next act. You would expect to see several pinch points in the first two acts of the film, and hardly any towards the end when the action speeds up. In *Apollo 13*, for example, the main point in the first act is the accident on board the spacecraft, but in addition to this we have further aftershocks such as the reduction in oxygen supply which serve to add to the tension and keep the audience engaged.[14]

Developing good structure

There is no right or wrong way of structuring your film, only ones that are appropriate to what you are making. Narrative film in the classic Hollywood mode has a well-established way of structuring stories and this is seen as the default method for many filmmakers. Using this method does not mean you are working in a non-challenging, conventional way; you may use classic structure but delay it, subvert it or otherwise change it in ways that surprise the audience. To make it even more interesting for you, you can use the presumed knowledge the audience have of classic structure and use this against them, by using the established method but now and then deviating from it.

Film View

The success of New Horror films such as *Scream* (1996) and *Scary Movie* (2000) is proof that filmmakers know you are expecting certain situations and certain chains of events to happen in standard horror. But, aware as they are that most of us are bored with formulaic horror films, rather than play along with these ideas they will take detours and wrong turnings, sometimes conforming to the formula, sometimes not.

Using a timeline

To map out a good structure to a movie we need to use a tool called a timeline. As can be seen in Figure 4.5, this is a long box, horizontal on the page, subdivided into seconds and minutes. Along the line shapes are placed corresponding to the length of the individual scenes within it. So, a scene lasting 30 seconds takes up about one tenth of the total line if the film is 5 minutes long. We can give each

---

[14] www.script-o-rama.com   Screenwriting information.
www.dailyscript.com/scripts/main.html   Screenwriting information.
ftp://ftp.loc.gov/pub/copyright/forms/formpai.pdf   Official government form used to copyright your script with the Library of Congress for US usage.
www.CreativeScreenwriting.com   Scriptwriting magazine.
www.ScriptMag.com   Scriptwriting magazine.
www.wga.org/WrittenBy   Scriptwriting magazine (Official Writer's Guild of America).

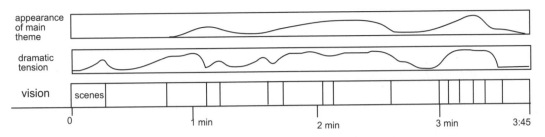

Figure 4.5 In this diagram, the timeline shows various aspects of the film. The first layer at the bottom represents the individual scenes, enabling you to see the structure of the film, reflected in the pattern created by the relative lengths of each scene. The next layer shows how the dramatic tension of the film will build in places throughout the film, reaching its climax in the final scenes, while the top layer shows how often the main theme is going to occur. For example, the theme could be good vs evil and this may become more and more a part of the story as the film progresses.

separate scene varying shapes or colours, enabling you to group them in terms of the three acts. You can now see the relative sizes of the scenes and notice which, if any, are dominating the film. Towards the end of the film, you might expect to see the scenes become shorter than at the start. You can also use the timeline to map out the peaks and troughs of dramatic tension throughout, so you can see how to pace the story and deliver key scenes at regular intervals.

See the film at a glance

First-time filmmakers often talk about the problems they have in maintaining sufficient grip over the film throughout production, avoiding wrong turns and diversions. Many also talk about the effort in keeping sight of the main point of the film, rather than letting the action take over. The timeline allows the director to see the film as a whole and, most importantly, see each component as relative to the rest. It is this ability to stand back and view the film from afar that gives many the clarity they are seeking in defining how to structure and pace the film.

The timeline in action

As a good structure starts to develop on paper, you may start to see a pattern emerging. We could take a look at *The Wizard of Oz* (1939) to see patterns at work. On a timeline, you would see a particular shape at the start representing Dorothy at home in Kansas, in scenes filmed in monochrome. Throughout the first hour you would see a pattern emerge of Dorothy encountering more characters to join her journey. At regular intervals we have a song and at further intervals we have interventions from the wicked witch. The structure changes in the last act, where we see the group enter the wizard's palace and here the action hots up, so we see a greater turnover in scenes. At the end of the film, Dorothy is returned to Kansas in monochrome scenes again, so we would use the same shape used to denote the opening scenes. Looking at the timeline we can see a very pronounced pattern, representative of a strongly structured film and typical of movies aimed at younger audiences, where the need is to conform to traditional storytelling forms. Even in later, more radical films such as

Reservoir Dogs (Quentin Tarantino, 1991), we see a pattern emerge as we go to and from the warehouse to encounter various points of the story told in flashback.

Other uses for the timeline

You can use this method to reveal the presence of just about any aspect of your film:

- Recurrence of characters.
- Highs and lows of tension.
- Possible dominance of types of scene, such as exteriors, interiors and so on.
- Uses of flashbacks.
- Recurrence of sounds or music.
- Stylistic changes.
- Points of action and points of reflection.

Further variations on the timeline could include drawing it as a circle, with degrees within it representing minutes and seconds of the film, in a clockwise fashion. There is also a variation using children's coloured building bricks in which a three-dimensional line can be built and rearranged to get the right structure.

Scriptwriting and structure

When looking at structure in other films, it is easier to look at those which are more transparent, in other words, which have their structure and pace written all over them and which conform to some cinematic conventions. Films such as *Jurassic Park* (1993) and *Armageddon* (1999) are instructive models because they do not attempt to alter the established formula and positively revel in living up to it, with the result that you can see the nuts and bolts and rivets of these films after just a brief look. Some of the ideas that follow can be seen in these and other movies. The tight structure of these movies is perhaps more a credit to the scriptwriter than the director.

Embedding the purpose of the movie early

The aim of this is to stake a clear aim of the film, apparent to the audience, right from the start. In the opening scenes you could suggest what it is that will drive the film. Separate this idea from the one described earlier on identifying the 'key scene'; the key scene is more likely to occur later and will go some way to resolving the questions and challenges raised in this early scene. This early scene may include some line of dialogue or some symbolic event which sets up the themes and aims of the film, while also giving us some important exposition. The difference between good and bad scriptwriting is whether the audience knows that they are being handed these points or whether this scene is fluidly and seamlessly embedded in the opening sequences. To use a restaurant analogy, this early crucial scene is like putting in your meal orders while the later centrepiece scene is like getting the food and maybe reading the recipe.

Film View
Sometimes embedding the plot is done in an obvious way, sometimes not. In *The Sixth Sense* (M. Night Shyamalan, 1999), the first shot we see is of a light bulb gradually illuminating. Only when we have seen the film, and its concluding twist, do we see that this is a good metaphor for the way we suddenly understand something in the plot.

Each scene should have conflict within it

This refers to the detail of the film and means taking a close-up look at how every scene works. Each scene needs to have a goal of which the audience is aware. This has to be something fairly obvious

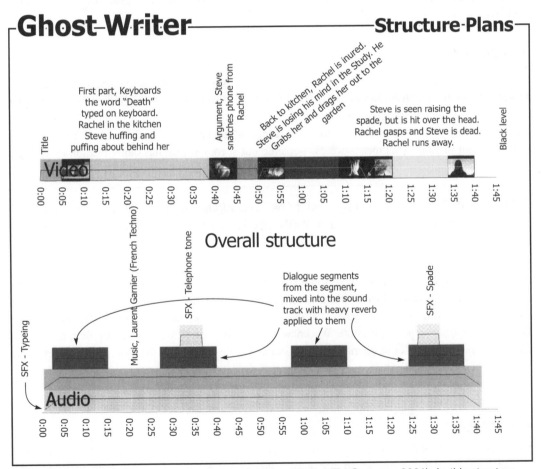

Figure 4.6 Overall structure chart for the movie *Ghost Writer* (Ed Spencer, 2001). In this structure chart, the filmmaker is trying to lay out the whole movie at a glance to see how the different parts of it work together. Below, the audio tracks are displayed to reveal the pattern emerging in the dialogue segments.

and solid rather than something abstract and ambiguous. The Indiana Jones series of films are masters of the art of setting minor tasks for Indy to complete in each scene – get the aeroplane, run out of the labyrinth – and then placing numerous obstacles in his path such as pits of snakes, the lone armed guard and so on. This is a simple example and the more sophisticated the film the more you may play with our expectations, raising hopes and dashing them.

In our Hollywood model, a typical scene climaxes as disaster strikes and the goal of the main character has been frustrated. This leads to an interruption of the way the overall action is heading. This is good for two reasons: it surprises the audience and it leads with neat continuity on to the next scene, with its own conflict and own goals. Think of a particular scene in *Star Wars* when the three main characters – Han, Luke and Leia – cannot escape from the attack by the stormtroopers and bail out into the garbage shoot. Unable to complete the goal of that scene they have been forced to change direction. In the garbage pit they have a new goal – to get out. But they are again frustrated when the walls start to draw in.

The sequel

Creative writing teacher, the late Dwight Swain, of the University of Oklahoma, put forward a cause-and-effect concept which applies as well to novels as to screenplays. Swain suggested that the disaster or obstacle that places the character in the next scene leads to a sequel, a chain of events which follows, leading directly but subtly to the next scene. In this case, it is useful to think of a scene as a beat, or unit of time. This means we can separate out scenes within the same location or setting.

Tip   Read Swain's highly regarded book, *Techniques of the Selling Writer* (1981, University of Oklahoma Press, ISBN: 0806111917).

At first, the main character must have some sort of reaction to the obstacle that has frustrated their goal. This reaction is determined by the kind of personality you have evolved for the character. To go back to the *Star Wars* garbage scene, Han delivers a sardonic comment aimed at the others while Princess Leia tries to get a solution. We knew they would react this way; if we didn't, then the characters have not been built up into credible people. On this last point, the more your characters are like real people with real experiences informing their decisions, then the more opportunities there are for further conflict, as the individual personalities clash with each other.

The dilemma

Swain goes further and points to the need for a *dilemma*, something which causes the character to choose between two courses. In an action film this is usually the choice to fight or take flight. Prolonging this decision can add tension; there should be a clear difference between the two options and this must be apparent to the audience, so this is a good moment to show exactly how bad it would be if *x* happens and how great it would be if *y* happens. The action taken to exit the character from the conflict of that scene immediately leads him onto the next. For example, in *The Fugitive* (Andrew Davis, 1993), the wrongly accused Harrison Ford escapes and is chased along a water outlet, hundreds of feet above a river. The cop closes in, Ford looks down at the long drop, then back to the cop, and so on. In a matter of seconds we sense his dilemma, between capture or freedom, and are made to wait while he decides which to take.

Characters

In your screenplay you should be aiming for a group of characters who are real in a number of ways but are, significantly, not human beings. McKee believes that 'a human being does not have the richness to become a protagonist'. This is because a film character needs to be a compression of lots of ideas and lots of people, a metaphor. The danger here is in making the character into a stereotype similar to other characters seen in lots of other films. The way to prevent this is to avoid the obvious, introducing elements which are counter to the stereotype – the piano-playing, art-loving serial killer (Hannibal Lecter) – and make his or her aims unlikely – the poor boy who wants to escape the ghetto. Furthermore, add lots of contradictions. These surprise the audience and help you to add new elements into the story as it progresses in the form of skeletons in the cupboard, leading to people or situations which potentially obstruct the characters. They also help to make the characters more fallible, more human.

> **Tip** If you are writing your own script, limit the number of characters in the plot. Dealing with just two or three main characters simplifies the action and yet is enough to allow each to set off character traits in the other. Whatever you do, don't exceed seven main characters.

Finally, if you have secondary characters in the script, make sure that these are slightly less interesting than the primary characters. Secondary characters are there to draw out the qualities of the focal character by asking the right questions and setting up situations to which the main character responds.

Sub-plot

In thinking about pace and structure, it is useful to be able to have something which acts like a brake now and then, taking the audience's attention away from the main plot and into a diverting smaller story which simultaneously seems to help the main story. A sub-plot is a refrain, a time to breathe a little and reflect on the scenes in the main story. The James Bond franchise has managed quite well without this element but, to make up for its absence, needs to go frenetically from place to place, incident to incident. In *Star Wars* again, we see the sub-plot continue into the sequel, namely, who will win the heart of the princess (see Figure 4.7). Clearly, this is not the main plot and is not intended to be the well-hidden, true meaning to the film. It is absolutely secondary to the main story and in this case does a perfect job in taking us out of the fast action and into quiet exchanges, when the dogfights and light sabres become too much. These parts of the movie also serve to deepen our understanding of the characters and show another side of them.

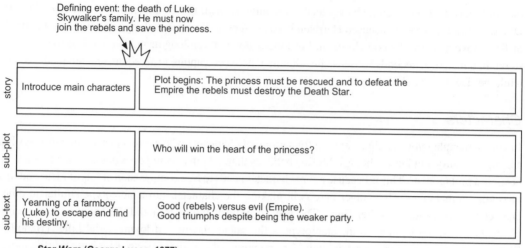

Star Wars **(George Lucas, 1977)**

Figure 4.7 Structure. In *Star Wars*, there are several levels going on simultaneously. The story is the most dominant part of the script, with the sub-plot appearing only occasionally. The sub-text is the least noticeable part of the film and may shift as the story advances into the main plot.

Sub-text

Many scriptwriters advise putting a sub-text under every text. What this means is avoiding writing lines which mean what they say and nothing else. A very instructive scene is seen in Woody Allen's *Annie Hall* (1977). In this film, the two main characters, played by Woody Allen and Diane Keaton, have just met and are making small talk. At the foot of the screen subtitles reveal their true thoughts. Your screenwriting should involve the same 'double-speak' and you could even try typing with gaps between the lines for you to write your thoughts on the sub-text.

Revealing the sub-text is done carefully and only partially, allowing the audience to think about the implications of the script. Ambiguity is acceptable; if you are working with good actors, they will be able to reveal sub-text through body language and the way they deliver the lines. The way Jack Nicholson's character talks to his son in the first few scenes of Kubrick's *The Shining* (1980) suggests a whole history of menace and familial tension in some very innocuous lines. This is good double-speak, saying one thing and meaning another.

Pace in the script

Tempo and beats

Pace is also useful to look at here in relation to structure and scriptwriting. We can define it as being the tempo of the film, the rate at which the aims of the plot progress. The pace at which your film runs is determined by a number of factors, including the length of the movie, the subject matter and the style you have in mind. If we are going to talk about tempo it would be useful to have some way of measuring this, just as we can with music when we talk about beats per minute. With pace, we can describe scenes in terms of beats, which may be less confusing because actors will talk about scenes in terms of the 'French Scene', in which each new entrance starts a scene and each exit ends it. In filmmaking, it is easier to talk in terms of 'units of time', and these could be anything from 20 seconds to a minute. If this sounds vague, think of each beat as like a footstep, advancing the plot, even slightly, towards conclusion. This analogy also helps us to think of these footsteps as rhythmic, determining the pace throughout the film.

How fast?

The pace or speed at which the film goes is entirely up to you. There are no rules which say that one particular rate of progression is better than any other, that sombre subject matter should naturally run at a slow pace nor that comedies should be frenetic. As with all aspects of the filmmaking process, and most arts in general, you need only justify it in terms of what you are aiming for. It is again all about good advance planning.

Action and pace

Pace determines the flow of information to the audience, how much they receive and how often. A dense storyline requires a quick pace to carry all the events within the film's duration. In *Die Hard with a Vengeance* (John McTiernan, 1995), for example, a series of encounters take place in the last quarter of the movie, any one of which would have served well as the main conclusion to another action movie, yet here they form part of a dense line of situations which pile action on top of action. This frantic pace is at odds with the slower, more measured pace of the first *Die Hard* movie, in which the sub-plot – of McClane's relationship with his former wife – and the sub-text – in which a downtrodden man rediscovers his self-confidence through triumphing over conflict – both help to delay the action and serve it up in portions which leave the audience keen for more.

Changing pace

In Kubrick's films, pace is majestically slow, even in action scenes, but this is with a purpose. In these films, events can be seen to have more meaning and more implications if there are fewer of them. In *The Shining* (1980), this is illustrated where several scenes lead to false climaxes and where long, slow tracking shots take us relentlessly towards the bloody conclusion, hinted at in sparse, brief nightmare images. In this case, the viewer quickly becomes accustomed to the slow pace and it in no way deflates the action.

Terrence Malick, in all his films, also avoids the obvious and goes for slower pace even in action, plot-based films. In *Badlands* (1974), the murderous couple on the run seem more isolated from us, more in their own world, as the slow, objective pace shows them in a stark, cold light.

At the other end of the scale, Todd Solondz's *Welcome to the Dollhouse* (1995) uses a brisk, unsentimental pace to show the tragicomic events occurring in the life of 11-year-old Dawn Weiner. This upbeat tempo belies the film's very poignant themes and rescues it from soap opera cliché.

In all these examples, you can see how pace matches not the story itself but the filmmaker's interpretation of the story; it can give a subtle new twist to an otherwise straightforward telling.

The Crunch

- Write your own script.
- Get to know classic structure.
- . . .Then break the rules.
- Use the three acts.
- Use a timeline to work out overall structure.
- Get to know your core scene.
- Use sub-text throughout – it makes it more satisfying.
- Use a sub-plot – give the audience a break now and then.
- Think in terms of beats within each act. Push the tempo up or down according to the action.

Project 4. Core scenes

Sorting out priorities: find your core scene

This very brief exercise is aimed at working out the priorities in your films, about which parts of it are more dominant than others, and can be done when you have a film outlined and planned up to visualization stage. To test it out, you can also apply it to a feature film you know well. The aim is to locate that part of the movie which is the centrepiece, on which the whole film pivots. When you find which scene it is, you can build the film around it and use it as a moment when some of the main features of ideas in the film come to the fore.

Stage 1

First, get hold of a packet of sticky stationery notes. On each note draw sketches of the main scenes in the film. If you can get to at least seven, the exercise works more effectively, but applies to shorts as well as to features.

Stage 2

Look at all the notes and try to find the one which you feel is the most important in the film, the one which you could not do without. This is usually not the big, climactic scene, nor does it have to be the one which explains the story. It is more likely to be the one which seems to sum up the film in that one, single scene by acting as a focal point for the dominant emotions, themes or aims of the film. This centrepiece scene is recognizable by the way it may connect, thematically, to all the other scenes in the film. Borrowing from the theatre, films tend to use a similar idea in which the revelation of the main purpose, theme or message of the film is buried in the middle rather than relegated to the conclusion, where it might be misinterpreted as a mere end-of-story sermon.

Stage 3

Place this image in the middle of a sheet of paper and draw a circle around it. You now have the core of the film, around which all the other parts will revolve.

Stage 4

Now try to divide these scenes into two lots: those on the inner band and those on the outer, drawing a circle between the two. Then take the others and place at varying points around the core scene, at various distances from it depending on their relative importance.

Now you have a core scene, surrounded by scenes of primary importance, surrounded in turn by scenes which are of secondary importance, including those more functional parts which take the audience from one part of the story to the next.

Example of a core scene

A good example of the key scene that is not necessarily the most loud or impressive is one found in the Michael Mann film *Heat* (1997). The film looks at a gang of crooks and a police officer who is hunting them. The gang is led by Robert De Niro while the police hunt is led by Al Pacino. Mann knew that the crucial scene of the film would occur when these two charismatic actors confront each other for the first time, although the scene itself is anything but turbulent, taking place in a dreary diner, and is more an oasis of calm in a sometimes violent film. But in terms of the main themes in the film, this scene is indeed the pivotal one, as it brings together the main opposing forces of this duel, while revealing their shared qualities and the more realistic ambiguity of the usual good versus evil equation. The whole film seems to run up to this point like two lines being drawn ever closer. Following this point, the film takes on a different tone, signalling the importance of this moment.

Knowing which scene fulfils this role in your film is important in knowing how to structure the film up to and after that point. Take your time deciding which scene occupies this place, since you are actually settling on the main thematic focus of the film in doing so.

Project 5. Silent movie remake

As we saw right at the start of this chapter, screenwriting structure is like the skeleton of a movie. If we follow that analogy further, we could say that this next project is going to help us identify the individual bones in a film. To do this, we are going to make a film where we have to take very specific decisions about what is a main scene, what is sub-plot and what happens within each scene. In making a silent movie we will be forced to consider the structure of the movie more clearly and make it transparent through the use of caption cards to denote the various stages of the plot. We will see how to convey information that advances the story and how to spread the feed of this information to the audience in such a way that leaves people expecting events and guessing the next move, involving them in the movie.

A brief diversion: silent movies in Hollywood

To define the silent movie we should first agree that these were never in fact silent. Musical accompaniments or the voice of a theatre narrator would have helped the audience to understand the film. Later movies would use caption cards to distinguish scenes and to show important dialogue. The first scripts in movies of this period had no detail, consisting of merely a list of the scenes that would be in the film, but allowing for further adding or subtracting later. A title card covered the gaps in between, and the form of the present-day script has arisen largely because these early lists of scenes treated the film as being made of chunks of narrative, telling the story in blocks. These cards had to be limited in their use, so as not to detract from the main visual aspects of the cinema as an attraction, and the placing of them was a skilled craft. The young Alfred Hitchcock worked as a caption card writer in the 1920s and his experiences in deciding when to insert a card and what it would say were instrumental in developing his later ability in structuring and spreading out the action in a movie. Alfred Hitchcock was arguably at his happiest when dispensing with dialogue and relying on the tricks of the silent movie.

Film View

Watch classic silent movies *The Cabinet of Dr Caligari* (Robert Wiene, 1919) and *The Crowd* (King Vidor, 1927).

'The truth is that with the triumph of dialogue, the motion picture has been stabilized as theatre. One result of this is a loss of cinematic style. Another is the loss of fantasy. Dialogue was introduced because it is realistic. The consequence was a loss of the art of reproducing life entirely in pictures.'

Alfred Hitchcock (Hitchcock on Hitchcock, Faber & Faber, 1995)

Film View

In *Rear Window*, vast tracts of the film are silent but for the background noise of the street, and yet a complex plot is developed through careful use of visuals.

If we can go through a similar but much compressed training in the use of structure in the silent movie it may be possible to understand more about this essential part of filmmaking.

Stage 1: Story

To begin with, we need to find a narrative. The film needs to have a very limited, simple plot with a straightforward linear progression which is obvious to the audience. This means a physical movement from A to B, involving perhaps a journey, a chase or an escape, but its simplicity will make it easier to insert a little sub-plot here and there. This is the easiest way to approach the project, but by all means make it harder for yourself by making the story more complex. In any case, make the movie short, perhaps 5 minutes in length.

Borrow a scene

A short way to arrive at a useful, action-led scene which involves simple progression of plot is to lift something from a film that you know well. For example, the great Wes Craven horror films contain many scenes which play on the idea of paranoia and pursuit, especially within a normally safe, suburban setting. Take something you have seen a number of times and which relies more on visual impact than dialogue.

Film View
Try *Wes Craven's New Nightmare* (1994) or *Scream* (1996).

A silent movie in three acts

The aim is to make a short movie which uses the ideas talked about in this chapter and consists of just three short scenes, corresponding to each of the three acts. So, to use as an example, a simple chase could have as Act I the main character before being chased, perhaps suspicious that something is about to happen; Act II shows the main action of the chase; Act III takes us to what happens when the chase reaches its climax in the capture of one character by the other.

Use a sub-plot

Don't forget, we need to include a sub-plot which will act as a diversion from the main film. If possible, try to avoid the use of flashback as this may dilute the drama and tension in the film. For example, you could try introducing other characters into the chase who each serve to divert the pursuer from their task, or the pursuee from their escape. Break the scenes in Acts II and III, after the action has kicked off, down into small sections, giving each scene:

● a clear aim (to swim across the swollen river);
● an obstacle (he can't swim);
● a dilemma (escape but possibly drown);
● and a reaction (finds a way of crossing without drowning).

In practice, it's going to be hard to cram more than just one or two of these obstacle–dilemma scenes into the short movie. As long as they serve the film's structure, as Act II or III, then you will have gone through the right sort of experience.

Title cards

For the titles it would be useful to have a text generator on your editing software. The vast majority let you do basic titles, but there are one or two that don't and in this case you could add titles by directly filming boards with captions written on, as was the method in the silent era.

Stage 2: Planning

Visualizations

Go through the process as we have seen in the previous chapters in developing the film on paper. Produce a set of visualizations which allow you to devise an overall look to the film and follow these through into storyboards.

Storyboards

At the storyboard stage you can start to consider the way you unravel the action. When you feel you have all the right scenes drawn on paper, cut these up into separate frames. Bunch them together into the beats or units of time we saw earlier in this section. Now you have chunks of the story laid out you can notice the structure of the film. Each chunk becomes a main structural piece, and within these will be smaller pieces involving the actions of the characters. Although you are not committing yourself just yet, try adding a line which suggests the upcoming action before each beat. This encourages you to distinguish between the main plot, the sub-plot and the smaller divisions within.

Stage 3: Shooting

When shooting this sort of film it may be useful to see the solutions that early cinema used to address the absence of sound. Actors tended to act a lot more with the whole body and more dramatically or extravagantly than today.

Use strong lighting

Use lighting much more dramatically to focus attention on the important details in each scene. Rather than set up realistic lighting, try instead something more akin to what you may see in a theatre, with higher contrast between the dark and light areas, strong shadows and exaggerated colouring. You could even go the whole way and use the kind of devices used widely in silent films such as the keyhole wipe (blackening the screen except for one small circle, and wiping out from this point or towards it) to draw attention to a particular part of a scene. The result of all this is to allow the visual elements to do the talking, so that you can more effectively put across the information the audience need. Use the camera far more as an 'explaining' tool, showing the audience clearly what is happening (without going so far that you hand it to them on a plate). Be explicit in what camera 'language' you use. Probably without being aware of it, you possess a wide knowledge of what certain camera angles mean simply by having seen so many movies. The tilted camera, for example, suggests something wrong within the scene, while the camera viewing a subject from above can make it look more vulnerable.

Go to: Chapter 5:8 for more ideas about how to get the right sort of lighting and how to avoid the camera reacting badly to creative lighting.

Stage 4: Editing

It is at this stage that we need to become absolutely sure about the structure of the film, which is not set in stone until you start assembling the movie. Paper preparation helps you some of the way, but there is no guarantee that you will get the shots you wanted. When you have logged the footage and assessed which are the good and bad takes, start grouping the footage as you did with your storyboard in the planning stage. It would be useful now to plan the editing of this film on paper so you could prepare an edit decision list (EDL) or do a brief, shorthand storyboard. The latter is always preferable if you want to stay aware of visual style throughout the film. Certainly, you need to start to become familiar with the timeline as a tool for assembling the movie on paper and revealing the inner skeleton of the movie.

Go to: Chapter 6:2, 'Preparing to edit'.

Where to insert caption breaks

This next stage involves the breaking up of the film into pieces. We are using caption cards which serve to hint what has happened or what is about to happen. These will require us to decide exactly where the *joints* in the film's skeleton are, as it were. In other words, where the key elements in the structure of the movie begin and end. These points will articulate between one scene or beat of the film and the next, but their use is going to have to be strictly rationed so that the overall flow of the movie is sustained.

Let's consider the following example:

Scene 1. Bob is seen sitting on his sofa, with beer and TV (*caption explaining where we are*).

Scene 2. The door rings. Bob thinks it is his ex-wife who he argued with that day and we realize he has had a bad day, amidst a complicated life. He looks at the photo of a woman on the mantlepiece and we see that normality for Bob is not good (*caption explaining his thoughts*). After a second ring, Bob casually looks through the curtains and, with a look a horror, steps back, turning off the light and searches for a blunt instrument (*caption as he tries to find something to use*).

Scene 3. Cut to the figure outside Bob's door. He/it rings again and fingers a pistol held in his jacket.

Scene 4. Bob slams the back door and tries to exit quietly. He knocks over the bin and attracts the figure's attention (*caption articulates Bob's desperate thoughts*).

Scene 5. Running along the street, Bob flags down a neighbour's car (*caption shows Bob's relief*). The neighbour thinks he is drunk and drives on (*caption explains the driver's thoughts*).

If we take the scenes above, we could agree that the first scene is slow and casual. A caption card establishes this scene as one of normality for Bob. Dragging out this scene a little by detailing the homely detritus of his small room allows the audience to sympathize with Bob, essential if we are to be cheerleaders for his journey and escape. The relatively sparse spread of captions indicates a slow pace at this stage. This scene also introduces a sub-plot as he looks at the faces in the photograph. Sub-text, on the other hand, could be more challenging without sound and in such a short film, but is possible with carefully worded captions.

- When Bob finally breaks out of the house we are on to a whole new part of the film, a new structural block where suspense and tension are punctured slightly and replaced by the action of running. Within this block, we see a few encounters, one of which is with the disbelieving neighbour.
- A further caption appears as Bob encounters the neighbour and gets a chance to end the chase, but is foiled by some hint of a previous problem between the two men. Is he a disturbing element in the neighbourhood? Is the neighbour colluding somehow with the mysterious figure? These questions allow us a diversion for a moment and make us see another potential side of Bob, even questioning whether the house we saw at the start is Bob's at all or whether it belongs to his former wife. This momentary stillness in the action allows the film to pause before the next plunge.
- He carries on with his escape. A caption here could indicate that the nightmare is far from over.

At the end of the exercise we can see how the film has been paced by the caption cards, which have allowed the action to progress but have now and then slowed it down. Towards the end of the movie we see more captions than at the start, but these will have fewer statements and may be more punchy and precise.

Evaluation

This project has allowed us to see how a film can be broken down into chunks and that these pieces are precisely moulded and shaped to fit the purposes of the film. Some are short, some long, some fast, some slow, but all play a part in pointing the film in the right direction but not taking us there so quickly and predictably that we can guess the next moves.

- Plot a timeline chart showing the peaks and troughs of drama throughout the film. Is the film too slow at the start? Is the action over too quickly when it gets going?
- How did you use the caption cards? They should not interrupt an event but should signal its imminent arrival. Did you find they were placed more frequently at some points than others and how did the wording of these affect the way other people may read the film?
- Using a different timeline, map the appearance of each character in the film. Do insignificant characters take up too much time and is the main character on screen enough?
- Look at your editing. Does the purpose of each segment of the film match the kind of editing you adopted for that bit? For example, does a slow, introductory scene use fast, accelerated editing, or does a scene with lots of action have long slow cuts?

- Take a microscopic look at the film. Have a look at one particular scene and see whether it breaks down into the kind of parts we outlined earlier: goal, obstacle, reaction, next scene and so on. Produce a timeline of that scene and try to see how you have edited the different shots together and whether the purpose of that scene was served by the shots you included. Watch out for sudden diversions mid-scene, or interruptions that break the chain of cause-and-effect that you have set up. If this cause-and-effect seems unclear in the way you have recorded the shots or the way you have edited them, try to find out which shots are at fault or which are missing.
- Finally, as with every film, look for the way the various elements of your film synthesize into one artefact. Does the lighting reflect the mood of the film? Does the sound or music add or detract from the aims of each scene? Does your framing of each scene convey information or does it leave too many unanswered simple questions about the plot? In summary, is everything in the movie pulling in the same direction?

5. Visualizing a film

Planning a film is different from director to director. Some will insist on a very clear idea of what they are making before production; others will opt for the more risky approach of letting some elements develop on set. At one end of the spectrum, some directors find that the actual process of committing a story to film is less interesting than the long gestation period, over a year or more, when they are able to invent and re-invent the film, subtly changing it and deepening it with layers of meaning. Other directors prefer to organize the film as a set of bases to touch, leaving the precise look and detail of the film until shooting.

The process of production for most art forms is centred on the personal; the artist is in direct control over a painting, as the writer is over a novel. The absence of people or technology to get between the artist and the artefact allows much greater freedom in how such works are developed. In film, however, the number of people involved, even a very small crew, can depersonalize the work. If you are not careful, the resulting film can be the sum of several individuals working with their own ideas rather than several people with one idea. This is not to say that working creatively with other people is unwise; on the contrary, it is the involvement of others that forces a film towards its highest peak of development. But at the tip of this pyramid of creative people and ideas there needs to be one single vision to carry the film forward. This can be the result of one person's efforts or several, but it does need to be fixed in advance of production, on paper, as a blueprint.

Interview
'On any low-budget film, planning is crucial to the success of the project. Every second the camera is running it is costing you money, so you do not want to waste valuable time and money re-shooting. It is no good simply turning up on the day and making it up as you go . . .if you try that it will only lead to stress and a bad film.'

David Norman, filmmaker, UK

Translating words into images

One of the most difficult aspects of developing a film is trying to translate the words you may have that describe your proposed film into images that can be realized on camera.

This inevitably involves much compromise and change as the ideas form themselves into a workable, practical list of shots. This aspect of development is one where you partly make it up as you go, noticing the shape your ideas take as you commit them to paper. It is only later, when you have studied the visualizations, that you come to select the shots that will go into the final storyboard.

Visualizing involves sketching ideas. You do not have to feel confident about being able to draw; the aim of sketching in this context is to communicate information as clearly as possible about the angle of the camera and the arrangement of objects within the shot, so you need only draw as you would for diagrams.

Visualizing methods

- Begin by being as precise as possible about the ideas you are trying to convey.
- Find several words that describe the scene you are trying to visualize and these can be as abstract or descriptive as you like.
- From these words, sketch images that show how you see that scene in your mind. It is better to sketch without first drawing a frame; just freely doodle on paper as you might when your logical mind is otherwise engaged on the telephone.
- When you have finished a set of sketches regarding a scene, add rectangular frames that show what you would leave in the frame if you were shooting.

The advantage of drawing first and adding boxes later is that it allows you to toy with several ideas for frames on the same sketch, as can be seen in Figure 4.8. The key here is being relaxed and not hurrying the process; you need to filter the idea for a scene through your subconscious, allowing it to pass out with a shape unique to your particular view.

Different views

As an example, you could ask five people to each visualize a scene of a figure on a beach. The first person might draw a figure in a crowded, colourful scene with blue sky and sea; another may draw a solitary figure, set against a dark sky. Your own particular take on this scene shows where your preferences lie and indicates what you could call style. As we will see throughout each project, it is the pursuit of self-knowledge as a filmmaker that will characterize your development.

What do you draw?

When sketching, you are trying to depict a range of elements in the film. These include:

- The arrangement of the various props and actors in the scene.
- The intensity of direction of light cast.

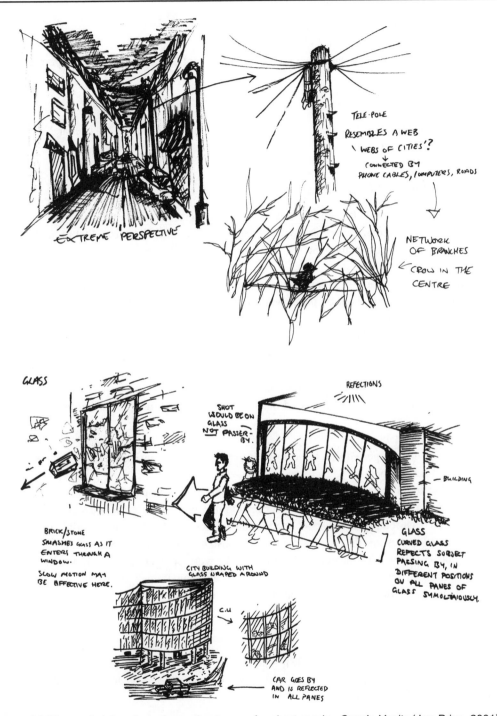

Figure 4.8 These sketches from the early stages of a short movie, *Crow's Vanity* (Jon Price, 2001), detail the filmmaker's attempts to develop images to match a poem. See more of Price's visual work in Chapter 4:6, 'Storyboards and visual tools'.

- Colours that may dominate a scene.
- The amount of contrast between light and dark.
- Possible camera movements such as sideways (tracking shot), rotation from a fixed point (panning shot) or zoom.
- Images or text layered over the main image.

You may not be aware of each of these as you draw, but may go back to sketches later and add to them to include most of the above.[15]

Developing ideas into pictures

When visualizing, the aim is to take fast steps towards the very best ideas you can come up with. It is rare that these are the first ideas you have and there are ways of getting from that initial blunt idea to a more defined, less predictable one.

This process rests on the route of going from a first, obvious idea through to a more advanced version of it. To do this you have to work on paper; you can't expect to do it purely in your imagination. The following is an example of one filmmaker's thought processes on a particular scene. The scene required that a man enters a house, intending to steal whatever can be found. It's very straightforward, but the filmmaker did not want to film this sort of overused scene in a predictable way.

- **Idea 1** (most predictable idea, thought up in a second or so)
  This suggested that the camera is placed outside, looking at the man, recording in a fairly direct way.
- **Idea 2** (less predictable)
  A second drawing suggested that the camera instead looks from inside the bedroom, as the man attempts to force it open.
- **Idea 3** (other ideas are rejected in favour of something more unusual)
  The third drawing takes it a step further, suggesting that instead the camera dwells on something else to cut to occasionally. In this case, the filmmaker thought of someone preparing a meal in the kitchen. Besides showing the prospective thief, we also cut to and from images of cooking. When the thief breaks the window an egg goes rolling off the worktop; when he later leaves the house we cut to an image of a meal in an oven burning. This disrupts something – the meal – we can all relate to and suggests the disruption to the house rather than actually having to show it.

Film View
In *Fatal Attraction* (Adrian Lyne, 1987), a similar device is used: a boiling kettle smothers the noise of an attack in an upstairs bathroom, almost stopping Michael Douglas from saving his wife from the murderous Glenn Close.

[15] http://drawsketch.about.com/cs/figuredrawing/   Basic guides to sketching.

The aim of developing an idea further is to get into the habit of a more advanced way of communicating.

Sketching with video

Although development on paper affords you the chance to think wildly and come up with diverse ways of shooting a scene, there are other ways that can help you to visualize. Try using the camera as a sketching tool. This means losing the idea that each frame you take has to have some purpose and simply seeing how locations or people look on the screen. It is difficult to imagine how a scene will look until you shoot it and by that time you have already invested heavily in time and money. It would be more useful to have produced some rough video shots of the place where you will film, under certain lighting conditions, with or without the actors, to see in advance how it looks when viewed on the rectangle of the screen. In many cases, a place or person can seem mundane until viewed through the lens; they then reveal their cinematic qualities. Video sketching in this way enables you to experiment with new camera angles which you could not necessarily sketch on paper.

Play with the camcorder

There is also a great deal to be gained from simply playing with the camera, seeing how the world looks through the lens. The more you get used to the way filming alters the world, the more you are able to recognize locations, settings, people that work well on the screen. A location such as a train station is a good example. Seen as a participant in the chaos and movement, standing on the platform, you may be deluged with visual information coming at you from all sides. But when you look through the lens on your camera you order that environment and you start to notice, for instance, how the roof structure of the station helps you form a good composition or how the perspective lines of the track look good with people standing alongside.

> **Tip**   There is a (perhaps unlikely) tale about how the young Steven Spielberg learned about camera framing by cycling while looking through a cardboard frame, seeing all the time how to order what was in front of him.

The Crunch

- Planning is crucial.
- Don't let the film stay in your head until shooting; you must see it on paper early.
- Sketch basic images without thinking about scenes.
- Develop words into images.
- Progress your ideas further by more sketching.
- An hour of planning is worth a week of shooting.
- If you start filming and have not done enough planning, your crew and actors may lose faith in the production.

6. Storyboards and visual tools

In the last section we have seen how a film needs to be visualized first on paper before you pick up a camera. In this section we need to see how to collate these visuals together into a coherent whole.

Why plan?

Planning helps to devise ways to show the events of a film more clearly, and images in such a way that shows the world afresh. It is rare that images arrived at on set with no prior thought can achieve a level of interest and meaning of images conceived on paper, rejected and superseded by better images.

Through film we can make sense of the world, whether this is in confirming our sense of disorder or arranging it into a neat narrative. It is no coincidence that many films have sight as their central theme. Ridley Scott's *Blade Runner* (1982) and Nic Roeg's *Don't Look Now* (1973) are two very different examples, and many of Hitchcock's films hinge on the lack of sight or perception of its characters (*Marnie, The Birds*). At the heart of this preoccupation is a recognition that the power of film lies in opening our eyes to the world. Film professor and writer Haig P. Manoogian suggested that:

> 'It is often remarked that people listen but do not hear. What is true of our hearing is also true of our sight. We see, but do not perceive. The successful filmmaker must see for us [and] must open our eyes, provide meaning for what we see and thereby break through our isolation.'

Different ways of preparing

A film needs design and it needs it in the sense of an aim, a purpose, a destination, if it is to become a fully developed movie with its own inner logic, structure and style. How this design is arrived at has many variations, from the detailed plan which can be executed by any assistant director, to the sketched outline of images which the director will try to work with when shooting. We could think of a film plan consisting of the various elements – mostly visual as similar to a map, depicting the route between the start and end of a journey. If we take this analogy further, some people would prefer a very detailed map on a small scale, showing not only the overall route but where the possible problem areas are and get to know exactly what the journey will look like. They will then be able to reassure themselves that the journey will be successful before committing time and money.

Interview

'I find storyboards essential – I need to see how my story is looking. Drawing up the shot-list and having a storyboard means that you are beginning to see how your film looks. I work out quite a lot in the storyboard stage, but with no budget it does mean that as ideas change these aren't necessarily reflected in the storyboard.'

Debra Watson, filmmaker, UK

'It's a really good idea to get a great storyboard artist so that you can create the film on paper before shooting to see how it might look. This gives you time to plan the shots to get the most from the camera.'

Paul Cowling, executive producer, Starving (2000)

On the other hand, there would be still others who would prefer a map showing only the main points on the journey, the must-visit places and general compass direction of the route. This person would be more likely to make the journey precisely for the reason that it is unknown territory and would provide surprises. They work in terms of the main direction rather than the precise route; they know they can deviate from the route now and then, safe in the knowledge that they are generally heading south-west, for instance.

How much planning is right for you

These two approaches could represent two very different ways of approaching the movie planning stage. You need to find out what level of planning makes you comfortable, and it could be argued that you should strive to reduce this level of planning to its minimum, asking yourself what aspects you can live without. Certainly, there is no right way to develop a film and it is to the benefit of the film that the creative process does not stop at the planning stage. Each stage of filmmaking presents its own opportunities for creative decisions, ones that affect the entire purpose of the movie and its overall success. The pressure that goes with this informs you that you cannot afford to run on automatic when shooting and editing, merely following the orders you drew up on paper. If the film sticks too closely to its plans, the result may be artificial and contrived, with the realization of the filmmaker's ideas made too literal.

To arrive at the best method for you, try working with varying degrees of looseness from the initial plans. However, no filmmaker can afford to depart on the journey of making a movie without reference points. How much detail you include in between these points is up to you.

Storyboards[16]

A storyboard is the blueprint for a film. It is not the final look of the film but it is the best you have right now and it provides a list of all the information you need to include throughout the film, including sound, music, images and the effect that each of these have when juxtaposed with one another. The example storyboard illustrated in Figure 4.9a shows a typical page layout. Three or four frames are drawn on the left side of the sheet, in accordance with the aspect ratio you will work with.

---

[16] www.geocities.com/storybords/ Home page of storyboard artist Dan Antkowiak with examples of work.
www.movies.warnerbros.com/twister/cmp/storyboards.html Good example of action storyboards for the movie *Twister*.
www.famousframes.com/artists/laartists/pb/extra/bws/01.html Site of artist Paul Binkley containing examples of work.

2 CAN PLAY AT THAT GAME - STORYBOARD

Storyboard Frame	Details
	SHOT No............SCENE............ACT............ LOCATION:............ ACTORS:............ SHOT TYPE: 1. LS. STATIC 2. CU. STATIC CAMERA-INSTR: STILL ON TRIPOD DESCRIPTION: PLAYER 1 DEALS THE CARDS FOR HIMSELF AND PLAYER 2	PROPS: CARDS DIALOGUE............
	SHOT No............SCENE............ACT............ LOCATION:............ ACTORS:............ SHOT TYPE: MS STATIC CAMERA-INSTR: STILL ON TRIPOD DESCRIPTION: PLAYER 2 RECIEVES CARDS	PROPS: CARDS COSTUME CIGARRE DIALOGUE............
	SHOT No............SCENE............ACT............ LOCATION:............ ACTORS:............ SHOT TYPE: CU STATIC CAMERA-INSTR: STILL ON TRIPOD DESCRIPTION: THEY EXAMINE THIER CARS	PROPS: CARDS + COSTUME DIALOGUE............
	SHOT No............SCENE............ACT............ LOCATION:............ ACTORS:............ SHOT TYPE: MCU STATIC CAMERA-INSTR: STILL ON TRIPOD DESCRIPTION: PLAYER 1 DEALS HIS MONEY	PROPS: MONEY COSTUME DIALOGUE............

Figure 4.9(a)

2 CAN PLAY AT THAT GAME - STORYBOARD   Page: 5

SHOT No..........SCENE.....................ACT...........
LOCATION:
ACTORS:
SHOT TYPE: STATIC MS
CAMERA-INSTR: STILL ON TRIPOD
PROPS: CASH / GLASSES
DIALOGUE

DESCRIPTION: PLAYER 2'S CARD LANDS. 1 tips his glasses

SHOT TYPE: PAN
CAMERA-INSTR: PAN SLOWLY FROM LEFT-RIGHT, GIVING TIME FOR ACTOR TO SNEAK BEHIND CAMERA INTO 2ND SEAT
PROPS: GLASSES CIGARRE, CASH

DESCRIPTION: A PAN FROM PLAYER 1 TO PLAYER 2.

SHOT TYPE: STATIC MS
CAMERA-INSTR: PROFILE, STILL ON TRIPOD

DESCRIPTION: PLAYER 1 SHUFFLES AND DEAL CARDS

SHOT TYPE: STATIC CU
CAMERA-INSTR: STILL ON TABLE
PROPS: CARDS

DESCRIPTION: HE TAKES CARDS

Figure 4.9(a) continued

(b)

Figure 4.9 Storyboards (a) and photos (b) from *Two Can Play At That Game* (Jon Price, 2001). Use the storyboards to link in with the relevant photographs, and vice versa.

These may each be the size of a credit card, with similar dimensions. On the right, linking to each frame, information is given about that shot, concerning sound and music, dialogue, camera movement, and any other elements that cannot readily be depicted in the diagram.

You don't need to be an artist

In drawing the storyboard you do not necessarily need to be a good draughtsman; it is enough to show the image clearly and precisely to the extent that you could give the storyboards to someone else and they could go ahead and make your film. As an interesting exercise, a film course once tried this and the participants were startled to discover the differences between the movies that resulted. Everyone sees an image through their own eyes, regardless of how much information you give. Another issue that arose out of the exercise was that storyboards which gave a clear idea of the director's intended meaning for a scene were more inspiring to work with than those drawn in a vague, ambiguous way; the new director seemed to need someone else's interpretation of the idea to spark off ideas of his or her own.

If you are not confident with your drawing skills the tendency is to use pencil, but this serves only to reveal skill weaknesses. Try using a bold, black marker pen to give the image more impact and help you to show shadow and light.

Make images with meaning

In your storyboards and visualizations you can also develop a sense of what each image means. Every scene must show more than just the passing of the events that make up the plot; the shot must lead the audience to the view that this is not just an image but that it has meaning, revealing more about the central theme of the film. For example, if you have a shot of a figure sitting in a chair in a room, you can alter the meaning of what we are seeing simply by changing the lighting from dim to bright, or from changing the actor's expression from passive to agitated, or by including objects or colours in the shot that suggest meaning. All these subtle variations in one simple shot are the result of what the camera sees; there is a whole other set of opportunities for more meaning when we look into sound and editing, but for now it is enough to realize the impact you can make with imagery. Every element forms a set of signs which the audience are cued to look for and which they will assemble into meanings whether you want them to or not. When planning and storyboarding the film you place yourself in control of this process of reading signs, giving the film more depth and pointing the audience towards a certain interpretation of the movie.

Go to: Chapter 9:3, 'How films work', for more details on the uses of signs, symbols and motifs in movies.

Get in control of the images

The successful filmmaker knows the power of the image and judges what information can be used in a scene and how to temper it for effect. Unfortunately, there is no opting out of this. When an audience sees your film they will read into the information they are given and attach meaning to it whether you intend it or not. Being a participant in this dialogue between you and the audience is better than being a mute presence. This does not mean that you have to dominate this dialogue, by prescribing how people should read the film, and some of the alternative planning methods mentioned here will all encourage sequences that allow the director to relax control now and then.

Alternatives to the storyboard

The storyboard has evolved as one of the best methods for seeing the film as a whole before you start shooting. Although you can rarely afford to leave anything to chance if you are working with a large budget and large crew, in digital video you can allow more flexibility and use chance and improvisation now and then to give the film some spontaneity and spark. You can start to loosen up a little.

Reducing control

Various directors use techniques which allow them to reduce their control over the film while still retaining an overview of it. The benefit to these directors is that they feel the resulting movie is a better product, that it is less artificial and more vibrant than the more thoroughly planned. Making a film in this way becomes a risk-laden business, but also has a thrill of uncertainty which can bring out the best in some people.

Using a timeline

One way to prepare is to use the timeline chart, and a more advanced version could resemble the timeline used in some editing packages, such as Adobe Premiere. Several tracks are used to depict images and audio, including simultaneous clips such as text or layers of image. As you can see, this method uses blocks to show where certain scenes will occur and presumes that you have first developed an idea of the

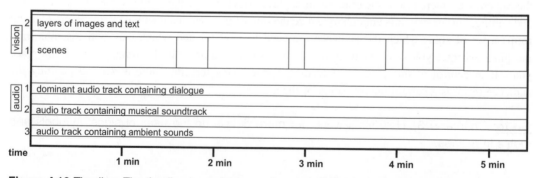

Figure 4.10 Timeline. The timeline is useful for seeing at a glance how each of the elements in the film combine together. Scenes are shown as boxes and their size reflects how long the scene lasts. In this example, smaller scenes in the middle of the film represent flashbacks and the scenes overall become shorter as the film reaches its conclusion.

images you want to use in sketches and visualizations. The development of images is purposelessly left only partially resolved so that the rest of the process can occur during filming.

The timeline is useful in showing how the tone or atmosphere of the film evolves, or how sub-themes or meanings evolve throughout. More important is the main, underlying theme of the movie, whether this is 'betrayal', 'escape' or 'triumph over evil', and without this it is not just a case of not having a map for your journey, but of not having any starting point or destination – a true definition of being lost.

It must be stressed that this method is not just aimed at being risky for its own sake, like some kind of extreme sport. For many, this approach is about getting the kind of buzz described by those who work on live television, where the knowledge that anything can happen, and you are not always prepared for it when it does, forces the director to be more ingenious in responses to problems.

Key frame method

A second, less risky method involves the use of what could be called key frames. In this approach, you lay out 'signposts' showing the route the film will take by devising a series of scenes which you want to include, roughly in the order they will appear, but with gaps allowing for the inclusion of further images and scenes. This originates in animation techniques, where the overall movement for a character would be sketched out by an artist with the main movements, or key frames, shown and this would then be passed on to animators who would fill in the movements in between.

> **Tip**   This method takes its cue from aspects of digital editing. In some packages you can alter a special visual effect or motion setting by noting what the image looks like at the start, compared to how you want it to look in the middle and at the end.

In practice, this means drawing storyboard frames depicting the main parts of the film and cutting them out to resemble a deck of cards. For example, five frames could show the development of a train terrorist plot:

1 Man receives call.
2 Man takes suitcase to train station.
3 Man boards train.
4 Man leaves suitcase on train.
5 Man jumps off moving train.

You may only have five main scenes but would place these on a sheet of paper with large gaps between each, allowing you to make notes of the kind of shots and atmosphere you want to use to connect these key scenes. You could show what encounters the man has on the train, what obstacles

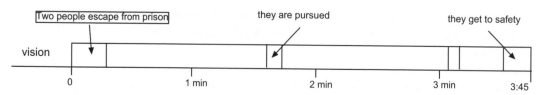

Figure 4.11 Key frame method of ordering scenes. In this method, the story is mapped out in vague terms so that the main events are placed in at the points in the film at which they occur. But the precise detail of how each scene is connected is left open.

he has in jumping off the train and whether he is seen; all of these allow improvisation on set and yet do not detract from the main plot.

Image circle method

This method takes a completely different approach, designed to suit the needs of the more theme-based, non-narrative movie, including music videos. In this sort of film the linear arrangement of scenes is not too important. Instead, you need to be able to see the whole set of images at once and look for connections between them.

Prioritize your images

To try this method, draw a set of visualizations depicting the scenes or images that will appear in the film. Take a large sheet of paper – at least 24 inches square – and draw a large circle on it. Place the

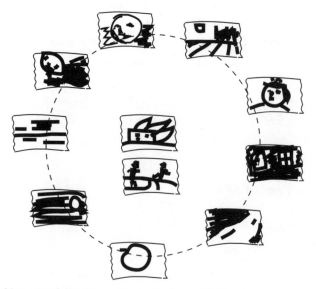

Figure 4.12 Circle of images. Separate scenes are placed around the edges of the circle, with the most important scenes at the centre.

images around the circle, placing the most important ones, most central to the film's theme, towards the centre. The less important ones are placed at various points around the circle, indicating their relative importance to each other.

This method allows you to arrange all the scenes from the film without regard for their linear appearance. You are prioritizing the clips, instead of showing the order in which they appear, allowing you to treat this in a more intuitive way when you start editing. This form of movie doesn't sit comfortably with the traditional arrangement of shots in a storyboard, but with this method the film can be built by seeing the way all the shots react with each other.

Image circle in action

For example, one particular filmmaker was making a music video on the theme of jilted love. Rather than show just a simple narrative, the filmmaker wanted to have various scenes in which this theme was developed: loss, betrayal, love and hope, all of which play a part in the overall theme and were reflected in the soundtrack. Using this method of planning allowed each part of the film to develop equally, but allowed the filmmaker to see how each element affected the rest. It's an organic way to work which may not suit everyone, but if you find that the usual way of doing storyboards seems to restrict your thoughts, then this may help.

The Crunch

- Find the amount of planning that is right for you.
- Visual planning carries on sometimes during shooting.
- Plan to improvise.
- If you can, do visual planning yourself.
- Visual planning and storyboards help you develop structure.
- ...and they help develop meaning in the images.
- Try different methods of planning (storyboards, key frame, image circle or timeline).
- OK, you know a lot of it is going to change when you start filming, but with a base to start from you can at least keep track of these changes.

7. Making a schedule

In a feature film, the idea of planning how much time each part of the process will take is crucial to the smooth running of a production, and has a huge impact on marketing and subsequent profit margins. In short film production and in micro-budget filmmaking, a schedule is less rigid. The reason for this is the amount of variables with which the micro-budget filmmaker has to contend, from the availability of non-fee actors to the demands of day jobs. The smaller the budget, the more flexible, and changeable, the schedule.

Many filmmakers have made films over a number of years, filming at weekends while they earn the money to buy film stock or tape, reliant always on a complex set of timetables of each crew member as they juggle their commitments around the demands of the film. For many, the short film is more likely than longer productions to result in a piece of finished work. Actors are less likely to get called away to more attractive paid work and crew are more likely to be able to commit themselves if a shoot lasts just a few days. Morale can easily sink when you have a half-finished production and no way of knowing when you can get your crew back together to finish it.

Enough good footage

To assess what your schedule is likely to be, you need first to look at your experience. You can think in terms of usable footage, or shots that can possibly be used in the final film. For many people starting their first film something like 10 or even 20 per cent is good, the rest blighted by shaky camera, bad sound or missed cues. After the first film, and indeed sometimes during production of the first, this rate rises in accordance with the ability of the filmmaker, but is usually in the region of 50–60 per cent after two or three short films. Short films allow you to learn more quickly than more cumbersome productions by letting you see your mistakes more quickly.

How much you need to re-shoot or re-draft is a big factor in determining how much time your film will take, but is not necessarily a factor in its quality. Stanley Kubrick would frequently shoot up to a hundred takes for minor scenes, and it has been suggested that he used this as a method to push his actors further and get more out of them. To be cautious, consider that in one day's filming only a few minutes of final footage will be achieved, less if it is action, much more if it is simply-staged dialogue.

Length of each stage

In terms of overall schedule, planning the length of time to allow for planning, shooting and editing, it is useful to think of the relative times each stage will take. Planning may take an indeterminate time, given that it is rarely produced intensively over a period of days, but it would be safe to assume that it will take twice as long as the time allowed for shooting, which is often the shorter of the three stages. Post-production may last up to four times the length of the shoot. So a ratio of planning, shooting and editing could be 2:1:4. The editing stage is prolonged when working in digital editing with your own unit at home, as it allows you to play with alternative versions and tweak the final film, perfecting it to a high degree. However, to many editors schooled in the old linear, analog methods, better editing occurs when you are pushed for time and need to make fast choices.

In between the stages mentioned above, there will be other tasks that need attention. These include casting, rehearsals, design, props buying, and viewing daily takes and rough assemblies during shooting.

Pre-production schedule

This stage is the most flexible in that you can wait until your film is prepared before you commit to a shooting date. However, the tasks to be covered need to be prioritized. Drawing up the budget is the primary task, as it dictates how much time you can spend filming, how many actors (if any) you can hire and what props you need to buy.

Make a continuity breakdown

To assess your budget you need to make a continuity breakdown. This is an outline of what is needed for each scene in the script, a list of what each demands and its associated costs. For example, a shot involving several cast members will require greater catering costs. It should also include for each scene:

- The amount of the script that is being covered by a scene. Note that each page of script is 1 minute of movie time. Partial pages are counted as eighths, so $2\frac{3}{4}$ pages would be 2 and six eighths, running at about 2 minutes and 45 seconds.
- Details of location, including transportation costs, accommodation and catering.
- The time of the shoot, noting whether it is day or night.
- Any extra equipment or props that are required, such as cars, additional lighting, costumes.
- Which members of the cast and crew are needed for that scene.
- Any additional cast or extras needed.
- Set plans showing an aerial view of a location with details of where cameras, props and lights could be situated.

You don't necessarily have to stick to the above, but it is crucial to the smooth running of the production that others have faith in your organizational abilities or you may lose members of your crew. Plans that change, particularly as a result of the input of your crew, are better than no plans at all.[17]

Shooting schedule

One of the logistical problems of filming is trying to arrange that all scenes set in one location are shot together. Ideally, you should try to arrange a schedule like a tour, placing locations together according to geographical proximity, and shooting separate locations on separate days, trying to avoid changing locations halfway through the day. Many low-budget filmmakers find themselves having to film at inconsistent times according to when the cast and crew are available, often weekends or evenings, and this can play havoc with attempts to maintain a smooth flow to the film.

It is also likely that your co-workers are simultaneously working on other projects and you may have to devise ways of reminding cast and crew about the key points of the film before each shoot. It is easy to lose track of the kind of film you are working on when you have several on the go, and it is common for you as director to want to change and adapt the script between shooting dates. Make plans well in advance that everyone – cast and crew – have the opportunity to place in their diaries before they get involved in other projects. If you have the choice, try to get everyone together for a condensed period of shooting over several days, rather than spread work over weeks.

---

[17] www.pgh.net/~pwquest/prescr2.html   Detail on breaking down the script.
www.film.queensu.ca/250/250ScriptBrkdwn.html   Useful template for script breakdown.

How long is a shoot?

Shooting times vary widely between different sectors of the film industry. Twenty years ago, a 90-minute feature film would take 40 days, whereas now it is common for the same length to take 60 days. Bear in mind, though, that this is studio production, where filming is in line with union requirements regarding working hours and breaks. But in the independent sector it is wise to adhere to similar working arrangements, as your crew will function more happily and efficiently on good rest, average food and a day or more off once a week.

In studio filming it is common to shoot roughly 2 minutes a day, although some directors will work more quickly if, for instance, working on television drama, which averages six pages per day. Clearly, some scenes will take longer, such as action sequences, scenes involving special set-ups or those with more cast members or extras than usual.

Bear in mind during the shoot that there will be enormous pressure on you to extend a schedule or to re-shoot. Remember that footage of the day's shooting rarely looks good; it's messy, it is interspersed with bad takes and is dominated by unusable tape. Resist the temptation to re-shoot without taking advice from others in the crew, or people with a more detached view of the project, and try not to judge the daily takes of a scene too harshly without seeing them in the context of the shots preceding and succeeding it.

Using the script as a guide, and informed by the restrictions of your budget, it is possible to be fairly accurate about the length of time you estimate your film will take to shoot.

The Crunch

- Be realistic: allow more time than you think. Think of a period and add 50 per cent.
- Plan in advance for your crew.
- Make a continuity breakdown: be in control of the schedule.
- Keep crew and cast informed of any changes. Check their availablity.
- The size of your budget will affect how long it will take.
- Avoid re-shooting hastily.
- Don't overspend by filming more than you have to.

5 | Production

1. A condensed guide to shooting

This chapter is going to help to get you filming quickly, taking you through the basics of filming so that you can start working on the projects detailed in this book. Refer to this chapter before you start each project so that you go shooting with more confidence, aware of the various obstacles that could arise.

Preparing yourself

As we saw in Chapter 4, much of the filmmaking process is about how to deal with problems – minor and potentially larger ones. Every day you may encounter some obstacle to your plans, some person, some rule, or act of God that puts everything on hold. The sorts of skills you need to overcome these problems are the kind that you use every day to deal with many situations – those vague, transferable skills that enable you to negotiate a pay rise, calm a distraught friend, try to do three jobs at once, sort out a problem on your car. All these hurdles are the kind that have been secretly preparing you for the process of shooting. You already have the most important skills needed to accomplish the task of making a movie, and when you put these to work with your technical knowledge of cameras and your ideas about what you want to express on video, you are on your way.

Equipment

You need:

- *Video camera.*
- *Power supplies.* Batteries or mains connection cables.
- *Videotapes.* Take four or five for a day's work, although it is unlikely that you will accomplish this much shooting.
- *Camera support.* Take a tripod or the other suggestions in Chapter 5:2.
- *Microphones.* A boom or shotgun mic should cover most situations, but take a unidirectional cardioid mic as well if you have one. A lavalier, clip-on mic will help with close-ups, or if you want to exclude other noises when recording dialogue.
- *Lights.* If you only have one lamp, make sure it's a powerful key light such as a Redhead (a brand name, but people will know what you mean if you refer to it). But you can make great-looking films

using just one strong, purpose-built lamp. Avoid using lamps that clip on to the camera. If you have the budget to use a good range, see the list in Chapter 5:8 (the ideal kitbag), but also refer to this list for the extras you will need, such as gaffer tape.

- *Monitor.* If you want to be sure that the film you are shooting maintains the highest technical standards throughout, consider using a monitor, a small television hooked up to show you what you are recording.

Interview

'One real "must-have" is a monitor, and one that you can calibrate [colour, contrast and other settings]. You will then be able to see what your picture will look like on a screen, not down a grubby viewfinder. £30 a day is well spent on a small unit with full controls. Once it's calibrated, get some camera tape and stick it over the knobs with the legend, "anyone who twiddles here dies".'

John Wildgoose, filmmaker, UK

The camera

- *Focus.* Don't shoot constantly with automatic focus as it plays havoc with interesting compositions. Use manual focus and check that the frame looks sharp and in focus often, even after the slightest movement of camera or actors.
- *White balance.* See Chapter 3:5 for details of white balance.
- *Aperture* (iris control). Automatic settings will again affect your best laid plans with lighting. See Chapter 3:5 for more about this.
- *LCD display.* Don't forget, it uses more power to use the LCD display than the small viewfinder.
- *Timecode.* See Chapters 3:3 and 6:6 for more details about timecode.
- *Continuity.* Keep notes, take Polaroids™, use video shots – anything to make an accurate record of the location of props, the arrangement of costumes, the kind of light.

Using audio

- Record sounds separately if you want to be able to manipulate them later in the editing stage.
- Use a mixing board if you have one.
- Don't record with the built-in camera mic, but if your mics fail and you have no choice, go ahead and use the camera mic, as you can use this as a guide track if you need to dub sounds later.
- Look at the hierarchy of sound recording techniques in Chapter 5:7. Use this as your default guide to every situation.
- Use headphones to be sure that you hear the levels of audio correctly.
- Use XLR adapters on the mic cables to minimize interference.
- Always record at the highest possible level before the sound starts to distort.

Working with actors

- You may get far more out of actors if you treat them as part of the team; involve them in discussions about the direction in which the film is headed.
- Don't skip on good, plentiful food on set – for actors and crew. Aim for cheap, filling food that suits everyone : pizzas, fried food and so on. ('I was nearly fired for taking two donuts when it was made clear that one was the maximum per day per person' – Harrison Ford on the set of *American Graffiti*).
- Listen to your actors, they may have as much or more experience than you about filming.

Interview
'Share your ideas; some of the best ideas came as I was telling people what I was doing and then a little brainstorm would happen and things would develop a new layer. Also: write everything down; trust your crew to do their jobs; but when recruiting, make a back-up list of every member of the crew, even two or three. Don't make new decisions on set without taking a two minute break to think things through, and don't hesitate to ask for help when you are stuck – there were a few points when I was in a tight corner and one of the crew came up with a really elegant solution.'

Debra Watson, director, Animal–Vegetable–Machine (2000)

Getting help

What happens if you are filming and you come up against a technical problem you cannot solve? The downfall of many filmmakers is a lack of experience of technical issues; it stops a production in its tracks and undermines your confidence.

- Get to know your retailer, from who you buy your filmmaking gear. They make a living working out what each bit of equipment does, how useful it is and why you need it. They may help with your questions to make sure you come back and buy more goods.
- Get involved, in advance, with local filmmaker networks; one of the strong points about the independent sector is that people help each other, on the whole. Exchange of information and help is the commodity it thrives on, as much as Hollywood does on dollar bills.
- Use the Internet for quick advice. If you can wait 24–48 hours, post a notice on one of the excellent filmmakers' notice-boards such as Shooting People (UK) or Indiewire (USA) and wait for a response. It's common to see urgent ads asking for replacement actors, legal queries or technical problems. No question is too stupid and, in any case, answers are posted on the site and benefit everyone.

How much to shoot and how long it will take?

This one has no answer but it deserves attention because it is so frequently asked.

- Shoot as much as you like, but bear in mind that economical use of your tape helps focus your mind. If you shoot everything and anything, you may end up with 10 slightly interesting, unfinished films. Limit what you film and you make better decisions. But also remember that some of the most useful shots which add spontaneity to the movie are found by being more relaxed about how much you shoot.
- If you want to be able to compare what we could call the success ratio of useful to useless footage it would be good to aim for something like 1:10. When independent feature films are being shot it is common to try to complete shooting of about 2–4 minutes a day, or 4 pages of script, but will vary according to the complexity of the sequence.
- If you work a whole day you might get in about 4 hours of shooting solidly. Short films tend to overrun more than features because there is the tendency to make each scene perfect.
- Build a good, fair schedule that reflects both your experience and the amount of available time you have and you will remain on time and, consequently, on budget.

But bear in mind that some schools of thought recommend gathering far too much footage, leaving the shaping of the whole movie to the post-production stage. George Lucas took this route on *American Graffiti*, and the result is a vibrant drama with a documentary feel.

Interview

'The day before shooting was spent sorting out last minute details, including catering. We felt that as we couldn't afford to pay our actors the least we could do was to feed them. The first day of shooting was on the Friday. We all met at some unearthly hour with our crew and began setting up equipment. This took slightly longer than was anticipated but after a while we were up and shooting. We managed to finish at a reasonable time and Saturday was pretty much the same. We decided to do two takes for each shot.'

Daniel Bogado, filmmaker

Insurance

If you can stretch to the cost of this, it could be the one outgoing which enables you to carry on making movies. Ask your insurer about large-item cover for your basic equipment and check to see how you are covered if you borrow other people's gear. If one of your actors breaks a leg during work and cannot take the next acting job, you need to be sure that you are covered either by written, legal mutual agreement or insurance.

Permission

If you are shooting in public you may (perhaps inadvertently) film someone who objects to being filmed, or would not like their image to be broadcast. A written consent form will cover you and save you from costly re-cutting or shooting later. Prepare a form which you can use on set should the need arise. Children will need the consent of their parents or guardians. In general, you can film anyone in a public place provided that footage is not improperly used, or shows them in a derogatory manner.

Emergency funding

What happens if you run out of money during filming?

- Credit is one option, but investment from people who believe in your project is better. Credit has the potential to stop future projects, even if it helps your current one.
- If you run up against the possibility that you cannot finish your film, don't consider abandoning the whole project. Shoot certain key scenes and consider applying for completion funding.

Film View
For example, *Go Fish* (1994), a brilliant debut from Rose Troche and Guin Turner, was shown to Island as a collection of black and white scenes from varying parts of the proposed film. Further funding was offered and the movie was finished.

The Crunch

- Plan the shoot well and you will achieve more.
- Remember: power, batteries, headache pills.
- Listen to advice.
- . . . But you are in charge, so be bold and decisive.
- Improvise and think around a problem.
- Be calm and relaxed.
- Make the shoot fun for you and the crew: warm food, music and mutual support.

Project 6. Modern fairytale

The aim of this project is to try out some ideas in narrative filmmaking which can help get you further into this area and give you a few starting points. We are going to look at fairytales – but before you turn the page, take a few minutes to see what this can offer. George Lucas acknowledges his debt to myths and tales and the role they played in developing his first *Star Wars* screenplay. He has successfully incorporated many of the types we see in these tales and blended them into a formidable sweep of references and symbols. Maybe his young audience don't pick up on this symbolic underworld, but a glance at the film gives us a princess to be rescued, an evil father, good versus evil, an old wizard, and so on. Lucas's trick was to convert these age-old archetypes into believable characters and forge a convincing scenario in a science fiction setting. Other films, too, rely on reinterpreting myths and tales into a modern setting. David Lynch 'adapted' *The Wizard of Oz* for a late-night, strong-stomached audience in *Wild at Heart* (1990), while *O Brother, Where Art Thou?* (Coen brothers, 2000) takes apart ancient Greek tales and crash-lands them into depression-hit America, complete with floods, strange vanishings, escape and redemption.

Film View

In *The Company of Wolves* (Neil Jordan, 1984), a bewildering mix of legends are served up with the latent symbolism and dark, erotic nature of some stories moved to the fore, making the movie a surreal and fascinating display of the strange underbelly of myth and tales.

Stage 1

Find at least a dozen tales or myths. Try anything from Hans Christian Andersen to Native American myths, from Red Riding Hood to Rapunzel. Read everything you can find.

Stage 2

When you have digested each story, start making a list of the varied ingredients found in these stories. For instance, there may be:

- a cave;
- a figure in a cloak;
- a poison apple;
- a deep valley;
- a house in the woods;
- a man in search of his destiny;
- a woman leaving the path in the forest;

and so on.

When you have these elements, write each one, or draw them if it makes the idea clearer, on separate pieces of paper. These are now what we could call 'the building blocks of narrative'. Each one is a specific element which carries much symbolism or shared meaning, and when combined they make a heady brew. The aim of this project is to bring these elements into the present: out of the fantastical, ancient setting and into the recognizable modern world.

Lay out these pieces of narrative and look for elements which you know you could reasonably film – either because you have access to locations or to particular actors who could help you. Treat the individual pieces as a deck of cards: shuffle them around until you have an arrangement which looks like the bullet points of a narrative. So, using the selection above as an example, you might have a story in which a man leaves his village to make his fortune; he meets a figure who offers him an apple which turns out be poisoned. He staggers to a nearby house . . .and so on.

Carry on building up the story until you have something you like and can shoot.

Stage 3

Proceed on through the stages of planning the film, developing the look of the film (its use of the camera, of colour, of lighting) in one particular direction. To find out what direction this should be, take one particular element you picked out for inclusion in your story, perhaps the one which seems to suggest the most atmosphere, such as the dark forest. Take this one image and build the style of the film around it so that, in this case, all aspects of the film are infused with darkness and the menacing feel of a deep forest.

Stage 4

Shoot the film, following the ideas suggested in each of the sections on production. Look at lighting and sound recording in particular. Having made a few films already in previous projects, you may now be building up a sense of what you like and what you don't, of what kind of narrative film you would like to make. If you prefer emphasizing underlying elements of symbolism and deeper meaning in your films, choose a story which involves few events, leaving you room to use more sequences which give us the atmosphere and ambience of each scene. If you prefer strong narratives, do the opposite.

Stage 5

Editing this film will involve a look at the next chapter on DV editing, or you could wait until you feel more confident with editing before you start cutting it together.

The kind of editing you feel is right for the film – fast and action-packed or slow and lingering – is up to you and does not affect the outcome of the project.

Evaluation

The main emphasis of this project is on the planning and building stage rather than on shooting or editing. You can almost evaluate this project through looking solely at the screenplay, looking at how the story has been constructed. The project works on several areas:

- How a narrative is pieced together from key elements.
- How to structure these elements into a story and plot.
- How certain elements take a dominant role in the film.
- How the story tells you what look the film should have.

Look closely at how you interwove each of the story elements together. This takes some skill and it may be something that you return to after you have gained more experience in editing. It can be a difficult challenge to provide enough information for each part of the story and yet keep events moving briskly. It was probably the easier option to tell this story chronologically intact, without resorting to confusing devices such as flashbacks or visions of the future.

Decide how well you have managed to update the myths and legends you used and whether they fit together into a smooth-flowing stream of events. Have you brought these individual parts of the story into the present but kept the symbolic aspects of them intact? In practice, it is hard to shake off these additional meanings; your audience have grown up with these archetypal images and events, and to this extent the symbols will endure whatever you do to them.

Regardless of the quality of the film itself, does your story seem to go from place to place and event to event convincingly? Do your characters' motivations push them to do what they do? In short, is your story believable, within the bounds of the fantastical world you created?

Look at the degree to which you feel the story you devised is part of the film's style. If you followed the way of developing style suggested here, then you have probably evolved style out of the film itself, rather than letting a certain style push and pull you to certain story elements.

Finally, think about whether you enjoyed this experience. Aside from the subject matter, look at what this period has taught you in terms of the way you work with actors, plan your shooting, organize your crew, edit the film. Go back to Chapter 2:2 and go through the interview again to see what this film can tell you about your preferences and your individual, unique approach to filmmaking.

2. Better looking films

You've spent a while looking at how to stretch the potential of your camera without spending any cash on the film itself. Now you need to look at what kind of 'feel' you want in your film and how the overall look of it can be achieved. Working with a small budget, you may not be able to rely on well-known actors or sets to make your film stand out from the competition, so you need to become more confident about what you can achieve with those tools that don't cost anything: what the camera sees.

Make your camera work harder, make your film look better

The aim of this section is to go through some of the basics of getting the most from the camera; how to get the right shots and how to find those elusive, special shots that will make your film rise above the rest. But as well as knowing the short cuts to getting these kinds of shots, we need to look at how you can depict something in a professional way, to industry standards. This doesn't mean you are going to produce dull, uninspiring images; we are just going to concentrate on learning a few rules in camerawork so that later you can feel free to break them.

Use the rules and bend them

It may seem that if you know what kind of film you want to make you shouldn't need to know how other people work. It's true that no one knows better than you what kind of film you want, but this next step is not about copying how other filmmakers do it, it is about learning how to get your preferred shots more quickly. When you know how a certain shot is often filmed it gives you a starting point – you can either go with the norm or reject it. It can make you think faster. Furthermore, if you find yourself working with a crew of other people also committed to making films, they will expect you to know what works when filming – and what does not.[1]

Conveying mood

Mood is a nebulous concept, but to attempt some definition, we could say that it is the integration of the various style elements of a film with the core theme of that film. Lighting, music and camera angle are the main tools behind the camera helping you to achieve this. It may shift throughout the film, but a pervasive atmosphere will dominate if the film is to be coherent and consistent. Mood is something that is evoked rather than described explicitly, so you have to rely on subtle methods to add a particular slant to a scene. Being able to manipulate mood is useful because it enables you to specify what sort of emotions are dominating a scene and how we as the audience should interpret it.

Let's suppose you want to shoot a scene in a drama. There is a character who is afraid of something; he is in a dark room and is apprehensive about something that is about to happen. You decide you want lots of drama and you want to increase the sense of tension. Now your job as a director is to shoot that scene in the most effective way, conveying clearly the *atmosphere* evoked by this character in this room in this situation. If you know some of the ways other people have produced tension or fear in a shot, then it immediately gives you something to start with. When you know the rules you then start adding something of yourself to them; indeed, your own personal style is the way you respond to the rules and in what particular way you break, bend or stick with them. So, in this instance, you may use lighting with higher contrast and with the camera may use close-ups to exaggerate the facial expressions of the actor, or long, wide shots to emphasize the sense of isolation and vulnerability of the character in the room.

Film View
Many movies that seem to project a strong atmosphere come from a background of low budgets and few special effects. Try watching *Eraserhead* (David Lynch, 1976), The Terence Davies Trilogy (1974–1983) and *The Garden* (Derek Jarman, 1990). This is not to say that low production values make great atmosphere, but these films do possess a richer sense of mood, perhaps due to the budgetary restrictions.

---

[1] www.aber.ac.uk/media/Documents/short/gramtv.html   Detailed breakdown of camera shots and what they can represent.

Composition

Let's concentrate now just on what the camera can achieve in showing the plot and conveying mood. We can look at how shots are more effective if you think about how you are arranging the objects within the frame. The position and angle you select for the camera relative to the subject and its surroundings is called the 'composition'.

Composition in filmmaking has developed mainly from the ideas of painters in Renaissance Europe; many cinematographers will freely admit to being inspired by great paintings of this time. But the great filmmaker Eisenstein has suggested that we need framing for all our art because we tend to look at the world through windows.[2]

Tip   Sergei Eisenstein is credited with having established some of the fundamental ideas behind montage in his ground-breaking films such as *Battleship Potemkin* (1925) and *Strike* (1924).

Tip   Try looking at Renaissance works by Masaccio and Giotto to see where classic, epic staging originates, or look at the sumptuous attention to light by northern Renaissance artists such as Jan van Eyck or, later, Vermeer.

Composition helps a low budget

Going back to our scared-man-in-the-room scene above, it is quite likely your budget averages your monthly disposable income and you definitely can't stretch to dry ice or a specially composed score. The lower your budget, the more you must try to get your camera to work harder. It's no coincidence that directors making their debut feature will display quite high levels of ingenuity with the camera, showing off a number of different compositions to make up for a lack of expensive props or effects to point the camera at.

But don't show everything

You are also going to rely on the audience to imagine some images. A good director would not have to display all the action or spell out the whole narrative and will use imaginative compositions to

---

[2] www.agfaphoto.com/library/photocourse/9903/index.html 02   Excellent photographer's guide to composition equally useful for filmmakers.
www.azuswebworks.com/photography/ph_comp.html   Useful detail on photographic composition.

suggest and evoke, allowing the audience to fill in the gaps. But this sort of filming is quicker and more successful with a good grasp of the basic rules. If you watch *The Haunting* (Robert Wise, 1963), you can see how a small budget was somehow irrelevant. The film's scariest moments rely on clever composition, pointing the shadow at a certain shape, shadow or object and at a certain angle to give a feeling of unease. As if to prove the theory that what we don't see is scarier than what is spelled out for us, the remade film in 1999 (directed by Jan De Bont) made much of the implicit horror explicit and was widely condemned as not scary enough.[3]

Basic starting points in composition

- The clarity of the objects in view.
- The amount that is not in view.
- The use of shapes to denote particular theme or mood.
- The angle of the camera.

Within this there are certain kinds of composition which are more suited to certain situations. The eminent cinematographer Nestor Almendros used a lifetime of experience to describe the following principles:[4]

- Horizontal lines suggest serenity and calm.
- Vertical lines denote strength or authority.
- Diagonal lines suggest action or movement.
- Curved lines suggest fluidity and sensuality.
- Moving a camera forward to enter a scene suggests 'bringing the audience into the heart of the narrative'.
- The opposite movement, away from a scene, is often used as a way of ending a film.

(*A Man with a Camera*, p. 14, Faber & Faber, 1982)

Placing action in the viewfinder

To get to grips with composition, start by looking at the way you use the whole. Try a short exercise: get a sheet of paper the same shape as the screen you intend to work with (see Figure 5.1). The shape is what is called the 'aspect ratio' of your screen. Aspect ratio refers to the height and width of the screen. The common standard for European television is 16:9 – the longer measurement being the width. Most filmmakers like to work on a slightly rectangular screen because, in terms of composition, it is easier to get a more interesting arrangement than using a square. This shape has evolved over time as one which will most help you in finding a good arrangement.[5]

---

[3] www.filmmonthly.com/Horror/Articles/Haunting/Haunting.html   Article on *The Haunting* (1963 version).
[4] http://208.154.71.60/bcom/eb/article/7/0,5716,5937+1,00.html   Article on Almendros' work.
[5] www.hometheaterforum.com/home/wsfaq.html   Detailed look at aspect ratio in the movies.
    www.digital-digest.com/dvd/downloads/aspectratio.html   Download a calculator to work out your aspect ratio.

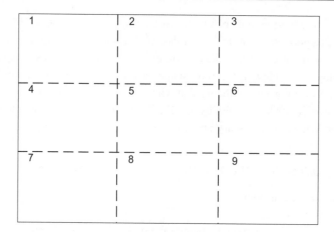

Figure 5.1 Divide a sheet of paper into nine equal rectangles, numbering each one.

An A4 sheet of paper is as good a shape as any to start. Fold it into thirds both horizontally and vertically so you have nine rectangles. Try to imagine the sheet as your viewfinder on the camera and look at any shots you have so far on your camera, noticing in which rectangle the action tends to be in each scene.

Lazy parts of the screen

If we number the rectangles as in the illustration, you might find that most of the action in your footage takes place in the fifth box – the centre of the screen. Whether you are shooting a very still scene such as a conversation, or a running chase scene, it is common to find that the focus of attention is in the middle and all the other boxes are unused. This is easy to shoot – you just place the subject in the centre of the screen and stand back – but it makes for bad composition. It's predictable and boring while your job is to grab an audience's attention as much as possible, even in quiet, subtle scenes. Have a look at some of your own: is box no. 5 doing all the work or are the others pulling their weight too? To encourage you to find new camera angles, keep moving the camera around until the action is spread throughout the nine boxes. Every box doesn't have to be used in each shot but there should be a spread throughout the film. After trying this method for a while you will soon find that you naturally want to compose the frame rather than just shooting into the middle of it.

You can be aware of this during the planning stage, so that when you do storyboards you can stop the bad ones in their tracks and redo that frame. But if you find that you have poor compositions when you are actually filming you need to rectify it on location, under pressure. If you have an LCD viewfinder you could place a sheet of clear acetate over it with a grid over it to keep a check on how you are dividing up the screen.

Figure 5.2 *Bernada Alba* (2001) by Naomi Lock. The composition in this is well judged: the arms of the figures provide a useful construction, while the upward camera angle allows strong, contrasting light, leading to clearly composed elements.

<u>**Go to:**</u> Chapters 4:5 and 4:6 for more detail on visual planning.

To assess how you use the screen, you could shoot a simple scene (such as making a cup of coffee) but avoid putting the action in box no. 5, in the middle. Avoid the tendency to depict the action squarely in the centre and try constantly to be aware of the whole screen. Although you would not want to avoid the centre box all the time when making a movie, this exercise of abstaining from the centre does force you to give added weight to other areas of the screen.

You can then try watching feature films and notice how much of the screen is used. You might start to notice some of the conventions which filmmakers use. For example, placing a character to the edge of the screen can heighten the dramatic content of that scene and tilting it can give a sense of unease. Don't forget, however, that there are many times when a centrally framed shot is just right for your film. The director Stanley Kubrick made this kind of shot his trademark as he found it gave some shots a kind of claustrophobic feel.

Film View
Watch *Paths of Glory* (1957), Kubrick's film set in World War One, to see how a one-point perspective shot can work as he takes us around the trenches.

Composition dividing lines

With a bit of practice you may now see separate areas when you look through the viewfinder, dividing up the image. But the four dividing lines that separate the boxes can also be very useful. You can start to use these as 'hooks' to peg your actors or action on. Let's use an example of, for instance, a simple dialogue between two people. When you watch other films you start to notice the most common composition for placing the face within the frame. Heads can be very difficult to place because you need to make sure the mouth is visible all the time and the eyes are prominent. Try putting the eyes on the upper line (see Figure 5.3) – don't worry about how much of the forehead you have to lose – then place the nose on either of the vertical lines.

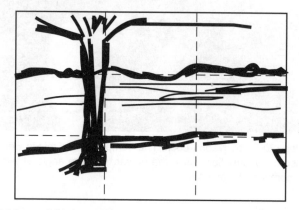

Figure 5.3 Use the divisions of thirds on the paper to place objects within the composition. 'Hooking' them onto the verticals or horizontals gives rise to depth in the image.

Feel free to break this rule, but it is a good place to start for a well-composed shot. Avoiding overusing the centre of the frame works because it moves the focus of attention away from the place where we lazily and automatically want to look and allows other objects or people to occupy the spaces left over, adding more interest to the film.

The same goes for landscape shots: place the horizon on one of the horizontal lines and any distinguishing features such as trees or a building on the verticals. You are making the audience look at different parts of the screen and this makes for a less predictable experience. If you make the audience look around the screen constantly it starts to work in your favour, as they will then start noticing everything in the shot. Of course, if it is done badly it is distracting but every kind of filmmaker tries to make his or her film more interesting to look at. In fact, now that Hollywood has discovered computer-generated images, directors can also achieve unusual, daring shots in large-scale action sequences.[6]

[6] www.cacr.caltech.edu/~roy/vermeer/thumb.html   Thumbnail shots of Vermeer paintings.
    http://mfadt.parsons.edu/~mcgomez/theAge/eu1.htm   Excellent interactive site on composition of the great artists.
    www.bc.edu/bc_org/avp/cas/fnart/HP/renaiss.html   Boston College site looking at Renaissance perspective: very useful for cinematographers.

Figure 5.4 In this shot, the screen is divided by the sea horizon line, the figure and the bar in the foreground.

Film View
In *Apollo 13* (1995), director Ron Howard was able to liberate the camera from the usual static shots of models in space through the use of computer-generated images. Look at the launch scenes, where the camera weaves in and out of the lifting rocket, to see the result.

Using depth in your shots

We have looked at how to use dividing lines to help you get good compositions. One of the things created by these compositions is something called 'depth'. Don't confuse it with meanings in your film; this is *pictorial* depth. Basically, depth is your way of inviting the audience into a scene. If you follow the ideas in the last chapter about dividing up the screen you will almost certainly have put some depth into the shot without trying. Depth is achieved where one object or person is close to the camera and something else is further away. The space you create in the middle is called depth. It is disarmingly simple, but if you are conscious of it when setting up your camera then you are going to get a much higher success rate in terms of getting great-looking shots. Once you've understood it you can then start to use it to your advantage, putting greater depth where you want a more dramatic scene.

Figure 5.5 *Cereal Killer* [sic] (2001) by Ed Spencer. This shot uses an extreme degree of depth, emphasizing the drama of the scene, detailing a hit-and-run murder. The dominance of the car in the frame powerfully symbolizes the event.

Figure 5.6 *Ghost Writer* (2001) by Ed Spencer. As in Spencer's other movie, depth is again used here, this time to increase the sense of tension between the two figures and suggesting their isolation from each other.

Using tripods for composition

The tripod is a very useful, essential piece of equipment but it is expensive. It can be very restrictive but on balance it's probably a good idea to have some sort of support for the camera occasionally. If the cost puts you off, try a mini-tripod, which is a shorter and smaller version but does need a table-top or other surface to rest on. Some wildlife filmmakers use a beanbag on which to rest the camera, as they enable the user to move quickly to various camera angles and don't require a flat surface. They also help you to get a range of steady shots without having to fumble around altering the tripod constantly. Alternatively, you could get rid of the tripod altogether. There is a school of thought which says that the tripod stops your film from having vitality and spontaneity. Filmmaker Robert Rodriquez suggests that: 'if you have a tripod you are going to leave the camera stuck on it. It looks nice . . .and your film is going to look dead.' Good advice for the lazy filmmaker, but remember also that filming without a tripod requires skill. Watch out for 'hosepiping', which occurs when the filmmaker waves the camera around without providing the audience with a firm place from which to view the action. Apparently, when watching *The Blair Witch Project*, more people felt ill from the violently moving camera than from the violent events it showed us. Keep the camera under control, giving us a view of the action from one viewpoint, just as if it is another actor, watching rather than participating in the action. Feel free to alter this viewpoint throughout the scene.

Tripods can inhibit good composition

The idea goes that as soon as you have placed your camera on a tripod you effectively close the decision-making process, removing the possibility of other ideas coming up which could improve a scene. So, if you are using camera support, you need to be certain that you have got the right shot before you get out the tripod. Try setting the composition to begin with without any support, looking continually through the lens to make sure you try out every conceivable angle and then, when you are sure you have found the shot that works best for you, set it on a tripod. This method ensures that the camera angle does not have to compromise to suit the tripod's limitations.[7]

Tip There are many other filmmakers who reject camera support. The Danish group, Dogme, believes that any use of tripods adds further layers of artificiality to a film and takes its audience one step further removed from it. For examples of Dogme movies, try *Julien Donkey-Boy* (Harmony Korine, 2000) or *Festen* (Thomas Vinterberg, 1998).

Finding and using unexpected shots

It is reasonable to suppose that if you have planned a film properly you should never need to find extra shots. Many filmmakers, however, believe that the combined energy and input of a lot of people on

[7] www.dogme95.dk/   Official site of the Dogme group.

set can throw up unforeseen opportunities for quite unexpected shots. It is already accepted that actors may ad lib in a scene, only to find that the director keeps their off-the-cuff lines and removes the written part of the script. It is the same with filmmaking; you have to be aware that there are many shots you are not getting because you are sticking rigidly to your storyboard.

In practice, one way to arrive at this is to try leaving the camera switched on more often between takes and during on-set rehearsals. You will, of course, end up with lots of unwanted footage of people moving lights around, microphones being attached and so on, and will find yourself with a great deal more footage to trawl through before editing. But this can have some striking benefits. When you are setting up a shot it is common to switch off the camera in order to be economical with your tape and power. Bear in mind, however, that shooting lots of excess footage is still seen as bad practice and is often dismissed in filmmaking courses as bad practice. The aim of this book, however, is to make interesting and original films – rules or no rules – and any method that helps in finding shots that make your film stand out from the crowd is welcome.

Spare shots

There is another good reason for allowing more footage to be gathered than first intended. When we look at editing in Chapter 6, you will see how useful it is to have spare shots with which to patch over parts of a scene now and then to add interest and keep the audience watching. The kind of shots that turn up when you are simply experimenting to find the right angle or lighting effect can add variety and spark to a film.

What kind of shots?

Inevitably, preparation work is capable of preparing you too well; you end up knowing exactly what you want and will probably end up making a good, honest movie. But filmmaking remains an art form as well and as such needs to have some allowance made for the unexpected during shooting. It is this that marks the line between the average, workaday movie and the one that grabs the audience and makes the movie a more dynamic experience. The kind of shots you can use to sprinkle over the movie later are the ones that you would usually discard, either because they don't fit in with the rest of the scene or because they have some slight fault in them. You might stumble across some of the most unusual compositions when you have occasionally departed from your plans and might have considered the result a mistake. But when you get to edit the movie later, revisit these unwanted parts of your footage tapes and give them a chance.

Let's take our earlier example of a straightforward scene with dialogue between two characters. Filming this scene will be relatively easy as you have to show only two actors, but after a minute or so you could start inserting the occasional shot of the two from a distance, or a shot taken in close-up as the actors were rehearsing earlier. However, don't show faces on these 'patched' shots if the actors are speaking as the new shots would be out of sync with the rest of the scene. Try to film shots of the actors' hands moving; this can emphasize drama in certain scenes and is vital for covering up the join between two takes of the same scene.

Film View
In *American Grafitti* (1973), George Lucas made his first full-length feature by filming virtually everything from every angle and leaving decisions about how the film would look to the editing stage. The result is a drama that has the realism of a fly-on-the-wall documentary.

The Crunch

- Make your films look good.
- Get to know the rules of composition.
- Know when to use the conventional approach and when to try something new.
- Good composition can give a low-budget film a high-budget look.
- Be aware of the whole screen when shooting.
- Use composition to allow for pictorial depth.
- Try unexpected shots, found during bad takes.
- Show you are a master of conventional filmmaking and a master of doing it your own way.

Project 7. Tell it like it is: portrait of a place

The next project is aimed at developing your ability to find great-looking shots and to notice the accidentally great ones when you come across them. To do this, we are going to place the whole weight of the movie on the shots alone. Although actors may be used in this film they are going to have no dialogue and in this way there will be little chance of your leaning on actors or plot to deliver you a great film. We will try to depict a place or a situation, an encounter or an event, capturing the atmosphere and the sensation of being there.

This could include:

- A deserted industrial estate.
- A crowded bar or club with a tense stand-off between several figures.
- A competitive, highly charged sporting event.
- An empty sea resort in winter.
- An eerie, empty house.

The aim is to devise shots where composition is everything, where you have worked hard on the arrangement of the frame to get just the right look, evoking that particular place. Try to describe what it is like to be in that situation, with those people, at that time. For example, if you depict a tense sporting event – easy to find and requiring no actors or props – you may show the anxious atmosphere by the use of close-ups and extreme depth, with figures set against the backdrop of the stadium, perhaps shot from below to show the strength of the competitors.

In all, try to get hold of at least 20 different shots depicting the place.

Stage 1

Choose somewhere to film. Paradoxically, the project is more effective if you choose a place that seems quite uninspiring, encouraging you to rely solely on what you can do with the camera rather than what the place itself has to offer. For example, Niagara Falls is going to look captivating wherever you point your camera, but a commonplace situation or place you are more familiar with is going to require a lot more ingenuity to make it interesting.

Stage 2

Once you have chosen your subject, write down several descriptive words that summarize the place. For instance, 'crowded', 'noisy' and so on.

Stage 3

Take these words with you and bear them in mind every time you set up a shot. One or more of them should imbue every shot you take. For example, a sea resort in summer might suggest the word bustling, so you might look through the lens constantly, trying to find a shot which best sums up that word, as well as others. Bear in mind also the points on composition made earlier about using all areas of the screen.

To get you started, it may be useful to take as a starting point some of the shots described as common compositions. Take a look at the ideas suggested by cinematographer Nestor Almendros earlier in this chapter. These shots are a kind of shorthand which filmmakers have evolved to show events or situations in a certain way. For instance, a tilted angle to your shot will suggest to the audience that something slightly disturbing or negative is happening, even if the actual content of the shot is showing something very different.

Use music

You may find it useful to keep an overall sense of atmosphere to the movie by finding a piece of music which also sums up the place you have chosen and listen to it while filming. This can help you to find and keep the right sort of atmosphere throughout the film.

Tip   Director Martin Scorsese was, for a time, a great believer in this method and would often rig loudspeakers on set to play the track aloud that would later accompany that scene, thus helping the crew to focus on one particular mood.

Stage 4

You are going to edit this film as you go along. Record each shot you want in the order they will be seen, just as you did in Chapter 4:5 (visualizing and the in-cam edit), but bear in mind that once you have the shots you can return to them and edit for real later.

Evaluation

- When you look at the shots you gathered, don't think about the ratio of good shots to bad just yet and instead think about how you got the good ones.
- What sort of decisions did you make while filming, and what kind of practical process did you go through to arrive at these shots? You may have found, for example, that you needed to take time to explore the possibilities before committing yourself to a shot. Regardless of how anyone else films, you need to pin down exactly what works for you in getting to the good shots.
- This film did not involve visualizing or storyboarding the movie in advance, but having seen what kind of shots work well through the lens, you may find this part of preparation easier and more fruitful in future films.
- Look at whether the shots in the final film resemble each other or whether there was a wide range of angles and compositions. These should have been dictated by the demands of the place, so there may be some resemblance to a certain extent as they all link to the same subject, but check whether there is too much similarity and too little interest.
- Did the end result suggest the place you portrayed? It is all too easy to be diverted from the initial words that set the film in motion and this is an important test in being able to stick to your own personal view of a place and portray it through film.

In addition, look at:

- How you used light, shadows and the iris of the camera itself.
- Was the image exposed properly? In other words, was it frequently too bright or too dark?
- How the contrast of light and shadow was used and whether greater contrast helps.
- How many shots incorporated depth in some way.
- How you used the nine areas of the screen we talked about earlier.
- Look at how you used the vertical and horizontal lines mentioned earlier. Did they prove useful in helping to decide where to place objects within the frame?

3. Continuity

Continuity refers to the way shots go together to create a seamless chain of events. It is going to be the invisible tool that helps you bind the film together and link it as a single, whole experience. It is going to hide the nuts and bolts of filmmaking, creating an illusion of reality and merging separate pieces of film – sometimes recorded days, weeks or months apart – into one stretch of fictional time.

The need for continuity arises only because the audience do not see everything. Time is compressed and space is shown only selectively, cropping the imaginary world we see. To illustrate this effect, try a test where you look only through a small tube, with tunnel vision. You start to feel the need for information to tell you about your environment, being able to look at separate parts of it at any given time. If someone leaves your small frame of view, you want to know whether they have left the room. Add to this the effect of editing, where shots are broken up into small pieces, and it becomes essential that some way is devised of maintaining the smooth flow of events on film.

Continuity is disrupted easily; the slightest object out of place, a confusing camera angle or a shift in the style in the film can all break the audience's involvement with the illusion. The effect of broken continuity is unusually shocking; it momentarily drops the viewer from the fairground ride experience of watching the film and sends them back to earth with a knock. Of course, with such a noticeable effect, discontinuity is just one more trick for the filmmaker to utilize. If you are aware of the positive and negative effects of keeping continuity and disrupting it, you can choose when and how you employ these tools. To use the fairground ride analogy again, you can choose when to keep the ride smooth and when to give an unexpected jolt to the passengers, without risking the whole ride falling apart.

Narrative continuity

In narrative film, continuity is crucial. Various elements have the potential to cause problems during shooting and editing, including:

- technical factors such as changes in picture quality;
- plot factors such as omitting crucial explanatory scenes;
- prop and set factors such as clocks out of sync;
- style factors such as a shift in the look of the film.

Know the rules, know how to break them

It is worth noting that bad continuity is not necessarily good discontinuity. In other words, simply ignoring the rules of continuity will not automatically lead to a ground-breaking film that has its own innovative look. Every film needs to have an internal logic where any disruption of the basic ideas of continuity is planned and incorporated into the film as a whole, so that it corresponds to its own rules. This may sound vague because each film has its own individual needs but, in general, rules are broken in a planned way rather than arbitrarily.[8]

Avoiding bad continuity

How do you set about ensuring that continuity is under control? A range of issues need to be considered, as outlined below.

---

[8] www.theworkshops.com/shared/courses/Continuity_Script.html   Filmmakers' workshops in continuity, US based.

Tape quality

This is less of an issue for digital tape but is important nonetheless. Use the same quality of tape throughout production, new ones if possible. Digital tape degrades far less than analog tapes through reuse because it is built very differently, but there are other ways in which tape can be affected through length of use, so it is safer to buy new tapes and use a consistent number of times, usually less than 10.

Camera features

Make sure you remain with the same camera settings throughout production. If you start the film using, for example, an aspect ratio of 16:9 (sometimes called 'cinema' on the camera), stay with it throughout unless you have a scripted reason to change. Set the white balance to the same values each time you shoot. White balance is often automatic on many models but check before every shoot; any unknown changes in lighting and you could end up with one shot having a warm, orange cast to it and the next having a cold, blue cast to it. Altering the white balance on purpose can be a valid tool, of course, allowing you to change the look of a scene.

Plot disruption

Even a minor absence of some small part of a plot can be baffling for an audience. For example, a shot showing a character in one location, a beach perhaps, followed by a cut immediately to the same character in an entirely different location, perhaps back home, needs some explaining. We have soon assumed that the character jumped in a car and drove home, between the two shots, but we need to be shown it or told it with a subtitle, even if it is just a glimpse of the car speeding on the road for a couple of seconds, or a title saying 'later'. A narrative is like a ladder; its upward, linear progress depends on having all the rungs in place. Miss out a few rungs and the ladder still works but requires considerable effort to climb, and eventually you lose faith in the overall structure.

Closure: the viewer fills in the gaps

However, before we start handing the audience everything on a plate, there is a concept called 'closure' which refers to the ability of the mind to fill gaps in a narrative to make it into a coherent whole. If you draw a circle but leave out a few degrees of it or draw one with dotted lines, you will still recognize it as this shape, but the crucial point is that enough information has been given for us to conclude that it is a circle. Just a few lines *in the right place* and we can fill in the rest, just as in the example above we needed to see only a fraction of the car journey to see that it had taken place. Leave out the scene that connects the two locations and you risk losing the shape of the film as a whole.[9]

Sound

One of the more subtle but still noticeable continuity problems is in sound. Sounds recorded in the background to each scene will differ greatly, even those recorded on the same day in the same place.

---

[9] www.movie-mistakes.com/   Light-hearted look at continuity mistakes in famous movies.

The reasons for this are looked at more fully in later chapters on sound, but bear in mind that ambient sound or presence has the capacity to make or break continuity. The use of devices to smooth over the changes in presence are one of the hallmarks of professional filming.

Go to: Chapters 5:7, 'Sound recording', and 6:4, 'Sound in editing', for more details.

Style disruption

Style is something which naturally occurs as a result of the numerous decisions you make about camera angle, composition, music, editing and so on. Once you have noted the constant elements in the film, such as the kind of shots you use, dominant colours or style of acting, you need to nail these down and stick to them. There will be times in the film when you want to disrupt this conformity of style, for instance in dream or fantasy sequences and flashbacks, or to denote a radical change in the film's pace. At these points you will certainly devise a very different look to the film, but it is a constant style throughout the rest of the film that allows you to lift other sections out of it so neatly. Try to establish the look of the film early on in the planning stage. Use a timeline to indicate the dominant style and where it is to be broken.

Film View

In Woody Allen's *Annie Hall* (1977), disruption of style is worked into the fabric of the film from the start. At one point, this seemingly straight romantic comedy veers off into an animation sequence.

The action line

Among the devices we have looked at to ensure smooth continuity, one of the most useful regards the placing of the camera. This rule is also known as the 180-degree rule and has evolved to ensure that the fictional space created by a scene is sustained throughout. Both shooting and editing play a role in this. Every new shot has the potential to suggest that we are in a new location or at a new point in time. The purpose of the 180-degree rule is to reassure the audience that we are in the same place and that the events are happening in the same short space of time.

How the action line works

It works by drawing an imaginary line between characters in a scene and drawing a semi-circle that runs 180 degrees around them, on one side only. The camera must shoot from one side of the line, from any position. If we look at Figure 5.7, we can see what the camera records by staying on one side of the line. In this shot the two actors are on opposite sides of the frame, actor 2 on the right, actor 1 on the left. The audience note the position of the two actors and set up a kind of internal map of the room accordingly. But if the camera goes onto the other side of the line, the actors seem to have changed sides, with 1 on the left and 2 on the right. The audience then ask questions: Did an actor move? Or did an edit go missing?

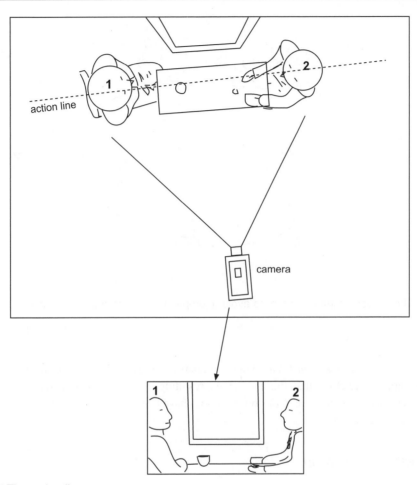

Figure 5.7 The action line.

The action line and the jump cut

A further use of the line is in avoiding the 'jump cut'. A jump cut is an abrupt cut between two clips when the camera of each gives slightly different views of the subject. When framing a figure we will notice a disruption of our view by moving the camera slightly to the side and cutting between the two shots. It is as if you had filmed a tracking shot and left out a small piece of tape as the camera moves, as you may expect to see in badly preserved old movies. The effect does not destroy the scene but does introduce some hiccup in the flow of the film. As with all discontinuity, this is also a useful tool as it produces dissonance against the harmony of the overall continuity and, as anyone working with music will tell you, dissonance is a valued element in music composition.

The 30-degree rule

To avoid this effect, however, cameras are placed at certain places around the action. Imagine a semi-circle radiating around the main action, as if the camera is in the auditorium of a theatre looking at

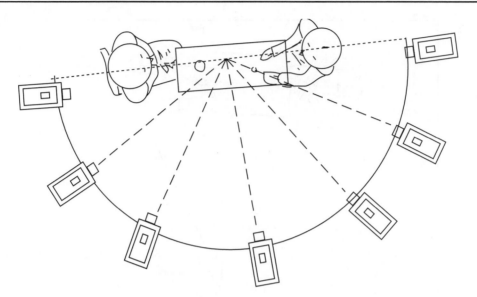

Figure 5.8 The 30-degree rule. In order to avoid a jump cut, cameras are placed at least 30 degrees apart.

a stage. Cameras can be placed *at least* 30 degrees apart from each other around this semi-circle, but no closer. If cameras are closer than this and the two resulting close shots are edited together, the effect will disrupt the space of that scene. Cuts to new angles have to be sufficiently different to justify their occurrence (see Figure 5.8).

Motion within the screen

The rectangle within which we see the film, whether it is a television or projection screen, is also a tool in achieving continuity in that we construct a map of the invented world of the film. Movement within and off screen needs to be handled particularly carefully. Explaining this gets a little complicated and abstract, but here goes.

There is a difference between scenes that are stationary and scenes involving forward movement, such as a chase or journey. Let's take the first kind to begin with. Say you have a scene involving, for instance, some people within a room or in a particular defined space. If a figure walks off the screen we adjust our internal map of the scene and place a mental marker regarding where they are now. If they go left, we expect them to return from the left; if they exit right, that's where they should re-enter. Ignoring this makes for an unholy mess in continuity. At worst, your audience are going to lose faith in the whole movie and start watching for more such continuity errors. Even a simple plot is then in peril, as now nothing the filmmaker is offering to the audience can be relied upon.

The other kind, and you were warned it gets confusing here, involves the reverse of this. Suppose you have a scene in which one character is chasing another. Maybe a policeman is pursuing a villain, or

(a)

(b)

Figure 5.9 *Two Can Play At That Game* (2001) by Jon Price. This short used one actor to play two parts and required careful control of continuity to link scenes shot on separate occasions, giving the appearance of simultaneity.

a *Tyrannosaurus rex* is chasing a jeep. In these kinds of scenes the participant will exit right (usually) and re-enter left, showing us that the journey or chase is constantly in the same direction, left to right, left to right. If you follow the piece on the action line earlier, then much of this problem is solved.

There is a convention regarding the direction actors will be moving when filmed. If a figure is going forwards or onwards *metaphorically*, in the script, perhaps to a new location or new part of the plot, we expect the figure to travel consistently from left to right across the screen, and the reverse when seen to be returning from somewhere. There are times when you need to imply onward or returning motion and this device becomes even more useful when you have few location landmarks to help orientate the audience. In David Lean's *Lawrence of Arabia*, the exhausted Lawrence is journeying across a barren desert, and we see him go from left to right. When he later learns that one of his party has fallen from his camel many miles back, he returns for him and we see him go from right to left across the screen. With no landscape elements to help us to judge which direction he is going in, this becomes essential.

> **Film View**
> Another interesting example can be seen in David Lynch's *The Straight Story*, in which an ageing and car-less man travels hundreds of miles on his only mode of transport, a lawnmower, to visit his long-lost and ailing brother. In every shot, Lynch places him travelling from right to left, thereby hinting that the man is returning home, travelling back to the place he needs to be.

Light quality

Since light is one of your tools for showing the passage of time, you need to ensure that light is constant throughout a scene if the audience is to view the events of that scene as contemporaneous. Lighting used in a scene should be maintained at predetermined levels; if you are unhappy with the lighting of your scene, do not change it halfway through, redo that whole scene. If filming takes place over days or weeks, make careful notes of the position and intensity of lights. Similarly, daylight is notoriously unpredictable; a temporary cloud can radically alter the colour and lighting of a scene. The weather may influence the day you shoot a lengthy scene. Search for consistency. Hollywood grew up where it did because it enjoyed near-perfect clear, blue skies almost every day. Continuity becomes easy, even if two parts of the same scene are shot days apart.[10]

Continuity in non-narrative movies

Non-narrative movies demand a very different approach to narrative. They require that you embed continuity as a part of the whole structure of the film, not as an afterthought during filming.

---

[10] www.rochester.edu/College/FS/Intro/Continuity/sld001.htm   Slide show detailing history and uses of Hollywood continuity editing.

Non-narrative movies, such as music videos, abstract movies and multimedia projections used in live concerts, are particularly susceptible to looking fragmented. At their most out of control, they look like you are channel surfing, looking at a number of clips of movies by different people. Of the following ideas, the more effective ones are those that are part of the planning and shooting stages rather than those placed over the film in post-production.

Single filter effect (edit software filters, not camera filters)

If your edit software has special effects which you can use to alter the look of clips, for instance, to make them change colour, stretch or change contrast and tone, you could apply one of these to the whole film, or at regular points. Restrict yourself to one filter only.

Tracking

A tracking shot – where the camera moves while it shoots, tracking the action – can make a good way of connecting shots. Decide on a constant speed of tracking and stick with it throughout the film. To enhance the effect, keep to one direction in the screen, for example, left to right. For example, you could show a slow, left-to-right movement of the camera along a beach, cutting then to a similar constant shot along a busy street.

360-degree movement

This device is particularly effective in linking shots. Decide on the height of the camera and the speed of the camera as it moves, then shoot everything while moving 360 degrees around the subject, at every location, throughout the film.

Common space

This involves including an object or space in the background which is present in each shot and could be as simple as a fireside with picture frame. This is commonly used in scenes with dialogue where it is useful to be able to locate two actors within the same space by showing some common space or object in each actor's frame. In a non-narrative film you could choose a single prop which is present throughout.

Transitions

At the editing stage, you will need to decide how you cut between scenes. The most common – the straight cut and the cross dissolve – could be developed by trying something a little more noticeable. An example could be to fade fast to white as the picture cuts, suggesting flash photography.

Did you know?
A transition in digital editing refers to any method of connecting between two clips, other than a straight cut.

The length of the shot

A style of editing which uses short cuts, with a high turnover of shots, will encourage the viewer to see the clips as linked in some way, even if the subject matter is not. Therefore, we tend to find a montage sequence consisting of a lot of quick images. But what is a 'long cut' or a 'short cut'? In this case you could think of a quick cut as half a second or less, and a slow cut as anything from 3 to 5 seconds, but your subject matter will dictate how fast your cuts will be.

Motif

In non-narrative films, a motif can be used with some thought to what kinds of objects or colours add to the overall theme of the movie. For example, in an interpretation of the word 'anger', we could justifiably use the colour red as a motif in the film. To stand as a motif you would have to see the object or colour recur often enough to be noticed. Alternatively, you could use images of a clenched fist or a brick hurtling towards a window, letting us see more and more of it as the film proceeds.

Linked imagery

For this idea we could take a look at Kubrick's *2001: A Space Odyssey* (1968). After a lengthy start, where we see ancient pre-human apes, Kubrick needed a way of jumping tens of thousands of years into the future without disrupting the flow of the movie. If ever there was a time to use a continuity device, this was it. His response was to have the camera follow a bone thrown high into the air, and immediately cut to a similar-shaped, bone-like spacecraft, occupying the same space in the frame. This is a daring way of connecting two shots that could not be more dissimilar, visually. While shooting, you could look for parts of the scene that visually resemble a part of another, with the aim of linking the two later.

Sound

This is a last resort method of connecting shots and is not the most effective way. A single piece of music is dubbed over the whole film, as with a music video. If you want to use sound in this way, try to use a particularly noticeable home-made soundtrack of sounds, rather than music, and one where you have altered the sounds or looped them, producing a repetitive, rhythmic effect.

The Crunch

- In narrative, continuity is crucial.
- In non-narrative, broken continuity can be a useful tool.
- Get to know the rules of keeping continuity and break them wisely.
- Continuity is developed both in the script stage and *also* while shooting.
- In non-narrative movies, beware that the movie doesn't look fragmented: use continuity devices in editing or shooting.
- Get to know the action line and the 30-degree rule.
- Use good quality sound and take care about ambient sound (see Chapter 5:7 for more details).

4. Narrative movies

The aim of this section is to look into narrative more closely and address the problem of how to tell a story effectively. Narrative is about telling the audience about a series of events and engaging that audience to sympathize with one or other party in those events. To achieve this, you have to be able to convey all sorts of crucial information relating to different parts of the film. Questions of why, what, when, where and how are essential if the cog-wheels of the film are to turn correctly and if the audience are to stay with you. You are in control of the information, but the audience need to take part in the plot; give them too much and they will feel patronized and bored, too little and you lose them.

One of the most difficult aspects of narrative is the necessity to compress time as you juggle the wide-ranging elements of the story against your resources and the duration of the film. In most films, this is achieved through editing to suggest the passage of time or to suggest parallel events that were actually recorded weeks apart. Biographical movies often have to deal with this on a large scale, such as *Raging Bull* (Martin Scorsese, 1980), in which details of the life of boxer Jake La Motta are compressed into 129 minutes, or *Godfather II* (Francis Ford Coppola, 1974), which attempts to unfold two lives stretching 60 years in 200 minutes. Stylistic elements are commonly used to show that one scene is set in a different time from another, as seen in *Godfather II* when a sepia tone colours scenes set at the turn of the century.

Plot vs story

Before we talk about narrative in detail, we need to look at the terms we use. A story refers to the whole sequence of events from the opening moment of the movie to its close, while the plot refers only to those events that take up the main focus of the action. For example, in *Taxi Driver*, the film concerns a semi-literate Vietnam veteran, Travis Bickle. For the first section of the film we encounter daily life for Travis as he contemplates the dark side of New York street life. This is the story, but the plot only kicks in when Travis meets Jodie Foster, whom he wishes to rescue from prostitution, and Cybill Shepherd, whose rejection of him leads him to plan assassination of a leading political candidate. In these and other cases, the plot takes on a slightly different pace to the rest of the film, increasing the tempo and providing a focus for confrontation and resolution.

Devising stories for low budgets

For the low/no-budget filmmaker, the most compelling factor in drawing up a script is what level of funding is available for the film. As we saw in Chapter 4:1, it can actually be a source of creativity to be starved of funds. Many filmmakers are forced to be more ingenious than their better-salaried peers because they know they have to grab attention through good filmmaking craft rather than expensive props and effects.

Narrative costs

Regarding the actual story you choose, working with a low budget requires you to handle certain restrictions to the kinds of movies you can make. If you visit film festivals you quickly become aware of an absence of potentially expensive genres in debut films. Character-led movies are more common than science fiction; films set in the here and now are more common than period costume dramas. Don't immediately drop plans you may have which seem to contradict this; there are always ways around problems of resources, locations and costumes, but the low-budget filmmaker needs to be far more ingenious in finding solutions than their studio counterparts. Independent filmmakers are noted for their dogged way at working within a frustratingly tight budget. Imaginative shooting and editing will go some way towards this, and optical effects are increasing viable through digital software. You may also find that when people find out that your film is a low-budget, do-it-yourself production, made outside of the normal production framework, they may be prepared to help out, give free access to locations, props and so on.

Potentially expensive story elements

- *Historical setting*. Costumes and dressed locations are expensive. Films set in the future can present less of a problem if you agree with the visions laid out in, for instance, the *Mad Max* movies, a post-apocalyptic world of decay.
- *Uniforms*. Anything official and realistic will need to be hired.
- *Stunts*. You should always use a trained stunt performer for any stunts, not only to prevent actors' broken limbs, but also because legal issues and insurance are easier to deal with if you employ an experienced stunt person. If you can't get a stunt performer, cut that part of the script.
- *Insurance*. You can't avoid it but you can limit scenes which are high risk, avoiding potentially dangerous situations for actors or crew (most accidents on set involve crew, not cast). Check also what cover you have for equipment on your existing personal insurance.
- *Heavy make-up and prosthetics*. Expensive, if you want good quality. If you need unusual make-up effects try recruiting students from theatrical make-up courses, who may be willing to work for costs only.
- *Too many locations*. Transport and hospitality will add much to the budget. Stay local, where crew can return to their own homes. If you need to visit locations, don't plan to go to more than one each day.
- *Permission for street filming*. If you are working with more than a small, half-dozen crew, you may need to get permission – and pay for it – for filming in public places, especially metro lines, streets, public buildings and so on. Smaller towns and cities can be much more co-operative than well-used main cities. For example, the Scottish city of Glasgow has tried to welcome filmmakers to the city, aware of the benefits of boosting tourism.
- *Extras (crowd scenes)*. Even if your production is rained off you still pay the extras for turning up. Try recruiting local people, or place notices with amateur drama societies, some of whom may be willing to appear for more manageable fees.[11]

[11] www.communicator.com/scriptip.html   Detail on devising low-budget stories.
www.davet.freeserve.co.uk/articles/tips.htm   Filmmakers' ideas on low-budget stories.

Making the most of a low budget

Use what you have

Many low-budget films have taken shape purely in response to what the director has access to. *Clerks* (Kevin Smith, 1993) is a good example, made for less than $28 000. If this film was made entirely on digital equipment today, the budget could probably lose a zero off the figure. For this very successful debut feature, Smith was able to use the convenience store he worked in late at night and involved many friends as the cast. The action is entirely within the shop, and it is the witty, sharp dialogue and perfect timing that makes this such a classic of independent film. Using this approach should encourage you to make an inventory of the locations and props (and even people) which could be used to make a movie. It takes filmmaking out of the studio and makes it a more flexible ground-level art form; as one filmmaker said: 'my garage is my Hollywood'.

Low-budget ideas in action

To put this to the test, let's try a few examples of the very basic ingredients that make some movies:

- **Idea 1**. An empty warehouse available free for a couple of weeks, some (slightly mean-looking) friends and some suits. The result: *Reservoir Dogs* (Quentin Tarantino, 1991).

Figure 5.10 *The Debt* (2000) by Ed Beamer. This micro-budget short relied heavily on unusual camerawork to compensate for the absence of expensive sets and props. In this shot, the aim was to describe the dark personality of the leading figure, with the reflection in the dustbin lid hinting at his nature as a low-life character.

- **Idea 2**. A cheap mask, a house, a babysitter and a few friends. The result: *Scream* (Wes Craven, 1996).
- **Idea 3**. A bunch of interesting-looking friends, but not much else. The result: acclaimed independent movie, *Happiness* (Todd Solondz, 1998).

This exercise may be half-serious, but it does reveal that underneath quality filmmaking with great ideas, the actual potential cost of these movies is minimal. Clearly, with 90-minute films, expenses are going to rise no matter what you do, but compared to a large studio you have the ability to turn in a film like those above on a very small budget, and that is a skill the large studios would pay you dearly for, so nurture it.

Tip   When we talk about cost of a movie, we need to think in terms of 'negative cost', which refers to the cost of making the movie before distribution and marketing. In Hollywood, typical negative cost is two-thirds of the overall budget.

Write your own screenplay

As we saw in Chapter 4:4, many filmmakers prefer to use stories they have originated themselves, enabling them to maintain more control over what they make. Free software is available on the Internet to help you compose a screenplay in a conventional format.[12]

Acquire a published story

It is not really advisable in the low/micro-budget sector to use published work, but if you are determined there are many people, as you can guess, who will help you part with your money.

Optioning
It is less expensive to take what is known as 'an option' on a story than an outright acquisition. Optioning means that you have said you are very interested and need to go away and raise the finance. Options usually last for 18 months and you will need to engage an entertainment lawyer to handle the contractual side of the process. Working with a story will usually be far cheaper than acquiring a finished screenplay, for the reason that you are not buying a finished, ready-to-shoot product.

Out-of-copyright stories
But don't forget the ultimately cheap option: older stories may be out of copyright under the 100-year rule, but before you commit yourself check with the estate handling an author's work if you are unsure whether copyright has expired; such estates can be highly litigious.[13]

---

[12] www.scriptware.com   Scriptwriting software.
   wwwga.org/tools/ScriptWare/   Writers Guild of America site.
   www.writerstore.com/store/screenwriting_software.htm   Full list of available software.
[13] www.groton.k12.ct.us/mts/pt2a.htm   Copyright information.

True stories

Again, this option is more expensive than simply coming up with stories yourself. If you have read an article or heard about a true story which you would like to use as the basis of a film, you need to tread carefully. There is no doubt that such stories can and do make fascinating – and award-winning – films including *Erin Brockovich* (Steven Soderbergh, 1999) and *The Insider* (Michael Mann, 2000). But beware of the subjects of these stories taking action against you during or after production. In the seminal documentary *The Thin Blue Line* (1988), director Errol Morris pursued a death row convict's story, eventually proving his innocence, but only to find himself being sued for the return of the life story rights by newly freed Randall Adams. Stories told second-hand, where the original protagonist is masked in some way but the general thrust of the story is retained, include *Taxi Driver* (Martin Scorsese, 1976) and *Rope* (Alfred Hitchcock, 1948), but you cannot guarantee that the participants in the real-life events will ignore the potential reward from following you through the court should the film make large profits.

The Crunch

- Narrative films need careful handling so we know what is happening.
- Build a story around props or places you have available for free.
- Write your own screenplay.
- Small-scale stories are low-budget stories.
- Avoid expensive genres: make films about people, not falling asteroids.
- Use the close-up to learn about telling a story.

Project 8. Close-ups

This project concentrates on the use of the camera and how it can help you in conveying narrative. In this project we will be making a straightforward movie using a simple plot, but will be doing it with a particular restriction: the entire film will be filmed using close-up shots only.

If narrative is concerned with information, then the purpose in working with close-ups is to focus attention on what is important in a scene and prioritize the various elements within. In conveying the story you develop, you should be able to see in the final film a positive linear progression of the plot through the use of this device. The close-up enables the viewer to see what is important in the shot and demands that you determine this in advance of shooting, with implications for the way your story is conveyed. As an example, in filming a dialogue between two actors, some people would be inclined to show more of the human reaction to a set of events, training the camera on the faces and hands of the actors to show the emotion behind the story. Others may prefer to focus on the mechanics of the action, with more emphasis on how the actual events are occurring and perhaps delivering a simpler reading of the action.

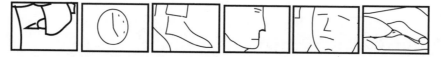

Figure 5.11 Close-up frames. One frame can contain many pieces of information. In this example, a frame of two figures with the suggestion of confrontation has within it six frames which could be shown in close-up, each of them telling the audience vital parts of the narrative.

Controlling information

Visual and stylistic aspects of filmmaking are described in Project 7 earlier in the chapter, and help in describing the means with which we convey the story. This project, however, focuses entirely on the ability to control this drip-feed of information making up the narrative to the audience, and when used alongside the previous projects may help you deliver not only the plot, but also much more.

Stage 1

In preparing the plot for this film, it would be more effective to find something simple, a familiar plot that an audience can relate to. But if you want to try more advanced versions of this project, make the narrative more complex. Use simple linear stories, taking the audience from event A to event B, such as a delivery, a heist-and-getaway or a confrontation between two people.

Stage 2

Developing this film is going to be slightly different from other projects. When you have completed the visualizations stage and are ready to move on to the storyboard, work instead on much larger frames. Draw a frame the size of a CD box or larger.

When you have completed a first draft of the storyboard you will then need to start drawing smaller frames around certain parts of the image, trying to home in on the essential parts of that shot. To do this, you could try making a number of window frames out of paper, at anything from one-quarter to one-sixteenth of the frame size. The aim is to see if you can isolate images within the frame which convey the primary information in that scene. Look at what is the most important section of that frame, what is the next most important and so on.

Multiple shots in one frame

As can be seen in Figure 5.11, the single frame here contains several frames which are telling different parts of the story. The primary source of information is probably the gun on the table and the hand resting on it. But a close second are the two frames showing the faces of the actors. After this, you could look at the foot tapping nervously under the table and the clock ticking on the wall. All these sections of the frame give portions of the overall information contained within and it is for the director to prioritize each part when deciding how to point the camera. Does the hand on the gun need to be centrally placed in the frame? There are infinite ways to order the shot depending on what you want to show the audience and how much you want to 'spoonfeed' them the plot. Bringing unlikely elements to the fore now and then can add layers of meaning to a scene. Hitchcock demonstrates this many times as he draws our attention to a minor part of a scene, often showing human quirks and frailties in the process.

Stage 3

When you have completed this exercise with all the frames in the original storyboard you are ready to begin sorting the new images taken from the larger frames into some kind of order. We need to build a new storyboard out of these images, paying careful attention to the order in which the close-up shots appear and the frequency with which they recur. It is likely that you will need to have more shots of shorter duration than in a similar film made without this device.

Stage 4: Shooting

Shooting this film is going to take slightly longer than other narrative films. Although you will be setting up more shots than in other films, you can make your task much simpler by asking your actors to play a scene several times while you take various shots from different angles. If you have access to additional cameras this would save time and make continuity problems less evident by shooting different parts of the scene simultaneously.

In obtaining the close-up, it is better to move the camera closer to the action rather than rely on the zoom control. Zoom tends to increase camera wobble and removes the opportunity, to a certain extent, for you to track or pan the camera.

Shooting tips for this project

Focusing

Like just about every aspect of filmmaking, even something as technical as focusing can be a creative tool. When working in close-up, the aspect of focus is even more emphasized due to the laws of optics. You can choose which part of the screen the audience look at when you decide which area will be in sharp focus; the focus tool is like an arrow pointing to the crucial part of that shot. But there is no reason why you should not challenge this convention by settling attention elsewhere in the scene. The director Kieslowski has some memorable images in his films obtained through a creative use of focusing.

Film View

Near the start of *Three Colours: Blue* (Krzysztof Kieslowski, 1993), for example, we see a doctor enter a ward containing the victim of a car crash. Seen from the point of view of the victim we see a close-up, focused on a few feathers on her pillow moving with her breath, while the doctor is a blurred figure in the background. This tells us that the victim is alive, but also conveys something of the sense of bewilderment felt by her. The next shot is equally impressive: the camera fills the screen with her right eye and we see the pupil contract as a reflection of the doctor appears in the iris.

You may also find that some camcorders are designed to focus the object in the centre of the frame and reject your attempts at creative focusing, particularly if you want something on the side of the frame in focus and the main object in the centre not. If you do have a manual focus option, see the instructions in Chapter 3:5, 'Operating a camcorder', for getting round this problem.

Camera wobble

When shooting close-ups you will find that the camera is going to reveal more shakes and wobbles than in other shots. Although a tripod is advisable for many shots, it would be useful to devise a more flexible solution that did not restrict the range of angles available to you, such as using a beanbag or similar moveable, soft support.

Lighting

When you are working close to the action, lighting becomes an important factor. There are some lighting conditions that will aid you in trying to convey information and some that may confuse the scene. Avoid flat, dispersed light from fluorescent lights and household bulbs. Use light that is sharper and more directed at the action, so that the shapes of the subject are revealed and contrasting shadows are thrown. This will help to reduce the amount of extraneous information we see and draw attention quickly to what is important in the shot.

Go to: Chapter 5:8, 'Lighting', for more help with how to show the subject clearly.

Extra shots

Finally, when you are shooting, it would be useful to get additional shots you had not previously planned for. When you feel you have shot all the parts of a scene you needed, look around the scene for anything else that could be used to break up the rigidity of the final edit. If we are constantly given crucial information the film becomes hard work, but if you can occasionally cut away to something not so crucial it may make for a more rounded, less frenetic film.

Stage 5: Editing

There are a number of points to consider when editing this sort of film with its dominance of close shots. As well as having a greater number of shots than other films, these may be shorter and you may find that it is useful to use cutaways – cutting to and from a shot repeatedly. For example, if we consider Figure 5.11, you may cut from the hand on the gun, to the face of actor 1, to the face of actor 2 and back to the gun. You will need to avoid bewildering the audience, however, and include regular longer cuts: too many short, sharp edits can be physically hard to cope with. To vary your shots when filming, you could try tracking and panning to link two close-ups together.

Evaluation

Much of the evaluation for this project can be seen as assessing how you told the story and what you emphasized. This project reveals your individual preference in how a story can be told, as well as encouraging you to focus on the essentials of a scene, simply by asking you to draw our attention to what you feel is the most important part of it. This sort of self-knowledge is worth a lot in helping you towards a personal approach to the medium.

- When you were shooting, were the shots you filmed close to the storyboard you prepared? You don't lose points for deviating; it is more useful to assess which is the better document: the tape or the storyboard. For many filmmakers it is the former, since the camera shows you what you can achieve while the paper version only shows what might be achieved.
- How did your use of light alter? Did you become more aware of where you were placing lighting to reveal certain parts of a scene? Did the use of strong, directed light help you in simplifying the frame and making better compositions?
- Focusing will also have been a useful tool for composition – did it prove useful in close-up?
- When you were editing the movie, how did you feel the flow of the story was interrupted by the need to cut between the elements of the scene? You may have found it useful to use one particular shot as the dominant one and insert others now and then. The length of each shot itself tells the

audience something about your priorities for the story and determines how viewers will read it, according to which shots are dominant. You may have decided to dwell on a particular, seemingly less significant, part of a scene in order to challenge the presumed priorities for that scene, changing the way we expect a scene to be shown.

5. Working with non-narrative

If the idea of working within an established form of film knocks your enthusiasm then there is no reason why you shouldn't start to combine ideas usually seen in more unusual areas of the media. This section is concerned with the kinds of film that don't rest on story, which are more reliant either on images in an abstract sense or on themes, and don't need to organize these deeper ideas underneath layers of plot. Non-narrative is not as scary as it sounds; you are not cast adrift without any centre to the film, endlessly turning out weird images that no one wants to watch.

Film View
For a glimpse of the original surrealist movie, in which ideas and images are the only motivation, watch *Un Chien Andalou* (Luis Buñuel/Salvador Dali, 1929).

On the contrary, non-narrative is probably the form of video and film that you are in most contact with daily. Music videos, advertising, concert projections or website animations are all vibrant, evolving forms and yet do not rely on story and, in fact, it would be an impediment to them. Even in feature films, it is no longer the case that stories with a beginning, a middle and an end are the only way to make films. For the last 50 years at least, filmmakers have tried to develop new ways of communicating which they are more comfortable with. For the majority, this has meant letting the film take on a different look occasionally, whether it is to show a dream sequence or just to show everyday reality in a more interesting way.

The development of devices such as montage tells us that merely to show something objectively does not always capture it as we feel it to be; some uses of montage dispense with linear story in favour of a deluge of images. We can look at even the most mainstream Hollywood films, supposedly far removed from non-narrative, and there is evidence of the need to allow a film to loosen up now and then. There are times in a movie when the story takes a temporary back seat and the underlying messages and themes in the film come to the front.

Non-narrative helps your narrative movies

To achieve this, directors use reflective moments, refrains, time out from the plot, to take stock of what the whole film means. If you intend to work within narrative then being able to work with just the theme will give you greater confidence in handling the plot itself. After all, those parts of a movie when short diversions arise, music takes over and the film seems to drift into a reflection of what it is trying to communicate are what makes the movie stand out. It also gives your narrative work much greater depth. So, even if you don't think you are going to veer away from storytelling in its conventional form, non-narrative is still going to be of use throughout many films. Still other filmmakers will relish the idea of letting go of the restrictions of plot and seeing what happens when images and ideas take over.

Non-narrative sequences

To illustrate this we could look at some films where this occurs. In all great films there are such moments and it is here that audiences often form their bond with the film; for a while they don't have to take on information about *x*, *y* or *z*, but can concentrate on relating to the film in a more sensual way. To be realistic, though, many films only use these segments as a method of lowering the pulse of the film before the next big bang.

- *Taxi Driver* (Martin Scorsese, 1976)
  In a sequence seen occasionally in the film, the eponymous driver, played by Robert De Niro, roams the New York streets in his taxi, seeing what goes on late at night. A combination of images, music, some slow motion and voice-over lead us to the main ideas in the film, which show a man appalled by city night life and suggest menace in the way he will encounter it.
- *Manhattan* (Woody Allen, 1979)
  In this comedy, Allen takes several refrains from the story in lingering sequences of the city set to music by Gershwin, implying that the subject of the film is as much the place as the people who occupy it.

Film View
Also try watching *The Ice Storm* (Ang Lee, 1997) and *Apocalypse Now* (Francis Ford Coppola, 1979) – two very different films, but both convey a strong narrative while taking regular poetic detours into non-narrative.

What makes non-narrative?

Films that rely wholly on this kind of idea tend to have in common:

- Camera framing: more emphasis on the individual look of each shot.
- Images: significant imagery of symbols, colour and motifs.
- Images grouped together to reinforce a certain theme.
- Theme: with no plot, theme can assume centre-stage. We could define theme as a broad concept which links all the scenes together.

- The film progresses usually only through a series of variations on a theme – without a plot to help it move forward it needs something else to show development over the film's duration.
- Structure may be more simple than in narrative films. It is often reliant on a cumulative structure based on repetition of themes and images to bring the film to a climax.
- Stylistic elements, such as camerawork, images, location, lighting and music, become important as the main vehicles to convey theme.
- Editing may not conform to narrative conventions.[14]

Images and non-narrative

What makes good images?

Images are meant to stick in the mind. A good shot should be able to withstand being freeze-framed on your VCR and looked at for a while, just like a piece of art. It is often pointed out that the reason that Stanley Kubrick makes films with such memorable images is that he was for several years a photographer and was used to isolating an image and seeing its worth. The images we are looking for are the ones which tell a lot in just one shot, condensing lots of information to convey something important about the film.

One way of isolating these images from a film is to look at film posters. The images displayed on the main poster possess a combination of symbols and motifs which describe the whole point of the film and summarize it in a simple way.

> **Film View**
>
> As an example, in *Psycho*, one particularly memorable shot is that of Norman Bates looking up at the house where his 'mother' is. The sky is high contrast and stormy, the shape of the house looks menacing and we see, isolated, one room lit. The main ideas in Hitchcock's film – the themes of twisted family life, a dark secret, a volatile place – are well summed up in this one shot alone.

> **Film View**
>
> *The Cabinet of Dr Caligari* (Robert Wiene, 1919) is a very useful film to look at, though a little hard to find in your video store. The look of the film is defined by German Expressionist painters and every shot has been designed to enhance the atmosphere of the film, though without the self-consciousness that this implies. Doors are twisted, landscape is exaggerated and shadows are painted onto the sets.

[14] http://filmdb.t0.or.at/FilmMakers/default_e.htm   Australian avant-garde filmmakers' group. www.film-makerscoop.com/core.htm   International distributor of non-narrative movies.

Lighting

In this kind of film we are looking for lighting which adds atmosphere to a shot. This often means deep shadows and stark contrast, and at this stage it is going to be easier to achieve what we want by trying this out first. Keep your lights bright but keep them directed in small splashes, pointed at one particular part of the shot. If you have directional lights that have barn doors on them then you will be able to block out the light from parts of the shot and place it where you want.

Go to: Chapter 5:8, section on 'Types of lamp'.

Motifs

A motif is a recurring element to a film which helps advance the main ideas or theme of the film. A motif could be an object, a colour, anything which recurs and fits in with the meaning in the film. In Chapter 9, we will see how, in Nic Roeg's *Don't Look Now* (1973), the colour red appears throughout the film. In many scenes we see this colour and soon come to see how it represents danger and alarm, a main theme in the film. Motifs do not have to dominate a shot, in fact they are best used subtly; it is the recurrence of it that makes it significant. Choosing motif for a film is often something that arises out of extensive work on the script; the ideas you have put into the script start to present themselves to you clearly and you may then devise objects or colours which represent them.

Symbols

Symbols are neatly connected to the last point and are crucial to the filmmaker's art. They can be just about anything but don't need to recur and to that extent it is often hard to notice symbols as they arise in a film, but if you are tuned in to the main ideas in the film you will start to see certain images, objects or situations as being symbolic.

Another layer of meaning

Symbols are easily read by the audience and yet are effective because they involve the audience in forming them; the director gives a few clues and we add them up into a sign of something. Using symbols also allows you to extend some ambiguity into a film; no single reading is correct, letting several readings of it coexist, depending on the individual viewer's ideas. Problems occur when a filmmaker starts to put in conflicting symbols, or a cacophony of them, usually because the ideas behind the film were not explored in enough detail. If you can develop an ability to use symbols and motifs within strong imagery you have at your disposal a range of ways of expressing what you want to say, rather than just relying on what the actors say. Similarly, we all use non-verbal means to clarify what we are saying when we talk by gesticulating and using other forms of body language. Psychologists estimate that when we communicate with each other, visual communication, or body language, makes by far the greatest impression. Visual language is not only the most effective, but is the more subtle and the more richly imbued with layers of meaning.[15]

Go to: Chapter 9:3 to see how other filmmakers use symbols.

---

[15] www.koyaanisqatsi.org/   Site dedicated to this non-narrative movie.

What does this actually mean for the film we are going to make? It will lead to a movie which is without dialogue, is reliant wholly on images and will succeed on its looks alone. It will be a film of symbols and motifs, expressing a coherent, underlying theme. Bordwell and Thompson defend non-narrative form by suggesting that it helps us see reality afresh:

> 'some viewers . . .think of abstract films as frivolous. Critics may call them "art for art's sake", since all they seem to do is present us with interesting shapes and sounds. Yet in doing so, such films often make us more aware of such shapes and sounds – and we may be better able to notice them in the everyday world as well.'

> *(Film Art: An Introduction, p. 121, McGraw-Hill, 1993)*

The Crunch

- Non-narrative movies are everywhere: music video, advertising, the Internet.
- Balance this kind of movie: if you let go of plot, tighten up on structure.
- You deserve a time to play, to experiment and re-invent the world around you. This kind of movie allows this.
- Themes count more than plots in this territory.
- Non-narrative is heavily reliant on images.
- Concentrating on images and visual meaning helps you in other kinds of movies; narrative movies use non-narrative to add depth.
- If it sounds too weird, think of it as songs without words, relying more on mood and tone than specific words to carry its meaning. Try it out.

Project 9. Music video

The aim of this project is to put into practice the ideas covered in this section and to make a movie that relies wholly on images. A music video offers you ample chances to work whatever you want into the film, linking a wide array of unusual images together under the umbrella of the music track. You can be experimental, creative, and try tricks and ideas you normally can't work into a more straightforward movie.

As with most videos, the aim is to convey the ideas and atmosphere of the piece of music with images that complement it, or set off new meanings in it. Avoid the kind of music video which focuses solely on a band performing, as this will restrict your creative opportunities.[16]

---

[16] www.futureffects.com/   Music video online magazine.
www.internetv.com/html/music.htm   Download and watch music videos; caters for any player format.

Stage 1

Decide what piece of music you will be using. Bear in mind at this stage that if you intend making this part of your showreel, the tape that hopefully gets you accepted in festivals or offered other work, or if you want to show this movie itself, you are going to need copyright clearance from the band or its music publisher. In almost all cases this is going to cost huge sums, so your options are to use this movie as a stepping stone to learning how to make better films, not expecting it to be seen beyond you and your friends, or to use the music of a local or unsigned band who may welcome a free music video in return for waiving any copyright fees.

The kind of music you need to use is that which you already know well, which sparks off images and ideas in your mind whenever you listen to it. If you feel you can relate to the song and get a sense of the atmosphere it conveys then this will lead to a good range of images to match.

Stage 2

Get a piece of paper and, while listening to the track you will use, write down descriptive words which you feel convey the song. Then write these down a vertical column and start sketching images which match the words, similar to the process used in Project 7. In that project, you were trying to convey something more tangible: a place or event, while this project asks you to try to put into images something which you imagine in your mind, triggered off by the piece of music.

When you have attached images to each word, define and select these sketches, redoing some of the more obvious, predictable images (to get an idea of the range of music video clichés, watch a few hours of cable music television).

Stage 3

When you have enough images to sustain the 3- or 4-minute film, you can start to forge the underlying theme in the film. We need some constant thread that runs through each shot to connect the film and stop it looking like a collection of unrelated images. This means looking at the images you have evolved on paper and trying to find connections between them. For instance, you might find that all your images have a certain claustrophobic feel to them, or are dominated by the colour red, or use a similar prop or setting throughout. Get to know your images. When you have decided on the kind of theme running through your images, label one particular image as the central one. Use this one image as the main focus for your film and one which you return to now and then.

Stage 4

At this point you might start to work on a storyboard, working out the order in which these shots will appear, but in this instance it may be more useful to instead move directly onto shooting, leaving open the possibility to add to or expand on shots.

When you are shooting this movie, you will need to be aware of visual elements far more than on other kinds of movie. To a certain extent, a narrative film that uses images so dominantly may look overworked and contrived. A non-narrative movie, however, with only images to make it work, actually requires you to make images more compelling and dominant than any other aspect of the movie. Shooting, then, is going to need a great deal of attention to detail, in each and every shot, in each setting.

Working without storyboards, you need to remain in control of what you shoot by referring to your visualizations constantly. These are your base point, the central ideas that run through the film, and you need to be reminded of them often.

Stage 5

Editing a non-narrative music video is more enjoyable than other kinds of movie. There are many ways in which the film can be developed even at this stage, rearranging your shots, setting off one against another to see the ideas that arise. It may be useful to take a look at Chapter 6:5, on montage, which goes into more detail about what happens when disparate shots are combined.

Unlike other kinds of movie, place the soundtrack on the timeline *before* you work on the images. This is to enable you to tie-in certain images with particular parts of the song and time the whole movie so that it is the right length.

As with shooting, use the visualizations to return you to the central theme of the film, the main images which dominate it. If these have changed significantly while filming, don't worry – check that you were aware of these changes during production and your decision making in following them, and that they are not having to compete with your previous theme for dominance.

In terms of structure, try using one particular image as the central point in the film and use it as an image we cut to at regular intervals.

To make the project more effective, try to avoid using special effects in the editing stage, including unusual transitions (ways of cutting from one clip to the next).

Evaluation

- How far did your ideas develop during filming? Were they fully formed when you picked up the camera or did you perhaps allow for more development during filming, preferring to keep some options open at this stage?
- In terms of images, look at how they compare with each other. Which ones are the most successful in terms of composition, subject matter, colour, camera angle, lighting?
- Looking at lighting in more detail, what kinds of lighting did you use? Maybe you focused on dramatic, high-contrast lighting or low-key, naturalistic lighting. Are there some lighting effects which you felt worked well in terms of the atmosphere you are trying to convey?

- The structure of this movie is not determined by story, so you were free to put it together in any way you feel best illustrates the music. Look at the arrangement of images in the film: Did you place some images repeatedly throughout the film and was this successful? Were there moments when the film seemed to be going in a completely new direction? If there were, try removing these sections and viewing the film again, as they may have been contradicting the main purpose of the video.
- Finally, leave the movie for a few days or more and watch it without its soundtrack. Does it still evoke the same atmosphere or theme as the song?

6. Making creative non-fiction movies

Many of the projects in this chapter deal with ways of working in narrative or non-narrative forms and the various shades in between. But aside from these areas, there is the vibrant and fast-changing form of non-fiction film, using elements of narrative storytelling, non-narrative sequences and news within the same movie. Trying this hybrid kind of work can lead to a better grasp of other forms we have covered and opens up a further market for you to get involved in. For many filmmakers, non-fiction is an entry point in to the wider film industry.

Documentary vs non-fiction

Before it gets complicated, however, we need to distinguish this form from the straightforward documentary, whose name implies that it is just a recording of events, impartial and without prejudice. Today, though, filmmakers recognize that it is acceptable to use other means when relating real events, reflecting the belief that there really is no 'truth', just interpretations. So, these filmmakers would argue, since we can no longer claim to be objective, we might as well make these movies more creative too. Add to this the need by broadcasters to make factual programmes more entertaining and you have enough encouragement for a more creative approach to showing real events.

For those people working at the lower end of the budget scale, this offers some attractive ways of making films but avoiding the costs often inherent in fiction. Using reality as your setting, with 'real' people as opposed to actors, you immediately find that the prospect of making a movie is less costly and perhaps less daunting. Removing the need to recreate events can slice large chunks from your budget, from script, props, actors and locations. Furthermore, working in non-fiction movies does not mean that you take a break from all the ideas talked about in these chapters, including great camerawork, evocative lighting, well-paced structure and so on. It's the opposite, in fact, since this form is one of the few ways of bringing together creative filmmaking, good storytelling and visual surprise.

What is non-fiction film?

At this stage it would be useful to agree a definition of what documentary is. In the mid-1980s, Errol Morris, director of *The Thin Blue Line* (1988), was single-handedly responsible for reviving this form and at the same time re-inventing it as something that only partly resembled its former self. Morris preferred the term 'non-fiction' to describe his film, reflecting his sense that it signalled a departure from previous films in this form. It also allowed him to enter the film in festivals where the term documentary would have barred his film.[17]

The term itself was not coined by Morris but by a group of influential documentary filmmakers of the 1960s, Drew Associates. Within this group, working primarily for television, were the brothers Albert and David Maysles and Donn Pennebaker, who made *Don't Look Back* (1967), a portrait of Bob Dylan. Prior to this group we could go back further to a group of French filmmakers in the 1960s, who for the first time admitted that the presence of the camera made a difference to what was being filmed. This '*cinéma-vérité*', as it was known, changed the way documentary was perceived and led towards the form becoming more subjective, perhaps more honest about its capabilities in that it could not claim to be entirely impartial and dispassionate.[18]

> **Tip**   *Cinéma-vérité* takes its name from a Soviet newsreel, '*kino-Pravda*' (film truth), and refers originally to a kind of documentary in which it was accepted that truth had to be told in a less objective way, in opposition to the earlier 'cinema direct', which rejected editing and almost all filmic devices.

Broomfield and Moore

A further step has been taken by the work of British filmmaker Nick Broomfield and the American Michael Moore. They have placed themselves firmly within their films, showing how the presence of the filmmaker affects the subject of the documentary and trading on this fact, making it into a positive element. In Moore's *Roger and Me* (1989), the director tries in vain for 3 years to track down General Motors chairman Roger Smith in order to confront him with the human consequences of GM corporate policy. Moore jumbles chronology and places his own feelings about the subject at the heart of the film – both these ideas would have once been outside the parameters of documentary.[19]

> **Tip**   For further viewing try the following, though they are not easy to find in video stores: *Medium Cool* (Emile de Antonio, 1969), about the 1968 Democratic Convention; *Hearts and Minds* (Peter Davis, 1975), about the US involvement in Vietnam; *Italianamerican* (Martin Scorsese, 1970), a portrait of the director's parents; *Day of the Fight* (Stanley Kubrick, 1953), a portrait of preparations for a boxing match.

[17] www.errolmorris.com/   Morris' own website, including filmography.
[18] www.drewassociates.net/   Information point for documentaries by Drew associates.
      www.popped.com/articles98/cinemaverite/index.html   Five interviews with *cinéma-vérité* directors.
[19] www.nickbroomfield.com/   Broomfield's own site with trailers, stills and information.
      www.michaelmoore.com   Moore's home page with information and news.

Non-fiction film since then has gradually incorporated many of the elements we expect to see in narrative film, including montage editing, the reconstructing of events to *show* what happened rather than simply *tell* it, the use of unusual and challenging structure, and imaginative use of the camera. To some extent, the non-fiction film is becoming more challenging and provocative than the narrative film, stealing from other forms but doing so with the aim of a truer representation of the events it is portraying.

The result is a form that is more attractive to the aspiring filmmaker. The low costs and opportunity to be as creative as with narrative film means that this form is a valid place for a filmmaker to work; it can teach a great deal about all forms of filmmaking.[20]

Camera language

Camera language is something that is going to apply as much to narrative films as to non-fiction work. We have seen what good composition can do for a film, but here we need to know how the camera can convey certain meanings and use these as part of a repertoire of shots to say what you want without having to use words.

- *Camera framing*. Camera language is, in this project, the most important way of conveying your ideas. Without narration or text, you will need to find the right way of framing a shot in showing the viewer the various aspects of the subject. Subtle changes in camera angle, height or movement all affect what you are showing. Over time, a broad vocabulary has been established in which certain angles of shot correspond to certain feelings, or views of a subject. Much of this has been developed by the early masters of narrative cinema, such as Hitchcock. Being aware of this language is useful in being able to adhere to, or subvert, convention.
- *Close-up shot*. This kind of shot will often raise the dramatic tension in a scene. It evokes intimacy and sensuality, but also suggests enclosure or claustrophobia. Directing the viewer's attention so tightly to one aspect of a scene also makes clear your own interpretation on the subject.
- *Tilt*. In this shot, the camera is tilted so that the viewer sees the world at an angle. The general effect is to suggest imbalance, a situation not quite right, a character unable to find his bearings. A slight tilt of perhaps 70 degrees will give a more subtle indication of this state, while more exaggerated angles increase this feeling.
- *Camera looking down on the subject*. This can suggest vulnerability in the subject. It indicates that the viewer is higher than the subject and is therefore more powerful than the subject.
- *Camera looking up at the subject*. As the reverse of the above, this shot can suggest that the subject holds power by placing us below.

---

[20] www.documentaryfilms.net   Excellent resource for the documentary filmmaker today.
www.dvshop.ca/docscanada.html   Canadian state funding for documentary filmmakers.
www.fracturedmedia.com/main.htm   New York group; view movies.
www.documentaries.org/   Independent group promoting documentary work.
www.d-word.com/   Site focusing on non-fiction film and video.
www.documentary.org/   Independent resource for non-fiction filmmakers.

Camera language is similar to spoken languages in that it evolves and is a result of its usage rather than being formulated in advance and adhered to. Certain devices are seen to work but change considerably over the years, partly as result of the increased sophistication of the audience. So-called 'Hollywood grammar', popular in the middle of the twentieth century, has evolved so far as to be unrecognizable.

Multiple meanings in camera language

As with narrative film, non-fiction film takes full advantage of the uses this kind of camera language bring and enjoys subverting one sign with another. For example, a happy, optimistic image can be altered slightly, suggesting some underlying unhappiness by slowly withdrawing the camera from the subject to reveal an isolated subject. One way to illustrate this is to look at spoken language. When we listen to someone, we take on board what they say but also watch the way they move their arms, their whole body language. Interesting juxtapositions can be made when one form of communication contradicts the other.

How we read images

Another factor is that the image the camera gives us is read as both a mental and optical phenomenon, hitting the brain in two ways. James Monaco provides an excellent description of this (see *How to Read a Film*, p. 176, OUP, 2000). When we see an image, we read it both culturally and as a simple array of patterns. Take, for example, a shot where a character is standing in a doorway with strong light on the face, the door framed by black shadow. We can track how we perceive this image by focusing on both the mental and optical.

Optically, we see the figure before we see the blackness, and we respond strongly to the impact of the bright light shining on the face and the high contrast of black and white. We feel a need to decipher it and will pursue whatever little information we are given, and yet our interpretation of what we decide the image is saying is influenced by the impact of the optical effect the image has on us. This is why some camera compositions and lighting effects are particularly useful for the filmmaker.

On a mental level, an image will strike us for other reasons. We have preconceived *ideas* regarding shadow and others regarding faces lit in the darkness. An air of mystery may surround it, or a sense of something spiritual or perhaps menacing. The face may also have a particular expression, drawing in our memories and feelings about the particular emotion we are seeing; one section of the human brain has the sole function of analysing every other human face we see, for recognition of the familiar tribe or family, so we also search for anything that resembles a face, linking also into the optical view of the image. Our response is determined by our culture, affecting the significance of certain signs in the image.

As Monaco points out, it is the combination of both mental and optical that work together to come up with a single idea of what is being signified. The signifier is nearly always visual, while the signified is necessarily a mental outcome.

When you frame a shot, you are, therefore, setting up a range of responses in the viewer. Being able to control all of these responses is outside anyone's reach, but it is possible to manipulate response to a certain degree.

> **Tip**   For more reading about this area of perception and art, try *The Hidden Order of Art* by Anton Ehrenzweig.

The Crunch

- Documentary film has evolved into other forms.
- Non-fiction is a great place for the filmmaker to build knowledge about filming. Try it out.
- Non-fiction film often requires you to use narrative filmmaking methods, so it's going to help your narrative movies too.
- Always tell the truth (at least your own interpretation of it anyway).
- Get to know how to convey ideas and opinions through images, through the way you use the camera.
- Use non-fiction as a low-budget method of making movies (no actors, no sets).

Project 10. Interviews

This project is going to cover a few areas: sound recording, documentary/non-fiction work and structure. The aim is to produce a short film consisting of interviews centring on a particular topic. You will gather many opinions on a subject and piece them together in an entertaining, or provocative, way.

Stage 1

Choose a topic that you feel would encourage people to talk, something that most people have an opinion on or can reflect on. Choose something related to personal issues, such as:

- your first love affair;
- the worst day you ever had;
- your idea of perfect happiness.

Or try social issues:

- What do you think about (insert relevant local or national issue)?
- What's wrong/right (choose whichever elicits the most response) with this country?
- What would you do if you were Prime Minister/President?

Or try less serious topics:

- Are there aliens out there?
- Have you ever had any paranormal encounters?

Stage 2

When you have decided on the single question you want to ask, look for possible candidates. It's going to help keep interest in the film if the interviews are conducted with as wide a range of people as possible, in very different locations. So, you might have a traffic policeman explaining how he was abducted by aliens, and then cut to a very different scene of a window-cleaner, high up on the side of a building, detailing his experiences.

Stage 3

Recording each interview is going to require you to take another look at the section on sound recording. Use the right mic for each interview, trying to block out other sounds so we can hear clearly what is being said. If you are doing more than simply stopping people in the street, which will require just one directional mic, you may find it easier to use a lavalier. This will maintain the very clearest sound quality, and although it can sound artificial, this is fine for non-fiction work.

For each interview, do a short sound test before you start filming and play back with headphones to make sure it sounds correct.

When the interview is over, we also need to ask permission to get hold of some shots that set the scene for the interview, and which we can paste over bits of it to make it more varied. For instance, if you have an interview of a man recorded in his garden, this could get dull after a minute or two, so we could cut now and then to shots of his garden ornaments, or the expensive car in the drive. In addition, ask a few more questions, but this time focus the camera on the hands, getting a range of hand gestures which can also be added later. Inevitably, you are going to tell us something about the interviewee by the objects and gestures you draw our attention to. But keep it subtle, or else the film will appear unsympathetic to its interviewees (unless you specifically want us to dislike them, but even then it can backfire).

Stage 4

Editing this film is going to be straightforward. First log all the interviews by transcribing them and noting the relevant timecode points. When you have each interview on paper, you can start to reassemble them, taking interesting sections and placing them next to others, composing a paper edit of the movie in which we cut back and forth between different responses.

Go to: Chapter 6:2 for more help with the paper edit.

How should you cut the film? Extract sections of the interviews which match and arrange the order of the clips in a way which corresponds to the question. So, if we look at the question 'the worst day I ever had', gather all the responses to the first opening sentences. Something like, 'It was raining; I was then working for a company selling . . .', followed by, 'I was in London for the day on a conference; there was huge plate glass being carried across the road right where I wanted to park the car', and so on. This makes us want to carry on watching to learn more about what happened to each person.

When you place clips in the timeline, consider how to cut from one interview to the next. Cutting too fast can leave the audience bewildered so you could try giving a few seconds over to establishing who we are with each time we cut to a new person. If we have never seen that person before, spend longer setting the scene. As the film goes on, you can lose this device as the narratives or opinions of each person reach the most important points.

You may also find that the ambient sound of each interview disrupts the film slightly. To get round this problem, try fading in and out rather than simply cutting straight to speech. A quick fade of less than 1 second is a good starting point.

Use the information given by the timeline to help tell you how fast the cuts are becoming as the film nears the end. Individual clips of each person may be getting shorter and you can look for a pattern emerging to see how much air time you are giving to each person, keeping a balance throughout.

When you have the interviews in place, you can start to insert cuts here and there which will break up the monotony of long sentences. This is where you use all the extra shots you gathered after each interview. This can be a particularly interesting task, as you are able to suddenly alter the meaning of what is being said simply by juxtaposing an image we wouldn't expect. So, if a person talks about how being abducted by the aliens was a good experience and hasn't harmed them in any way, you may cut to a shot of their hands, wringing with tension and anxiety. The likelihood is that we will believe what we see more than what we hear, so with this kind of cutaway you have a tool of subtle but particular power.

Evaluation

This project is a good chance to try out more than one skill, seeing how you cope with having several different aspects to deal with at once: sound recording, interacting with the interviewee, while looking for the image that tells us more about this person. It is a sensitive area to work within, but if you can make people feel at ease with the camera then this is a skill which helps you work with actors too. It also shows just how complex it is to remain focused on what someone is saying while also checking that the recording is technically correct.

The editing stage is the most revealing. As you will have seen, editing is hugely influential on how we interpret what we see. Understanding the nuances of when to cut and when to insert other images is a vital skill.

Review the film and ask yourself how each person is conveyed. Look at the effect of different settings, different camera angles and how this influences our impression of the interviewee.

Look at your own presence in the film. It may be almost absent or you may have preferred to reveal the inner workings of the film by, for instance, showing you approaching your subject and setting up the interview.

7. Sound recording

Video filmmaking is cheap, enabling you to make movies at a fraction of the cost of those on traditional celluloid film. But for most filmmakers using basic, consumer digital equipment, picture and colour resolution are poorer than high-level digital video or film. In one particular area, however, you can compete with the very highest quality: sound. The sound quality of your movies can equal the best by using 16-bit digital stereo signal, and an interesting layer of sounds. If you can master good quality sound recording, you can give your film the best possible start in life.

Interview
'Often people don't consider sound as an important factor – it is. Design the sound fully before the shoot. One or two badly framed shots will not ruin a film but bad sound will; it will lose its audience. Sound and image work together to create the film's atmosphere as well as giving the audience dialogue to listen to.'

David Norman, filmmaker, UK

Recording with the camera mic

The easiest way of recording sound is by using the mic that comes built-in with your camera. Even at the low-end consumer level of digital camcorder, sound quality is surprisingly good. You will get clear sound, relatively free of hiss and with tracks that are not prone to bleeding – that is, the leaking of sound from track to track on the tape. But for most filmmakers, built-in mics present problems due to their inflexibility in dealing with creative work. Most camcorders do not offer you many choices for recording sound; sound goes in from mics only, to both stereo channels, and you cannot adjust the level of sound.

Cam mics boost sound levels unnaturally

The problem with built-in mics on camcorders is that they boost sound levels automatically, even if there is not much to hear. This is very frustrating when encountered for the first time and results in costly re-shoots or extensive post-production cleaning up. For example, if you film a quiet room with whispering voices, the camera will push up sound levels and end up recording the background, ambient sound too loudly. This doesn't mean that it records low-level voices at perfect volume, but that it pushes up the whole range of sounds in the room, and not just the one that you actually want to hear. The result is a hissing and clunking soundtrack; listen to the voices on your telephone answering machine and you will hear something similar.

Get a range of sounds

The camera wants a steady range of sound for it to fill the meter. To play safe, then, cater for the full range of sound. Include dialogue or loudest sounds – sometimes referred to as foreground sound – and take middle, less important sounds, right down to the lowest on the register. Think of it as you do when composing lighting for a shot: there should be a few shadows, a few bright spots and some grey shades within. Sound can be handled like this so that you have some strong areas, but not too much, complemented by lower, bass sounds. In general, give the camera mic lots of strong sound dominating over background and the result will be adequate.[21]

Three reasons to avoid recording with the camera mic (most of the time)

You can't tell if the sound levels are correct

The problem with camcorders, and the reason why these methods of recording are preferred above the cam mic, is that cameras do not usually have any way of seeing the sounds levels you are recording. This means that you have no visual way of accurately telling whether sounds are being recorded at the right level, which should be as high as you can get it without the sound distorting. Level meters exist in some cameras, such as Canon's XL–1, but are a rarity in most models at the lower price range. If you have an external device you may be able to see levels and record more professionally.

Unbalanced cables

Linked to this is the problem of balanced and unbalanced cables and mics, which camcorders at the consumer end have. Balanced audio is referred to as low impedance, or Lo Z; unbalanced, as with camera mics, is referred to as Hi Z. High-quality mics usually use what is called XLR as connectors, which affords it a balanced signal – that means you hear no interference or hiss – even over long distances of cable. It works by having two opposite wires, one positive and the other negative, and when electrical interference is picked up on the cable, that noise is heard by both wires. Because they are opposite, they each cancel out the offending signal. XLR, then, is good. But if you look at your camcorder you will see that it has a mini-plug input for sound, so you need to buy an XLR adapter, enabling you to get the quality you want into the camera. Don't get hold of a cable that has XLR at one end and a mini-plug at the other; a transformer on it to convert the signal is superior.

---

[21] www.kodak.com/US/en/motion/programs/student/handbook/recording1.shtml   Brief history of movie sound.
www.filmsound.org/   Excellent movie sound site.
http://filmsound.studienet.org/bibliography/littlist.htm#journals   Good bibliography of articles on movie sound.

Interference

A third reason to record without the camera mic is the common problem of interference. Different mics may produce a noise on tape sounding like a low hum or buzz and this is very hard to remove later. This is often caused by electrical interference from the power supply to the mic and is more frequent when you plug the camcorder into the mains supply via the AC input. Get round this problem by switching back to battery supply and by disconnecting an external monitor, if you are using one. Also try wrapping a rubber band around the camera casing to stop the wire moving around, but if these don't sort out the problem you could invest in an adapter cable that knocks out interference from the camera power supply itself.[22]

Recording with external mics

Recording with a slightly more expensive camera may allow you to alter the levels at which you record. Loud sounds can be reduced and low ones omitted. These kinds may also allow you to plug in a mixing board so that sounds are recorded at a higher and clearer level. Mixing boards are good for filmmakers; they enable you to have far greater control over what you record and how it is mixed, so that different mics can be used simultaneously for the situation. The constant aim, regardless of what equipment you have or what production you work on, is to get the strongest possible signal without getting distortion, so any device that allows you to boost or reduce signal is going to make life much easier on set. One of the best principles of sound recording is to get the microphone as close to the subject as camera framing will allow. This way, you will get more of the sound you want and less of the sound you don't.

For the professionally minded filmmaker – even if not professionally funded – external mics are going to be a necessity. There are basically six common types:

● *Personal mic*. Also known as a lavalier or clip-on or tie-mic, this is a discreet small mic that can be easily hidden from view, clipped onto the actor's clothing. For dialogue these give great results as they pick up a full, deep, resonant sound from the chest.
● *Hand-held*. A common mic used in close proximity by on-camera interviewers.
● *Boundary effect*. These are used to pick up reflected sound bounced from hard surfaces and are sometimes known as PZ or PZM mics.
● *Contact mics*. These are used for attachment to musical instruments or the picking up of any other sound in physical contact with a surface or object.
● *Shotgun mic*. A very useful mic for location shooting, as it picks up sounds at a moderate distance from the camera.
● *Studio mics*. This encompasses a range of mics used for studio filming, including television work.

---

[22] www.prostudio.com/   Magazine on movie sound.
www.thx.com/skywalker/skywalker.html   Site focusing on the work of Lucas Films sound studio.
www.thx.com/skywalker/skywalker.html   Professional sound site.
http://mpse.org/home.html   Motion Picture Sound Editors site.

Let's go through the uses of these and look at what sort of mic you will need and what you can manage without.

Basic level

If you are working at the most basic levels of equipment, you need a *dynamic microphone*. This is a rugged type often used in news reporting and can cope with a wide mix of recording situations. A really useful feature is that it does not need a power supply, unlike the next category we will look at. If time is at a premium and you don't want to be re-shooting, you need to avoid the mic battery running out during a scene. Dynamic mics don't necessarily give the best quality but are easy to manage and will give you clear sound if you are not sure what to use.

Mid to experienced level

Once you get more experienced, you can start using the more sensitive and vastly smaller condenser/capacitor mic. These are not so good outside in poor weather and do need a small power supply coming through the mic cable itself, from a mixing board or an AC power supply. They also run off batteries which can be a more flexible, convenient option but will, to the fury of you and your crew, run out of power without informing you.

Which microphone?

Within the categories above there are a number of types, for situations ranging from recording all sound in a given area to that just within a small range. We refer to mics according to their directional characteristics, in other words, the range of the angle they will pick up. This is similar to lenses, where a wide angle will see everything within a wide range whereas a macro lens is better at picking up small, close objects. There are three types: omnidirectional, bidirectional and unidirectional.

- *Omnidirectional*. Omnidirectional mics are sensitive to sounds that they hear all around them. They will pick up these sounds equally, so they record what you want plus all the other sounds going on around. This may sound good for busy, crowded scenes where you want the actors to be heard amongst a crowd, but it is rarely as clear as that. This mic will not distinguish between sounds and will record everything as an even mix, which can be adequate in some situations if there are no other sounds around to interfere with what is your main sound. You are almost always going to want to avoid this kind of mic because control of sound is your primary aim and this simply gives free reign to whatever happens to be around, including sounds behind the camera.[23]
- *Bidirectional*. These mics are open to sound coming from two directions and can be used in two-way interviews or, occasionally, when working with stereo. But achieving clear stereo is not easy to accomplish using these mics without some skill, and in any case it is better to play with directions of sound in the editing process, when you can alter the track of all sound sources (when recorded separately).

[23] www.dpamicrophones.com/ Detailed technology information about mics.
http://home1.pacific.net.sg/~firehzrd/audio/mics.html Guide to mics.

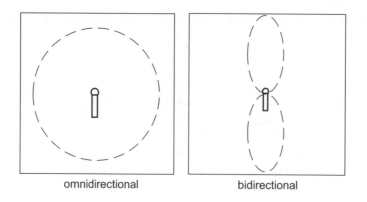

omnidirectional   bidirectional

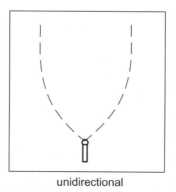

unidirectional

Figure 5.12 Mic ranges.

- *Unidirectional*. These really are the ones you need for your DV movies. If you go into a store and ask for one, however, you will be asked what kind you want from a range of four types. They all pick up sound coming from one direction, in decreasingly narrow ranges of sensitivity. With movies shot on DV, unidirectional affords you the most control over what goes onto the soundtrack.

Sound environment

Think of your whole 'sound environment' as consisting of separate sources, even if what you want is a cacophony or jumble of sounds. Recording each part of your soundtrack separately lets you amplify or reduce aspects at will, either on a mixing board on location or when you edit later. For example, a situation such as a street scene with two policemen talking would probably need their dialogue to be heard clearly. They then need to respond to a police radio in a nearby car. Recording this with an omnidirectional mic would pick up everything you want, but would distinguish no single part above the rest, so you would hear the dialogue reasonably well but would hear equally well the sound of background traffic and the footsteps of the camera operator.

Did you know?
The sound environment refers to the different layers of sounds that make up the soundtrack, not just those that are present on location, and these are arranged in order of priority. A simple sound environment could consist of dialogue as the loudest, clearest sound we hear, followed by sounds relevant to the setting, followed by music, followed by ambient sound.

Record separately

Recording with a single unidirectional mic would be fine to a certain extent, but you would have no way of amplifying the radio message or of making the traffic sounds seem realistic, since the tiny range of the mic would all but ignore the mêlée around the actors. If you recorded the street sounds separately you could then layer these on in editing and control the level of their intrusion on the dialogue. Every aspect can be mixed at precisely your instructions, although parts of each sound may bleed into the next unless using very-narrow-range mics. But bear in mind that it is not necessarily damaging to have some seepage of sounds as this can give a more realistic sound. For example, if some traffic sounds can be heard in the back of the track containing the dialogue these can be blended with the specially recorded traffic sounds later.

Tip   This can have its uses: in *On The Waterfront*, Marlon Brando tries to explain himself to Eva Marie Saint and excuse his earlier actions, but the rising sound of a boat-horn drowns him out at precisely the point when he apologizes, with bad results. Using a separate track brought forward at the right moment, the result is impressive.

Types of unidirectional mic

Unidirectional mics involve a wide range of types and we need to look at these in some more detail:

1 *Cardioid*. The least narrow unidirectional mic is the cardioid. It is named after the heart-shaped look of its range pattern. It picks up sounds in a relatively wide range in front of the mic, but is less sensitive to sounds from behind the mic. For many situations, even this is too wide, as it will pick up reflected sound bouncing off the walls or other surfaces, in addition to the original sound. You can reduce this by moving the mic to within 5 feet (1.5 metres) from the source of the bounced sound.
2 *Supercardioid*. These mics record sound on a narrower range than the cardioid. The shotgun mic described earlier is an example of this type and is widely used on location shooting. They are useful

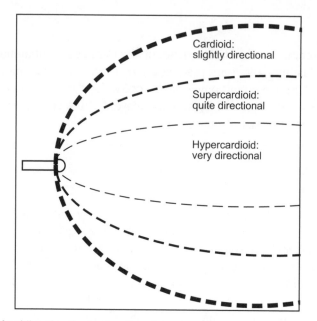

Figure 5.13 Types of unidirectional mic showing pick-up range.

because you can stand back from the source and point the mic from a distance of up to 13 feet (4 metres) – safely recording sound of an actor while avoiding placing the mic in view of the camera.

3 *Hypercardioid.* This is even more narrow than the supercardioid and is useful for some work where distance is required and you may have lots of off-axis, or unwanted, noise to avoid. These do need careful handling; move a little to the side – or if your actor moves – and you lose pick-up.

4 *Parabolic mics.* These are the most directional of this range of mics. To be exact, this is not exactly a type of mic but a way of using other directional mics. You can fit a parabolic reflector which

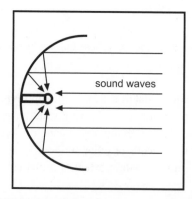

Figure 5.14 The parabolic reflector bounces sound waves towards the mic from a range of up to 60 metres and can be fitted to any unidirectional mic.

allows the mic to pick up only those sounds along a very narrow line in front of the mic. If you use one of these reflectors, running from 35 cm to 1 metre in diameter, you will have a very accurate angle of recorded sound. But, as with the hypercardioid, any movement of source or mic needs to be closely accommodated and headphones should be worn to notice unwanted changes. There are not many situations when you need a parabolic mic for movie location work, so you can skip on these unless you intend to shoot a remake of De Palma's *Blow Out*, or record field sports.[24]

Good sound recording on location: the hierarchy of microphone techniques

There are ways of achieving good, clear sound from all your diverse sources on the movie set. Knowing how to get this when working at a fast pace is going to make your production move smoothly. In larger productions, there is a concept known as 'the hierarchy of microphone techniques' and this model can be used as your default method for recording a scene and then be altered only when you encounter unusual recording situations.

In this technique, the top method of recording – number 1 – is going to work most of the time in most situations, while the method following it can be used when the first won't work and so on.

1 Overhead boom/shotgun mic.
2 Shotgun from underneath.
3 A shotgun mic placed in one position.
4 Lavalier (personal) mics in one position.
5 Lavalier mics on the actor.
6 Lavalier mics without cords.

1. Overhead boom/shotgun mic

If you want good quality sound with minimum effort and minimal mixing later and if you want it to sound natural and not overproduced (in other words, artificial or too clean), the shotgun mic is the best option. This elongated mic is held, typically, above the heads of the actors out of view of the camera. This is even more helpful when you start working on a scene that has more than two actors speaking. Actors can move about, enter or leave the scene, stand up, or whatever they need to do and still be heard, the mic operator adjusting the angle of the boom to focus on the right person. Furthermore, there are no cables to get in your way. This approach will work in almost any scene and allows for great flexibility in what you record, depending on how close the mic is to certain sounds.

2. Shotgun from underneath

There are times, though, when obstacles on set get in the way of an accurate reading of all sounds and you may need to hold the boom from beneath the actor. This does alter the tone of the sound as the lower,

---

[24] www.moviesoundpage.com/msp_cl-faq.htm   Information on movie sound recording.

bass sounds are located in the lowest parts of the chest and are nearest to the mic. It is less common to do boom recording this way, as you are more likely to get the mic in shot and it reduces the freedom of movement of the actor, but it does have its uses because it is quick and easy to set up.

3. and 4. A shotgun mic placed in one position and lavalier mics in one position

There are occasions when it may not be convenient to hold a mic above an actor – for instance, if the camera is recording a wide angle – and it is easier to secure it to a stationary part of the set. You can secure a large boom mic or a small lavalier at a given point in a room, set or location to pick up a particular sound. There are times when this is the most favourable method when a boom is not feasible – as in a car – or when you need to pick up a sound on one part of a set only occasionally, allowing you to hold the main boom mic over the main action or dialogue.

5. Lavalier mics on the actor

Although not your first choice, a lavalier mic, or tie-mic, situated on an actor's body offers a good method for recording dialogue. Some people prefer this mic as it gives a strong signal with lots of bass when using a standard consumer-level camcorder. These cameras record high-quality sound but do not always allow you to alter the tone of the signal – something which can, in any case, often be achieved in post-production with very basic sound software. Attaching a mic to the body gives you deeper sound but is prone to interference when clothes rustle or other objects or actors obscure sound. On the whole, if you want natural sound it is better to record with hidden rather than attached lavalier mics. Bear in mind that if you do use lavalier mics a lot in your dialogue, the result will be clean but may be a little too clean, and you may need to add ambient sound later to create a more natural effect, as achieved by a boom or shotgun.

6. Lavalier mics without cords

If none of the above work then you can resort to the radio mic. These bring a disproportionate amount of problems with them despite their usefulness in capturing a fast-moving, unpredictable source. These mics use a weak FM signal, as weak as possible to avoid contravening national guidelines, and so tend to attract interference from other radio transmitters. Local taxies, security walkie-talkies and other radio users near your location can often cause disturbance. Many radio mics allow you to alter the channel you use for transmission and it is usually possible to find a clear path free of interference, often in the UHF (Ultra-High Frequency) ranges, but you may still have problems with metal surfaces obstructing transmission. There are two types of radio mic: hand-held and clip-on. Radio mics are getting better at eliminating interference and some camcorders have built-in antennae for picking up this sound. The convenience of the radio mic is obvious, but it is the method most prone to causing problems.[25]

[25] www.filmsound.org/articles/designing_for_sound.htm   Article on location recording.

Line feed levels: getting the mixture right

If you can invest in a mixing board to combine the various sounds being recorded you will achieve high-quality results. As we have seen, one of the main advantages is being able to see the levels – the power – of the audio signals and adjust accordingly.

Using an audio mixing board

An audio signal entering a mixing board is boosted above that coming in from a standard mic, usually at the 600-ohm level. However, most camcorders can't function with sound this powerful, so you will need to reduce the signal by about 30–50 dB, although some mixing boards have a simple switch to set the levels at the right point for camcorder mic inputs. Again, make sure you check for interference on the signal the camcorder picks up, not just that which the mixing board hears. Testing is crucial to see whether your levels are correct and whether you are experiencing problems with interference, so record a test scene and play the sequence back using headphones. Don't rely on what you hear on headphones as you record, as sometimes you may hear a buzzing sound on the tape that you couldn't hear when recording.[26]

Location recording in action

To summarize the ideas we have covered so far, it may be useful to look at a few different situations and see how you would use mics and how you would record the signal. There is no typical scene, every film has different needs and will present different problems.

Example 1: two figures, interior

A scene involves two actors, A and B, situated in a room. They talk and at a particular point a third actor appears at the door, after which the scene cuts. For this sequence you can assume that the dialogue is important and needs to be clear and audible. As the two actors are sitting throughout the scene in the same position, you could use a stationary shotgun or boom mic which picks up their voices. Actor C appears later and we will need to pick up what is said by all three. Actor C will stand at the door entrance and say a few lines before departing, so we can safely attach a hidden lavalier cardioid mic to the side of the door frame.

You will also need to record the extra sounds to be placed behind these tracks later, when editing. You would first record ambient sound or presence, which acts as a continuity device, smoothing over the subtle alterations in background hum as you film each part of the sequence. Record just a few minutes of this using omnidirectional or cardioid mics, and loop it when editing. Each of the other separate sounds are recorded including, for instance, street sounds outside the room, footsteps of actor C coming up the drive and a slightly exaggerated door opening and shutting.

---

[26] www.modernrecording.com/articles/soundav/link25.html   Mixing board basics.

Example 2: several figures, street scene

The scene is set in a narrow street with several actors, all of whom are talking simultaneously. There is a strong sense of atmosphere as the rich sounds of a street market, traffic and cathedral bells in the distance combine. To record this complex scene, use a shotgun mic mounted on a pole or boom, situated a little higher than usual above the actors' heads. The shotgun is good for giving you a sense of sound perspective (sounds far away are less powerful) and will pick up other background sounds to give a more natural sound, but will not drown out the main voices. If one actor above the others needs to be heard at one point you can direct the mic the right way. Even though you are recording good, natural sound with the voices, you still need an overall ambient track to iron out the differences in the various takes later. You will, don't forget, be shooting over a period of time during which the sounds of the street may change. With this scene, you could use a dynamic mic to record everything if you want to stick with basic equipment; it should pick up sounds in all the various conditions present, but may compromise quality.

Example 3: two figures, a car, exterior

A scene involves two people in a car. A third is to talk to the others as they arrive at their destination and get out of the car in one continuous take. This is tricky as it involves different situations, dialogue and potential problems with situating the mics.

To begin the scene, place lavalier mics in the car. Hide one each on both driver and passenger sun visors to pick up dialogue clearly. Attaching it to clothes would cause problems with seat-belt or clothes causing rustling sounds. If you can't attach it to the sun visor (a soft-top with the roof down?), try attaching to clothes but soften the clothing and take out the starchiness that causes the noise by damping a small section of cloth, out of view.

When the two reach their destination we need to have one take in which they get out of the car and talk to a third actor. Record this by using an overhead boom mic angled to pick up all three at the same time. The noise of the car engine will also appear in the background of the shotgun track, adding realism. The lavalier will pick up the last of the conversation in the car, while the shotgun picks it up from there outside. In this case, you actually need a difference in sound to reflect the move from interior to exterior, so the alteration in what you pick up is satisfactory. If you want one continuous recording, try a radio mic attached to the actor's body, but switch to a more reliable mic as soon as you can in the scene.

Example 4: three figures, exterior, sea front

Continuing on from the scene above, let's assume the three actors then walk down to the sea front and talk further. Recording this scene presents problems because of the need to keep crew and cameras well back from the actors as they walk further along the beach and the potential of wind noise to interfere with quality. Although parabolic mics are going to do the job more cleanly, a hypercardioid may be easier to use as it does not have to be so pinpoint accurate, and if your actors are moving around this is going to be crucial. If you are restricted by your equipment, and do not have an accurate long-distance mic, you could consider overdubbing voices if you cannot actually see clearly the actors speaking their lines. You may still want natural sound, with all the ambient sound of the beach location, but this could be more easily handled if the actors are close to the camera. This would be a better option than radio mics in some ways, since the latter will tend to give sound that is too clear and neat, requiring you to lay over much ambient sound to 'rough it up' sufficiently to convey the location.

Recording extra sounds

On videotape

If you have relatively little experience of sound work, it is better to record all your sounds on videotape at first and then, in the editing stage, import and alter sound clips in the same way as you would for vision/sound clips. This method for recording background sound or particular effects such as footsteps or telephone rings is straightforward, because you can simply use your existing edit software and don't need to yet get involved in specialist sound software. The timeline in most software offers a useful visual guide to the layers of sound on the soundtrack. On the negative side, capturing these clips at the editing stage is less than economical as video clips are far larger than sound files, but you can, of course, delete vision from these files as you use them.

There are two formats available if you choose to record sound separate to the camcorder: mini-disc and digital audio tape (DAT).

DAT

Digital audio tape was created in 1987. The quality of the DAT format is such that professional studios very quickly adopted it and made it the digital standard for recording. It offers 3 hours of digital sound on a tape half the size of an analog audio cassette tape, with the same format as a CD (44.1 kHz sampling frequency and 16 bits). While both Digital Compact Cassette (DCC) tape and mini-disc use data compression, DAT is the only consumer recording standard that does not, meaning that the whole signal is held on the tape. DAT is easy to use on location; indexing of the tape and rewinding are extremely fast (50 seconds for a 120-minute tape), so you can quickly access any place on the DAT tape. For clarity and purity of sound, DAT rivals the compact disc (CD).

Mini-disc

Mini-discs were created by Sony in 1991 as a disc-based digital recording medium that is as near to CD quality as possible. There are two types of mini-disc (MD): pre-mastered MDs, which can be recorded on once only and are similar to CDs in operation and manufacture, and recordable MDs, which can be recorded on repeatedly and employ magneto-optical technology.

DAT vs mini-disc: which format is better for filmmaking?

Bear in mind that while both DAT and MD are digital formats, MD stores audio signals using a data reduction or compression technique and there are data quantity differences between the quality of a

CD recording and an MD copy of it. But this doesn't mean that anyone listening will hear the difference; most people will assume the CD and the MD recording are the same. So, for filmmaking there is going to be a negligible difference between the high-data DAT and the compressed MD. However, the one disadvantage of MD is that differences from the original increase with each generation copy, even though it is recorded digitally. There is a build-up of 'artefacts' (picture disturbance caused by technical limitation) as data are re-compressed.[27]

The Crunch

- You may not have the best model of camcorder on the market, but you can have sound quality to match big-budget productions.
- The camera mic is almost never a good solution to your sound needs.
- Use good quality mics with XLR transformers and adapters to attach to your camera mic input socket.
- There is no need to buy the whole range of mics unless you can afford to right now; a good shotgun cardioid and a lavalier will cover you for most situations, while a hand-held cardioid mic will help record individual sounds.
- While you are building up experience of how to record sound in varied situations, use the hierarchy of recording techniques.

Project 11. The chase

This film is going to put into practice a few ideas we have covered so far. This doesn't mean it is necessarily harder than other projects, just that it starts to challenge you on several levels. Here's how.

This project asks you to make a film in which we don't see the main aspects of the narrative. We are going to use the powers of suggestion in sound to imply what is happening rather than showing it directly, allowing us to make a drama that relies less on a big budget and more on what comes free, namely, your skill and imagination.

The film centres around a figure running through a series of dark streets, running into different obstacles, possibly being chased by something we cannot see. We only hear what the figure encounters throughout the film. In addition to your use of sound, we need to use the ideas brought up in the earlier parts of this section, on using the camera. Use the whole range of camera angles in this one, and go as far as you need to suggest the tension and drama of the events of the plot. In order to keep your options open as to what the figure encounters, try to avoid complicating the plot in any way. It's enough to use the figure's journey as our sole purpose of watching the movie.

[27] www.solorb.com/dat-heads/   DAT enthusiasts' site.
www.minidisc.org/   Mini-disc information and links.

Stage 1

Since we have the story worked out in its essentials, you need only at this stage to think of what the figure will encounter in its path. The specifics of this are down to you: you can make it a comic film, a serious scary movie or a futuristic fantasy. Indicate what the character is going to run into, for instance, 'wild animal sound' or 'weird flying object'.

The kind of movie you make may be influenced (as it should be) by the locations you have access to. If you know of a place you can film with a labyrinthine set of corridors, or a series of narrow streets, or an industrial site, then let that be your deciding factor in where it is set. Add to the air of mystery by keeping several facts from the audience: Where are we? What year is it? Who is the protagonist?

Stage 2

Complete a set of visualizations and storyboards which detail how you film is going to look. Since we have few details to go on, it is going to be easy for the audience to become lost, so we are going to have to remain in control of continuity issues. This means making sure that the lighting you use (refer to the next section on lighting to get more help with this) is constant throughout, so that we get a sense of the chase taking place in one continuous flow of events. Keep the costume the same throughout and make sure that the direction of the figure running is maintained: this means he or she will probably go from left to right, exiting right but reappearing left and continuing on right. This will help to show that the movement of the figure is in one main direction: away from whatever is threatening.

Stage 3

Shooting this movie may feel artificial, or at least more artificial than it usually does. It's going to be like Sam Neill ducking on a film set from an imaginary, but soon to be computer-created, *Tyrannosaurus rex*. But bear with it. Indicate to your actor points on the set when particular reactions are required and, since we don't have to use sounds recorded actually on set, you can shout as much as you need.

To maintain continuity of lighting, choose a set-up you like and stay with it. If you are unsure what to opt for, choose a strong single lamp stationary on the set, casting a light that the actor can enter and leave, revealing facial expressions and yet keeping the majority of the set in shadow, allowing us to fill the shadow, as it were, with sounds. Now and then, step back and take a few shots of the overall scene, showing off a particular part of the set that looks good. These covering shots, displaying the actor in full and allowing us to notice the left-to-right direction they are going in, are going to be useful later in the editing stage, helping to stitch the whole film together easily.

Stage 4

Editing this film is relatively straightforward. But before you start piecing it together, we need to put into place some way of the action getting more intense as the film reaches the end. Keep the individual cuts on the longer side at the start, perhaps 4 or 5 seconds or more, while the last quarter of the film sees the cuts get quicker, indicating a speeding up of the action and an imminent conclusion.

At this point we can start to think of the sounds that indicate what the figure has encountered. This is a time to have some playtime with the microphones. Spend a few days investigating and recording sounds. Go into this with an open mind; it really is a revelation how something very ordinary sounds when taken out of context. For example, try recording how a cabbage sounds when cut in half; the crunching sound was often used in horror movie scenes of a guillotine. Record washing machines, dripping water taps, a cat howling, and make use of whatever you can do with your voice. The aim is to find raw sounds which can later be layered to create a full and menacing soundscape.

Stage 5

When you begin the process of inserting sounds, try layering a few together on the timeline. Import sounds directly into your edit program and play around with them on the timeline, listening to how they sound in conjunction with others. Look for the available tracks you have on the timeline and create as many as you need (see Chapter 6:3; also see Editing with Premiere 6, CD-ROM). Place the clips down first and make a complete silent movie. Many edit programs enable you to place visual markers on the timeline so that you can tie-in certain sounds later to particular shots. Also make sure that you adjust the sound levels of each clip.

Make sure that you have:

- A constant noise which will indicate to the audience that we are in one place.
- A suggestion that there is a 'something' pursuing the figure, again by sounds alone. Try footsteps or a howling.
- A particular sound which we associate with the figure, maybe a musical watch or panic-stricken breathing. We need to associate the pursuer and the 'pursuee' with two very distinct sounds.

> **Film View**
> Look at the closing scenes of *Blade Runner: The Director's Cut* (Ridley Scott, 1991) for a chase where we often hear Harrison Ford's pursuer.

Evaluation

This project requires much more work on the post-production side than shooting. You may well have shot everything in one evening but then had to spend many days perfecting the sounds and the way they match the visuals.

How was the sound layering? Success in this area can be measured by how you have managed to take the sound out of its setting and given it a new life. So, if a dog growling layered with a child's rattle, for example, sound like nothing else then you have hit the right mark. As you may have found, the plot of the figure being pursued and encountering different events along the way is no more than a vehicle to allow us to play around with sounds.

Beyond this, however, look at how you handled the potential continuity problems. Play the movie to your friends, ask whether they noticed any unnatural jumps in action, as if a section of time had been removed, or whether it seemed as if the events of the film flowed realistically.

When looking at your use of the camera, make a note of the kinds of shots you used. Did you use shots which resembled each other too much? Or was the range of shots varied, maintaining our interest in the film?

Whatever you managed to achieve, the main purpose of this film has been to see in this very extreme example how sound can be just as powerful as images, but at a fraction of the cost.

8. Lighting

Digital filmmaking is a double-edged sword: on the one hand, you are going to be able to make a movie for less than you ever thought possible, but on the other, you are going to have to be much more creative with very basic equipment. You don't just need to make the best of what you have, but make what little you have look like the best. In the area of lighting, this is certainly true. Good lighting has the ability to lift a film out of the limitations of its budget and into another league.

This task is given to the director of photography, whose job it is to light a picture. Even this role tells us something about the importance of this area; photographing a film is entirely tied up with how it is lit. You cannot pick up the camera without also considering how to use your lamps.

Lighting helps to:

- pick out relevant details and figures in a scene;
- tell the audience what you as director prioritize within a shot, and therefore the story;
- establish a set of values to what we are seeing, by throwing more and less light on the elements in a scene;
- enforce emotional pull in a scene, heightening mood and atmosphere;
- allow the camera to see properly, on a technical level;
- allow you to create a look for the film;
- maintain continuity between takes shot on successive days.

But before we can utilize the full potential of lighting, however, we need to understand how the camera itself reacts to light.[28]

---

[28] www.kinoflo.com   Informative newsletters on movie and TV lighting.
   www.3dlight.com   Lighting tutorial.

The camera and light

The video camera reacts to light in much the same way as the human eye. It has a sensor behind the lens, called a CCD (Charge-Coupled Device), which converts light entering the lens into digital information to be stored on tape. But unlike the human eye, if there isn't enough information coming into the lens, it compensates, resulting in bad quality, grainy pictures. Today's cameras are designed to see in almost any lighting conditions, but you cannot rely on this to give a clear picture. To keep picture quality high we have to feed the camera lots of light. This doesn't mean blanket lighting, but rather enough strong light in spots for it to maintain quality.

Go to: Chapter 3:2 for more details about the CCD.

Most video cameras are less able to distinguish between shades of light or colour than traditional celluloid film. Film is about 10 times more able to see the various subtle tints or hues in a shot than video. To make matters worse, the chips embedded in lower-end cameras are less able again, and need particular attention. You will eventually get great results with any camera as long as you know the limitations of the camera you are working with. Be aware that video – at least at the low to mid range of cameras – does not read subtle light to the degree you might like; what looks good to the human eye may not reveal itself through a camera lens. This means lighting your sets in a certain way that exaggerates natural light.

Automatic camera features: why you don't need them

Your biggest enemy on the camcorder is probably the automatic setting. This is useful for some conditions but on the whole you cannot rely on it to deliver when it comes to creative filmmaking – it's the fast food of lighting. Since the camera fills in the frame if it doesn't see the amount of light it would like, it is better to have a camera with manual override to switch off this feature – which the vast majority do. This means you can set the lighting yourself and be more creative about what you record. As an example, you may want to shoot a scene in which a group of people are in a room, with windows behind them with bright sunlight flooding in. On auto, the camera simply cancels out some of the sunlight, rendering the figures dark beyond all recognition, the sunlight just about right. But you may want the scene to be overexposed (too much light coming in) in the windows because that gives a certain feel to the scene, and in any case is the only sure way to still see the figures. Automatic will do it the way the manufacturer's handbook says, but manual allows you to do it your way.

Iris and light

Just as with the human eye, the camera has a small hole at the front of the lens which controls how much light is allowed in. In bright conditions, it closes slightly to block some out, while in darker conditions it opens to make more of what little light there is. On a technical level, the iris is important in stopping the inner workings of the camera from being damaged by too much sunlight, just as does the human iris. Too much light also stops the camera from reading colour correctly. But like other features on the camera, we can use the iris creatively. Allowing too much light, or restricting light, can be useful ways of adding atmosphere to a scene.

Figure 5.15 *Intruder* (2000) by Robin Whenary. In this shot, single source lighting is used from below to depict the face of the burglar, distorting the features and adding atmosphere to the scene.

Depth of field and light

Furthermore, the iris performs a quite separate job of adjusting how much of the frame is in focus. This is called depth of field and refers to the aperture of the iris. On some cameras these are expressed in numbers, such as f/2, f/8 and so on, the larger numbers corresponding to the smaller hole openings. As we have seen, the higher the f-number (or the smaller the opening of the iris), the greater the depth of field. Greater depth of field means that you get more objects in focus before and behind the main focal point. In some conditions, then, you may want to open up the iris for other reasons than just light.

Go to: the section on depth of field in Chapter 3:5.

Colour temperature

Something else that video cameras, particularly at the lower end, are not good at is balancing the colours they see, which is why they have a white balance feature which helps them take out the 'cast' of a particular lighting condition, that is, the particular colours given off by most artificial light. The human eye performs a similar routine every time you enter a new environment. A room lit by a domestic light-bulb, for instance, will not give off true light in the way we think of daylight, but instead is tinted by orange. Your brain can automatically compensate for this, but the camera will need your help. We need either to use light that does not give off unwanted colours or adjust the camera

Source of light	Degrees kelvin	Colour cast
Candle	1900	Warm, orange red
Sunrise / sunset	Between 2000 and 3200	Orange red
Household lamp	2800	Orange
Tungsten lamp	3200	Yellow, close to daylight
Daylight in Europe	5600	Clear, white
Cloudy day	Between 6000 and 8000	Cold, blue

Figure 5.16 Colour temperature.

to offset what it sees. On the other hand, like everything about filming, there are creative uses to colour imbalance, such as setting white balance incorrectly in outdoor daylight by setting it to remove the orange cast of indoor lamps, resulting in a cold, blue tint to the scene. The worst of all worlds is where daylight and artificial light are mixing in the same frame.

To understand this, we need to have a look at colour temperature. All light has a temperature, measured in degrees kelvin. In film, we refer to daylight as normal light – light giving a true reading of colours – and it resides somewhere in the middle of the scale, at 5600 degrees. This applies to sunny afternoon light in Europe, but in places where light is stronger, such as in California, colour temperature will be lower, whereas an overcast day with poor light will be a higher colour temperature. The point of looking at this is to be able to use certain lamps to light your scene effectively, with colour as true to daylight as possible. To this end, use tungsten lights, which have a colour temperature of near daylight, and avoid household lights for movies.

Good studio lighting

- Use lamps.
- Use lighting to help you with composition.
- Use contrast.
- Don't over-light.
- Use shadow.

Although a basic concept in lighting, video has some problems giving you the contrast you want. Contrast is the relative polarity of dark and light; the greater the distance between the darkest and the brightest, the greater the contrast. Camera composition is all about arranging elements within a scene to give the most visual impact and lighting with contrast is one of the most useful ways of achieving this. Frames that have large amounts of detail, depicted in a flat, grey light, have less impact than ones

Figure 5.17 *Coventry* (1998) by Dan McMillan. In this snooker game scene, high contrast was achieved by using the snooker table lights above the actor – a low-budget solution that serves its purpose well.

where larger shapes dominate, in which shadow and brightness select what it is we should be paying attention to. Deep, dark shadow is a way of ordering the frame, pointing the eye towards what we are meant to see.[29]

High contrast

Film noir made a virtue out of using lighting with high contrast and unusually placed shadow. For example, a scene with a detective standing in a doorway, looking ominously at a figure he is tailing, may be lit with just a few puddles of light scattered around, some of which is strategically placed on the detective's face but, by and large, the scene was underlit, relying on darkness to evoke a feeling of menace and uncertainty.

> **Did you know?**
> Film noir refers to a type of movie dominant in the post-war era of Hollywood. It is often seen as a sub-genre of the gangster movie, but it is more a visual style than a genre and is frequently picked up by today's filmmakers as a self-conscious style choice.

[29] www.exposure.co.uk/eejit/light/ Low-budget lighting article.

Softening contrast

Contrast is badly used, however, if you use it without regard to whether it suits the film you are making. Although its effects are to make compositions look stronger, it can flatten three-dimensional objects by removing the shades of grey that show form. At this extreme, it is as destructive as flat, low-contrast, all-over lighting, which also has too little shadow to reveal three-dimensionality. Use contrast to a degree but also add softer lights within the scene to make sure that the tonal values of objects are not lost. Use contrast as a tool to solve problems associated with composition or to help show depth and texture in a shot. But avoid using it simply as a style option as it can take on too prominent a place in your film; use it as a tool to reveal atmosphere in a scene and to mask an absence of expensive props and sets.

Use lamps

Realism is often the aim of a filmmaker. But you don't get realistic lighting by using just what is around naturally. If the camera was as sophisticated as the human eye then you could do this, but you have to help a camera to see as we see. This involves using additional light, whether you are outside

Figure 5.18 *The Invitation* (2000) by Emily Corchoran. This well-received short movie has been seen in several film festivals. In this shot, Sally Phillips as Sarah is lit by soft lamps, supplementing the candlelight in the foreground, since candlelight alone does not give sufficient light for the camera.

in natural daylight or in what seems to be a well-lit room. The level of light is not really the issue here; it is about directing the light, altering the intensity of it and removing it from some areas. Lamps will help you with this, but you don't necessarily have to go out and spend half your budget on the full range. Like everything, there are ways of using fewer.

Basic lamp technique

The basic aim of using lamps is to:

- pick out the primary object in a scene (known as the 'key light');
- reduce some of the harshness of the key light with small, softer lights (known as 'fill light');
- lift the background to increase depth and separate the main figure from it (known as the 'background light').

Key light

This gives what is called 'hard light'. It is clear, bright, full light, casting a strong shadow and is directed at the main subject of the scene to give importance to the part of the frame the audience should see. This doesn't mean showering it in light all over, however, as the direction of light is more effective if placed at an angle from the line between the camera and the subject. For example, with a figure, we may place the key light at a 45-degree angle from the face, so that it hits the side of the face, but not too much on one side. This produces interesting shadows on the face and helps the actor

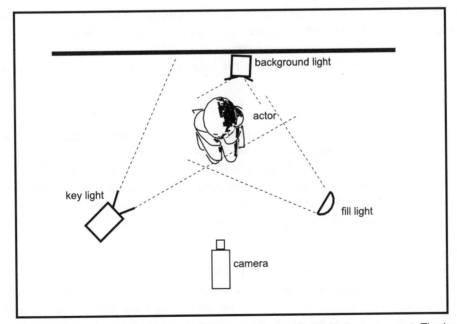

Figure 5.19 Key, fill and back lighting is placed around the subject 120 degrees apart. The key provides the hardest, strongest light, the fill takes away some of the shadows on the opposite side, while the back light lifts the background to provide a sense of depth.

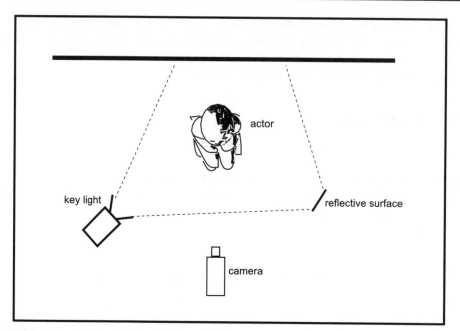

Figure 5.20 In this set-up, only one light is needed, a strong key light. A reflective surface bounces the light softly around the opposite side of the subject.

convey expression more easily by delineating the muscles on the face sharply (as well as revealing the signs of ageing). Move the key light at various angles and elevations to achieve the right effect for your film, but avoid at all times giving your subject two shadows from two strong lights aimed in similar directions. A strong light from below, for instance, gives the actor a menacing, devilish look.

Fill light
This kind of light is aimed at softening the effects of the key. But it also makes the lighting set-up more complex and rewarding as a composition. It is used as a lower-level light, washing over parts of a form and making shadows more interesting, by giving them some subtler shades within. A fill light will be a more diffuse lamp, sending light out in many directions, and must never be as powerful as the key, in general about a half to a third as bright as the key light. If you are unable to use a fill, you can instead bounce light around the room by using white, reflective surfaces.

Background light
This is just what it suggests: filling out and revealing the background of a set-up. Usually the background is hard to determine if you don't use background lamps and rely on residue light from the main lamps. It starts to blend in with everything else and this has a big impact on the sense of depth seen in the shot. We need depth because it offsets the inherent two-dimensionality of the screen and creates an illusion of reality. Soft lights picking out background allow you to be more creative with your compositions by giving you more elements in the frame to play with.

To achieve this, place lights behind the subject, in between it and the background. Avoid pointing it directly at the back of the actor as it will simply result in silhouetting. Instead, place the lamp pointing in the general direction of the camera but not right at it, so that it lifts both the back of the subject and the background areas.

Remember that every light produces a shadow of some kind. Firing more light at the shadow will never eliminate it, but moving the main subject further from the background will solve the problem of shadows. We can look at something called the inverse square law, which sounds complex but isn't: light reduces in intensity (quantity) in square proportion to the distance it travels. In other words, light is four times stronger at half the distance.

Types of lamp for key, fill and background

When using lamps we can break them up into categories, serving different functions. In different ways, each lamp will affect both the technical aspects of your production – for instance, by exposing too much or too little – as well as the artistic aspects, such as dramatic mood and atmosphere.

For each lamp, we should look at its:

- *Intensity*, i.e. how bright it is. This is determined partly by the amount of power going in and by the type of bulb it uses, such as halogen, fluorescent or tungsten.
- *Colour temperature*, i.e. what kind of colour cast the light gives when picked up on non-white-balanced film. Ideally, you should stick to lamps that do not have any inherent colour of their own, allowing you maximum freedom to add your own, with the use of gels, a transparent coloured film which is placed over the lamp (don't use anything but a film manufactured for use with lamps – something that can't stand the heat could be a fire risk).
- *Direction*, i.e. the degree to which you can point the light at the places you want. For many lights, however, you will have the option of shutters, or barn doors, which allow you to let the light diffuse outwards in many directions of fill just a small area of the set.

Further to this, you need to consider how simple each lamp is to use in exterior shooting in terms of how easy it is to move about and how much power it consumes.

- *Redhead*. A good workhorse and very versatile, this 800 W tungsten–halogen (quartz) lamp is named after the colour of the lamp top, although actually a kind of orange. It is the brand name of Ianiro, but its popularity has made it a generic term for this sort of lamp. Use this for hard light as your main lamp; it is too strong to use easily as background, but you can direct away from the subject by bouncing light off other surfaces to get adequate fill light.
- *Blonde*. So called because of its gold painted head, it is a 2 kW lamp from the same company as the Redhead. This is a versatile, strong and reliable lamp with uses for key and fill lighting.
- *Pup, Mizar, Inky-Dink*. These trademark names are all at the lower end of intensity and power. These are useful for lighting very small pockets of the set, with direct, focused beams. Use these for picking out specific parts of the set.

- *Dedo*. A set of lights probably out of the price range of most low-budgeteers, these are actually a set of lights that are small and versatile, and designed to add complexity and variety to a set. The name comes from the company, Dedo Wiegart Film.
- *HMI*. Using a special, high-pressure metal–halide bulb, this lamp is much more economical in terms of power use, and is brighter than a similar wattage Blonde. It has the colour temperature of daylight and so can be used to fake sunlight in interiors, or to just maintain good colour balance.[30]
- *Sun-gun*. This is a term referring to any battery-powered hand-held light, available in tungsten or halogen.

You should be able to find any of these lamps through specialist suppliers or via photographic retailers.

Lamps: the ideal kitbag

Whatever your budget, you still need to work with the same kind of range of lamps. Some of these lamps can be supplanted by those not specifically made for the film industry, but the range should be about the same as that used in a well-resourced production.

- Big, versatile lamps such as the *Redhead*. Get three or four if you can.
- A battery-powered, hand-held lamp: the *sun-gun*.
- At least two small, highly *directionable lamps*, such as Mizars or Dedos.

On top of this, you should carry:

- Many metres of *extension cable*.
- Some *distribution boards* or multi-sockets.
- A large flat, white, *reflective surface* such as card or polystyrene, or a folding, reflective panel called a Lastolite, to bounce light around, or complement lighting without too many smaller lamps.
- Some *coloured gels*, especially blue, so that your tungsten lamps will not upset colour balance in daylight.
- A few sheets of *tracing paper* to diffuse light but make sure it is heat resistant.
- Lots of *bull-clips or pegs* to attach gobos (opaque pieces of board to obscure light and make interesting shadows) and gels. Wooden clothes pegs are also good for this.
- *Spare bulbs*. You could change these more often than you need, to avoid a lamp blowing just in the middle of a crucial, one-off scene.
- *Gaffer tape*, to bundle wires out of the way and make your set safe.

Lighting alternatives: the Dogme way

The kinds of guidelines described above are not the final word on lighting. This applies only to those filmmakers who want their films to have a certain look and feel associated with traditional conventions of cinema. A group of filmmakers based in Denmark have challenged these assumptions,

[30] www.stagelighting.com/ltmhmi.html   More information on HMI lights.

producing films with no artificial lighting, other than what was present at the location. Dogme as a movement is aimed at 'undressing a film' (director Thomas Vinterberg), removing what they believe are the layers of artificial tools that remove vitality and realism from a movie. Kristian Levring, director of Dogme movie *The King is Alive* (1999), suggests that with no lighting: ' . . .the actual set-up of the scene is very, very fast. That makes it possible to concentrate on the essence of the scene, instead of spending 90 per cent of your time on peripheral things, so that when you're finally ready to shoot, the energy has disappeared. So, we were able to re-shoot a lot of scenes, just going on and on until we had it.'

The Dogme way

Dogme lighting is easy: don't buy any lights, don't borrow any, don't use any. Just use only what was actually on the location. If a place is dark, then that's the way you shoot it; if this reduces picture quality, so be it. In extreme situations you can attach a small lamp to the top of the camera, but nothing else. This may sound like a recipe for disaster, but take a look at the stunning images in *Breaking the Waves* (Lars von Trier, 1996), a dramatic portrait of misguided love set in the Scottish highlands. Von Trier puts his faith only in natural light and whatever else Scottish highlanders use indoors, and is amply rewarded with some richly poignant and atmospheric images. The Dogme philosophy would insist that although a particular standard of picture quality is breached, the result is less plastic, more poetic. Furthermore, Dogme has led the way for movies shot with digital video to gain acceptance, with *Dancer in the Dark* (2000) and Thomas Vinterberg's Cannes prize-winning *Festen* (1998). Dogme is like a siren voice in the distance, offering another way entirely to make movies; you won't know whether you like it until you try it.[31]

But even before Dogme existed, cinematographers have sought other ways of making shots more realistic without the need for the method described above. Nestor Almendros, director of photography on many acclaimed movies, incuding *Days of Heaven* (Terrence Malick, 1978) and *The Last Metro* (Francois Truffaut, 1980), often preferred just one light source, rejecting this key, fill and background light technique: 'The result [of this method] has nothing to do with reality, where a window or a lamp, or at most both of them, normally provide the only sources of light' (*A Man with a Camera*, p. 8, Faber & Faber, 1982). He used the key light as a functional source, directed by what light would be cast from sunlight or from an interior lamp. 'Once the key light has been decided, the space around it and the areas that might be left in total darkness are reinforced with a very soft, gentle light, until what is reproduced on film is close to what the eye would see' (ibid., p. 9).

The Crunch

- Get to know how your camera reacts to different lighting conditions.
- Keep control over your camera: avoid automatic features.
- Use high contrast for web films.

[31] www.naive.co.uk/movies/dogme95manifesto.html   Rules about Dogme lighting.

- Key, fill and background is the basic technique – add or subtract from here but don't forget it is just one way of lighting.
- Use a small selection of good lamps.
- Use lamps as near to daylight in degrees kelvin as possible.
- Avoid at all costs a scene where both daylight and artificial meet.
- Look at alternative methods of lighting: try lamps you already have, but also look for cheap alternatives for halogen (household security lights, for example).
- Feed the camera what it wants: strong light.
- Never place two strong lights close together: they cast two slightly conflicting shadows.

Project 12. Intruder

This project is going to put into practice some of the ideas described above, asking you to create several different lighting situations within one film. The film centres on an intruder breaking into and searching a house. It's a good low-budget story in that it involves nothing more than one or two actors and a house. The intruder is going to enter the house and explore what is in each room. At the end you could resolve it with a confrontation between the intruder and the occupants, but the main point of the film is the series of lighting set-ups in each room.

Stage 1

Begin by making visualizations of the scenes you intend to use, based on a brief, outline script. We don't need dialogue, so you need only describe what is going to happen and when. The opening scene could show the house as it is usually, at night and at rest. The next scene can then show the intruder making his way in. Draw your sketches using only a thick black marker pen, to encourage you to think in terms of shadows and contrast. Use colour also to hint at what kind of light is in each room.

Stage 2

When shooting, you are going to utilize whatever lights you usually have in the house, so we could see the intruder silhouetted against the outdoor security lamps, or partially lit by the light from inside the house. Maybe the intruder has a torch, which could be used to make quick flashes across the face of the dark figure, or acting like a keyhole for us to see glimpses of what is inside the house.

In each room the figure enters, try to set up a different lighting environment. One room could have a single lamp on the floor, casting shadows on the ceiling as the figure walks across the room. Another could be lit by candles, helped by a small lamp to give the camera a little more light. With each room seemingly only recently occupied, there will be a sense of tension and expectation that the occupants will appear soon. Keep the lamps close to the figure to maintain the strongest amount of light from what are usually very weak lamps.

In all, try to set up at least four rooms and in each one take time to explore the effect of this particular lighting on the intruder and on the objects in the room. Let the camera linger often. In one room, try in some way to make shadows move by having a swinging light-bulb, or a recently deserted rocking chair in front of a strong lamp. Or try using reflected light, for instance by bouncing a strong lamp off a bath of water, causing ripples to move across the figure. In all cases, however, remember to maintain enough light to keep picture quality high. If in doubt about what you can get away with regarding low light, do a few tests so you know what intensity and quantity of light is essential for your particular camera.

Your camera may not respond well to moving light, as its automatic functions will be constantly trying to assess how much light there is and compensating by opening or closing the iris. This causes havoc all over the place, so remedy it by allowing the camera to find the right aperture using its automatic facility, but then switching it onto manual when you start shooting. This will ensure that it does not try to adjust itself every time a large shadow or bright light appears.

Stage 3

Begin editing by logging all your footage, as usual, and sorting the good from the bad. Editing this film is going to involve a few tricks such as visual effects (if your software has them) or transitions (a way of cutting from one shot to the next). We need to let the camera do the talking and keep the editing simple and discreet. Avoid fast editing (we can say that anything less than 2 or 3 seconds long is a fast cut here) and let the audience enjoy the visual richness of the lighting situations.

Evaluation

Although we have covered many of the conventional methods of using lamps in this section, in practice many people just cannot afford to purchase this equipment. This project helps to identify the means by which you can get original, visually interesting lighting that suits a scene without having to overspend. One potential problem is the colour imbalance of household lamps, but for now we can ignore this in favour of what can be learned through necessary improvisation.

With this is mind, look at what you have managed to extract from cheap, household lighting. Success can be measured by how resourceful you have become and how you have transformed functional lamps into creative ones.

Look at the camera framing. Ask how each lighting set-up affected what the camera could see and how it affected the quality of the image. In particular, look at your lower-level light situations and assess how far you can go before there is too little light. One of the drawbacks of video is its sterile appearance when used in bright, clear light, and the impact this has on creating atmosphere. It is useful to track your experiments with shadows and low light, even if sometimes you go too far.

6 Post-production

1. Introduction to editing

As we saw in Chapter 1, editing is the most crucial stage in the film's development, since it is the moment when it becomes more than just the sum of its parts, more than a collection of scenes on a theme. The task is daunting: to compress time, to make events filmed days or weeks apart flow seamlessly, to make space contract or expand, or simply to suggest locations or events that are non-existent. It is, simply, deception on a grand scale.

It is impossible to lay down a rigid set of rules that lead to great editing; since the needs of each film are different, such rules would inevitably change for each movie. But there are points that can lead towards a better understanding of what your film needs. The ideas listed below are some of the most common points mentioned by editors, but all will be broken as and when necessary. The purpose of studying editing techniques is to know when you use these and when you break them. Since you probably want to get out there and make movies rather than spend a few years as an editor's assistant, you need to jump the queue of experience and look at how you make a film look good right now.

Editing: this is how it goes

1 Know your footage inside out, viewing it again and again to get to know where your strong points are and what looks (sometimes unexpectedly) good.
2 'Log' your footage tapes. This means making detailed notes, including the description of the shot, the timecode start and end points, its duration and whether the audio is of sufficient quality.
3 Make a rough paper edit. More on these early stages in Chapter 6:2.
4 Make a first real edit, consisting of all the right shots you want in the film, but without any of the frills such as text, special effects, colour alterations and so on. These separate clips may also be untrimmed, which means they may still be cut down further. Full details of digital editing are in Chapter 6:3.
5 View this first edit and go away and do something else. Go for a walk, do something physical, think about what you have made and consider all your initial plans, reflect on what you originally wanted and how this cut (or version of the film) relates to your intentions.
6 If you still feel good about it, go ahead and make the next version. This next cut is more defined, is smaller than the last and takes more time to compete. But at least you know that what you are doing is going in the right direction.

7 Leave it a week. In doing this, you are backing off from it emotionally, allowing you to make ruthless cuts if need be, and letting you see the film perhaps as others will see it eventually: objectively.

8 You still like the film. But beware of constant fiddling with the film, adding or taking away pieces as friends and crew see it and make suggestions, or new ideas hit you. The film won't survive as an artefact if you make it endure multiple rebirthing. Try to restrict your editing period to one specific term. After that, note down all new suggestions and ideas and make time for a reappraisal at some date.

Editing dos and don'ts

Say it economically

In narrative film, one of the purposes of a scene is to convey information. Your job is to show what a scene progresses in terms of the motivations of characters, events that have happened or any other detail needed to understand the plot. Your primary tools are the angle and movement of the camera, but how long do you allow to make sure that the audience have taken on board what is going on? The length of a cut is impossible to prescribe and the answer must contain the proviso that you may not want to hand the plot to the audience on a plate. Sophisticated audiences want to be made to work a little to uncover the goodies you are offering; films that demand something of you are often the more satisfying experience. As a starting point, however, close-ups will take up less screen time than log shots, for the reason that less information is contained in the former, more in the latter. The relative lengths of these will vary according to the pace and rhythm of your film, but you can decide in advance that a certain number of seconds becomes a benchmark.

To begin, you could start with the idea that for medium shots in an action sequence ask yourself to justify the length of a shot lasting beyond 3 or 4 seconds while dialogue will determine the length of cuts in other scenes, but even here you can break edits up into several shots, from varying viewpoints. However a scene is conveyed, whether it is oblique or straightforward, try to make the edit only as long as it needs to be to convey the necessary information, and this is equally true when that 'information' is more ambiguous or abstract. Cut away as soon as you can.

Tip However, editing length can be said to be cultural, with some traditions of filmmaking more likely to use longer shots and some shorter. In many countries, the impact of MTV, the music video and Hollywood action films has led to the speeding up of edits, as attention spans shorten, while European and Australasian film has felt more comfortable with the longer, stationary shot.

Show clearly what is happening

Unlike reading a book, the viewer will only get one take to ascertain what is happening in a scene. Although your aim is to edit economically, you also have to convey clearly what you want the audience to see. How much you want them to see is up to you: do you imply what is happening in a scene or describe unambiguously? As we will see later, montage is one way of opting out of this argument and making each shot quite plain and defined, but juxtaposing it with others, suggesting more layers of meaning than otherwise would be conveyed.

Use the close-up

As a starting point for describing action clearly, the close-up is the most useful tool. It draws the attention of the audience towards one aspect of an action and therefore tells them that this or that part of the scene is the most important to see. If you are in doubt about whether a part of a scene is prominent enough, use a close-up. Balance this with frequent medium and longer shots so that the audience can get their bearings as to where the action is and who is involved.

Each clip progresses the action

Equally important is the progression of the action. If a crucial part of the action is missed out or not given enough prominence, then a scene can be rendered meaningless. Take as an example a scene involving a chase through empty train carriages, with no dialogue. The aim of this scene is to show who is being chased, who is doing the chasing and what obstacles are going to get in their way. If we lose track of the information at any stage we lose interest in the film. The main instructive shots in this case are those that show the relative distances of the escapee and the chaser to each other and those showing how, for instance, the escapee jams a compartment door shut, opens a main door and climbs up to the roof. We need to see how the pursuer releases the door and finds the escape route. In fast action sequences, it will be crucial to make the delivery of information as punchy as possible. Therefore, in these shots, the close-up is going to be the most economical way to shoot, enabling us to see the essential part of the frame without having to scour the screen for it.

Go to: Chapter 5:3, 'Continuity', for more details of how to keep smooth continuity.

Don't use a shot just because it looks good

When you have invested time and money it is tempting, and inevitable, to become emotionally attached to it. You may start to enjoy the footage as individual bits, as great-looking scenes. You may also look at how well certain scenes go with pieces of music you have earmarked for the film. As any artist or writer will testify, being seduced by the work you are in the middle of constructing is a certain way to lose track of it.

Without doubt some scenes turn out to be better than expected and start to assume a more prominent role in a film, but this does not necessarily mean they take up more screen time. A scene on a beach with two characters is going to look even better when, unexpectedly for you, a great sunset appears from behind the clouds partly obscured by a flock of birds. All this does is to make that particular moment more memorable; it does not follow that you have to extend the duration of that cut. This should also apply to scenes that proved unexpectedly difficult to shoot, or cost more than you had planned.

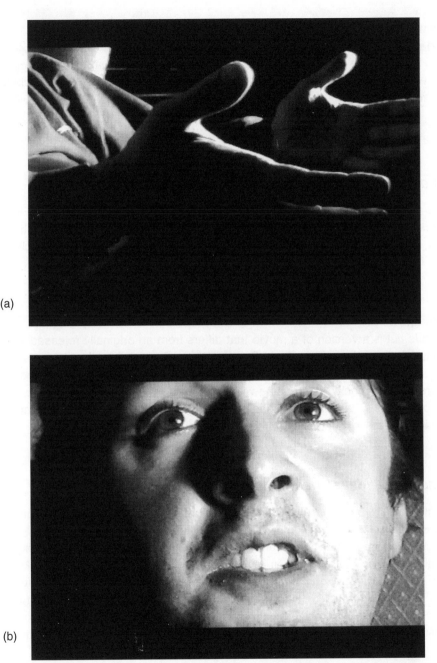

(a)

(b)

Figure 6.1 *Gabriel's Story* (2001) by Ed Spencer. This documentary centres on an interview which recounts the story of a car crash victim. Frequent cutaways to the interviewees' hands give a break from the main shot and add interest as we notice body language which sometimes contradicts the spoken words.

Interview

'A good editor will form the story using the best takes. He or she won't care that you waited 6 hours for the rain to stop, found 20 extras, paid a vast sum for the location, that the camera operator broke his shot getting a shot. The editor will look at it with objectivity and calmly say "so what?".'

John Wildgoose, filmmaker, UK

Make a director's cut if you can't decide what to edit out

If you have great shots but you know deep down that you really can't include the full glory of them, then go ahead and make a 'director's cut', knowing that this is an experiment. Reserve the cut-down version for exhibiting but retain what you have in the extended version. Noting which shots you consider to be better than others is crucial self-knowledge and will help you next time around.

Did you know?

A director's cut is a version of a movie that differs from an originally released version. One of the first examples was *Blade Runner*. Ridley Scott was under pressure prior to the film's release in 1982 to place a voice-over on the film to make the plot more transparent, and to include an ending which resolved the plot in an upbeat way. He did so, but in 1991, having established a strong position in Hollywood, released a new version without these elements.

Check how your ideas change during editing

Further to this, you may start to notice that the parts of a film which you really like are not ones you had first thought when preparing the film. If you have made an action film but find that you actually want to spend more time on the slower, more reflective sequences in between the action, then you have gained an important piece of information about what makes you different as a filmmaker. In truth, however, if you have a change of heart and try to turn one film in to something quite different *during* editing you are likely to come unstuck. You are likely to gain more from the process of completing a movie than you may lose in making one that is not quite what you wanted. So make your movie as you first intended but keep track of what you liked about those reluctantly discarded shots.

Keep rhythm

As we saw in the section on production, finding a rhythm for your film gives you an overall flavour, mood and pace, and enables you to modulate this rhythm according to the needs of the plot. Rhythm is one of the most important aspects of editing. Without it a film lacks any ability to evolve dramatically.

Arrive at the rhythm of your film in advance, looking at whether the film is to be fast-paced and action-oriented or slower and more contemplative. When compiling a scene, arrange the shots in order and start assembling them, noticing the relative duration of each clip. Assuming that you are trying to cut for continuity, notice peaks in the action or dialogue. Keep most of the shots surrounding these points at a similar length, but change when you come to these peaks.

Rhythm in the timeline

Use a timeline chart to work out the relative lengths of clips and try to establish some consistency in duration. Label the peaks and devise a different approach for those parts. In some ways, the rhythm of these detailed scenes – what we could call micro-rhythm – should mirror that of the film as a whole – macro-rhythm. In Kubrick's *The Shining*, individual scenes are edited with the same menacing, drawn-out consistency throughout. It takes a long, slow-moving pace towards the climactic action, like Frankenstein's monster, but it is this very consistency which makes it relentlessly tense. It is easy to crank up the action a gear when necessary, by shortening the length of cuts and increasing the frequency of cutaways.

Cut on movement

This means ending a cut while the subject or camera is still moving. It encourages the fluid transition to the next shot, sustaining continuity and flow, and is going to help maintain rhythm. In many of the points described here, the aim is to hide the mechanism of editing, to place the plot or theme at the fore in the viewer's attention and not draw attention to how the film is constructed. Often called 'continuity editing', this is the dominant mode in cinema. Part of the aim of covering your tracks as editor is to make the potentially jarring cut from one image to another as smooth as possible, and cutting on movement is one way to achieve this.

Don't plan too rigidly

Cutting together the shots for your movie has to involve, frequently, a certain amount of listening and watching. However well you have planned the film there will be changes and fluctuations as it passes through the hands of the people you are working with during shooting. Your own ideas may have altered and what was once the main theme in the film is now a sub-theme, or sub-plots may start to take more prominence. It is not uncommon for a director to continue changing a part of the script even as the previous one is being recorded. Viewing the daily takes give you a more objective view about how you are interpreting your material; it could remain very much as it appears in your plans or it could start to deviate. Be aware of these shifts in emphasis and don't reject them out of hand.

The need to remain with your plans and to see them through to fruition, no matter how tempting it is to deviate, is an important lesson but it is true that the film does not finish evolving at the planning stage. A film in its early planning stage is often a blurred, overall plan, without detail. The main themes, main events and outcomes are evident. But what we might miss at this stage are the ideas lurking in the background which might come to the fore during production. It is possible, of course, to prepare a film so thoroughly that every conceivable angle has been considered, but this degree of planning can sap the life out of a film at an early stage, and many filmmakers would argue that it is, in fact, desirable to make available some aspects of the film to be resolved during production and editing.

Allow, then, for alterations to occur when deciding how to edit. To put it in perspective, this will probably be more the shifting of priorities within the film rather than bringing in completely new concepts.

Edit in sympathy with the film

A key concept in editing is to be *appropriate*: that every aspect of a film must lead back to the aims set out by the director. Editing filters what goes into the film, so it is the most important opportunity you have to forge each aspect into a coherent whole. If you have, for example, a short, fast-paced action film, you would expect to edit using faster cuts. If parts of this network of filmic elements are out of sync to others then the film may fail, although, of course, there are times when out-of-sync is what you want, so even this is under the rule of appropriateness. Ensuring this is maintained throughout the film is achieved partly through having and retaining a strong vision of what its core ideas are.

Go to: Chapter 4:5, 'Visualizing a film', for more help with finding out what the core theme or idea of a movie is.

This fault was more common when the filmmaker was less in control of the final stages and needed to pass on editing to a third party, perhaps unconnected to the project until that point.

Film View
This occurs at all levels of the industry, a famous example being the editing of *The Magnificent Ambersons* (1942), after Orson Welles was obliged to hand the master print to the frustrated studio, RKO, and a probable masterpiece was ruthlessly cut to excise parts of the narrative, removing much of Welles' vision, and tacking on a false, sentimental ending.

The exceptions to this rule are the occasional necessary diversions (more often in feature films), such as sub-plots. But even here, the relative infrequency with which sub-elements appear will confirm the dominance of the main direction of the film.

Technical skill

As an artist you need to be a great technician in order to be in control of your film. Achieving this is down to practice. The more hours you have spent coming up against problems and overcoming them, the more you will be able to handle every task, manipulating your software and freely accomplishing your aims.

The Crunch

- Editing is good: you are in control once again.
- . . .But the wide range of options is tempting. Be decisive and sure-footed, rejecting ideas that seem to divert you from what you set out to do.
- Avoid editing too stylistically. Editing is subservient to your aims.
- Use rhythm to order your editing and take your cue from the overall rhythmic structure of the film.
- Become a technical master of your equipment or software; it stops you having to depend on someone who doesn't understand your film.
- Don't let your attachment to certain takes lead you to change your plans.
- Improvisation is OK.
- You won't always know what you are doing. Sometimes it is enough to say that a particular arrangement of shots 'just feels right'.
- Be aware that the arrangement of themes and ideas in the film may have shifted during filming. Edit according to what you have.

Project 13. Compressed movie

The aim of this project is to make a cut-down version of a sequence which holds the basic information of the original but conveys it at a fraction of the time. The purpose is to enable you to try out ruthless editing without being emotionally attached to the material, because you didn't shoot it. Within this, however, you still need to maintain a sense of the plot, but without the finer, subtler points of it. Show what happened, to whom, and when and where it takes place. This is not simply an exercise in draconian cutting – that would be a useless skill without first seeing what effect this has on a film.

We also need to understand the reverse – what happens when shots are extended and how one clip can change the whole emphasis of a scene simply by altering its duration.

Stage 1

To begin, select a movie to re-cut. Record something from television broadcasts. Any film will do, but an easier version of this project would involve an action film, with little plot or dialogue, while a more advanced would involve a film that places theme above plot. A sequence or film of about 10 minutes would be sufficient.

Tip   Copying movies is acceptable for your own educational use at home, but you will infringe copyright if you try to exhibit the cut-down movie in any form.

Stage 2

Next, view the film and pick out scenes which you feel are most relevant to the plot and the overall feel of the film, noting their placement in the film on the VCR time counter, and in so doing compile an edit log of the movie showing the lengths of each scene. The kind of scenes you will need will be a mixture of:

- crucial opening establishing shots showing where and when the action takes place;
- main characters;
- events which give these characters their motivation, such as the loss of the cash or the chance to escape their captors;
- ways in which the situation is resolved.

Try to avoid the kind of tricks used in film trailers, where only the flashiest, explosive or most impressive scenes are used; you are under no obligation to hide the plot ending or entice viewers to part with their money. Your task is to forge a new film that contains the same kind of information but which delivers it more economically. One of the first casualties of this exercise could be the more subtle sub-plots and sub-texts in the film, but even here skilful editing may enable these to be suggested.

Go to: Chapter 4:4, 'Script and structure', for more details about sub-text.

Stage 3

After you have chosen the relevant scenes, make an Edit Decision List (EDL) on paper, showing which shots you are going to use in the rough order they will appear. A more lengthy but interesting route is simply to choose the shots you are going to use in an intuitive way. This is going to result in several poor versions before you arrive at the final one. Practically, this method would involve the constant selection and discarding of shots until it is felt that the exercise is complete.

Stage 4

Edit the clips you have selected. At this point it may be useful to look at how you can convey the feel and mood of the film through the use of transitions, structure and pacing. One of the benefits of this project is the way it highlights structure; in taking the most significant elements from the film you start to notice the way the film has been constructed.

In *The Wizard of Oz*, for example, you would start to see how the tight structure of the film centres on the increasing number of characters meeting people on the yellow brick road and then breaking into song. This structure is within the bigger framework of the two black and white sequences that start and end the film.

Using transitions can help to define the film. Slow fades between each clip would suggest a thoughtful film, whereas straight, short cuts with no transition would suggest action. Equally, fading to and from black can suggest a mysterious, dark atmosphere to the film, as in *Seven* (David Fincher, 1995).

Your basic aim is to capture the story and retell it at a compressed, short-attention-span rate. If you manage to go beyond this and convey something of the mood of the film, then you are moving onto a more advance form of précis.

Evaluation

- Make a 2-minute movie showing as much as you can from the original.
- Use short cuts.
- Select only those images which are essential to understanding the film.
- Include an amount of material from the sub-plots in proportion to its presence in the full version, if you can fit it in.
- Suggest the overall mood of the film and maintain continuity by using a piece of music from the film as present throughout the cut-down version.
- Identify each important aspect of the film and try to see it represented. Develop characters in one shot rather than several scenes.

2. Preparing to edit

Although editing has been somewhat liberated by the arrival of the at-home, take-your-time desktop editing system, enabling the filmmaker to make infinite variations of a film, it pays to take some time before editing to consider how to go about it.

Edit log

The edit log is the first step to take. The aim is to identify and mark the clips on each tape that are satisfactory and make life easier by noting where to find them.

The log shown in Figure 6.2 contains four vertical columns. In the first vertical column note the timecode that the clip relates to. In the second column, note the tape on which this appears, if you are using more than one. In the third you may have a shorthand way of referring to each part of each scene, either describing a shot by name or numbering it. The last column gives a description of the shot, including notes on its quality.

Although we look at timecode elsewhere in more detail, there is a point worth noting here that affects your ability to use it in log sheets. Timecode exists as a continuous line of information, labelling each and every frame on your tape. If, however, you interrupt the tape, by pausing filming now and then, you may create a breakage in the timecode information and what you would see when playing it back would not be a continuous timecode but a series, with each new clip starting at zero. This is true of most domestic camcorders, but is easily overcome during shooting by coding the whole tape with timecode before you start filming, simply by recording continuously over the whole tape with the lens cap still on the camera.

Timecode	Format	Description	Notes
0:19:24	miniDV	Outside in garden. CU Rachel in foreground, Steve in background.	He pushes her head down
0:20:00		LS. Steve pushing Rachel's head down	
0:20:12		Raising spade from left	
0:20:32		Raising spade from right	
0:20:40		CU dropping spade	Rachel drops the spade
0:20:45		CU dropping spade	Closer than before
0:20:48		CU Steve's feet	
0:20:52		CU Steve's feet	
0:20:57		CU Rachel	Rachel raises her hand to her mouth, gasping
0:21:00		CU Rachel	Walks back
0:21:13		LS Rachel	Runs away from scene, Steve's feet not in shot
0:21:21		ECU Telephone	Very close shot of the handset
0:21:40		CU Keyboard	Hand comes into shot and types
0:21:56		CU Edge of keyboard	Focus throw
0:22:12		CU Keyboard	Letter 'D' in centre of shot
0:22:44		CU Keyboard	Letter 'E' in centre of shot
0:22:51		CU Keyboard	Letter 'E' in centre of shot, shadow pans across keyboard
0:23:07		CU Keyboard	Letter 'A' in centre
0:23:14		CU Keyboard	Letter 'T' in shot
0:23:19		CU Keyboard	Letter 'H' in shot
0:23:25		CU Keyboard	Card bounces up and down
0:23:34		CU Telephone card	Cord swings left to right
0:23:40		ECU Telephone	Shot of 'Redial' button
0:23:48		MCU Lamp	Turns on and off
0:24:12		CU Lamp	
0:24:17		MCU Rachel	In kitchen, Steve paces back and forth in background
0:24:23		MCU Rachel Take 2	Same as before
0:24:42		MCU Rachel Take 3	Same as before
0:24:50		LS Study door	Door opens, Steve walks through
0:24:56		LS Study door (Reverse angle)	Shot from Steve's point of view, he snatches the phone from Rachel
0:25:25		MCU Rachel	She knocks on the study door

Figure 6.2 Tape log for *Ghost Writer*.

Logging software

There are computer programs which are designed for logging tapes and which work along the same lines as those described above. The advantage of using a program is that you are then able to compile an Edit Decision List (EDL) by cutting and pasting each clip you want in the order you want, and if you have been able to label each clip with timecode then you have a fast and easy way of getting hold of those clips.[1]

Edit Decision List (EDL)

The EDL is one of the most useful tools for the editor. Although much is made of the need to edit intuitively so that you get to know how one clip affects the next and how your decision making changes throughout the editing process, it is important to be aware of the way most of the industry works. For today's editors, the EDL is a way of arranging the production as a set of plans for an editor to follow through later. Editing in this case is a technical operation rather than a stage in which possibilities can arise and changes made at any point.

If you are not using one of the many software programs for EDLs, it is equally effective simply to cut and paste the information for real on paper.

The paper edit

The paper edit consists of a series of notes laying out the basic order of clips for a movie. The paper edit is arranged using vertical columns to show the place where a particular clip is to be found in timecode on the footage tapes and the point at which it ends, followed by a short description of the clip, another column describing audio necessary for that clip or sequence and, finally, the length in seconds of this cut. It follows on from the 'edit log' in that the information you use for the paper edit is taken from the log you have made of each single take you shot on the footage tapes. In the paper edit you have simply extracted the good clips from the edit log and played with the order in which they occur.

There are many reasons for pausing a while and working some of the edit out in advance. It is never possible to predict exactly how the film will look after the final cut is in place, because you are presented with problems and choices all through this stage, each of which can affect the film in different ways. A more likely reason is that, although you may have a good idea of what kind of footage you've got, there is no telling how one clip looks when placed next to another. A 'paper edit' prepares you to make better choices and decisions and gives you a baseline point, a model from which you can deviate or remain with, but which gives you some idea of how close or far you are from the original plans.

---

[1] www.futurevideo.com/products.htm   Information on EDL software and hardware.

Practical uses

In practice – in the real world – the paper edit does not have to be an exact plan as such, but more a way of triggering off ideas about how to edit. If you go into the editing process blind, that is without any forethought about what kind of movie you are looking to create, you risk making a movie of pieces with no sense of the whole. In a way, the paper edit is like organizing the seating for a table of guests at a party; if you place certain people next to each other you can be sure that more interesting conversations or situations are likely to arise, none of which you can yet predict, but the overall arrangement will make it more possible.

Speeding up editing

If we go in to the paper edit in more detail, it becomes possible to save considerable amounts of time by working out the order of shots and the rough timecode points for each clip. You can then start to add up the clips and get some idea of the length of the film and choose whether to cut or alter the overall structure in some way. Trawling through the tapes seems like excessive work at first, but to demonstrate its usefulness, try 'editing' just a few minutes of footage on paper and then try trimming and editing the sequence for real using the paper edit; you may notice the speed with which you work now and the freedom it might give you to concentrate on the way the film is looking as a whole.

Alternative methods

Some editing software programs now include a feature allowing you to import a series of clips, arrange them quickly into an outline of the film and then export the whole plan onto the timeline. This is a useful alternative to the EDL, as it allows you to quickly move and arrange a film as a general plan, in big blocks, before going on to do a fine edit later. Since each clip is labelled beforehand and shows timecode, you don't lose any of the accuracy you might want with the traditional EDL.

The Crunch

- Make an edit log of all your shots.
- Use timecode to tell you where the best ones are.
- Make an EDL.
- Save time editing: do it on paper first.
- Plans always change, 100 per cent of the time, when editing for real.

3. Starting to work in digital editing

The more you understand about digital editing as a whole, the better you will be at seeing what it can offer you. Software designers do their best to make editing programs as versatile as possible, suiting every possible need, but if you look through the manuals that accompany these products, they are nevertheless aimed squarely at a large middle-ground of programme maker. They will not go out of their way to find the most creative uses of their products; it is for you to find what parts of their product suits you and what is superfluous. If everyone uses digital editing software in similar ways, the potential chances of the technology to broaden what filmmakers can achieve will be reversed.

It is useful to look at what kinds of technical issues you may have to deal with, what certain bits of jargon mean and, of course, how your needs can best be served. If you are new to digital editing, or editing in general, then this will also explain the kind of route you take in putting a movie together. But we will leave all the artistic ideas about what makes a good edit for another chapter. For now, let's get technical.[2]

Digital editing in six steps

Just about all software for digital editing involves the same basic chain of events. From the most elementary software that cuts and pastes your clips, to those with special effects and added features, the process is the same. Getting to understand this route from camera footage to finished film will give you the confidence to try out other software and will allow you to discover which kind of software is best for your needs.

1 Get hold of your raw footage. The tape will be played on either a camera or a VCR, depending on whether you are using analog or digital footage.
2 Choose the bits of footage you want to work with.
3 Get all your clips on to your hard drive.
4 Trim your clips to the right length.
5 Play around with the clips on the timeline or filmstrip.
6 Put the finished film back on to tape.

It's like shopping

To put it in context, you could compare it to a trip to a supermarket. Each stage can be described as part of the wonderful shopping experience that is the modern mall.

● When you get there, you choose what items you want (like stage 2 above).
● Put them in your basket (stage 3).
● Take them to the checkout and put some items back you don't now need (stage 4).
● Go home and cook something edible (stage 5).
● Serve (stage 6).

[2] www.digitalvideoediting.com   Resources and news on DV editing.
   www.wwug.com/forums/digital-video-editing/   Worldwide DV editors' forum.
   www.editorsnet.com/   Highly rated editors' site.
   www.postindustry.com/   Daily editing news.
   www.editorsguild.com/newsletter/   Professional newsletter.

The metaphor ends there, but experienced editors will have something to add, such as what happens when you change the recipe half way through cooking (editing), or what happens when you find you don't have enough ingredients.

Getting clips from tape to computer

As you know, there are only two types of information you are going to be working with: digital and analog. You can edit digitally with footage that is filmed in analog, first translating it into digital language – encoding. Digital tape is more straightforward and can be played directly into the computer, using a variety of different connections. The one you choose to work with is dependent on a whole range of factors, which we will look into in detail.

As for the actual device used for playing your footage, if you are working with digital tape you simply use the camera you shot it on to play the clips, although there are mini-DV players available at about the same price as the most basic, domestic camera. Using one of these would be useful only if you need to use your camera while someone else is editing, but it makes more sense to buy a second camera rather than a player.

About capture cards

With video still in its infancy among computer manufacturers, it is no surprise that some units make life easy for the filmmaker and some don't. Apple have stolen a march on most other manufacturers by including FireWire ports – the best way of hooking up a camera – as standard with all units, and now even bundle free movie-making and DVD burning software at consumer level.

But with most PCs the options are not sufficient to satisfy the quality and speed needed for filmmaking. This means you may have to invest in a few extras to get your PC connected adequately. A capture card is a small addition to the PC which enables video to be plugged in and 'captured' regardless of whether it is analog or digital. At its most basic it allows digital video to be connected to the PC or, higher up the cost scale, will encode analog in to digital, and beyond that may allow you to return digital films onto VHS in analog. Deciding which one you need depends on what your plans are for the movies you make, and how much you can invest, but the good news is that most now give you free editing software, whether it is the company's own unique software (usually a very basic package) or a copy of a leading program. For example, Dazzle (formerly Fast) produce the popular Fast DV.now range. The entry-level product DV.now go! provides a very basic cut-and-paste program, while the next level up, DV.now Lite, offers a version of the widely used Adobe Premiere, a program also offered on Pinnacle Systems' DV 500 and the Matrox RT2000.[3]

---

[3] www.dazzle.com/products/dvnow.html   Company site: capture cards at entry level and beyond.
www.matrox.com/   Company site.
www.adobe.com/products/premiere/6cards.html   Capture cards compatible with Adobe Premiere.
http://dvguide.sharbor.com/head-to-head/   Reviews of all major capture cards.
www.videoguys.com/vidcap.htm   Compare capture cards.
www.pinnaclesys.com/   Company site: Studio DV products popular with basic level editors.

Translate from analog

Although digital tape is the superior quality, you may occasionally have to work from VHS or S-VHS or another analog format. Even if you prefer to work from digital, it is useful to be aware of how to capture analog, because an overwhelming proportion of the world's video footage, such as business material and archives, is stored in this way for cost reasons. Somehow, you have to get the information on VHS tape translated into the digital language that the computer will understand and which will allow the film to be shown on the Internet or stored on CD or DVD. The capture card will translate your footage and hopefully not take too long about it.

Choosing the right capture card

This means choosing the right one for your particular needs, taking into account the type of film you might make and where and in what form you want to exhibit. Some of the most common options are:

- **Option 1**. Films for showing on the Internet or to be viewed on a PC, possibly also stored on CD or DVD.
  Choose this option if you intend to make and show your work on the Internet or keep only digital copies, on disc or digital tape. You will need a capture card that has an input port but no means of outputting the film back onto analog tape. These cards are cheaper than output/input cards but still have edit software bundled.
- **Option 2**. Films which can be shown on the Internet but also to possibly make VHS copies to show to potential agents or to enter in competitions.
  These cards have additional output ports for you to export the finished film back onto analog tape and are slightly more expensive. If you have ambitions for your work this is the better option, because the vast majority of agents, competition jurors and film buyers will watch your work on standard 12 mm VHS tape at home or at the office (but be prepared for requests for digital too). However, if you can only stretch your budget to a digital *output* card, you can make analog copies by connecting your digital camera directly into your VHS player.

Go to: Chapter 8:3 to see what festivals and competition juries need.

Did you know?
To connect the camera to a VCR, connect an S-Video cable to each and tune your VCR to an auxiliary channel.

Within these two types of card, there are further options regarding the kind of software you need and the way you compress the films down to fit on disc or tape.

Checklist: ask these questions before buying

● *Do you need to send the films to DVD-ROM or CD-ROM?*
  If yes, then you will need an MPEG–2 output, a way of compressing a movie so it is small enough to fit on disc.

Did you know?
MPEG is a standardized compression procedure for reducing the size of movie files.

● *What kind of processor do you need in your PC to run the capture card?*
  Check whether the speed of your PC is going to suit the card.
● *Has it got a FireWire port included?*
  There is no better solution to connect your camera to the PC.
● *Has it got a four-pin to six-pin adapter for FireWire?*
  You may encounter either size of FireWire, so an adapter is essential.
● *What kind of extras are bundled with it?*
  Many systems will offer you editing and music programs, CD authoring software or DVD authoring, but check whether you are getting reduced versions or trial-only full versions.
● *How much can I afford?*
  The most basic, entry-level cards are surprisingly inexpensive. Don't forget that the main reason you are buying the card is for the ports, not all the extras, and bundled editing software is rarely the full program. So, if you have to go for one of the cheapest, it will do the job as long as you get the right port.

Ports

Ports have their good and not-so-good points. Some of these you may have already in your computer, others you will get as part of a capture card.

FireWire

This versatile and fast link is a brand name devised by its inventors, Apple Computers, and is also known as iLink (mostly on Sony machines, with which it is popular). The standard name is IEEE 1394, the letters referring to the Institute of Electrical Electronic Engineers, the numbers to the 13th patent in 1994. It has grown in popularity rapidly in the last few years, but when it was first introduced to the market its power was seen as excessive. It was rare to own a desktop editing system and the digital video revolution was yet to take off. But its attraction was evident: you could, for the first time at consumer level, reliably receive information at a high rate using a very small and discreet plug. It uses either four- or six-pin ends, Sony preferring the former, Apple the latter, but you may come across either in any system. Adapters are available for connecting one to the other.[4]

---

[4] www.apple.com/firewire/   Apple information site.
   www.dtvgroup.com/DigVideo/FireWire/Adaptec/1394work.html   Detail on FireWire.
   www.xyznyc.com/   Site devoted to FireWire and other DV peripherals.

FireWire is about four times faster than USB, transferring information at a breezy 400 MB per second. The net result for the filmmaker is that, with a FireWire port, even the cheapest, most basic or free bundled software, like Apple's iMovie or Microsoft's Movie Maker, will produce better quality movies than more expensive software using USB. If you have invested in a good quality digital camcorder, it would make no sense to then use a port which loses some of that quality in transferring onto the computer. FireWire should be used if you are keen to maintain technical standards in your movie.

Tip There has been a growth in the range of basic editing software and some manufacturers now bundle a limited program of some sort. Apple's iMovie offers many more features than other comparable give-away programs, while Microsoft's Movie Maker is also a good option, allowing movies to be made in a basic, no-frills way.

USB (Universal Serial Bus)

The USB is flourishing in the domestic PC market because it is a cheaper alternative to FireWire and serves the needs of the videomaker doing home movies of weddings, parties or UFOs. It is hard to criticize this port because it has helped broaden the home video market by making it possible for cheap PCs to capture video, therefore encouraging software manufacturers to cater for this market. It is also ideal for small businesses aiming to show short commercial movies on the web, where perhaps picture quality is not an issue. USB is great for capturing video quickly, but only at the expense of full screen capture and smooth frame rate.[5]

It transfers information at a relatively slow rate of 800 KB per second to 100 MB per second. This will knock the screen size on your PC monitor down to about 2 or 3 inches square, with the implication that if you later want to stretch the image to fill a full-size television screen or to project the movie, you will be struck by a heart-sinking loss of quality. The standard screen size for UK (PAL system), for instance, is 720×586 pixels, but USB prefers to work with a screen around 320×240, roughly half the size, and works more smoothly the smaller it gets. You can try to alter this by enlarging the picture while cutting the number of frames per second from the maximum (25 in the UK, 30 in the USA) by half, but you have to be prepared to put up with the consequent loss in smoothness.

S-Video (Y/C)

This is used in many consumer analog VCRs and in some capture cards. Most output capture cards use S-Video as their analog output socket. Quality is greater than that offered by analog composite signals and digital USB, but less than FireWire. The wide use of this port in VCRs and cameras makes it a useful addition to a capture card that incorporates it.

---

[5] www.usb.org/   Site dedicated to USB news.

> **Did you know?**
> S-Video is known as Y/C because colour and brightness data are transmitted separately, Y meaning luminance and C chrominance.

Capturing video onto the computer

Once you are connected using a capture card, you can gather the clips you need to start assembling a movie. Capturing clips does not have to be a precise process; you really don't have to be concerned about how much you select. The aim here is to grab what you think you might use plus a little more, leaving the decision making about the precise length of a clip until later.

What to capture

There are different approaches to capturing. You may capture according to an Edit Decision List (EDL), where you will have clearly thought out in advance the shots you want and will have noted where you can find these on the footage tapes. Any larger production is going to benefit from this approach to some extent, simply because of the sheer quantity of material you need to trawl through to get to the useful takes.

Capture loosely

Alternatively, you may prefer to capture in a more intuitive way, gathering the footage you may or may not want to use as you go through the tapes, having first viewed them several times to build up an idea of what sort of film you are building. The advantage of this second method is that, while capturing the basic clips you need to edit the film with, you can also gather footage which may add spontaneity to the film. A more likely scenario is to use both approaches, staying to a well-documented path but allowing considerable room for spur-of-the-moment acquisitions; allow room for the film to grow and develop. Do not be too precise about capturing; if a clip looks useful, grab it. You can always bin it later.

How much to capture

When capturing clips, you need to know how much your PC can handle according to the amount of RAM memory and size of hard drive. As a starting point, you should have at least 128 MB RAM available, but double or triple this is going to make editing much easier. If you are working with the absolute minimum of memory, you can maximize space by splitting up a movie into smaller chunks, working on each part separately and storing digitally. If space allows, you may then be able to capture each section individually and piece them together as one movie later, using the space freed up by dumping all the clips you used for each section. But no solution beats getting a more spacious PC.

Systems and hard drives

Whatever computer you have, it is going to become too small for you at some point. Unless you remain working with films lasting 5 minutes, the internal size of the PC, what it can handle in terms of data, will start to strain under the weight of your movies.

- Get the fastest processor you can.
- Get the most memory you can, bearing in mind that some programs require at least 128 MB just to get up in the morning.
- Add extra hard drive space to that existing on your PC. You are going to need about 30 GB to make short films easily, moving up to 150 GB to make longer movies, allowing you to cope with most situations. Work on the basis of 1 GB taking up about a minute of video, allowing the same or more on top of that for footage stored on the hard drive while you edit.
- Use your PC for editing and nothing else, freeing up space used by other programs.

Tip Final Cut Pro needs 128 MB to operate, while Adobe Premiere needs 64 MB to run but 128 MB to run efficiently.

Interview
'If one's editing equipment budget is really so low I would suggest just borrowing a system for a while to get used to it before considering purchase.'

David G. Hill, filmmaker

Tips for better capturing

- When capturing, try to break a clip down into small chunks, provided you cut at the end of a take. Avoid capturing one long clip consisting of several takes, as it is easier to work with if you name each separately.
- When you save your clips, name them as descriptively as possible, as this is the title that appears on the timeline and project bin. For instance, rather than calling a shot 'Steps, take 21', call it 'Steps – best take with good audio, 21'.
- If using a mid-range program, you have the option to alter capture settings. Since you will be doing a top quality edit you need to use settings that maximize the equipment you have, capturing audio and video at the optimum rate. This is sometimes referred to as the 'on-line' edit.
- Some programs tell you if they drop any frames while capturing and give you the option to abort if this happens (get used to it, dropped frames is common with some programs), but if this gets to be too frequent, try switching off the 'Abort on Dropped Frames' command, as captured video often drops the very first frame. If you have dropped only one frame, the capture was successful.

Did you know?
On-line editing refers to the practice of editing with the highest level of quality that the computer can handle. This is probably going to become your default method for editing. Off-line editing referred to a stage where shots were compiled in the correct order but not in their final form. In practice, DV editing goes straight to the on-line edit.

Files and saving

As soon as you start to capture, you need to start putting them somewhere that is easily accessible. Create a folder to contain all your clips, placed in the main drive, rather than within the software folder itself (which is often the default place it suggests you save it). Within this, always save your clips into separate folders with, for instance, titles in one folder, establishing shots in another, master shots in another and so on. It is very easy to mislay files given the number you are going to create with each movie, and the ability to wade through files quickly to get to the one you want is paramount.

Storing clips as you edit

There are storage implications if you intend to capture all the clips for the whole film at the start of editing. While there is an advantage to this in that you can have immediate access to all your clips at the same time, if you work on a film longer than the average short (5 minutes or more), you will certainly need to have clips saved on something other than the hard drive to make room for the film itself as it grows.

Although the best option is to get more space by adding an external drive or upgrading the internal drive, the least expensive method is to store your clips on CD. If you have a CD writer you can 'burn' clips onto CDs and delete them from the desktop, inserting the right one when you need it. Note, though, that if you choose this method, you may find that the PC does not like having to trawl through the CD to find each clip. If the PC does seem to be performing more slowly than usual, make copies of the clips you want onto the desktop and eject the CD. This should make the files easier to find, but remember to delete these when you want to insert this, or another, CD again.

You can also store clips on digital tape, but this rather defeats the object as you then have to upload them onto the hard drive by capturing them each time you want to access them. If, however, you have captured from poorer quality analog tape, then this method has some value. For digital tapes, you may want to store on tape if you have had to trawl through hours of footage to get a bunch of clips to use later, making them easier to find and work with during editing. This process is similar to the off-line edit.

Importing your clips

The next step is to get the clips up onto the desktop, ready for use. In some basic software, this is called 'Get Clip', but more commonly 'import'. Look for your clips, which should be arranged in easy-to-find folders. Once you have imported the clips, they will appear as a list with some information about the length and date of creation. You can be selective at this point, choosing only those files you want to use right now. At the end of this stage you are ready to start building the film.

Trimming your clips

This part of the process is where you start making creative decisions. You are deciding which parts of each clip you want to use and whether you need to split them up further into smaller clips. The clips you captured to start with are rough around the edges and need refining before they can be used in the film. Trimming is an exact art. The tools for this are precise to the frame and, provided you can access the original again and again, you can try out several versions of clip if you are unsure of how to construct a sequence.

The obvious question here is why don't you trim them earlier when capturing? Why import a larger file only to cut it down now? The answer is that you need to try to focus all editing decisions into one

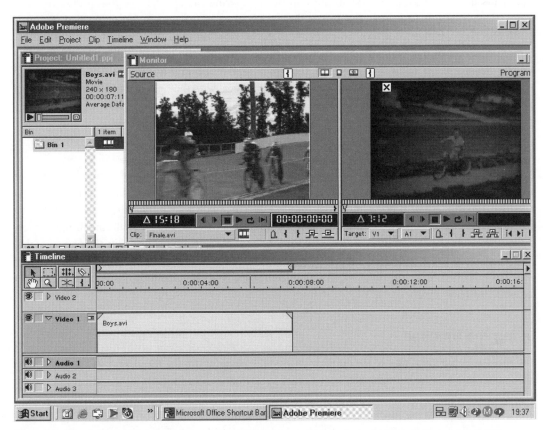

Figure 6.3 In Adobe Premier, as in most edit programs, three windows are used: a project bin containing clips, a monitor window for trimming and a timeline.

stage of post-production. Editing is a creative process which requires you to see treat the film as a whole; all decisions, such as the nature of the cuts and the order they appear, are creative and need to be undertaken in one process.

How much to trim

Choosing how long a clip will be depends on a number of factors and is influenced as much by the previous trim as by the look of all the clips on the timeline. You need to evolve a rhythm and energy to the film when editing, and to do this you should cast your net wide early in the process and focus on the look of the film now. It can upset your momentum if you find you have too few clips and have to go looking for them in the middle of an edit session.

Experiment in trimming

Trimming is similar to part of the old analog editing process and is devised as such to appeal to editors schooled in the old ways. The basic idea is to select 'in' points and 'out' points to denote the start and end of the new cut within the clip. In most software, altering the clip allows you to drag the new revised length onto the timeline, but leaves the master copy in the project bin untouched. But it is worth checking whether your own program alters the original, as does Windows Movie Maker. This is more common in free edit software, including those bundled with hardware. Clearly, this is not a popular feature as it takes away one of the great aspects of non-linear editing: the ability to experiment, for you to see first and make up your mind later, with the option to return to the original if you don't like what you see.

Look at other clips when trimming

One of the basic tenets of editing is that it is all about how one clip looks next to another, not how each looks in isolation. As we saw in some of the projects, clips change dramatically when placed next to others. Editing should become an organic process during which a film gradually emerges, in which decisions about each part of the film are made with reference to the whole. With this in mind, view the last few clips you just trimmed before you trim the next one and, if you can, view the one you think you are going to use immediately after it. In practice, this means looking at the effect of each clip on what has gone before, by playing sections completed so far, but allowing these sections to alter under the effect of later clips.

Using the timeline

The timeline is a central part of the editing process, the place where the film sits; it is assembled and is common to all software, though it is sometimes referred to as a filmstrip or storyline.

It is usually placed at the foot of the screen, a horizontal track running left to right displaying video and audio, looking like train carriages placed end to end on a rail track. The timeline is one of the most important windows in DV editing and it is worth taking the time to get to know what yours can do.

Software varies greatly here, with low-end units offering just one track for you to build a film on, others offering the opportunity to layer text and images in tracks of up to 99.

> **Tip** Having to operate on just a few tracks can severely limit the creativity of what you can achieve, but you can try outputting a sequence with two layers, then recapture and import it as a single clip so that it takes up only one layer. Then you can layer again and repeat the process, with no loss of quality provided you store the clip on DV tape or CD.

A–B tracks on the timeline

Another principle seen in software in the mid-range level is the twin, A–B track. Yet another aspect which will be a familiar feature to those who have worked with linear editing systems, this operates by allowing a film to be built across two tracks, track 1A and track 1B. This lets you place two clips together but choose how 'A' runs into 'B' (known as the AB roll) using perhaps a cross dissolve, a page tear or a simple wipe. Don't worry if your package does not offer this – great films are the sum of their images and the structure that binds them; if people notice your great AB rolls then the film may have little else going for it.

The method you select from the menu to roll from 'A' to 'B' is called a transition. A clip placed in track A will have a transition placed between it and the next clip, where the two overlap.

Play with the timeline

Part of the whole point of non-linear editing is that you can make the film in any order you like, starting in the middle and working outwards, or laying out the basic clips and returning to work on a particular section later, and the timeline becomes the main arena for this. Unlike linear editing, you now have a tool for experimenting, for trying out new ideas about how the film can look. Using the timeline as a creative, intuitive tool enables you to use it to its full potential; it is a place of play and trial and error, and no matter how detailed your plans are for editing, you cannot foresee the exact effect of one clip placed next to another until you see it played on the monitor. Be prepared to change your plans, using the timeline as the place to explore the possibilities presented by each clip.

The implications for this, of course, are that editing can potentially be a never-ending process, with endless variations and versions. Try to be aware of the danger of stirring the pot too much, of refining the life out of the movie. Give yourself a deadline for completing it, perhaps by setting up a first showing for other filmmakers or friends. The objective insights gained by looking at how other people view your film can be invaluable and at least give a solid reason to re-edit if you choose to do so.

Audio

Once the film has been assembled, you can begin to think about audio tracks. The advantage of non-linear editing is that you can see the audio clips and can link sound to vision more easily and more logically than on linear. Some of the lower-end software titles do not allow you to separate sound from vision or add music, but just about all in the middle lower upwards allow this.

The options for gathering sound are as follows:

- importing music from CD or another digital source onto the timeline;
- using audio from elsewhere in the film;
- using modified sound, created using one of the many sound packages available;
- using sound recorded yourself on a mini-disc player or other digital recorder.

If you have gathered the right audio tracks during filming, this process should present few surprises. The best option is to use sound which you have recorded rather than sampled from other sources. Taking sound from other sources stops you from having control over this most important of elements, and in any case, copyright implications should steer you away from it. However, if you don't want to record original sound effects yourself, there are some very good programs, some available as free downloads on the Internet, enabling you to generate sounds. Copyright-free CDs are also available, including a wide variety of sound effects. Be aware, though, that these often sound 'canned' or unreal. Natural sounds you have recorded will give your film added realism.[6]

If you are working on a music video (check you have a license from the copyright owner to use the track), you may find it easier to place the audio track on the timeline first and then add images later. This enables you to match images and sound correctly, with correct timing.

Rendering

Once the film is completed on the timeline, it needs to be assembled as one file. This process is called 'rendering' or building, or in some programs is called simply 'make movie'. Rendering takes time and is lengthened if your film has added filters (effects), titles or other layers and transitions, in fact anything other than straight clips.

Mid-range programs will allow you to render as you work through a film, saving you from the trouble of having to re-render the whole film just because you changed a part in the middle. In general, it is better to render in parts as you go, partly for time reasons and definitely if your package is not a real-time editing tool. Rendering is the only way to test the effect of filters, layers or transition; the movie won't play them until they are rendered. However, if you have a fast, powerful workstation then you will expect to render in a time that does not disrupt your evening – in the early days of DV editing,

---

[6] www.anvilstudio.com/   Free program for simple music composing.
www.threechords.com/hammerhead/   Free program for rhythm and drums.

rendering was an overnight job. With up-to-date processor speeds and an average or small memory space of 128 MB, you would expect short films to render during a coffee break, or two coffees if using 64 MB. RAM of 256 or 512 MB is ideal and will release the potential of your software more fully.

Output to tape

Once the film has been assembled in its final completed form, you will need to produce 'hard copies', digitally stored copies so that you can re-edit the film if necessary and VHS ones for viewing, as it is very useful to be able to see a movie's progress after each session. Seeing it projected or on a television screen enables you to get an opinion of the film as a whole and check that it is going in the direction you want, preparing you for the next edit session. It is therefore useful to be able to output the film occasionally as an analog VHS copy. It is also essential to have a hard copy of your film should anything go wrong with the computer during post-production. Output each new version onto something real: tape, CD or DVD.

Output options

Output to analog tape
Connect your PC to a VCR or camera and follow the instructions on your software to 'export' the movie to tape. If your capture card does not allow you to export directly to analog, you can still make VHS copies by connecting your digital camera to an analog VCR and setting the VCR to record while the camera plays.

Output to CD
If you have a CD writer, this is a good option, given the longevity of the format, but is limited by the size of the disc. Typically, a 650 MB CD will hold only a short film. Don't be tempted to compress the movie for storage; master copies should always be at the full frame and full pixel rate. If you really have to use CD and no other method is available but your movie is too big for the CD, store sections of the movie on successive discs.

Output to DVD
DVD, on the other hand, is a whole different story, but these are creeping into the marketplace only slowly, except for Apple, who are making a feature of the Mac's DVD-writing capability and have some excellent software bundled with new units. Films compressed using MPEG–2, the method used for DVDs, will retain excellent quality and can be reworked repeatedly, while the huge quantities that can be held – feature films plus additional material – make this by far the better storage option.

Output to digital tape
Once you have wired up your camera to the PC it is easy enough to be able to reverse the flow of information and get the finished film back onto the camera. Again, FireWire is the quickest and safest method at the moment.

Output to the web

If you have completed a film and wish to send it to a third party via the web or show it as part of a website, you can output to the web very easily. Most programs, including entry-level ones, have evolved greatly in this respect and allow a film to be saved in compressed form ready for viewing.[7]

Real-time editing

What's wrong with DV editing?

One of the drawbacks in digital editing is the need to render before you can see how a clip looks. If you have added a filter or changed the clip in any way you need to have a look at it before you continue, and most editing systems insist you render the film or that part of it you want to see. If you have a fast computer this is not too much trouble, but even the fastest consumer model will drag its feet at having to render more than one layer of video or altering a video track. Real-time editing is popular with many people because it does away with rendering. Clearly, this is one of the most useful tools for an editor as the savings in time are dramatic, even if the cost of these systems is higher.

Overall production costs could be lower in real-time editing, but only if you feel that your time needs to be quantified in money terms, something which most small-scale, low-budget filmmakers know is not a possibility. If you are paying for editing sessions, real-time is a bonus and will save you money; if you are not it won't and will only make a qualitative difference to the way you work, making life more comfortable during those long hours assembling the film. Real-time only really starts to earn its worth if your film uses extensive layers, filters or dissolves. A film made with mostly straight cuts and with clips unaltered – as most are – will not see much gain from the higher price of these systems.

Variations in systems

Real-time systems are all slightly different. Total real-time is something you have to pay dearly for and many units offer only a limited amount of real-time. On some units, real-time previews are available, but you have to render the whole film before you output onto a digital format (but may offer real-time output to analog). With others you cannot use real-time on filters or colour correction – you have to render them like any other program.

Most of the main capture cards offering real-time features do enough to live up to their name, but look first before you buy, and get some idea of what your own needs are before choosing. In general

---

[7] rec.arts.movies.production   Newsgroup on editing matters.
www.postforum.com/   Editing resources for Macs only.
www.ace-filmeditors.org/   American Cinema Editors homepage.
www.imperica.com/sofia/editing/index.html   Articles on continuity (Hollywood) editing.
http://members.optusnet.com.au/~matthewt/index.htm   Australian screen editors forum.
www.theeditcenter.com/   General editing site.

though, look for the tools you use the most: colour correction, titles, filters and transitions, and check that it outputs to digital – preferably to MPEG–2 – in real-time.[8]

The Crunch

- Digital editing is easy.
- Get the right capture card for your needs; don't overspend.
- Any edit program will do; it's what you do with it that matters, not the range of special effects it has.
- Use the fastest, most efficient port you can (FireWire).
- Try to get the largest hard drive and RAM within your budget.
- Make full use of DV's non-linear approach – edit in any order you like.
- Get to know your software and your system.
- Play, play, play. Experiment and try out anything with your software, whether it is in the manual or not.
- To improve your skills, try teaching someone else how to edit. It will reveal any gaps in your knowledge and, in any case, other people ask questions you haven't thought of.

4. Sound in editing

What does good audio do?

Audio is one of the areas of making a film that is often the last to be resolved. Since the nature of filmmaking is primarily a visual medium, it is often seen that music and sound are there to prop up the images; by the time shooting has finished and you view the footage tapes, it is not easy to consider that there is a further element which can radically alter the effect of the carefully won visuals. Too often, sound is an element that threatens to disrupt the edit-in-progress, but it is the path of least resistance simply to place a soundtrack that adds nothing new to the experience. Digital editing allows much greater creativity and control over audio than ever before, but few filmmakers take full advantage of its tools. The aim of this section is to encourage the use of sound as a central part of a film.

Compensating for low budgets

Sounds fulfil several roles in a film, beyond simply emanating from what is occurring on screen. One of the most useful for the micro-budget filmmaker is the capacity of sound to convince the viewer that more is present than we can see, suggesting a wider world outside of the frame. Cheap sets can be made to seem more realistic, small crowds of extras more populous and action scenes more dynamic, all by using more creative sound. The restrictions of your budget do not necessarily need to be reflected on screen.

---

[8] www.apple.com/finalcutpro/editing.html   Final Cut Pro information.
www.pinnaclesys.com   Real-time editing systems.

Helping continuity

In post-production, sound can be a way of rescuing a scene if unforeseen problems have occurred. A scene can be given a better sense of continuity and flow if a single audio track covers and links shots, acting as an ambient presence throughout. Jarring cuts can be made smoother by covering both with the same sound. Furthermore, a soundtrack can offer stability and continuity so that more abstract visual sequences are sustainable. Whatever the visuals look like when you have finished a rough edit, if you feel that they are not quite as exciting as you had planned, sound can start to turn them into something approaching a full cinematic experience. For the low-budget filmmaker, sound is one way of adding invisible dollars/pounds/pesetas to the value of a scene.

Editing programs and sound

In many edit software programs audio is not given a high priority, but in the mid-range this improves and the timeline is arranged so that you can work with audio and visual tracks simultaneously. Basic 'cut-and-paste' programs do not always allow the separation of sound from image, although most will allow sound from other sources such as CD. Creative filmmaking is only really possible in one of the more versatile programs. In Adobe Premiere, for example, many audio tracks can be added (up to 99) to bring complexity and depth to the soundtrack. You won't necessarily ever need to use all these, or even a fraction of them, but at least five could be used on a regular basis.

Building a soundtrack

Layers of sound

Building a soundtrack is going to be something that evolves over successive edits. The basic tracks linked to dialogue or essential sound effects will be placed early on in the process, but other layers could consist of a multitude of extras that add, paradoxically, a more natural sound to the film. In the earlier chapter on production sound, we saw how sound is dissected and recorded in layers so that it can be manipulated later. That 'later' is now and you may now start to see the value of having each part of the soundtrack on separate parts of a tape. Even simple scenes require several layers of sound to replicate the natural feel of real live sound. This illusion is necessary because in real life we are bombarded with many sounds constantly and our brain focuses only on what we think is important: dialogue when talking with friends, the sound of the underground train when waiting at a stop or the sound of a baby's cry to a parent. The way we layer sound mimics the way we order and make sense of the mess we hear. Your main tool is the relative volumes of each of the tracks in the scene.

As an example, we could take apart a sequence in which a figure is entering a room in expectation of finding a crime scene. In this, it is essential that a certain atmosphere is carefully built up, perhaps a feeling of apprehension, fear or anxiety. The actors have done their part, you lit the scene as well as you could and the camera framing is just right. But when played silently, the scene is rendered almost harmless. The way you layer the sounds that relate to each part of the scene will form the basis of how the audience views that scene. So, a list of the kinds of sounds that would be needed would include the main 'diagetic' sounds – the ones that are created from action within the scene as opposed to musical soundtrack or other invented sounds – and the range of sounds that you think generate the kind of atmosphere you are trying to evoke. It is this second part that is the most interesting to play around with.

Add atmosphere

The kind of sounds you could play with could include some extra effects to suggest the exterior atmosphere, outside the room or apartment building. Sounds of rain and wind, of sirens, car horns or other residents arguing in the block could all help create a sense of something wrong. Discordant sounds could be brought to the fore, such as the buzzing of a faulty neon light. In practice, this soundtrack could be composed of several separate sounds, most of which were not present on location when shooting and some of which were created electronically. For Hitchcock's *The Birds* (1963), renowned film score composer Bernard Herrman was hired to create bird sounds; no music was present in the film. Herrman used early electronic sound technology – quite unnatural in its effect – to accompany the bird attacks, preferring this to the sounds of real birds screeching. In this case, realism was not going to produce the sounds likely to correspond to our idea of what such an attack would sound like in emotional, subjective terms. And it is that point that tells us most about sound effects in film, that layers of sounds can be used to evoke the *sensation* of what it would be like to experience the action on screen.[9]

Film View
As a further example, listen to the careful use of silence during the initial beach landings in *Saving Private Ryan* (Steven Spielberg, 1998), which captures the bewildering sense of shock felt by the soldiers.

Prioritizing soundtracks

In every film it is necessary to consider which sounds are made most clear to the audience and which are less distinct. It is something which needs consideration before you start editing, as it needs to be consistent throughout. It can easily be described and arranged on paper, and these notes can be directly translated into what appears on the timeline when editing. When recording sound it is most useful to have recorded each element of the scene separately so that they can be given relative value later in terms of volume.

To see this in action, we could use a scene in which two actors are talking in a bar, with noisy customers and the television permanently switched on in the corner. Later in the scene, another character enters the bar. If one microphone was used in recording the action, the result would be a mess in which everything is heard but nothing understood. The correct way would be to mic up the

[9] www.geocities.com/Hollywood/Academy/4394/sync.htm   Good article on post-production sound.

actors, record presence or ambient sound, record the television and exaggerate the sound of the door opening. There would be a strict order of importance in arranging these sounds later, based on the effect the director wants to create. It is likely that we need to hear the dialogue, so that would be placed as optimum volume. Second billing would be mood music accompanying the scene, also heard over the din of the crowded bar, with ambient sound third. Sudden necessary sounds such as the door opening would be brought unnaturally to the front to signal their importance.

Go to: Chapter 5:7 for more details about recording sound on location.

Foreground and background

Throughout this process you are thinking in terms of foreground and background, with shades in between. Prioritizing sounds in this way makes editing far more straightforward, avoiding the chances of sounds pulling in opposite directions to the images, or sending out false messages to the audience. As an example of poor layering order, a scene in which two people are talking at the same bar could be disrupted by the sudden loud sound of an off-screen door being opened. As viewers, our response is to presume that this is significant and start to look for who has entered the room, but placed at a less noticeable volume it would be more natural to the setting.

Make it natural – *artificially*

This last point is crucial: that sounds must conform to what *seems* natural (in other words, what conforms to what we feel the sounds of the bar should be), not what *is* natural (in other words, sounds recorded by a mic placed randomly in an actual bar). Natural sounds appear artificial, but artificial sounds appear natural. On the other hand, the filmmakers group Dogme would argue that it is only our dependence how we expect sound to be heard in films that makes us feel one way is better than another. Dogme filmmakers use no ambient tracks, foley or other effects, relying solely on what was present in one track in the actual location at the time of shooting; sound and image are not separated. Initially, watching a Dogme film can be a jarring experience, but after adjusting to their methods, the viewer's involvement in the film is not at all diminished.

Getting to know audio – key terms

ADR

This stands for automatic dialogue replacement and is something you will hopefully avoid, but if audio for a scene is below standard you may need to re-record dialogue later and replace the existing track. This is more common when you are limited in the equipment you can use and cannot always record to the desired quality. For example, an actor performing lines near busy traffic needs a particular microphone that picks up only the voice, not the background sound. If it is a choice on set between shooting it with poor sound and overdubbing later or not to shoot at all, it is worthwhile doing the former. Make sure, however, that you have the agreement of your actors to return for post-production work if necessary.

The process involves speaking the problem lines again in a recording studio while watching the accompanying footage. The actor tries to synchronize the words to match. Most actors don't mind doing this, but some filmmakers remark that when you do this the emphasis is always on getting it in sync and not about getting the best performance, and the film suffers as a result.

Film View
At the start of his career, Stanley Kubrick shot a whole movie, *Killer's Kiss* (1955), without sound and then dubbed the entire soundtrack, including speaking parts and effects later. The movie is also startling for its high-contrast black and white photography and unnerving dream sequences. The making of this movie inspired Matthew Chapman to make *Strangers Kiss* in 1983 as a fictionalized account of the production.

Ambient sound

Also known as 'presence', this is crucial to providing a sense of continuity between cuts in a particular scene. It is nothing more than a quiet background track that acts as a kind of umbrella, smoothing the edges of editing and seeming to blur the boundaries between each cut. In first movies, this is one of the most common mistakes, possibly because it is such an easily overlooked, insignificant part of production and yet has the potential to create serious continuity problems, drawing attention to every cut.

When you shoot in a room or other location there is a constant sound reflecting the environment, a collection of sounds unique to a place. Each time you move the camera and microphone position for different shots, the ambient sound will change slightly. If you then edit these shots together with 'straight cuts', those sound differences will become very apparent. Unless a film is particularly poor, you should not notice an ambient track.

Another type of ambience is that which is designed to create an acoustic space for a scene. It is possible to add sound effects which blend together to suggest a certain kind of atmosphere in a place. For example, in Ridley Scott's *Blade Runner* (1982), Scott managed to create the sense of a city crowded and polluted with dense layers of sound. The restrictions of his budget did not affect his ability (or rather that of the sound designer) to suggest scale and density of population. Seventeen years later, *The Fifth Element* (1999) would employ every visual trick to emulate this kind of city, but still does not seem to match the claustrophobic effect of Scott's film.

To add presence tracks, record a few minutes of background sound for every scene while on location and loop this on the film later, at a constant volume. If you are filming an interior scene, simply empty the room and hold the mic steady, pointing at nothing in particular, but not too close to anything giving off sounds which could distort the overall track, such as computer fans or air conditioning. When doing this don't fall into the trap of recording it quietly, in other words, down on the decibel register. If you have a digital recording device, such as mini-disc, you will be able to alter the level at which you record, but you may have to use the camera itself for these sounds, and most mid-range or consumer-level cameras record on an automatic level. As with everything, record as high as you can go – usually 8 dB or zero on a meter. Reduce the volume in the editing stage later. For a more professional feel, record two presence tracks to add depth and to aid in creating a transition between two clips.

Sound perspective (direct sound and reflected sound)

This idea relates to ambient sound in that it concerns the way sound reacts to a given environment (although the term 'direct sound' is confusing as the original production sound is also known by the same name). The terms refer to those sounds coming straight from the source itself – hence direct sound – and those which are reflected by surfaces on their way towards the mic. We usually hear direct sound when the camera is in close-up. We may see a face near to the camera and expect to hear it as if we were standing close to the figure in place of the camera, because the sounds are hitting our ears – the mic – before they hit the walls or the floors or any other reflecting surface. If you record sound for such a scene you would use a mic that picked up only the foreground voice, right in front of the mic (use a directional mic or lavalier).

With reflected sound, you help to create a sense of the place in which the actor is speaking by recording the way the words bounce around the room. Hard surfaces such as stone, tiling or glass produce a strong reflection as they bounce the sound back, whereas soft surfaces such as upholstery and curtains will absorb sound waves, thereby deadening the sound. Recording this sort of sound is difficult as various surfaces at various distances from the subject reflect in different ways but, if recorded correctly, the effect of using this kind of spatial awareness in sound can add a real sense of three-dimensionality to a scene. Greater naturalism is obtained by recording in situ rather than digitally enhancing the sound later, even though some programs make it easy for, say, a voice recorded in a small room to appear as if in a large stadium, and these tricks nearly always sound sterile.[10]

Non-diagetic sound

This is a widely-used device in sound and is present in most movies in some way. It refers to sounds not emanating from what could be called the world within the film. For instance, words spoken by characters within a scene (on screen or off screen) and sounds from objects in the scene – known as diagetic sound – would all be present in the real world, should this scene take place for real. Non-diagetic sounds, however, could include the voice of a narrator, music or additional sound effects. Ever since the striking uses of subjective sounds in early films, the filmmaker has been able to heighten the dramatic content of a scene with non-diagetic sound.

Film View
Alfred Hitchcock made his first sound movie in 1929, *Blackmail*, and with it provided some innovations in his use of subjective sounds to heighten the drama of self-defence, murder and blackmail.

[10] www.film.queensu.ca   Article on sound perspective.

Hyper-real sound

This idea refers to the deliberate exaggeration of certain sounds to make a scene seem more realistic. In real life it would be hard to distinguish one sound from another in most situations, but in a film it is crucial to the story that some sounds are closer than they ought to be. An example is where a scene may need a figure walking along a street at night. In reality, the sound of footsteps would mingle into the other sounds of cars, people and so on. But in a film, that sound would be recorded separately or more likely be reproduced later by a foley artist, someone who specializes in recreating sounds for overdubbing in post-production. It is usually sounds that are important to the information conveyed by a scene that are treated in this way: car doors slamming, keys being turned in doors, phone numbers being dialled and so on.

Sound motif

Sound motif is yet another way in which the aural element of a film can reduce the load on the visual in telling a story. As with visual motif, this is used by the director to convey ideas that help the plot, giving it extra depth. In sound, its uses are often to associate a certain place or character with a sound and in so doing suggest some meaning to attach to it. As a filmmaker, you need all the tools you can get to convey your intended meanings. Ideas about characters or places are hard to put across to the audience, and this is one of those instances when the size of your budget is irrelevant. Sound motif can be a more subtle, almost subconscious way of telling the audience something and does not intrude in the on-screen action. Such sounds can be abstract and quite unreal, but can take their cue from a description of what is being depicted in the script.

> **Film View**
> In *Blade Runner*, the sound of a cat calling accompanies the arrival of Roy Batty, lending a slight air of menace and intelligence. In a film with a complex plot or with several characters to keep track of, the use of such signature sounds helps to maintain clarity.

Music

A music soundtrack undoubtedly helps create mood and yet this is an area where the filmmaker can find some pressing problems. For some directors, such as Martin Scorsese, music not only supports a scene but dictates some elements of it. Scorsese often filmed while playing a recording to the whole set of a piece of music he intended to use. If used well, as in *Goodfellas* (1990) or *Bringing out the Dead* (2000), it is hard to imagine a particular scene without its musical accompaniment, but for some filmmakers, music is a way of lending a film a purpose or style absent from the visuals, as a kind of short cut.

Permission

If you intend to use a musical soundtrack you need to look long and hard at the kind of sums needed to gain permission to use a track, as well as the legal hurdles to be jumped over. To use a track by an artist you need first to get written permission from the owner of the rights to that track, usually the publisher of the music and the company that releases it. You will probably not get free use of tracks unless you know the artist concerned personally and provided they have some clout with their record company.

Tip   Director Rob Weiss wanted to use many tracks by well-known artists for his first movie, *Amongst Friends* (1992). Although it was an independent feature, part-financed by Island, Weiss himself, and his relatives and friends, the director used up to $80 000 on licensing music for less than a dozen tracks. The burden this placed on the eventual cost of the film was part of the reason it failed to make any profit for its makers, despite a reasonable sale on video.

If you do intend to use licensed music, you need to get an entertainment lawyer on your side, to deal with potential problems such as how much the artist receives or whether a track can be used in promotional trailers.

Sampling tracks

Similar issues need to be addressed when a track is sampled. In legal terms, it is fine to use music that is sampled through no fault of the director, such as the sound of a radio as a character walks past it. If you are pursued by a publisher who recognizes their work in your track it is likely that you will need to pay a substantial sum. But there is no need for this situation to arise; you can use relatively inexpensive software to create unique soundtracks using samples of sounds you have collected yourself from videotape.

Use local musicians

Alternatives exist for adding music to your movie. If you contact an unknown (read: unsigned and not covered by copyright) local band or musician, it may be possible to involve them in your project in the same way you involve other members of a crew, either for deferred payment or as an investment-in-kind, for later reward from the film's profits. Given the exposure this would allow for an artist, it is a deal that works both ways.

Do it yourself

If you don't want to follow that route, it is possible to use music created without copyright, without having to create it yourself. Some software programs designed for use with video have a selection of music that can be used 'off the shelf'; in other words, music that is written to use within films, suggesting certain moods. Music is categorized by mood or situation (for example, car chase, suspense, dream sequence and so on) and you can change the tempo up or down according to your requirements. Critics of this approach suggest that such music is essentially elevator muzak and indeed you do need to think carefully about whether you want to let prefabricated soundtracks near your film.

DIY 2

Of course, there is no reason why you can't have a go yourself. Make your own sounds using a piano, guitar, tin can. David Lynch took this route when he made *Eraserhead* (1976), which has a richly dramatic score consisting of circus-style organs, vaudeville melodies, and industrial thumps and bangs. It is much better than this description, however.

Special audio effects

Many edit software programs allow you to modify a sound, or work with plug-ins which allow this. You can, for instance, give a sound an echo, reverse it, warp it or change the pitch. As with visual effects such as strobe and negative, these should be approached with care, and with the maxim 'if it ain't broke don't fix it'. Sounds should not necessarily need digital alterations if the original recording was correctly produced, and if you are using sound to make up for a shortfall in the quality of your shooting then this is best approached with layered sounds rather than by special audio effects.

Capturing audio

Audio clips are captured and used in the same way as standard video/audio clips and appear as different icons on the project window. You can use this stage to adjust the gain of the audio clips on the soundtrack. So, if a certain clip was too quiet when recorded, you can increase the gain so it becomes louder. But bear in mind that increasing gain too far will emphasize background noise or interference. The audio setting of a clip is set at 100 per cent for no gain, and anything above this increases the power of the audio signal. Some programs have a suggested gain feature which brings out the track to optimum level without distorting, but in general, try to avoid increasing gain above 200 per cent.[11]

The Crunch

- A £100 film but a £10 million soundtrack.
- Record sounds separately and layer them for maximum control.
- Create illusions through off-screen sounds.
- Ambient sound is a film-killer: conquer it in your film.
- Beware of unlicensed music.
- Sounds can be like extra actors: use them to add expression and meaning to a scene.
- Prioritize all the sounds in a scene.
- Become a technical master of sound in your edit software.

5. Montage editing

Montage is one of the most significant devices used by filmmakers in editing. It consists of a range of different ways of editing, but at its most basic it centres on the idea that shots do not have to match

---

[11] www.stonewashed.net/sfx.html   Free sound effects.
www.partnersinrhyme.com/   Royalty-free music and sound effects.

in order to be placed side by side, but can show seemingly unrelated images with the aim of heightening the emotional or dramatic impact of a sequence, or compressing information into a small amount of time.

In keeping with the spirit of montage, the rest of this section will look at a range of ideas in a different way. Feel free to mix them around, add them up later and make your own ideas about this section.

How does montage work?

In a sequence, shot 1 has one particular meaning – for example, a car journey at night – and shot 2 has another meaning – for example, a burning house in daylight. Both have separate and quite individual meanings and have potentially lots of symbolism. We may consider as separate the journey in shot 1 or the event in shot 2, but edited together they trigger all sorts of ideas. Together they create a synthesis that is now greater than the effect of either shot independently:

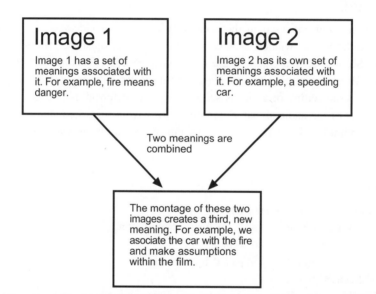

Figure 6.4 How montage creates new meaning out of combining seemingly unrelated shots.

Imagine a scene:

Burning house + more shots of house = burning house

Car + more shots of car = car

But if you try:

Burning house + car + burning house + car + man looking scared = Did he do it? Why is he escaping, if he is escaping? Is he the occupant of the house, reliving the memory? Is he alive? Is he dead?

Film View

In *Lost Highway* (1996), David Lynch uses montage to illustrate the disturbed state of mind of the protagonist, played by Bill Pullman, as he tries to make sense of his wife's infidelity. Watch it yourself to decide whether Lynch goes too far in his use of montage. Severe plot disruption and the use of music at odds with the film combine to make this either really profound or really pretentious.

Tip Montage has become more sophisticated since its beginnings in early Russian films such as *Battleship Potemkin* (1925) by Sergei Eisenstein. In its infancy, montage was criticized for being too literal, inserting shots that did not add to the meaning of a scene but merely underlined what we already knew, such as a cutaway to a shot of a lightning strike when a character falls in love. More recently, montage has begun to fulfil its potential, namely to create a third meaning out of two shots. It is this ability to conjure up new meanings that would not be attached to a single image by simply juxtaposing it with others that has revealed an enormous, untapped reservoir of poetic subtlety in film.

- Working with montage is somewhat easier with non-linear editing systems, which by their nature encourage the user to try out shots against other shots and view the possibilities.
- *Montage is a kind of anti-editing*, in that it is concerned with building up a sequence, amplifying meaning and effect through multiple cuts and images, whereas more conventional editing, in its classical sense, is concerned with discarding, with deselecting images.
- It has a geographical bias in that its greatest exponents are found in European film, while Hollywood has tended to view it as a disruptive influence, upsetting the steady flow of shots in classical 'continuity editing'.
- As with any other tool in post-production, montage editing should be driven by the content of the film itself.
- With montage, more is better. *Montage is a kind of anti-editing.*
- A montage sequence can convey ideas, emotions or a series of events more subtly than through purely verbal means, and the director is then free to add a particular twist to the scene, depending on the kind of shots included.
- Use montage in an almost improvised way, selecting and using clips intuitively.
- Montage is not a device as such to add some complexity when a film seems like it's becoming too obvious. Instead, as Scorsese's film professor and mentor Haig Manoogian put it, montage 'is the source for a film's power; it *is* editing' (*The Filmmaker's Art*, p. 215, Basic Books, 1966).
- 'Parallel montage' allows the director to show simultaneous events or stories by cutting from one to another and suggesting shared meanings.

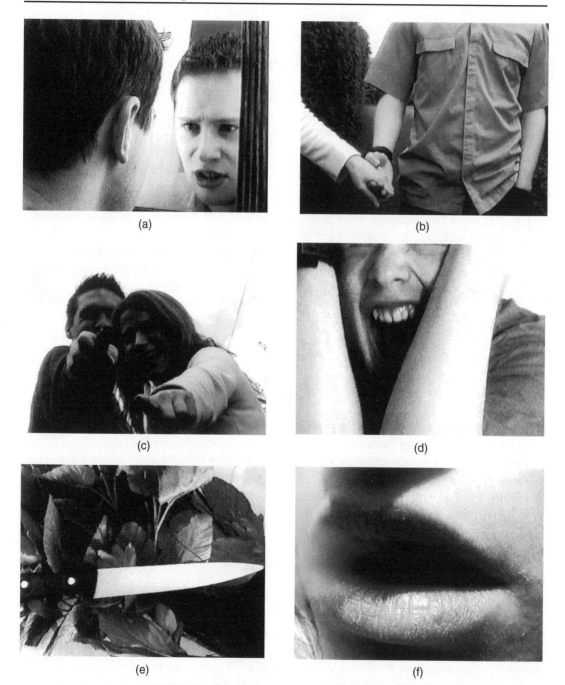

Figure 6.5 *Dreams* (2001) by Charlotte Clark. This short movie uses fast-paced montage of unnerving images to reveal the dreams of the protagonist. Starting with the image of the unnamed figure in the bathroom mirror, we cut quickly between images of fear, anxiety and eroticism, before finally returning to the image of the figure's reflection to close the scene. The montage occurs so quickly that we assemble and link the disparate images into a bizarre narrative.

Film View

In Sofia Coppola's *The Virgin Suicides* (2000), the director needs to demonstrate the strange, other-worldly closeness of the sisters. This is essential to the film because our involvement with the sisters who are shortly to embark on a series of inexplicable suicides depends on our empathizing with them, but also suspecting that this closeness is less than healthy. This complexity of emotion could be conveyed through mere conversations between them, but there is a limit to what words can convey. Coppola's answer is a montage of dreamy, swirling images of the girls dancing against a setting sun. If this method of conveying their relationship seems too open to interpretation, it is also true that words themselves are no guarantee of a definite meaning.

<u>Go to:</u> Chapter 9:2 for more detail on this. In his theories on montage editing in the late 1960s, film theorist Christian Metz suggested eight different types and described the interactions and uses of each.

- In 'accelerated montage', a sequence is built of a succession of fast clips of a bewildering array of images, trying to effect a particular response in the viewer.
- 'Involuted montage' allows a story to be told without regard to chronology, letting the filmmaker reveal parts of the plot and draw the viewer into a more complex reading of it than a simple a-to-b-to-c of events.

The Crunch

- Montage looks weird but try it: it is unpredictable and adds something extra.
- Montage takes many forms; try out each method and see what it can offer you.
- Look for montage in movies you watch – it's everywhere.
- Why should you tell a story straight? Give the audience something else to think about other than the story.
- You don't have to be in control; improvise when you compose a montage sequence.
- Car*burninghouse*car*burninghouse*carcarcar*burninghouse*car*burning*man*car*.

6. Timecode in editing

Timecode is one of the more complex areas of video and any explanation of it does veer into technical language. Although it is one of those tools in DV filming which you can live without, once you understand what it is you see the benefits for your production and the way it speeds up your work rate. 'Stripe', or timecode, your tapes before you shoot and your computer will really appreciate it; it makes it easier for the PC to locate each clip on your footage. Here goes.

Did you know?
To stripe, or place timecode on your tapes, prior to filming, simply put the cassette in
the camera, keep the lens cap on, press record and let the tape run, recording over
the entire tape, without interruption. It's like laying rail track for each clip to sit on later.

What is timecode?

Timecode is a way of numbering each and every frame of a videotape. Videotape – both analog and
digital – has a certain number of frames in each second. Timecode exists as a separate track – invisible
to the viewer when you show the movie – recorded on the tape. It is an eight-digit code consisting of
frames, seconds, minutes and hours. An example could be 03:16:45:12, which shows that the
particular frame attached to this code is 3 hours, 16 minutes, 45 seconds and 12 frames into the tape.
Those last three words give you a clue as to the purpose of timecode. It is a navigational tool, allowing
you to find the exact point of every take and every shot in your tape.[12]

Different countries, different systems

Unfortunately, to make it all more complicated, each part of the world uses slightly different amounts
for their television programmes. In Europe and the United Kingdom, a frame rate of 25 fps (frames
per second) is standard and is known as PAL, whereas in the USA a rate of 30 fps is used, and is
referred to as NTSC. This has no discernible effect on the programmes that are made, but it is true that
in terms of quality a higher frame rate is desirable.[13]

Go to: Chapter 3:1 for a complete list of international television standards.

Timecode in the USA and other NTSC territories

Timecode in the USA and other places using NTSC is 29.97 fps. It is OK to round this up to the next
whole number of 30 fps, but it may be useful to go through the implications of this if you intend to
make productions larger than an hour in length.

The frame rate of 30 fps is actually devised for black and white television, and for technical reasons
a slightly shorter frame rate was introduced for colour. If you edit assuming a rate of 30 fps, then you
will end up with a 3.6 second error every 60 minutes. The solution to this is something called 'drop-
frame timecode', which removes 108 frames – from the timecode *not* your film – per hour. This
requires your counter to drop out two frames per minute, but since this would lead us to drop too many
– 120 – we need to *not* drop frames every 10th minute. This is not something you have to think about

---

[12] www.philrees.co.uk/articles/timecode.htm   Technical article on timecode.
[13] www.equipmentemporium.com/introto1.htm   Article on timecode.

– your timecode counter does it all for you and when you watch the timecode counter you will see at the end of every minute it will jump suddenly over the dropped frames.[14]

It doesn't affect your movie

Don't worry at all about how this affects your movie, no actual frames are dropped, only the numbering of them. Nothing changes about the way it looks and there will be no sudden jump-cuts as the timecode jumps forward; it is simply a device to keep the numbers looking good. In most short productions such as news footage or short business videos, drop-frame timecode is not necessary, but it is important to opt for this rate when you first open your edit program if you intend to sell programmes or movies to television or cable broadcasters using this frame rate, and especially if working on productions over 60 minutes.

Timecode in PAL

In territories using the PAL system, timecode is recorded at a rate of 25 fps. As with NTSC, if you are working with a specific client or market in mind whom you know is working on a different system, alter the settings of your software before editing and those of the camcorder before recording. In addition to the 25 fps PAL, there is also PAL 60, which aims to be more compatible with NTSC territories.[15]

Ways of recording timecode

Timecode is recorded directly onto the tape so that it can be read on any unit, anywhere. There are, however, different ways of recording it, as outlined below.

Audio track timecode

In this method, timecode is recorded onto the audio track of the analog videotape using sound impulses in much the same way as a modem converts digital signal into sound to send down the wire. This is called longitudinal timecode and although it has improved over recent years it still has two problems: it can only reliably be read when the tape is moving and it can suffer from loss of signal when it is copied or played repeatedly.[16]

Timecode as part of the video signal

This is known as vertical-interval timecode (VITC) and is generally the best method to opt for. This method involves recording the timecode signal using the video heads rather than the audio, so that leaves all audio tracks available for you to use.

---

[14] www.inforamp.net/~poynton/notes/video/Timecode/   Technical article on NTSC timecode.
[15] www.24p.com/PAL_TC.htm   Article on PAL timecode.
[16] www.mindspring.com/~d-v-c/Timecode.htm   Article on various timecode formats.

Uses of timecode

This section started with the statement that using timecode could save you time in editing. Much of the technical information above is good to know but you are not often going to be called upon to use it. The value of having timecode on your tape is that you will need to spend less time shuttling around your tape to find the right take when you come to capture your clips.

Get around your footage tape fast

It is true that getting to know your footage by constant reviewing is a way of speeding up the editing process, but mistakes occur if you rely on notes such as 'good take of Marvin singing, third take after the car scene'. That may be sufficient for home movie family films, but anywhere up the scale from there and you desperately need a more exact and mathematical way of finding that good take. So, on your edit log sheet, you might describe the scene as 'Marvin singing good take: 01:49:12:17'. Now when you want to find that take there will be no mistakes. The edit log sheet is hardly worth the paper it is written on if you are unable to find the precise location of clips whenever you like and, similarly, the Edit Decision List (EDL) is only really a viable option if you use timecode throughout filming. With this degree of forethought, editing can become something you are more in control of and less frustrated by.

Continuous timecode in filming

It is crucial that you keep timecode as one continuous line, uninterrupted by filming breaks on the tape. If, for instance, you pause and then continue filming you may have created a break in the code and the new recording will start at zero timecode. The problem with this is that when you start to capture your clips ready for editing, the capture software starts to get very confused, as it soon realizes that there may be several clips each labelled, for instance, 00:00:20:43.

Stripe your tapes

The easiest way to ensure that you have timecode present is to place it on when you start filming. As we saw in the section on shooting, place the lens cap back on the camera and press record. When the camera has finished recording over the whole tape it will have placed continuous timecode from start to end. When you later go and shoot over this, the shots fit into the timecode that has been burned on. This process is called 'striping' the tape.

A further method, and the one to use if your footage was not shot on a pre-timecoded tape, is to make a copy of the tape containing your footage with new timecode burned on. You can do this by capturing large chunks of continuous footage and outputting it back onto digital tape, captured now with timecode. Copying in this way presents no problems with loss of quality, unlike analog.

The Crunch

- Timecode is good for your films.
- Get to know how timecode works in your camera.
- Get to know how timecode works in editing.
- Put timecode on all your tapes before you shoot on them.

7. Using DVD in editing

Store movies

One of the choices open to the digital filmmaker is how to store movies both during and after post-production. It makes no sense at all to make and edit a film digitally but then have to store the final copy as an analog version, with the resulting loss of quality, but for the low-budget filmmaker there are few options available. Keeping a copy of the final film on digital tape is essential but presents problems if you want to view the film anywhere other than a PC or camera. Copying the film onto CD is a good method, but this is really only practical for films of 5 or 10 minutes. Anything much longer becomes compressed out of all recognition. DVD, however, offers a way of storing your films in high-quality, digital versions and accessing them easily. Other formats cannot compete in terms of clarity and quality of compression.

DVD – or digital versatile disc – is basically a way of compressing a movie as an MPEG–2, one of several forms of squashing a film into a short space. With DVD, the film is compressed to the resolution of standard television sets, whereas VHS has never exploited to the full the possible clarity of the screen. The dramatic breakthrough for manufacturers was being able to squeeze a whole 2-hour movie on to the disc, and have room left for a few other goodies such as film information, subtitles or short documentaries.[17]

DIY DVDs

Until recently, however, the low-budget filmmaker has had no easy way of accessing this technology for storing and copying their own productions. Copying units for DVD – burners – have met some resistance from the video industry, as this format was seen as the last format unable to be copied by consumers. Thinking differently, however, Apple Computers have made a point of including DVD burners on their mid-range models and have actively pushed this as a domestic feature rather than a purely business one. If past events are anything to go on, Apple usually sees what consumers want and deliver it a couple of years before the big PC companies catch on (although Apple famously finds it hard to capitalize on their successes). FireWire is a good example of this.

In editing, the DVD burner will enable you to store works in progress and finished films, accessing them much faster than CD or through capture cards. The only blot on the horizon is the complexity

---

[17] www.apple.com/dvd/   Apple DVD products.
www.dvddemystified.com/dvdfaq.html   Many questions answered on DVDs.

of the way in which MPEG–2 compresses information, and whether this has implications for reading and continuing to work with a film. It remains, though, the most useful format for the low-budget filmmaker because it offers a way of viewing a movie in the clarity originally intended, without the losses inherent in VHS. Furthermore, juries at competitions and festivals will view DVD entries, where previously the only option was VHS cassette.

Tip Comparing DVD to CD:	DVD	CD
Diameter (mm)	120	120
Thickness (mm)	0.6	1.2
Data capacity (GB)	17	0.68
Possible sides	2	1

The Crunch

- DVD is a better way to store your films.
- Keep a copy on DV tape also.
- Make your own DVDs.
- Beware companies which say they will put your films on DVD.

8. Working with text

As we have seen, part of the task awaiting the low-budget, independent filmmaker is the necessity to use ingenuity and imagination to utilize what the medium can offer, before having to start spending money. When the main elements of the film have done all they can – camera composition, lighting, shooting, script, images – the use of text in a film can be a further way of supporting the ideas you are trying to put across. This applies as much to the traditional use of text in the opening credits as to their use throughout the film, setting off other meanings or adding a layer of visual density that the images alone could not supply. In this section we will be looking at the way creative use of credits and titles can bring a more professional look to your film and make its meaning more apparent.

On the whole, this is territory most often occupied by the more unusual, non-narrative films, including music videos, commercials and video art. As the projects on non-narrative film showed, there are many lessons for the narrative filmmaker that can be picked up from investigating non-narrative forms. So, stick with this section, even if you can't see a place for text in the films you intend to make; its benefits can be felt in many forms of filmmaking.

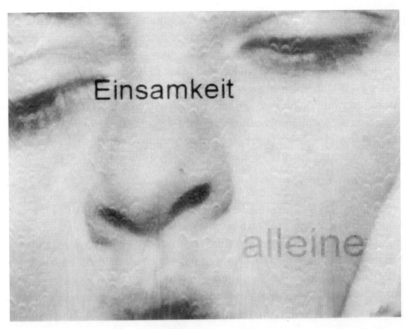

Figure 6.6 *Lonely* (2000) by Anna Brugger. This non-narrative short movie used German, the filmmaker's own language, to illustrate the feelings in the main theme. Brugger's use of the words is as much for design purposes as for meaning, as the words are placed around the screen and fade in and out with the images, sometimes clear, others obscured.

Better credits

Every film needs them, and they are most often the first indication we see of the style and mood of a film, but still some films look as if the opening titles are taken off the shelf, selected from a menu of pre-set examples and excluded from the kind of thought and attention that goes in to the rest of the movie.

Credits grow out of the movie

When the film has been completed and you are in the process of designing the right look for the opening titles, complete storyboards and visualizations just as you did when devising the look of the whole film. Take your cue from the images and colour schemes seen in the film. If you have been working on the film closely, covering nearly all tasks yourself, it is sometimes difficult to assess what makes the film look and feel the way it does. After a while you can't see what makes your film distinctive, so caught up are you with the glitches or negative aspects of it. Where other people see style, you might see the problems you encountered while shooting or how the scene was assembled.

To get around this, base the designs for your credits on the same notes you made at the start of the production, when you were deciding what constitutes the core of the film, what makes it tick. If we take as an example David Fincher's film *Seven* (1995), the extraordinary and distinctive credit sequence seems out of keeping with the rest of the film. The words flicker and move, are scratched and creased, and are reminiscent of words on a shaky Super 8 movie, filmed by looking at etched graffiti on a toilet wall. Given that the film itself is high on production values, this seems out of sync, style-wise. But both credits and film are working towards the same ends, and relate right back to the same theme, of a distorted and disturbed world, at its centre a figure sending out crude messages with violence. Looked at like this, the credits do not just fit into the film but offer a way of understanding the whole theme behind it. Like Fincher, you should be able to use every part of the film to advance your cause.

Stages in designing credits

1 Take the central theme in the film and describe it. Work out how you have manifested this theme on film. What devices did you use, such as colours, shapes, mood?
2 Take the image that you think defines your film. Look through the whole movie and try to see which single part sums up the aims of the film. Think of this as you would for choosing the defining image used for advertising the film.
3 It helps if you have a sense of graphic design or can hire the services of a designer, but try looking for the design characteristics of the credits: font, size, allusions to other films, colour and so on. If you are not sure, try looking through style or design magazines to work out what you do and don't like. If you are doing the designs yourself and have little experience, it is usually better to under-design, in other words, keep it low-key and simple.

Captions

Captions are sometimes used in a film to indicate the start of a new chapter. If your movie has a need to clarify the time or location of a scene, a caption can help the audience to maintain their involvement. In action films it is common to see them used to build tension towards a specific point, counting down to a meteor impact, an invasion launch and so on. In all cases, captions used to assist theme or plot should be kept low-key, with modest typefaces.

Other films use them to add further layers of meaning to the film, breaking it up into sections marked by theme rather than plot progress. For example, *Hannah and Her Sisters* (Woody Allen, 1986) separates the action by the use of seemingly oblique captions which later make sense. In one part, titled 'not even the rain has such small hands', Michael Caine ensures he runs into Barbara Hershey in a bookshop, who he is infatuated with. He insists on buying her a book of poems by ee cummings, from whose work the caption is taken. This technique is seen in early animated films in which a story is advanced by the turning of pages of a book, each signalling the start of a new part of the film.

The Crunch

- Credits grow out of the film.
- Credits are often the first part of the film that the audience see: make them good.
- If in doubt, go for clarity in terms of font, design and size.

Project 14. The journey

The aim of this project is to put into practice many of the ideas covered in the projects so far. In this project we need to push as far as possible what you can achieve and consider this project to be one which launches you into the distribution and marketing arena. This is the best you have made so far and shows everything you can achieve in this field.

The theme of this project is 'the journey'. It can be made within any of the forms we have covered:

- *Narrative*. Perhaps a literal journey towards a place or event.
- *Non-narrative*. Perhaps a music video on the theme of movement or on the idea of a symbolic journey, such as 'the journey through life'.
- *Non-fiction/documentary*. Perhaps in terms of a journey someone has made, either metaphorically (perhaps from part of their life to another) or literally (perhaps a real journey made, such as visiting a long-forgotten family member).

Other forms we have touched upon will fit equally well into the theme: video art, briefly covered in Chapter 9, or any of the minor forms looked at in Chapter 2:1, 'Forms and genres'.

Stage 1

Go through the process of developing the film on paper, according to the way you work best. The amount of gaps you leave in planning the film depend on how much improvisation you like to allow. Certainly, those forms in need of some lateral thinking and wild card ideas, such as the non-narrative film, will benefit from more improvisation.

Stage 2

In planning this film, consider the underlying theme in the title. Even the most narrative, straightforward interpretation of it would benefit from allowing a little sub-text show through. Think of what the idea of journey means to you. Is it like a journey encountering varied events and people, a kind of odyssey from childhood to adulthood? Is it more of a small-scale view looking at a certain journey that has an impact on us all, such as leaving home for the first time, going on a first date, moving to a new town. In all these situations, there are ample opportunities for the audience to empathize with what is happening. And if they empathize, then they become more involved.

Don't forget that the main path to success is finding your own particular view. How can you represent the ideas it contains? Montage contains some of the best opportunities for conveying big themes. A fast sequence of images can have great impact on an audience, provided you have a particular aim in mind and link the images in some way. Similarly, sound or music can help to define what it is we are seeing. You can radically alter a sequence simply by adding juxtaposing sounds or music at odds with what we see. In any case, use sound as a strong factor in this film.

Stage 3

Take your time with this film. Take time to build a crew, attract other people to get involved, balance one idea against the next, until you have something you believe in and have the commitment in to persist with through to a conclusion. Use this film as a test of your powers of keeping a project together. When you are shooting, take time to get it right, having built in to the overall schedule a realistic period to get the right shots and have enough breathing space to take some more if necessary.

Stage 4

Editing this film is another test: try not to spend too long picking through the detail of it after you have a final cut. It is tempting to re-edit and incorporate more and more suggestions, but give yourself a cut-off point, perhaps enforcing it by arranging a viewing for friends at a certain date.

Stage 5

When you have a film you feel is the best you can do at this point in time we can use it as the subject of the next two chapters (and don't be too hard on yourself: you are going to see a lot of faults in the film and will never be entirely satisfied but give yourself a break, it is the best right now).

Evaluation

Go back to the questions we looked at in Chapter 2:2. Try to answer honestly and take stock of the way this film was put together. Did you work differently knowing that this film was to be seen by many other people? Perhaps it added additional pressures to get it right, to allow no slip-ups during production? But that would be missing the point – the aim is not to make no mistakes and put in a flawless performance as director, but instead to get through, to remain undeterred by the numerous problems faced. Many productions fall at the first hurdle and success in this instance must be judged on having a result to show rather on what that result is. If you managed to plan, shoot and edit this film, you have proved that you can be flexible enough, determined and yet keep sight of the first idea that made you want to make the film. Sure, that idea changed along the way, but consider that the greatest achievement is your having finished the film. You made it.

9. Good editing software guide

This chapter looks at the range of editing software available and helps you decide what kind is best suited to your needs.

Before purchasing an editing package, consider carefully what you want to achieve with it. Each package is different, catering for the filmmaker who wants, at one end of the scale, to make short films without visual effects, no layering of images or sounds – in short, a cut-and-paste process. At the other end of the scale, you might want to eventually make more ambitious films, with no limit to what new technology can offer you. Either way, choose a program based on what your computer can handle and what matches with your plans for your particular films.

So, what is the difference between each program? Each will cut movies together for you. Each will allow you to put sound on these images. But beyond this, they start to vary in performance, in the amount of bugs in the software, in what effects they offer and how fast they operate (on similar computers).

This guide focuses entirely on editing software. Editing hardware systems are more expensive but may be worth investigating if you have a larger budget available. Software reviews are arranged roughly in order of expense, beginning with the cheapest.

Windows Movie Maker – not advisable for filmmakers, but it is free

Microsoft's bundled edit software is designed for the home video maker: someone who intends to use the camcorder for weddings, family occasions, holidays and so on. It is a basic edit cut-and-paste program, enabling you to put together a film with no effects, transitions, sound or image layers, but does include text. The big problem, though, is the absence of a project window: imported clips cannot be reused as they go straight onto the timeline, or 'filmstrip'.

Plus points: it's free; it is very easy to use; allows capture straight from anaolg camera.
Negative points: very limited in what it can offer; poor audio control.
Minimum processor speed: 200 MHz.
Minimum RAM: 64 MB.

For details contact www.microsoft.com.

iMovie/iMovie 2 – good beginner's choice, and its free with most Macs (not available for PC)

A freebie with Apple computers (except lower versions of the iMac), this capable edit program offers a real alternative for the no-budget filmmaker. Use this on a PowerMac and you can realistically put together quality films. It caters for the creative filmmaker rather than the tourist/family movie maker by including transitions, titles and a limited effects menu. It looks good and makes the process of editing straightforward, avoiding video-tech-speak terms in favour of plain English. iMovie 2 is a big step up from the first version and it is almost worth buying one, given also the widespread use of the Mac in the film industry.

Plus points: can be used to export straight to Premiere for finer editing; has an 'export to the web' option.
Negative points: limited for the ambitious filmmaker.

Details from Apple Inc.

EditStudio – cheap, accessible and easy to use

Pure Motion's EditStudio is an audacious attempt to break into the growing field of basic editing software, but the existence of free programs for both Windows and Mac makes it less widespread than it deserves to be. It offers a beginner's entry point to basic editing, but will prove less satisfying for those used to a wider choice of features.

Minimum processor: 200 MHz (350 MHz required for editing).
Minimum RAM: 32 MB.
Disc space: 4 GB.

Details from www.puremotion.com.

EditDV – good editing tool, some limitations

A good all-round program which resembles Premiere in many respects, it is a popular consumer choice. On the plus side it has a good layout, with Project Window for storing clips, Monitor Window for trimming clips and Sequencer Window for assembling the film. The Sequencer Window is awkward at times because it places special effects filters on a separate track below the clip, so if you move a clip, you have to remember to move the effect also. Trimming is easy and the design of the windows and controls makes it less daunting for the beginner. Audio is well catered for by the bundled version of Sound Forge that accompanies this program. The main problem for filmmakers is its inability to capture from analog using a standard capture card, but if you use DV only then this won't bother you.

Plus points: scrolling titles; audio fade controls; unlimited number of video tracks.
Negative points: no adjustable compression settings; does not support MP3.
Minimum processor needed: 200 MHz.
Minimum RAM: 128 MB.
Disc space for installation: 40 MB.

Details from www.digitalorigin.com.

VideoWave – a low-end tool, easy but not for experienced editors

The low cost and easy layout of VideoWave make this a good introduction for the beginner who finds iMovie or EditStudio too basic. It supports all major video formats except for Real (one of the most popular formats) and outperforms EditDV in many respects. It is inexplicably cheap and is therefore very attractive for the filmmaker who wants to start editing but cannot afford the high cost of Premiere or Final Cut Pro. It keeps language simple and untechnical, enabling those new to editing software to get straight to work and trim, compose and export a film with few problems. For instance, to make the film and save it the hard disk, you select the 'Produce Video' command. It lets you trim clips and apply a limited palette of effects at this stage, before committing them to the filmstrip at the top of the screen.

Plus points: very cheap; easy to use; good titling options including scrolling; adjustable compression settings; large amount of transitions.

Negative points: only one video and audio track; operates on a fixed 800 × 600 pixel screen (high resolution monitors have no impact on it); poor manual.

Minimum processor: 266 MHz.

Minimum RAM: 128 MB.

Disc space for installation: 45 MB.

Details from MGI Software: www.videowave.com.

Adobe Premiere – widely used, powerful, not too expensive

A powerful filmmaking tool, Adobe Premiere is a popular choice among low-budget filmmakers. It is widely used in education and has become one of the best known programs. It operates with three main windows: Project Window, Monitor and Timeline. The Timeline Window is easy to use and offers up to 99 video and audio tracks, enabling you construct dazzlingly complicated sequences. For beginners, the Monitor Window provides most problems, as many users report that it responds poorly to playing the movie and the dual monitor layout is confusing for some. However, more experienced editors, and those schooled in analog methods, will find this instantly familiar and logical. Version 6 has improved on previous versions by including more effects, an easier layout of (an increasing amount of) windows and the inclusion of the Storyboard Window, enabling you to roughly compile the film before exporting it to the Timeline for fine work. Version 6 has also made it easy for movies to be saved for use on the Internet.

Plus points: high number of visual effects; compatible with Adobe After Effects (special effects software) and Adobe Photoshop; high number of transitions; good title options; good audio options; adjustable compression settings.

Negative points: occasional problems with capturing; takes time to master it fully.

Minimum processor: 300 MHz.

Minimum RAM: 128 MB.

Disc space for installation: 60 MB.

Details from www.adobe.com.

Final Cut Pro – Apple's answer to Premiere

FCP (Final Cut Pro) looks very similar to Premiere in its layout and incorporates many common features. It, too, uses a Project Window, Monitor for trimming clips and Timeline for building the movie. It also has a dual-screen display for seeing both the clip you are working on and the full movie. However, FCP goes further in several ways: it has a series of special effects filters and a specialized scripting language called FX Builder which allows you to make your own custom-built effects. Premiere would require additional software such as Adobe After Effects to match this, but Premiere's version 6 goes some way to addressing this shortfall. Inevitably, FCP and Premiere fight it out for the attention of the majority of professional users, from low-budget to high, but ultimately it may be the platform itself that decides which you choose – FCP is not available for PCs so you would need to get a Mac.

Plus points: high number of filters; easy to use; suitable for the professional; good audio and text options.
Negative points: expensive; only available on Mac.
Minimum processor: 300 MHz.
Minimum RAM: 128 MB.

Details from www.apple.com.

Vegas Video – powerful but expensive

A powerful program made by Sonic Foundry, best known for their excellent range of editing software. It is a versatile program designed for the advanced user and semi-professional. It displays a lack of logic in some of its menus, such as the absence of an Import command, which is found in the File menu in Premiere, but here you have to go through the Explorer menu, which shows you the contents of the hard drive. A positive feature for filmmakers with limited disc space, seeking to maximize what they have, is the inclusion of an indicator, in minutes and seconds, of how much room you have on the hard disk. The titling menu is useful but is placed as a plug-in and is therefore not easy to get at.

Plus points: wide range of features; unlimited number of video and audio tracks; good audio support.
Negative points: manual is too big; very expensive compared to similar programs; low number of filters and transitions.
Minimum processor: 400 MHz.
Minimum RAM: 128 MB.
Disc space for installation: 20 MB.

Details from www.sonicfoundry.com.

7 | Using the Internet: promotion and profile

1. Film on the Internet: a brief introduction

What the Internet can offer

There is something rewarding about having finished your film – you can show it to your friends, play it over and over again and use it as a calling card to get further into the industry. But until the arrival of video on the Internet, this was about as far as you could hope to push a short film at the start of your career. Now, everything has changed and one of the primary aims of the next phase of the web is the movement of video films at faster and more convenient rates. Video streaming, as it is called, is here and is your friend.

On the plus side, the web is going to:

- Enable you to show your films to anyone, anywhere.
- Let you do this without the need for 'the middleman', such as distributors.
- Let you devise your own marketing campaign for a film.
- Let you communicate directly to potential buyers or other people you might want to work with.
- Watch what everyone else is doing.

All of which looks good until you see the potential downside of this technology:

- The net is unstable; its infrastructure is shaky to say the least.
- It takes too long to download a short film.
- The sort of connection you need to get hold of a film quickly is not the connection most people have.
- Picture quality is poor.

If you are starting to question the whole idea of using the Internet to show or promote your films, bear with it for a while. The rate of improvement in showing films has increased so quickly within just the first 5 years of its use that we can start to think of this route as one fast becoming viable, and soon to become practical for the average filmmaker. In your bid to reach people without the need for anyone else to give the go-ahead, the future is rushing to your aid with this technology.[1]

Video streaming

Video streaming has branched off from the net industry to become a field with its own growth rate, and millions of dollars of research are going into finding quicker ways of showing movies. In this section, we need to get to grips with this technology and find the best way of exploiting it for the use of the low-budget filmmaker. It won't solve your problems overnight or guarantee a great career – artistic merit is and always will be a deciding factor. But it does give you more control over your work than anyone working 20 years ago might have dreamed.

Tip   To be exact, streaming video is a method of sending files to you in which the video is sent frame by frame, much the same as television. This is the only way to ensure that the receiver is not waiting excessively for the video to start playing. However, on an intranet, streaming is much more successful where high bandwidth is more common.

What is web film?

Web film is basically any moving image which is downloaded as a single file or 'streamed' for viewing on a PC. At the start of the twenty-first century it is estimated that there are something like 300 million Internet users and although the net was once the preserve of information, communication and consumer services, the prime use of it for most people – 70 per cent on average – is entertainment. Chief Executive of Yahoo, Jerry Yang, estimated that in an average month in 2000 over 15 million hours of video were streamed. As use of home PCs evolves in this direction, the net industry has put more time and money into pushing it further, with better ways of getting these massive files over tiny phone lines.

File sizes

One of the issues at the centre of video on the web is infrastructure. Most people don't possess the right sort of connection needed to watch films at a reasonable rate. You can wait hours to download a short movie, since the size of a video file is far larger than anything the average modem was designed for. The

---

[1] www.internetnews.com/streaming.news   Streaming news.
   www.digitalwebcast.com   Broadcasting site.

kind of modem most people have is one which conducts data at a rate of 56 000 bits per second, but many people still use even slower ones, at 28 000 bits per second. Put this against the size of a video file lasting only a few minutes, which could be up to 650 Mb, and you start to understand why something had to be done to squash these files down into a more manageable size, and to find a way of starting to show the movie before the whole length of it has downloaded. Filmmakers and software designers have been ingenious in their approach to this problem, which has seen various methods develop on the data side and various techniques on the filmmaking side to make these films more easily viewed on the small, small screen. Two ideas are central to this pursuit: *bandwidth*, which allows more data to go down to your PC; and *compression*, which makes video smaller.[2]

What types of films are out there?

The rules and hierarchies of Hollywood have no currency here. In web film, it is common to see a site where first-time filmmakers are on the same bill as established, well-known directors. There is no limit to the kind of material seen, though the need to keep it short tends to point films away from established genres. The web has given birth to new forms, such as the 360-degree movie, and given a new lease of life to older ones, such as animation and episodic movies.

Did you know?
The 360-degree movie is a new development in web film, reflecting the interactive potential of the medium. With these movies, the viewer uses keyboard controls to zoom in or out from the action or pan left or right. At present, much of the content of these films is pedestrian, consisting of panoramas or sporting events.

Animation is popular, since web-specific software like Flash means that it is downloaded or viewed at a fraction of the time that video takes. Independent film dominates, and students of film courses use it as a way to get seen quickly. Interactive film has evolved, where you can zoom in or out on a scene, or choose the outcome of the film. Experimental artists have never had it so good; work usually destined for a poorly attended gallery now has wider potential. Film has become more of a fun 'hit' to be had at work or at home and web films are perhaps the espresso of the entertainment world: quality compressed into a short space.

Did you know?
Flash is a plug-in (an added piece of software) that enables you to view more dynamic web content such as animations. Some filmmakers are investigating the possibilities of using Flash to construct short movies, encouraged by the relatively small file sizes of Flash movies compared to video.

---

[2] www.smartcomputing.com   Many articles and tutorials on bytes, bits and so on.

Who shows films?

There are many sites that specifically show web films. After the initial adrenaline-fuelled rush to get on board, sites have become more diverse, more reliable and generally better at what they do. There are several high-profile sites, who are forging close links with the traditional film industry and attracting support from leading names in directing and acting. Most offer the viewer a small screen, roughly 2 or 3 inches in size, together with information about the film and a chance to comment on it. Many also offer other features. Atom Films has access to the back catalogue of the University archive that holds early films by George Lucas and Francis Ford Coppola; Getoutthere.com offers a parallel site up for audio, with unknown bands able to submit music and reach the public.

The evolution of the web film would not be forced along at such a fast rate if it were only low-budget filmmakers and artists using it. Inevitably, it is the profit motive which has pushed this technology,

Figure 7.1 Ifilm.com is one of the leading sites for showing short films. It differs from most others in that it is also active in other areas of the film industry, including a partnership with the cable network The Independent Film Channel for weekly broadcasts of online films. It also shows a broader range of material than its main competitors, including experimental and non-narrative films.

namely in pornography and business. But as more people are using it for film in its widest sense it is becoming a standard feature in PCs and from ISPs.[3]

The Crunch

● The Internet can help your movies.
● Get to know about video streaming.
● Investigate web film-showing sites.
● Don't let the poor quality of web films discourage you: it's a quickly evolving area.
● Watch lots of web movies: they are free, new and tell you what's going on.

2. Video compression

Why are you doing that to my movie?

Short films are too big for the Internet and need to be squashed right down to make the process of watching more practical. Until both connections and cables for the majority of users have improved, this is the only viable way of using the Internet for video.

The great parable of the ants©

The problem is like this: suppose you look at thousands of ants crawling through a tiny hole in a wall. They all get in an orderly single file but progress is still slow. They can do one of two things: make the gap bigger or get rid of some of the ants. Web film is working on both these fronts, the former in the long term and the latter to make do until then.

So, until cables get fatter or more efficient, we will have to compress movies for the web. With some editing software programs, this is easy as they are increasingly designed for use with web films, enabling you to select from a range of compression rates. But even here it pays to know what the process is and how you can adjust it according to the type of film you are showing. There are different parts of the video that you can compress and decisions to take on how you do that. You need to get to know what kind of compression method is best for what kind of movie. These methods are called codecs, or compressor-decompressors, and have been designed to suit certain films more than others.[4]

---

[3] www.atom.com   Major web film broadcaster.
   www.reelplay.com   Web film broadcaster.
   www.getoutthere.com   British web film site.
   www.macromedia.com   Flash home site, download for free.
[4] www.bmrc.berkeley.edu/index.html   Multimedia research articles.
   www.adsl.com/adsl_tutorial.html   Detailed tutorial on adsl lines.
   www.abovestream.com   Video streaming centre.

What's a codec?

Codecs are all designed to work on two fronts: temporal and spatial compression. That means they both compress the picture in terms of the amount of information used, but do this in different ways. Beyond this, there are other ways to compress further, by reducing colour quality, audio, pixel rate or frame rate.

Within these two formats, codecs are found in either hardware or software form. Hardware codecs are fast and more efficient but more expensive, and require that the receiver of the images has the same codec device. Software codecs do not have the same quality as hardware versions but most are available free on the Internet, and are more widely used on editing programs.

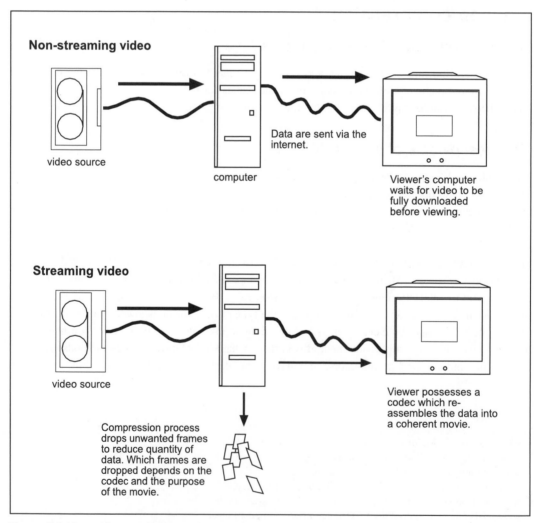

Non-streaming video

video source

computer

Data are sent via the internet.

Viewer's computer waits for video to be fully downloaded before viewing.

Streaming video

video source

Compression process drops unwanted frames to reduce quantity of data. Which frames are dropped depends on the codec and the purpose of the movie.

Viewer possesses a codec which re-assembles the data into a coherent movie.

Figure 7.2 How video streaming works.

The good codec guide

H.263 – use for video conferencing

This codec is a good choice for the business community. It's ideal for a video conference where you do not need high-quality pictures, and audio is going to take priority. It is best with low movement films, so a more or less stationary talking head is going to be just perfect. The data rate for this would be small but, of course, you lose quality all round. Perhaps the only use of this codec is if you wanted to send a quick version of a film for viewing by a co-worker; you may not worry too much about the way it looks as you just want quick feedback.

Advanced tip

There are two ways of compressing a film. Here's how it works:

1. Temporal compression

Temporal compression takes out lots of information that you don't miss by comparing the individual pixels in a frame – for example, if a frame looks almost the same as the last, perhaps with the same background colour, it recognizes this and hangs on to only those bits of information that differ from what was in the first frame, called the key frame. All other frames after the key frame it names 'delta frames' and only starts a new key frame when the scene changes significantly. In this way, it manages to remove much information and reduce the overall file size.

2. Spatial compression

Spatial compression works differently but still on the basis of looking for information that appears more than once. It does this not by studying each pixel of the frame, but by defining areas of the whole picture and looking for patterns of repetition in the pixels. So, if a piece of the frame contains blue sky and is the same on many successive frames, these data are repeated so it would be excluded. It saves space by not having to describe each of these pixels as the same colour blue, but by mapping an area and describing the whole group – or space – as blue. Many compression methods that use this method offer the ability to alter the values for spatial compression so as to avoid losing too much sharpness and definition.

Cinepak – use for CD-ROMs

This is a good, well-established system which works best with small image sizes. This codec is outperformed by many others even though its small size, at 120×90 pixels, is now getting bigger as computers improve. It is better used on low-end machines but is not usually the first option for web film, being more suited to CD-ROMs.[5]

---

[5] www.icanstream.tv/CodecCentral/index.html   Excellent index of all codecs.
www.4i2i.com/h263_video_codec.htm   All about H.263 codecs.
www.cinepak.com/begin/html   Cinepak information.

Compression	Picture quality	MB/second	Minutes for 1 GB
1:1	Broadcast	18.5	0.5
2:1	Direct transfer TV	9.3	1
3:1	Beta Digital SP	6.2	2
4:1	Beta SP Pro	4.6	3
5:1	Beta Semi-pro	3.7	4
5:1 in camera	DV	3.6	4
7:1	Hi-8, S-VHS Pro	2.6	6
10:1	Hi-8, S-VHS	1.85	9
15:1	VHS	1.2	14

Figure 7.3 Video compression, quality and hard disk space. This table shows how much space is used by different kinds of video signal. VHS offers the lowest quality and therefore you will get more minutes of film on the computer per gigabyte, while those at the top of the scale take up more disk space. The numbers in the left column refer to the rate at which data are sampled when they are recorded. Less compression, of 1:1, offers the greatest picture quality. Consumer-level camcorders are known as DV and sample at a rate of 5:1.

Tip A useful method of working out what compression you need for delivery onto CD or DVD is:

Disc space [measured in KiloBytes (KB), not MB] divided by movie length (in seconds) = KB of final movie.

For example, a film which is 10 minutes long, squeezed onto a CD-ROM with less than the full space left over, say, 450 MB: 450 MB = 450 000 KB, divided by 600 seconds, equals 750 KB per second. This lets you know that you then need to compress the movie down to 750 KB or less to safely get it onto the disc.

RealVideo – good for most uses

This codec has many admirers. It has 'temporal scalability', which means that the result for the user is smoother than others even on a wide range of machines; basically, it plays at a high frame rate for fast machines and a low rate for slow ones. This codec is hard to beat in terms of the number of users who may have access to it and the ease with which the rest can download it (for free). It has few drawbacks, but one is that users must have the most up to date version of RealVideo as the sender.

Sorenson – good, but more upmarket

This is a really good, high-quality codec. It looks better than most at a screen size of 320 × 240, but does require the user to have a fast connection, at least 100 kb per second, which is almost double the rate most users possess. The Sorenson is a good solution for movies that are going to be viewed over high bandwith connections, but some editions (notable the Developer Edition) cater for the rest of us by using scalable streaming, as with RealVideo. One aspect which puts many people off using this codec is the length of time it takes to encode a movie in this way, but a bigger problem is the fact that it tends to make areas of highly saturated colour look blocky and unrealistic.

Intel Indeo 4 and 5 – good, but mainly for high power

With this method of compression you get a good result with high picture quality, but it is only viable for high-powered PCs or Macs. Version 5 allows for progressive downloads. Intel's codec is generally better than Cinepak but cannot match the picture quality of Sorenson.[6]

MPEG – use MPEG–2 for DVDs

It is worth knowing about MPEGs as a standard that the industry as a whole is using, even though they are not codecs as such. MPEG stands for the Motion Picture Experts Group, a body trying to offer common standards for widespread use, for the benefit of all users.[7]

Advanced tip
How MPEG works

MPEG works by using a complex system to allow greater quality with lower amounts of data. It looks at the information on several frames at a time, a Group of Pictures (GOP), what is known as Interframe Compression. It does this by breaking up information it has collated into I, B and P frames. I frames are index frames and contain all the important information of a frame. MPEG's trick is to perform different levels of compression on different parts of the frame, so that, for instance, the centre of a frame is compressed less than the outer, permitting about 15 per cent reduction in the size. B frames are bidirectional frames and contain only the differences between a frame and the next or the one before. Again, data can be reduced further in this way. The P stands for predicted frames and these are compressed on the basis of those which have been compressed so far.

Of all the MPEG levels, MPEG–4 is the most useful way of decoding multimedia files such as video. You won't often have to deal with MPEGs directly, but knowing how they work is to understand some of the fundamentals of video compression.

---

[6] www.real.com   Company site.
   www.sorenson.com   Company site.
   www.apple.com/quicktime/technologies/indeo   Indeo information.
   www. intel.com/ial/indeo   Indeo information.
[7] www.mpeg.org   Main site for MPEG formats news.
   wwwam.hhi.de/mpeg-video   Overview of MPEG.

Formats

There are various ways of decoding the information once it has been coded for sending over the Internet. Computer manufacturers have adopted different formats for codecs.

Video for Windows – short films and CD-ROM, not for Macs

This kind of file will have an '.avi' suffix at the end. The advantage of this one is that it comes as standard with Windows operating systems, but on the downside cannot be read on Macs. This format is primarily aimed at the CD-ROM movie, for short films stored and viewed on disc. Microsoft is not supporting this format and is moving towards a more accessible and reliable format. Reliability is an issue here as this format is notorious for putting audio and vision out of sync. The preferred codec for this format is Cinepak, which has widespread use but is poor in picture quality, but for better quality it can use Intel's Indeo system, version 4 or 5.

Microsoft Windows Media – good streaming tool, flexible

This kind of file has an '.ask' after it and is designed to cope with almost any user, from the snail's pace 14.4 modem to the motorway that is DSL. This format supports best the H.263, MPEG–4 and Intel's Indeo codecs, such as Netshow. Netshow servers are designed to maintain speed of data delivery even if demand increases, what is known as true streaming, but it does so by reducing the quality of the images seen by the user, first visual and then audio.[8]

QuickTime – flexible, highly rated, free

This format is seen with an '.mov' or '.qt' after its files and is Apple Computer's answer to the format race. It is a flexible format, ideal as much for CD-ROMs as for DVDs or the Internet. Unlike earlier Windows formats, this also performs on Macs and best supports Sorenson, Indeo, Cinepak and MPEG–1. QuickTime uses RTSP, or Real-Time Streaming Protocol, which means that it delivers the movie in real-time, as does RealG2 and Netshow.

RealPlayer – free and very widely used

Real Networks Real Media (with an '.rm' at the end of the file) format is by far the most popular on the market and has earned this degree of use by being accessible – it's free to download, as is QuickTime – but mostly by being able to alter its streaming level to suit the machine it is being viewed on. This means you don't have to create multiple versions of a movie for the user to choose from.

RealPlayer is a flexible format that copes well with content streamed live as part of a webcast or through a progressive download. The only negative point is that on low bit-rates the film can start to look decidedly blurry and featureless, but compressing to this degree is to be avoided anyway.[9]

---

[8] www.microsoft.com/windows/windowsmedia   Microsoft site.
[9] www.apple.com/quicktime/download   Download for Mac and PC.
    www.quicktimegazette.com   Newsletter of QT developments.

Interview

'We use Real Media Player for our viewers. This seems to be the most popular and screens the clearest. We use the highest resolution possible while converting [compressing] to preserve "the look" the filmmaker intended. Eventually, we want to use MPEG, the best and largest file format; space and money have been an issue.'

Rob Moretti, curator, iflicks.com, Internet movie site

Customized compression

Compression is available either in ready-to-go forms (fast food version), whereby you simply choose from a selection on the edit program and in a few moments have performed the task, or you can use an additional piece of compression software to do it for you (restaurant version), which is slower but more exacting and more responsive to individual needs. If you choose the latter you need first to know something about the process to see how to get the most for your films. In practice, there are occasions when you will be able to send a movie straight to the web, with no complications and little work involved on your part, but it is more likely that you may need a separate method for each film you make, depending on content, style and where you want to send it. This gives you more control over quality and how people view the film.

Using compression software

The growth in video on the web has led to companies specializing in products whose sole aim is to find better ways of encoding your movies. These act as 'plug-ins' placed within the edit software and are a recognition that the program's own compression facilities are not as good as those offered by more specialist products.

You don't need to get technical

These plug-ins make the process of saving a movie for the web a process more suited to the filmmaker who wants good results but wants to be able to adapt compression according to need. It is also good for those who aren't confident about setting data rates themselves. Compression software gives you the widest possible range of choices, allowing you to compress for all types of user connection, and allows you to save for all other formats, such as CD-ROM and DVD. When using this kind of software, take a look at the settings wizard, enabling you to take a slow pace through the whole compression route. It will ask you many questions in plain, filmmaker language.[10]

---

[10] www.terran.com   Information on Cleaner.
   www.adobe.com/support/techdocs/9a86   Adobe support.
   www.mp3.com   Free download of mp3 software.

> **Tip**   Try Cleaner, a piece of software which has taken a lead in the compression game. It lets you choose from a range of settings designed to suit every kind of movie and recommends a particular path if you are unsure.

The main choice: frame rate vs resolution

One of these choices concerns whether you want smooth-flowing video at the expense of picture quality or vice versa. Let's look at the uses of this. In a film where you have a lot of fast-moving action to follow but the precise picture details are not a priority – for instance, no text or detailed close-ups – then you may want greater smoothness, in terms of higher frame rate. A film which involves less movement but has a lot of detail which needs to be seen clearly could benefit from the reverse: a lower frame rate but greater picture quality.

Audio settings

For audio settings, you can also make choices. In most cases it is beneficial to reduce audio from 16-bit stereo – if the film is going to be viewed on a PC rather than in a cinema – down to mono at perhaps 8-bit. Obviously this is going to reduce sound quality but again you have the choice: do you want to get a better soundtrack by sacrificing some of the vision quality? Video conferencing, for instance, may require better sound at the expense of vision.

Why can't everyone watch my movie on the web?

As we have seen, many viewers will have slow modems. The 28.8 kilobits per second (kbps) modem is still very common, although many of these users may have access to far faster connections at their place of work. If you are compressing a movie you need to aim for a general data rate that is fast for

Modem type	Data rate in bits/second	Data rate in bytes/second
28.8k	20 kbps	2.5 KB/s
56.6k	32 kbps	4 KB/s
Dual ISDN	96 kbps	12 KB/s
T1, DSL and Cable modem	300 kbps	40 KB/s
WAN/LAN	160–800 kbps	20–100 KB/s

Figure 7.4 Modem rates.

those people with good connections and yet still within reach of the slower. A good rate to aim for is somewhere in the middle of the two rates, between 56 and 28, perhaps at 35 kbps. The reason for upping the rate here is that with buffering a 28.8 modem will deal fairly well with higher speeds of data, so you are not leaving them behind. Buffering can speed up a signal by about 20 kbps.[11]

Did you know?

About data rates

We have talked a lot about data rates as it is one of the most important elements in compression, but there are some important facts to be aware of when talking about data. This basic computer science stuff has a potentially huge impact if you use the wrong terms. To begin with, there is a difference between a KiloByte (with K and B in capitals, represented as KB) and a kilobit (lower case, represented as k and kb). Multimedia and video tend to go with KiloBytes, where 1K is equal to 1024 bytes, but telecommunications tend to use *bits*, in which there are 1000 to the kilo. The byte consists of 8 bits, so you must adjust the way you calculate the downloading ability of a modem. For example, a 28.8k modem (notice the lower case) will provide 28.8 kilobits per second (kbps), but if we measure it in bytes we see that it is 3.5 KB per second when we divide it by 8 (the number of bits in a byte).

The Crunch

- Compression is ideal for transmitting a DV movie on the web or putting it onto CD or DVD.
- Know what kind of movie each codec is best suited to.
- Customize your own compression to suit your movies: use compression software.
- View your movie when compressed to check quality.
- You don't have to get involved with all the computer/data/technical stuff. Just work out what aspect of the film is most important.
- Compression is complicated – agreed – but it can help send your movie around more places.

3. Shooting for the web

There is no doubt that the web opens up new possibilities for the filmmaker. But like any new medium, some films look good when shown on the Internet and some don't. The same is true of the difference between showing films on a television or a cinema screen. The small scale and intimacy of television means that shooting for this medium imposes certain restrictions; television is described as a close-up medium, requiring the filmmaker to bring the viewer close to the action and avoid large-scale

---

[11] www.high-techproductions.com/ntsc.htm   Guide to broadcast standards.

panoramic scenes. The aspect ratio also changes between theatrical and video release to make use of the maximum amount of screen in the smaller medium.

Web movies are different

Filmmakers work within these restrictions to obtain the best results for a production. It should come as no surprise, then, that the web has other restrictions which you need to bear in mind. These are useful only when your film is going to be seen primarily on the web and you don't expect to show it theatrically. However, the results of these guidelines on non-web films are not without merit; many films can benefit from the ideas suggested here, such as a simplification of image.

The effect of altering the movie or the way you make it, to accommodate the limits of the web, is a little like working with live music. Studio music is always going to sound clearer, neater and more subtle, but playing live requires a band to make a song understood despite the poor acoustics of an auditorium. Usually, this means making it more explicit, musically, and less subtle.

Shooting web films

Length of the movie

Short films fare better on the web, for obvious reasons; anything less than a few minutes in length is going to be more suited to the extremely slow connection rates most people still have. If you want to make something more ambitious, try dividing the movie up into small sections and turning it into an episodic series in which viewers can download a few minutes and watch it as part of the whole series.

Audio vs video

Bear in mind the choices you may have to make about the priority of audio or video. If a film needs both very smooth, clear images and a complex, layered soundtrack, you may run into problems.

If you decide to lose some picture quality in favour of sound then the Internet is going to be kinder to your film. Fantastic sound quality is far easier to compress than pictures and you will get more quality for your data bits with sound rather than vision. If sound is not a priority, avoid relying on stereo as it will be flattened into mono in most compression methods. This won't get rid of any sounds but, together with the overall reduction in quality, it will make them harder to distinguish from one another. Avoid complex layering of sounds. Keep interference or excessive ambient sound to a minimum. If you think in terms of sound perspective, in which sounds occupy various levels in terms of foreground and background, web film offers you less depth, so keep sounds obvious and clear. In general, use lavalier mics for clear, if slightly unnatural, sound. Imagine playing the movie to someone over the telephone; you would need strong, obvious sounds.

<u>**Go to:**</u> Chapter 5:7, 'Sound recording'.

Clear-cut stories

As a whole, the story and/or themes must be more apparent, lucid and defined. Think of the live music analogy: subtlety may be lost by the time it reaches the viewer. This is not to say that you must hand the film to the viewer on a plate, but you will have to make the information more obvious, given the reduced size of that information.

Beware of text

Credits are still going to be legible but should be placed on straight colour, which should not be too highly saturated. Place credits one at a time on separate frames rather than bunched together and with a slightly larger font size than usual, maybe set at 24 point, at least. Text within the film, either as subtitles or as a design element layered over images, is more problematic. It is likely to be lost if the frame starts blurring, and the reduced screen size is going to make it blend with the background images.

Simpler imagery

This is going to mean making your compositions sharper and better, but this applies equally well to all your movies, not just those intended for the web. Try to eliminate extraneous parts of the frame, so it tells what we need to see and virtually nothing else. Use plain backgrounds to lift out from the screen the elements you want the viewer to pick up on. Compositions should be bolder and more 'blocky', in other words, with greater use of larger shapes and fewer details. In most instances, this is going to bring us back to the idea of dominance of the close-up. One way to define the kind of clarity we need is to look at design. There is a rule of thumb sometimes used by poster designers which says that a good poster needs to still make an impression through a dirty bus window, viewed in passing, and this applies equally well to web film.

Go to: Chapter 5:2, 'Composition' section, for more help with stronger compositions.

Use close-ups

The film is to be seen on a small screen, at roughly 5 cm across, so you need to radically alter the way you depict action. The close-up will need to be utilized much more frequently than in other productions. If a scene requires some depiction of the expression on an actor's face, an extreme close-up is necessary, perhaps even focusing on parts of the face in turn.

Go to: Chapter 5:4, 'Narrative movies', for more help with using the close-up in your movies.

The right lighting

Thirty-five-millimetre celluloid film has better resolution than video, and straight, uncompressed video films have better resolution than web films. Being at the bottom of the heap can be resolved

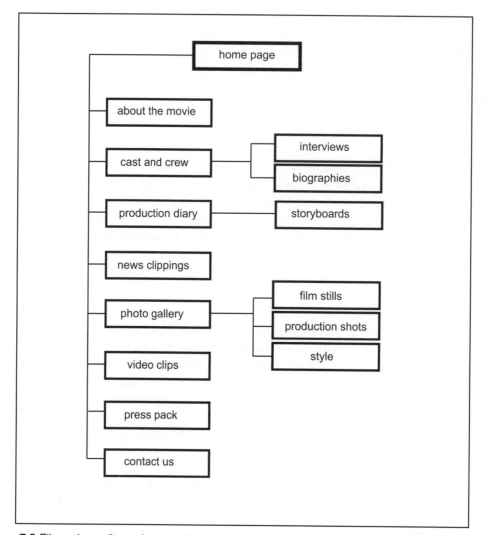

Figure 7.5 Filmmakers often rely on a dedicated website to spread the word about their work. This diagram shows an ideal website plan. Go to the CD-ROM to find out more about websites for filmmakers.

somewhat by a certain use of lighting, offsetting some of the detrimental effects of picture clarity. Strong contrast is crucial; flat, vague lighting is going to enhance detail, but heightened shadow and light will make a frame more easy to read, while improved composition may also enhance a sense of drama. Use a key light to pick out the main subject and use some fill lighting to separate the figure from the background, but above all avoid fluorescent lighting, as this flattens the picture. To test how your scene will look, take five paces back from your camera and have a look at the LCD monitor showing your movie.

Go to: Chapter 5:8, 'Lighting', for more detail on lighting techniques.

The right colours

Some colours don't travel well. Just as website designers use what are called 'web-safe colours', so films can also suffer from colours merging into another that are similar in hue or saturation. You will, on the whole, be safe with colour as long as you do not rely on it to convey important parts of the film; subtle differences between colours may be lost. This would have an impact, for example on text, if the text and background image colours were not dissimilar enough. Note also that strongly saturated colours cause some problems with some formats or player regardless of the image, though this is decreasing as an issue as software codecs become more advanced.

Use of the camera

Since clarity is a constant requirement, one of the biggest obstacles is camera shake. Despite the creative possibilities in shooting with a hand-held camera, the results on the web could be disappointing. By dropping the frame rate, the video becomes slightly more jerky and anything which increases this is to be avoided. A stationary shot is going to look better than pans, tilts or tracking, as these all increase the blurring or make the picture more blocky.

Aspect ratio

As with normal video movies, try at all times to shoot in the aspect ratio (screen shape) you want to edit in. This means that if you want a widescreen look, shoot in it. In practice, you should choose the aspect ratio best suited for your film, perhaps because a television broadcaster wants it a certain ratio. Try to avoid using widescreen as a style choice; it rarely improves poor images and usually simply heightens the bad result, cropping the frame unnaturally. However, if you film from the start in this aspect ratio then it is embedded in your compositions and looks natural and well suited to the film. Web movies are usually shown in screen shapes resembling television screens, a 4:3 ratio. If you film in widescreen, no matter how natural it looks, you lose a portion of the screen at the top and bottom. Unlike the cinema, the web broadcaster doesn't stretch its screen to accommodate your aspect ratio.

> **Tip** Aspect ratios for video are measured in pixels. Standard 4:3 PAL picture is measured in 720×576 pixels for video monitors, but for computer monitors a slightly different ratio is used to take into account the computer's square pixels, resulting in 768×576. You won't notice any difference; the different pixel ratios are there to maintain the same aspect ratios between television screens and computers.

Creative web movies

Looking at the list above, the don'ts far outweigh the dos and it must seem as if there is little artistic point to using the web for making films. But part of the progress within the medium of film over the last century has been the result of filmmakers pushing the limits of what can be achieved. Hitchcock pushed the very limited resources of sound when he made Britain's first sound film, *Blackmail*, in 1929. Even earlier, Georges Mellies devised the first special effects by accidentally using the camera for multiple exposures.

Push technology

Part of the task of the low-budget filmmaker is to look at what can done with the available technology, work with it as far as possible but at the same time push it further by experimentation, discovery and, basically, doing what the manual says you shouldn't. A quality that many independent filmmakers possess is that of being able to see possibilities within a tightly restrictive framework, whether this is budgetary or technological. Given that the web offers a filmmaker a direct way of reaching the viewing public, the constraints of this route are worth working with.

Some of the innovations seen in movie websites are testament to the fact that the filmmaker is a lateral-thinking, irrepressible artist. Many films make direct connections to early film experiments, conducted in the first decade of cinema. In that period, the theatrical movie was not the dominant form; people also wanted to see events they would not normally witness, like a train rushing overhead, filmed from the track, or burning barns crashing down. The pioneering spirit within film was a result of the desire of filmmakers to push the limits of this new form of communication and steadily turn it into an art form. That process was happening within a tightly confined space, in technology terms, yet produced a launch pad for generations of directors.

The Crunch

- Web movies are an evolving form, but they are still in their infancy. Get in on the history of them from the start.
- You're an artist – you like new ways of working and new forms of movie.
- Watch your movie through the camera LCD monitor from a few feet to check how it will look.
- Decide whether you sacrifice picture resolution, frame rate or sound.
- Keep it short and simple.
- Use strong lighting.
- Use a steady camera.
- Avoid small text.
- These restrictions imposed by web movies are good for your other movies too.
- Be experimental.
- Don't let it sit on the shelf: send it to a broadcast site.

4. Using Internet broadcast sites

Submitting films to a site

Getting a film accepted on a high-profile web movie site has acquired some prestige, with sites such as iFilm.com in the top 20 most visited Internet sites (statistics: May 2001, *Hollywood Reporter*).

Submitting films for these sites is straightforward. The most popular sites ask you to complete a registration form and pay before submission. Each site offers different incentives to attract filmmakers and has different terms; check on the specific requirements of a site before submitting.[12]

Film specifications

- Most films tend to be less than 20 minutes in length. Shorter ones are more popular with viewers due to download times.
- Films should be reasonably fresh, made within the last 2 years at least.
- Films should have all clearances and rights available. Make sure you have cleared the rights for any music in the movie before submitting. Some sites, such as AtomShockwave, distribute successfully to airlines, television and hand-held devices, and they will insist that no rights are going to be infringed elsewhere.
- Some sites screen only narrative work (Atom), while others include sections on experimental film, spoof and animation (iFilm).
- Tapes are mailed to the site operator on DV tape or Beta SP, although some will accept S-VHS or VHS. The preferred format for digital submissions tends to be CD-ROM and DVD, with the whole file on one disc only.
- All screen formats are accepted, including PAL, NTSC and SECAM.

Did you know?
Betacam SP is the highest grade analog video format, producing quality that far exceeds consumer-level VHS. Sony have also introduced a Betacam SX system, a digital version which records broadcast quality video.

Go to: Go to Chapter 3:1 for a complete list of which countries use each standard for broadcasting.

Interview
'I made a short film which has been screened on the Internet – *"This Ain't Your Business"*, a very low budget, tongue-in-cheek gangster film. I didn't sell the film [to the site] but I do think it is an advantage to have a film on the Internet. First, it is something to put on your CV (résumé). You've made the film and in a sense you've distributed it. You can also direct people to watch your film without having to send tapes. Second, there are so few outlets for short films, it would be crazy not to take advantage of what is offered.'

Carlo Ortu, filmmaker

---

[12] www.hollywoodreporter.com   News from Hollywood.
www.berlinale.de/en/f_main_einst.html   English version of Berlin Festival site.

Rights

The better sites will offer individualized deals based on the market potential for your movie. You don't lose any rights simply by submitting a movie, though check that you don't have to give any undertaking to this extent in online registration forms. The larger sites look to acquire worldwide rights and will actively seek to exploit markets for mutual benefit, though you need to check what percentage the distributor takes in each market, weighing up the benefits of signing over rights to an online distributor and losing the chance of selling through more traditional distribution methods.

Interview

'Use the Internet when trying to get your short film shown. There are a number of sites that showcase short films. Be careful, though, as many have an annual fee and some demand all world rights to the film. You may get some payment for the film but by losing your world rights you are giving up a lot. Go for sites that let you keep the rights to your film.'

David Norman, filmmaker

Paying to show your movie

Some sites ask for a fee to show your work, though on some of the larger sites with more industry experience and contacts in the wider distribution field, you are effectively getting a sales agent as well as a screening; they will actively push your film towards wider sales internationally. If you want this sort of site, look for ones that have evolved out of existing distribution and marketing companies (for example, Atom Film). Depending on the quality of the format used to screen your movie, costs can vary between $50 and $300 for a specific run of 3–12 months. Getting the film online may take several weeks, though some sites will offer 'express options' (read: more expensive) to get it screened more quickly.

Bear in mind that not all sites ask for payment to show your movies. The sites that offer more, such as a dedicated home page for your movies, do so because filmmakers are willing to pay for these services. Sites such as Atom view films and select only those they feel that have marketing potential – which is different from, though not always opposed to, artistic quality, so don't be discouraged if your film gets rejected.[13]

---

[13] http://Panushka.absolutvodka.com   Experimental animation.
www.alwaysindepenedentfilms.com   Great independent shorts plus some classic silent movies, but most cannot be seen on Macs.
www.AtomFilms.com   Comprehensive and widely popular.
www.bijoucafe.com   Cult movies.
www.binarytheater.com   Selection from US film schools.
www.thebitscreen.com   Web-specific movies.
www.dfilm.com   UK site offering one film per month.
www.directorunknown.com   Dogme-style movies.

The Crunch

- Showing on the web can help you: the feedback you get helps you move on.
- Keep movies short.
- Beware losing your rights to the movie.
- Not all sites ask for a fee.
- Aim at the best sites first.
- Capitalize on your successes: tell everyone you know to watch your film on a site. Post a message on a filmmakers' bulletin-board to say 'watch my movie'.

www.flashfilmfestival.com   New York annual festival of Flash movies.
www.heavy.com   Music-based and underground movies.
www.lalive.com/hollywoodshorts   Cinema-style site showcasing just a few movies each month.
www.hypnotic.com   Unusual and experimental movies.
www.ifilm.com   Possibly more comprehensive than Atom as it includes non-narrative and experimental work.
www.newvenue.com   Web-specific movies showcased.
www.pitchtv.com   Latin American and Southern European movies.
www.reelscreen.com   Shows new and archive movies by mostly British filmmakers.
www.shortfest.com   Excellent short movies site, but you need QuickTime or RealPlayer.
http://cherry.switch2.net   UK site offering short movies.
www.undergroundfilm.com   Mostly USA short films, independent and original.
www.urbanentertainment.com   Black-oriented site.

8 Distributing and promoting your movie

1. Guide to distribution

What is distribution?

One of the most challenging tasks awaiting you is to embark on pushing your film out into the wider world, and it comes when perhaps all your energies are drained by the process of getting the film made in the first place. Distribution – the art of finding someone somewhere to show your movie – is nevertheless a time when you must be prepared to make decisions that affect whether the film has any life beyond your immediate friends and family. Going into the field blind is not an option; luck plays no part in this end-game, except to say that the better you are prepared, the more you increase your chances of being lucky. You need to know what kinds of deals are common, what you can expect to get as a first-time filmmaker, how deals for short films differ from features, and what each route – whether theatrical, video, television or the Internet – can offer.

Distribution is going to take many forms. Despite the obvious kudos of seeing your film in a cinema, theatrical receipts account for only a small part of the overall gross a film could return. There are other options which are going to bring in revenue, including:

- Theatrical release.
- Terrestrial national broadcast television.
- Terrestrial local broadcast television.
- Cable television.
- Satellite television.
- DVD.
- The Internet.
- Sell-through VHS tape.

No single potential market alone is likely to bring any significant return for your investment, but a combination of these will be the best possible way of getting what you can for the film. But there is a hierarchy to which you approach first: theatrical release is the first step, followed by the small screen, followed by the Internet.[1]

Try cinemas first

Most filmmakers are predisposed toward getting their film seen in a cinema; films usually look and sound better on a big screen and there is a certain buzz from watching with an audience. If you share this view, make it your aim regardless of other avenues you wish to pursue, because if you don't show theatrically as your first option, it may be a great deal harder to take this route after sales to television or retail, as most theatres are not going to show movies that have been broadcast. And why not aim at the top to start with? You are the only person who is going to champion the movie at first and there is nothing gained from selling yourself short right at the starting blocks. Furthermore, the experience of seeing your film with other people gives you a chance to gauge reaction to it and to take a step back from it, enabling you to be more objective in your views.

Distribution options

If you have a feature that you want to sell, you need to make decisions about how to go about it: are you going to seek a distributor who will hawk your film around to get it seen, or are you going to do it yourself?

Interview

'Yes, it is difficult to get picked up. We will shop *"Blood Kiss"* (2000) around for a few months, then we will move into distribution. Most times, even if a film does manage to gain distribution, the contract greatly favours the distributor and the filmmaker hardly sees any profit. But by controlling (or self) distribution, we can offer our movies a real chance at being profitable. It is moving to a time of self-sufficiency for filmmakers. Not only can we make movies for less than what Hollywood spends catering a movie, we will also be able to sell the movie as well.'

Alex P. Michaels, filmmaker, prelude2cinema.com, USA

---

[1] www.film.queensu.ca/links/festivals   Guide to Canadian festivals.
   www.amamedia.org   Non-profit media organization offering distribution contacts.
   www.marklitwak.com   Entertainment attorney's site with much useful information.
   www.business.com/directory   Film distributors.
   www.assistantdirectors.com/financial/distribution.shtml   List of international distributors.
   www.rightsmart.com   Site for sellers to list their movies.
   www.films4auction.com   Auction site for movies to find buyers and distributors.

Self-distribution

The tough option

Marketing movies is a complex, unstable field. The market-place changes rapidly according to the most recent successes and is subject to geographical and economical variations. It is, therefore, undoubtedly difficult to attempt to market your film yourself unless you have knowledge of what each market offers, of what constitutes a good sales price, of foreign sales, of percentages, and you have the contacts to make this happen. This route means you will be involved in the business side of filmmaking more than ever before and that takes away valuable filmmaking time from your next project.

Domestic theatres

With domestic theatres, you will be negotiating directly to place your film for a limited run, but this is unlikely to yield results. Theatres specializing in independent movies are going to be more open to this possibility, but usually will want you to have some exposure at a film festival first.[2]

Handling advertising

You will be responsible for advertising. This means compiling a press pack and other promotion material used by theatres. Don't spend unwisely on advertising, because it is likely that you will receive less than 30–35 per cent of gross box office takings from a theatre. In real terms, this means that if a 200-seat theatre sells a quarter of its tickets (it is an unknown film, don't forget) at £10 apiece, with a revenue of £500, you receive something like £150, which is going to cover only basic publicity.

Terms

You will need to negotiate with theatres how much of the box office gross you will receive, but be aware that a theatre taking 65 per cent of gross receipts of mainstream films is probably going to increase this if they think the risk is greater for an unknown movie. You need to ensure that the deal you have negotiated tells you when your movie will be shown, and for how long. Some independent cinemas show short films for free before a main programme, or have unknown features as part of special slots in a programme and these functions are built into their educational programme. University cinemas, arts centres and local film societies are also likely to be more receptive to flexible rates.

Projection

A theatre's method of projection must match your print. A theatre equipped to show 35 mm film may not have the facilities to show a digital film, nor even a 16 mm film, although some smaller independent chains or campus theatres may be equipped to show S-VHS video. But the move towards digital

---

[2] www.bfi.org/showing/regional   UK guide to independent cinemas.
   www.digitalprojection.com   Specialist company showcase of new media.

projection of digital films is inexorable and will lead eventually to more and more theatres accepting this format, though it is more likely to be larger, high revenue cinemas leading the way for some time. Digital projection is going hand-in-hand with digital broadcasting, and films are being broadcast directly to some theatres. Studios are very keen for theatres to pursue this, with more films being made within the digital domain, and the massive costs of producing prints would be all but abolished.[3]

Tip   The pioneer in digital projection to cinemas was the very-low-budget independent movie *The Last Broadcast*. In October 2000, it was broadcast to selected theatres in North America by satellite.

Movie premiere

Marketing your film could be more difficult if it is yet to play in a theatre, and this is more so if it has not first premiered at a national capital venue, or at a prominent festival. This would mean Los Angeles, New York, London, Berlin and other places with a reputation for strong festival entries. Even a small showing at a venue specializing in low-budget movies is worth seeking if it is in a capital city.

Foreign sales

Distributors estimate that sales in domestic theatres (cinemas in the country of origin) will bring almost no chance of recouping a budget for a feature film, regardless of the production costs. Foreign sales, television and cable, DVD or video sales will bring home the best returns. The sort of film you have made affects which market is the more successful, with short films less likely to sell than a feature for theatrical release, but more likely to be sold for television broadcast or the web. According to Roseann S. Cherenson, Executive Vice President of Distribution at Phaedra Cinema, the short film is seen as:

> 'a calling card towards getting a feature film or television career. I have to say that while there is the possibility that you could make some money domestically or internationally from your short, the vast majority do not make any money, just get the filmmaker good festival exposure and hopefully prizes (maybe even Oscars) that help boost a filmmaker's chance of getting full-length gigs.'

Sales outside the country of origin may account for up to 75 per cent of total world sales (much higher if yours is a low cinema-going nation, but these figures are more correct for the USA and Europe) and are considered key markets, so you will need to be considering where and how to get your film seen in other countries. Handling distribution yourself means being confident about tapping into this market.

---

[3] www.teweb.com/lastbroadcast   Site looking at digital satellite projection pioneer movie.

> **Tip** The main film-going markets are, in order, the USA, Europe, the Far East, Latin America, Australia/New Zealand. Within these areas, the countries spending the most on movies, which would be at the top of your marketing list, are as follows. Europe: United Kingdom (25 per cent of European market); Far East: Japan (60 per cent of that market); Latin America: Brazil and Mexico (25 per cent each of that market). Of remaining foreign markets, Australia and New Zealand together take up about 5 per cent.

Getting a distributor

The better option

If you decide that the brief outline above is more than you wish to handle, you may want to find someone who will take the strain, for a fee. Many law firms and PR agencies will take on films, helping you find the right exposure for your movie. This would include trying to get the film seen at screenings and festivals, but there are also a network of reps within the film industry who may take on your movie, either at the pre-production finance stage or in marketing of the finished product.

What is a distributor?

A distributor is a person or company who will try to sell your film to markets you could not have previously reached. They will have extensive knowledge of each market, from theatrical to home rental, and will, more importantly, know how to pitch your film to achieve the highest levels of exposure at each event or screening. They will take a sizeable cut of your receipts and they will have many other movies they are trying to sell, but if you want to make any money at all from your movie, the service they are going to provide is extremely valuable in terms of getting you seen by the industry.

Actually getting a distributor to act for you is an uphill struggle. They receive dozens of unsolicited tapes each day and as many scripts and unfinished movies. If you win a slot in a festival, and get some raised profile from this, distributors may seek out a deal with you. The main festivals are populated by hundreds of international buyers and sellers each trying to make deals with each other, based on what critics, film juries and audiences claim to be the best of the crop.

If your film is noticed, most of the buyers you encounter will offer a distribution deal involving either an advance or no advance.

> **Interview**
> 'My distributor did not pay for my film. He raised the money we needed to finish and release the film. The reason he did it is because he now has a cut of overseas sales. Without that he would not have taken the film at all.'
>
> *Piotr Skopiak, director, Small Time Obsession, UK*

Foreign distribution

Foreign sales will account for a substantial part of your overall revenue and should be explored fully. As we have seen, domestic release is not something to rely on in recouping costs and may prove to be in the region of only a quarter of overall theatrical receipts. Furthermore, some films have specific appeal to markets outside of their country of origin and return a far greater percentage of overall sales, boosting revenue. For example, the British director Mike Leigh is particularly well received in France, while British cinemas have tended not to show his films widely.[4]

Distribution routes: where you can show your movie

Terrestrial television: local and national

While feature films are more suited to theatrical release, the short film succeeds more often on the small screen. Broadcasters are showing more short movies than they ever were, the number of accessible slots growing steadily in many countries. In the USA, there are several venues which may show your movie, but for the most part these are in local stations. At the top of the league in terms of prestige and audience numbers is PBS, in the United States.

Did you know?
PBS (Public Broadcasting Service) is a private, non-profit corporation operating 349 non-commercial television stations across the United States. To Americans, PBS offers a respite from relentless ratings-led entertainment shows on commercial stations and instead focuses on educational, arts and community programming. Available to 99 per cent of American homes with televisions, PBS serves nearly 100 million people each week.

They run a slot for documentaries – *POV* – and another for both fiction and documentary – *Independent Lens*. PBS provides fees for films it shows and the exposure you would receive is a great confidence boost.

Local PBS stations offer other slots for shorts, including:

- Reel New York on WNET 13 New York.
- Image Union on WTTW Chicago.
- ViewFinder on KPBS San Diego.

Acquisition fees for these local stations are low compared to what you could receive with larger broadcasters, although they are often up to $100 per minute, so submit your film to as many as possible simultaneously.

---

[4] www.filmfestivals.com   Comprehensive listings of film festivals.

In Britain, Channel Four's *The Shooting Gallery* acquires films directly from the filmmaker and may also offer considerable back-up in completion costs. Submission to this and other slots is straightforward but highly competitive and can be accessed through their websites. If you encounter a slot that asks for payment before viewing your film, think again. Most slots are free, or even pay you a small fee on transmission.[5]

Cable television and satellite

In cable television, there are more specialist programmes offering the chance to show your work, but to a far smaller audience. For documentaries, HBO/Cinemax run the *Undercover* and *Reel Life* series, which pay the filmmaker far above the usual rate and 'place you alongside a very eclectic and interesting group of documentaries' (Greg Pak, filmmaker). The prestigious film festival Sundance is also involved in broadcasting and its channel, The Sundance Channel, buys short films from unknown directors. Acquisition fees are up to $2000, but although prestige is high, actual audience share is low. A similarly discerning and prestigious cable channel, The Independent Film Channel, is also a good venue to submit for.

Before submitting a film to a broadcaster, make a few decisions first about the kind of 'return' you want. You need to decide which has priority: prestige, audience numbers or pay. If it is audience numbers you are after, national television is the route, while prestige and good acquisition rates are sometimes to be found in the same station. A good rule to follow, whichever route you intend to take, is to start with the biggest, most well-known, highest-paying stations and then work down. Many of the larger slots prefer it if your film has not first been seen by local audiences, though this will not automatically preclude you from selection.[6]

Educational

A further market, though considerably smaller than those looked at so far, is educational sales. This may include university courses and community groups who may be particularly disposed toward your film through subject matter. You could attend screenings as part of a discussion or lecture. A film dealing with racism, for example, could bring sales on campuses and communities where this is an issue. Another dealing with industrial relations could arouse interest from union groups. However, this market is not easy to engage with, as its buyers will probably not be a part of the usual buying/selling community at film festivals, although a distributor may have appropriate contacts.

[5] www.clermont-filmfest.com   Short film festival site (needs translating from French but some servers do this for you: try Google).
www.pbs.org/independentlens   Linked site to PBS television slot.
www.pbs.org/pov   Linked site for documentary slot.
www.filmfour.com   UK Channel Four film site.
[6] www.hbo.com/reellife/index.html   Site for TV documentary slot.
www.hbo.com/americaundercover   Documentary slot.
www.sundancechannel.com   Details of how to submit your movie.
www.ifctv.com   Independent film channel.

> **Tip** A cautionary tale is that of the influential documentary *Roger and Me*, by Michael Moore, focusing on the effect of General Motors' closure plans in unemployment-hit Pennsylvania. Moore was keen to preview the film in the town shown in the story, but was disappointed that few of the town's inhabitants attended.

Internet distribution

The number of sites offering to show your movies has increased in line with the comparative ease with which video can be downloaded on the web. This route can offer some very strong audience figures, outstripping that which can be achieved in a theatrical release, and some sites have developed enough of a profile to lend considerable kudos to the offer of a showing.

Broadcast sites vary widely, from those at the top of the scale offering payment and the chance to place your résumé and contact details to those offering no fee, some of whom are online only intermittently. In the short time that web film has been a possibility, a handful of sites have come to dominate the field, but this is not to say that smaller sites have nothing to offer.

> **Tip** The British site in-movies.co.uk has built up a large selection of short films and, unlike Atom, takes only Internet rights, leaving you free to seek sales elsewhere simultaneously. This site has set new standards for others to follow by commissioning shorts, paying for filmmakers to make and show their movies.

Jess Search, co-founder of Shooting People, a widely used site for filmmakers in Britain, believes broadcasting on such sites is becoming more important to filmmakers:

> 'It will only increase in importance as a distribution medium as quality improves and it does remain an easier way to refer people to your work than sending out tapes. iFilm and Atom have a certain kudos – a bit like being accepted for London/Edinburgh/Berlin Film Festivals – and it certainly helps to say your film is on their site rather than just your own site, just as it helps to be shown at a festival rather than your own screening in encouraging busy industry people to take the time to look. There are still huge limitations to web viewing to be sure: the things that work best have been shot for web – not too much movement, music sequences (music videos work well) and more heavily lit than usual – but the only way is up, especially as broadband becomes more popular.'

Low return on deals
The larger sites have struck deals with television broadcasters, passing on shorts originally shown on the web, and have supported filmmakers by offering a percentage of advertising revenue according to

how many downloads a film generates. The financial return of these deals tends to be very low, but the reviews which viewers post, and the use of such sites as part of a larger promotion plan, makes it a worthwhile option.

Festival links

Some sites are also linking up with festivals to show short films and in return lend sites the credibility that tight festival selection offers. The US festival South by Southwest in 2000 selected 10 short films to show on Atom for 3 months. Although there was no payment to filmmakers in this instance, it has set a precedent that others follow.[7]

Internet rights: protecting your movie

Just as you sign over the right to show a film with a particular distributor in theatres, so the Internet also works by giving all or some of the rights over your movie to a particular site. In the rush to sell a movie, you may be tempted to accept any deal, ignoring some of the finer points in a contract. You need to consider some areas very carefully.

Distribution agreement

If you are offered a showing on a website, you will receive a 'distribution agreement'. Check whether the site is offering to actually broadcast your movie, as opposed to selling video copies of it via the Internet, or doing both. This sounds like an obvious point, but if you later strike a deal with a foreign buyer to sell video copies of your movie in a certain country, the fact that the consumer can buy your cassette already from another country over the Internet may affect your deal.

If you have already allowed your movie to be broadcast on television, or in theatrical release, regardless of how limited this may have been, you must be open about this when agreeing your contract. Similarly, a television company will need to know whether your movie has first been broadcast on the Internet. Withholding this information could lead to problems later, if the TV company perceives that you have violated their exclusive rights to show the film.

Royalties

Royalties have yet to be standardized on the Internet. Choose a site that offers you a cut of the advertising revenue generated by people viewing your movie. Check whether you are receiving equal share with other films, although some sites include confidentiality clauses restricting filmmakers from revealing what their cut is. If a film is your Internet debut, and you have no profile in the wider industry, you have no real bargaining power and will probably have to take what you are offered. Bear in mind also that disparity of rates is inevitable, since some filmmakers regularly generate many more downloads than others.

---

[7] www.sxsw.com   Join mailing list for South by Southwest festival.

Rights

In signing a contract, you are granting rights to that website, exclusive or otherwise, and you need to ensure that you have the authority to do this. If your movie has music which needs permission to be included, or literary rights which must be acquired, have you first obtained the necessary permission? Some sites offering broadcast or video and DVD sale don't let you past the home page without first asking whether you have music or screenplay rights to your movie. Music is usually the biggest hurdle, as some makers of short films are unaware of the need to obtain permission for even a few seconds of music, or perceive that an unknown musician with few sales won't be aware that their music is being used on a movie.

Written agreements

If you do sell a film for viewing in any setting, you must make sure that you have full acceptance from your actors and anyone else who appears in the film. To get your film shown in a prestigious venue or television slot and then have to withdraw because you don't have clearance would be heartbreaking. To free your production from these potential problems, ask everyone who appears in the film to sign a written agreement that they accept your right to exhibit this film in a 'public showing'. You need this for any kind of movie, including documentaries. Written agreement may have special relevance where young, up-and-coming actors subsequently become famous overnight, and in documentaries tackling outlandish and extreme subject matter. Certainly broadcast television would expect to have complete clearance from everyone who took part before transmitting your film.[8]

If you are in a position to offer rights, look at how those rights are arranged. Some entertainment lawyers suggest seeking a reversion clause in which rights are returned to you after a set period, perhaps 6 months or a year. Rights could be retained by the site only if a certain amount of revenue is generated during that period.

Use the Internet for marketing, not financial return

In general marketing terms, remember that since a film shown on the Internet can be accessed, theoretically, from any territory in the world, just about all your future marketing deals will be affected once you have shown the film on the web. Since it is unlikely that you are going to see any reasonable return by selling to the Internet, it may be more prudent to seek deals first with markets offering higher rates, such as television and video. In addition, copyright laws vary enormously from country to country, and if you are at all protective about your movie and the possibility of its being copied and sold, think twice about Internet broadcast. The Internet should not be seen as a way of recouping costs or making a profit on your movie, rather it is an effective marketing tool, enabling people to see what you do, remember your name and check out the next movie you make. Although it certainly lacks any financial gain for the filmmaker, it somewhat makes up for this by offering the widest possible return

---

[8] www.fairuse.stanford.edu   Statutes relating to copyright on the net.
   www.a-w.org   Useful non-profit organization dedicated to Internet copyright protection and education.

of opinion. Many people find the comments and suggestions made by viewers enlightening and encouraging.[9]

So, to recap, decide in advance what your aims are in seeking Internet broadcast. Since financial gain is unlikely to be high, viewing figures are the main attraction, and that means going first to sites with high profiles.

DVD and video

This is more likely to be a route you pursue after you have first investigated the possibility of theatrical and television release, but if you look at this area after or before other routes, consider carefully who you deal with. There are many companies now offering to make copies of your movie on DVD and purporting to sell these. Don't forget that a company saying they will try to sell your DVD is not the same as a company saying they will go out and actively push your movie, advertising it and making sure it gets seen at the right markets. Given the ease with which DVDs can be produced, in very small numbers, there may not be much investment on the part of the distributor and you may well end up being part of a mail-order list with low sales. It is possible to burn your own DVDs, with Apple Computers leading the way in making this a consumer-level tool. Doing it yourself may prove to be no more expensive than via an Internet DVD distributor, with the advantage that you can include additional material such as commentary, interviews and other marketing tools.

Contracts and distribution deals

In each of the routes described above, you will have to deal with contracts. It depends on the cost of your movie as to whether you hire an entertainment lawyer or decide to rely on advice from other filmmakers and your own judgement.

Tip For fair advice from other filmmakers and industry professionals, try posting a query on a filmmakers' Internet bulletin-board, such as Shooting People or Indiewire.

Advance deals

If you get an offer with an advance, the buyer takes their distribution fee from any money your film makes – often around the 35 per cent mark – and then take off the advance you were paid at the start of the deal. It doesn't stop there; they then start to recoup their expenses, which may be considerable. For most filmmakers taking an advance, that is the last return they see from the movie, so it is important to make the right level of advance to begin with; calculate your figures based on the idea that this is all the money you will ever get for the movie. In calculating the advance, the buyer is not

[9] www.loc.gov/copyright   US information about copyright.

plucking figures out of the air, but thinking coolly and with much experience about the revenue this film is likely to generate. They take into account all costs and then think about making some profit for themselves. If this seems like a tough deal, bear in mind that the exposure you receive is going to be more helpful in the long term. Tarantino's *Reservoir Dogs* made more of a splash culturally than it did in terms of actual box office receipts, and the rest is history. If you do receive an advance, make sure that you stay in communication with the buyer to make sure that you receive your 'overages' when or if your movie starts to make profit beyond the expenses outlined above.

Non-advance deals

The other kind of deal, with no advance, means you don't see any returns for some time, at least 6 months after release. If the film starts to make good returns, you will see more of a share of it than if you had an advance, but only after the distributor has taken a cut and taken expenses. However, you will have negotiated in advance what you both agree is a reasonable amount to spend on advertising and other expenses, referred to as capped expenses.

The cut they take will vary but as a baseline figure, in North America the figure is 50 per cent for theatrical, roughly 40 per cent for video and television, and 20–40 per cent for foreign sales. Films will almost never recoup what they cost and then have enough to share around to the crew if you rely on domestic theatrical receipts alone, even in countries with a large population. The most likely chance of seeing returns – overages – is from video or DVD sale and television, with the only obstacle to this being whether the film had more spent on paying for theatrical release than was recoverable in the cinemas. Any other possible markets which could generate returns are opened up only after theatrical release has been fully mined. If you are relying on sales other than theatrical to recoup your costs as director/producer, you will have a long wait if the film performs poorly in domestic release, but the spread of these other markets is enough to raise the possibility of some return.

Check your contract

Whatever deal you look into, make sure you understand the whole contract and the kind of terms used. Ask for clarification on any term you are unsure about and insist that standard terms are agreed upon. For example, theatrical release may be agreed, but you need to know within what time-scale this would happen, and if the words 'reasonable period' are the answer, insist this is put in terms of months, years, centuries or whatever.[10]

Agree acceptable cost limits

One of the valuable services of the distributor is in advertising and pushing the movie to the right places, such as film festivals. These costs soon add up and you need to agree in advance how much

---

[10] http://store.yahoo.com/fmstore/frefilmuscon.html   Free sample contracts.

is a reasonable amount to spend on marketing. Take into account the cost of the movie and what you expect a low estimate to be of the return from all markets. Then agree a cap on expenses above a certain amount. If you don't cap you may not actually have to pick up the bill for disproportionate expenses, but it does mean you will have to wait far longer before any revenue comes your way. Don't let the unscrupulous distributor use your movie as a free travel pass, recouping more than they should from your sales.

What is your share?

Ask for clarification about what part of the potential revenue is being divided up when your percentage is worked out. You need to know whether you are sharing in the producer's share or whether your share comes from total profits. As an example, take the case of a producer from New York who was in dispute with a filmmaker reluctant to give much of a slice of the profits, should there be any. Starting at the top of the chain, the theatre takes 65 per cent of gross receipts and gives the rest back to the distributor. The other 35 per cent which the distributor received was the net money and had to be big enough to recover all advertising and print costs. The producer was seeking a deal in which he received 12.5 per cent of gross receipts, leaving that 35 per cent which the distributor received diminished down to 22.5 per cent. This set-up would have been unlikely to attract interest from distributors, but if the producer was asking for 12.5 per cent of the distributor's share, a deal would have been possible. Alternatively, the producer could have sought gross receipts of theatrical release only, which as we have seen accounts for only a small proportion of total revenue; the distributor will be more concerned about video and television rights.

If your film does the unexpected and starts to make money at the box office or in other sales, you will receive statements from the distributor detailing what money is coming in from what source. But if you decide you want to check up on the progress of your film if you feel not enough revenue is coming your way, you should not be asked in your contract to waive your rights to audit these figures and you should not be required to audit before enough time has elapsed for the film to make some profit. If you think that your share of profits is not forthcoming, an audit can be costly but the only effective way of recovering money from the distributor. Your contract should allow you to ask the distributor to cover the costs of an audit if it reveals that they have withheld money owed you, although this is rare and often down to mismanagement rather than malice.

If the distributor forwards you an advance, check whether you are paying interest on this money. If so, check whether interest is being gained by the distributor from money received in advance from theatres. If you can't eliminate interest, try to reduce it.

Arbitration

If you disagree with your distributor and are unable to resolve an issue, you need to have a clause on arbitration built into the contract. Lawyers' fees will hurt you far more than they hurt the company, so it is in your interests to have a binding arbitration agreement, avoiding costly court battles.

The Crunch

- Decide whether you distribute it yourself or involve a distributor.
- If you do it yourself, are you sure you can handle every market?
- If it's a feature, try theatrical release first.
- If it's a short, try festivals, TV and cable first.
- Avoid the Internet as the first option.
- Check your contract.
- Don't sign away all your rights to an Internet site.
- Foreign sales and DVD/VHS will bring more revenue.

2. Strategies for promotion

These chapters on promotion and distribution are aimed at pointing out the possible routes available to get your films seen more widely. Before entering into the world of publicity, press relations and profile raising, we need to take a step back and look at how to devise a coherent approach so that the time and money involved is worth it. You will only get one chance to promote the film; if you get it wrong, you can't ask people to give you a second chance, with so many filmmakers vying for the same attention from public or buyers. Whether you buy into the whole idea of film as a commodity or not, you must still accept that people won't see your work unless you compete with every other piece of culture trying to catch their eye. If you ran a business, you would expect to have to actively promote your products and would not rely on the maxim: 'If it's good quality, they'll find it.' Any movie that involves an outlay of time or money needs to have behind it some promotion plan.[11]

Get a plan

Promotion must be worked into the overall production plan right from the start, as a part of the overall budget. You will then spend only what is appropriate to the size of the production and won't feel too bad spending it because you have allocated it specifically for this purpose. If you involve investors in funding your film, they will take you far more seriously if you include in your costings some budget for selling the product they are supporting.

Before you move on to a plan, decide first what is it you are hoping to achieve in marketing your movie. We could narrow down the options to the following:

1 I want to get the film seen but I don't expect to make any cash this time around – I'm building a profile.
2 I want to get the film seen and I need to make a small amount of money to recover costs.
3 I have not yet made this movie and I want to attract support to get it made.

[11] www.efp-online.com/   European news on film promotion.
www.telefilm.gc.ca/en/affint/marches/marches.htm   Canadian film marketing information.
www.film-connection.com/resources-l-showcases.html   Details of low-budget showcase sites.

Beginner's route

This is likely to be the aim for those at the start of their careers, possibly making short films for entry into festivals, competition or cable television stations. In this case, the right route is to approach festivals, television short film slots, independent cinemas and websites with the aim of securing some small exposure for the movie but which you can then build on. Just one showing of your movie at whatever level and in whatever format is enough to launch your campaign of getting recognition for this or the next movie.

Beyond short movies route

This second route is likely to be followed by those who have made movies with a bigger budget than the average short and are aiming to see some return from their investment. They may have already made a few shorts and have some experience of showing them at festivals or on television. The more profitable routes will involve gaining entry to television slots that pay for the right to show the movie, or others that commission further projects. Retail sales will be crucial, centring on limited DVD and VHS release, and these must be spread over as wide a geographical base as possible. Theatrical release is a possibility for feature films but may drain any profits that could result, and would need to be well placed in the right cinema. You do, however, need to be realistic about the chances of making any return on your movie; getting it seen does not mean making money and even getting a distribution deal doesn't necessarily mean that the future is bright. For most producers, the advance is all the money they will ever receive due to the distributor first taking out all costs from the producer's portion, leaving very little left over as 'profit'. For this reason, get the highest possible advance on offer.

Features, advanced route

This last route is more likely to attract those people who have more experience of filmmaking and have now decided to move towards more elaborate, fully funded feature-length films. They may have made a small section of the movie and hope to get finance for completion costs. If this is your position, you may need to find a producer's rep, with the aim of securing a financing deal with a distribution company. A round of hard selling is going to centre on how well your film can perform at festival screenings or special screenings for selected agents. In many cases, there is the expectation that you have first invested heavily in the film yourself, demonstrating your commitment by having raised some finance and gained the confidence of investors. Festivals may put you in the right place to find a rep willing to push your movie and conscious of the right route for you, nationally and internationally. Don't expect to be able to handle the detail of foreign DVD sales or other unfamiliar markets without some outside help.

In all these options, it should be recognized in advance that there is a long-term goal – to make more movies and eventually enter profitability – and there is a short-term goal – to get a profile, with any exposure at all. If you make any profit at this early stage, consider it just the icing on the cake.

Interview

'The best way to get publicity is to never take no for an answer! In this industry, you have to push and push and push. If you believe you can get your film screened at the local cinema, then do it. If they say no, then ask again, ask at a different cinema. The media is about who you know rather than what you know, so make friends with people in high places; just being friendly can reap dividends when you need something from them.'

Kevin Lapper, filmmaker, ReelRaine Films

Marketing strategy

Research screenings

You need first to get views on what sort of movie you have made, since you are the last person entitled to be objective about the strengths and weaknesses of it. Maybe psychologists should coin a term to describe viewing one's artistic efforts in an exaggerated positive or negative light, where a filmmaker can no longer see the film, only the time and money invested in it (how about chronic artistic dysmorphia?).

Screenings

Arrange screenings of the film with friends and other filmmakers, on a small level at first. Try to recruit a range of viewers, with different expectations, but don't make life difficult for yourself; choose people for your pre-screening with care, preferably people who see independent movies often. Ask them to write their positive and negative comments about your film on a postcard, or hold a discussion if you have a thick skin. You need to know what kind of audience is going to respond best to the movie, what issues are raised in it and how they are conveyed, and whether any part of the movie is unclear, including parts of the plot.

Listen to other filmmakers

Although the practice of using focus groups by Hollywood is frowned upon in the independent sector, it must be remembered that our aims could not be more different. In Hollywood, it is possible that the film's conclusion may be altered if focus reports suggest so, or that certain characters be excised, all with the aim of avoiding alienating any section of the viewing public.

But in our own case, we are looking at defining the film, assessing how it is viewed, and may not consider cutting unpopular parts. However, if you have investors on board, think carefully about this sort of screening as the investor may insist on changes as a result of unfavourable pre-screenings. For wider audiences, try a screening at a film school, university film clubs or local filmmaker groups. Attend in person so you know at what point people started to walk out or how much applause there was.

Form a company

Project a more professional air by forming a company, perhaps with other filmmakers. Forming a production company can force you to become much more organized about your marketing and encourages your tax department to see you in a more favourable light, offsetting costs against tax if and when your movie takes off. The company could be a long-term venture to support all your movies, or could be formed for one project only. Go the whole way: get a company logo and headed paper. It won't legitimize your work as great film but does legitimize you as a filmmaker.

Set up a web site

This is as crucial as your calling card and as useful as an office full of assistants. A huge amount of information can be displayed and accessed by those you want to impress.

Go to: CD-ROM for a complete guide to setting up a filmmaker's site.

Make a press pack

Prepare material you can mail to the media to garner publicity for the movie. Use it also at festivals, in meetings with possible deal-makers and financial backers.

Go to: CD-ROM for details of preparing the press pack.

Tell the acquisitions exec about your movie

This is the first stage to getting a deal. Although getting a deal is not easy, getting an acquisitions executive to look at your film is not too hard. They are always looking to buy films, for theatres, home rental and television, in domestic and foreign markets. Various factors give you a head start, such as having a known actor, or having had a good response in a festival. Since most films have neither, the job of attracting the attention of the acquisitions executive is difficult.

Use the following ways to achieve this:

- *Tell everyone*
  If there is a dedicated filmmaking press or trade publications in your country, alert the paper to the existence of your project, usually in the last few weeks before shooting begins. In the USA, for example, this would include *The Hollywood Reporter* and *Daily Variety*.
- *Film Finders*
  Place a notice with *Film Finders*, a resource for buyers and sellers to get information about movies in production in the independent sector. This is a publication run by a successful former acquisitions executive, Sydney Levine, and is available online. It has established a strong reputation as a meeting point for filmmakers and buyers and helps to create a profile for the movie before completion. The service is free, just download a questionnaire and return. Set up links to your site

from well-visited sites connected to the film industry, including online trade press such as *The Hollywood Reporter*, which welcomes such links as they direct visitors to their own sites in return.[12]

Submit your film to an online buyers/sellers site

These sites offer the chance to show your film to distributors directly and are primarily for completed movies. They usually ask for a fee, but this does not guarantee that the film gets viewed any further than an initial submission stage. Before passing a film onto selection committees, the initial selectors will need to be convinced that your film is legal. Prior exhibition will greatly harm your chances of being considered.

Tip   For example, Films4Auction.com is a well-established site and asks for a $50 fee to cover the selection procedure.

Did you know?
A film that is referred to as 'legal' has a clear chain of ownership and no aspect of the film is part-owned by anyone else. Music licenses are also looked at to check that you have clearance to use music.

If your film makes it beyond these first stages, panels of filmmakers or industry people then view these movies and grade them according to suitability for the market, technical quality, story and so on. You may then be invited to submit your film for viewing by distributors or other buyers. However, most insist that the movie is at least 75 minutes long and is finished. Some sites are more directly geared towards selling and have some prior reputation in the distribution business, while others offer a wider service, with news, reviews and industry statistics. These sites act as galleries, selecting the best unsigned, legal, independent films and directing them at distributors. For the buyer, they offer a filtering service, making the process of seeking new talent more focused.

Tip   For a list of these sites, see links at *The Hollywood Reporter* site.

If your film is only partly financed, in other words, you don't yet know where the funding for the rest of the movie is going to come from, you can still place notices in *Film Finders* and the trade press.

---

[12] www.ifilmfinders.com/ *Film Finders* site.

Acquisitions executives and sales agents may negotiate to finance a movie that is only partly made in return for an equity stake in the movie, but usually you must expect to have something that entices them, such as a known actor or previous festival success.

Get a producer's rep

These people work hard at putting together finance deals for independent movies, but also act as agents to finalize distribution deals after completion. They are highly experienced individuals who will devise a strategy for marketing the film, so that it reaches the right festivals, is screened to the right people and is positioned correctly so all marketing possibilities are realized to the full. Producers reps take between 5 and 10 per cent of revenue.

Create a buzz

There is no hard and fast way of doing this, but it remains the most effective way to attract the attention of the acquisitions executive. A 'buzz' means that industry people are talking about your film and suggests that there is some mystique surrounding it, an air of excitement and expectation. You will find a 'buzz' at festivals, at its centre a film that has in some way created attention because of who is attached to it, or what others say about it through advance screenings – that single most effective of marketing tools: word of mouth. Since everyone tries to create a buzz surrounding their film at markets and festivals it is a scarce commodity, but a producer's rep will greatly help, with the most well known creating interest about a project simply through being involved in it.

Free publicity

Finally, mine every possible route through which you could raise the profile of your movie. Does it, for instance, have a particular minority-interest angle which may attract certain publications or news agencies?

Shorts are different

The options are different for a short film or a feature. Distributors do indeed buy shorts for theatrical release, but they are more difficult to sell. On the other hand, television and cable slots for new filmmakers almost always prefer to screen short films. Theatrical release is rarely the right route for a short film unless it is picked up for exhibition alongside well-known movies. In many ways, however, the availability of outlets for shorts has dramatically increased in recent years as a result of the Internet and a rise in public broadcasting slots for new filmmakers.

Web film

Although web film sites are visited by acquisitions executives – the people who buy films for distributors – it is very rare for any to be offered deals as a result. Getting a film entered into the wider market of theatre exhibition, television and home video or DVD sales involves a more circuitous route. In this option, there is no limit to the amount of time and effort you can expend on getting the right people to see your film. You have to be prepared to believe in your project without question, moving on relentlessly after each rejection. At every step of the way there are stories of filmmakers who have persisted when all avenues seemed closed. Not getting a deal at all is not the end of the story; some filmmakers go on to sell a film direct to theatres, or market DVDs direct to the consumer.

The Crunch

- Decide what you want first: be realistic and aim to get a small amount of exposure first time, then get more next time and so on.
- Don't aim for Hollywood: develop your filmmaking slowly and surely without aiming for the stars yet (or the pits depending on your point of view).
- Get opinions on your movie from filmmakers.
- Choose your ultimate aim for the movie, then select the right route.
- Prepare all the information you need in advance as if you expect a deal to be made.
- Don't be caught out: interest from an acquisitions executive is more common than you may think – they call even if they are only slightly interested and will keep calling to ask for information until they have everything they need.
- Work out in advance the route you see the film moving along and check whether you rule out other options in the process; for instance, broadcasting on the web may preclude a television deal.
- Set up a website.
- Enjoy it: you've earned it because you made a great film.

3. Film festivals

Pushing a film around the festival circuit is described by some filmmakers as one of the most important moves they made in marketing the film. Greg Pak, a filmmaker based in New York, found it essential, as he described in this diary entry:

> 'I met many great people at the [South by Southwest] festival, several of whom have made distribution offers for my movie. I'm keeping my mouth shut till I nail things down but it looks like I'm pretty close to achieving my distribution goals for the film. The experience has confirmed for me the importance of going to festivals and meeting people face to face. I might have gotten these offers had I not been at the festival but there is nothing like meeting people in the flesh for establishing real trust.'

Entry into some festivals is considered to be a huge boost to a career. The most well known rarely act as simple showcases for great and upcoming movies, but are the points at which buyers (distributors) and sellers (reps and agents) meet, with filmmakers hoping to be in the crossfire. In the independent sector, the festival is a chance to test public reaction in screenings. Critics may attend and review films not yet signed to a distributor, increasing or decreasing the chances of its sale.

For feature films, this route is crucial, but for shorts also the festival is a great chance to market your film and obtain a deal in markets other than theatrical. Some festivals specialize in shorts, while others offer special short films among the feature film screenings.

Film festivals as markets

The main festivals are also markets, helping the acquisitions executive spot unsigned films that could be picked up. This is the place where you and your sales agent can start to cash in on the buzz that you have worked hard to create through screenings at smaller festivals. There are five major markets, spaced throughout the year:[13]

● European Film Market in Berlin in February.
● American Film Market (AFM) in Santa Monica, also in February.
● Marche International du Film in Cannes, France in May.
● London Film Festival, in October.
● Mercato Internazionale Filme e Documentario, in Milan, Italy, also in October.

Finished product vs short clip

If you are trying to sell a movie to potential distributors, it helps if you have a finished product; surprisingly, up to 80 per cent of films submitted to Sundance are incomplete. However, incomplete projects are bought in special forums at most of the main film markets. For example, the Independent Feature Film Market each autumn in New York attracts buyers who are able to see special screenings of partially completed work. Incomplete movies are inevitably less attractive because the producer usually asks for completion funds, but distributors are well versed in deciding whether to buy based on just a small section of a film; even in full screenings, potential buyers make up their minds from just short sections of a movie and may leave midway through in order to attend other screenings.

Did you know?
Sundance is the most prestigious festival for the North American independent sector. Its filmmaker workshops, in which unknown directors make and shoot a sequence for viewing by well-known directors, have been the springboard for many careers, including that of Quentin Tarantino.

---

[13] www.berlinale.de/   Berlin Film Festival site.
   www.afma.com/   American Film Market site.
   www.lff.org.uk/   London Film Festival.
   www.italiannetwork.it/cinema/cinema30/cinema.htm   Mercato Internazionale site.

Trick or Treat • FireBird Production

Figure 8.1 *Trick or Treat* (2000) by Anthony Straeger. This witty micro-budget short has been successfully exhibited at several film festivals, including York Film Festival and Cannes 2001.

Interview

'I went to the Edinburgh Film Festival and put the film into what was then the NBX section, a section within the market part of the festival that lists all the UK films made the previous year and allows all those films to be booked out and viewed in a video room. Buyers and distributors then look through the booklet they are given and they can choose to watch any film at their own leisure without pressure.'

Piotr Skopiak, director, Small Time Obsession, UK

How to submit to festivals

Many larger festivals deal with huge quantities of submissions. Sundance, Montreal, Berlin, London and NewYork, for instance, are all intensely competitive but are worth entering on the basis that you have nothing to lose aiming at the top and working your way down to smaller festivals. There is certainly no lack of festivals; just about every capital city has its own, with up to 40 each month in the United States alone. Many larger festivals do not need to advertise for submissions and yet still receive thousands of submissions each year.

> **Interview**
> 'We asked for submissions on VHS in the first instance, and then made our selections as to what would be shown after our preliminary viewing sessions. For us, it made no difference whether publicists, agents or filmmakers themselves approached us – the film itself was more important than who sent it.'
>
> *Lydia Wysocki, curator, York Independent Film Festival, UK*

Specialist festivals

Further down the scale, at regional or state level, applicants are more likely to be successful. Some festivals focus on certain types of work or specific formats. For example, the Chicago International Film Festival shows the full spectrum of film in October, while more challenging work appears in the Chicago Underground Film Festival the previous August. Other festivals specialize in much more particular works, such as the H. P. Lovecraft Film Festival, which shows only adaptations of the novelist's work. Others still offer an outlet for those filmmakers rejected by the rest, such as the Reject Film Festival. Make sure you check out the kind of festivals that best suit your film and the level at which it sits within the industry as a whole. A film centring on gay issues should also be entered in Gay and Lesbian Film Festivals, such as the annual London or San Francisco international events. Other festivals specialize in ethnic groups such as Latin American or Asian or religious groups.[14]

Short film festivals

The number of short film festivals has increased over the last few years. The Shorts International Film Festival in USA and the Clermont-Ferrand in France are two of the most highly regarded, with distribution deals made in a competitive environment. Most general film festivals also have special screenings and awards for shorts.

[14] www.chicagofilmfestival.com/ Chicago Festival site.
www.cuff.org/ Chicago Underground site.
www.rejectfilmfest.org/ Reject Festival site.
www.frameline.org/festival/ Gay and Lesbian Film Festival site.

Interview

'Keep to under 12 minutes. Keep to as short a story as possible; many people make the mistake of making what is essentially a 10-minute short and dragging it out to 20 minutes. A cohesive short story with a beginning, a middle and an end. Precise and clean edit. And of course, original ideas, innovative style and creativity.'

John Wojowski, curator, Kino Short Film Festival, Manchester, UK, on what helps get a film selected

Getting information

Getting hold of listings will vary from country to country, but details are available on filmmaker notice-boards. In the USA, the Association of Independent Video and Filmmakers has listings in its magazine, *The Independent*, though the West Coast is better served with the Film Arts Foundation magazine, *Release Print*.[15]

Tip filmfestival.com provides the most comprehensive guide to festivals in dozens of countries.

Fees

Most festivals demand a fee for looking at your movie, but this varies between those asking for enough to keep the festival running and those operating more on a profit basis. Submit your film at least 3 months before the festival, using their application form; never send unsolicited tapes. Some festivals operate an office throughout the year, while others open for business in the quarter prior to the festival. When you submit your movie on VHS tape, make sure you have available a copy more suitable for screening, such as DVD, and which you are able to lose for up to 3 months. In response to the move in the industry toward digital technology, many festivals, particularly the larger, will have digital projection facilities.

If you are accepted, devise a thorough marketing plan, and consider hiring a publicist or sales agent. A publicist may cost you dearly but may be a worthwhile investment if you are accepted at a high-profile festival where there will be press attention and you are against wide competition from other filmmakers. A sales agent, on the other hand, is likely to have a more lasting commitment to the movie and will be more specifically geared toward the film industry, knowing how and when to cash in on festival success and translate this into sales.

Go to: Chapter 8:2 for help with devising a marketing plan.

---

[15] www.aivf.org/index_enhanced.html   Association of Independent Video and Filmmakers.
www.filmarts.org/   Film Arts Foundation.

Prizes

Festival prizes are given to encourage and reward talent, rather than provide the sort of money needed to make further movies, and are a great boost to your promotion of a film. Buyers will be more inclined to take a look at your film if a festival draws attention to it.

Online festivals

There are a growing number of festivals operating solely online, broadcasting films in specific periods, attracting mainly short films. One such is the Webdance Film Festival, and throughout the year up to 500 films are submitted from an international array of filmmakers.[16]

Interview

'Technically, lighting and camera movement are currently important for compression reasons. However, I believe in the importance of what's being said by the filmmaker. First, make sure that the film is only as long as it needs to be, that means convey the meaning of the film as quickly as possible. Keep the subject matter and locations simple; less is more when making a digital film. Be clever. In a short film, you don't have time to be really profound. Just convey a simple idea simply. Be original. There are tons of films out there and making them is difficult. If you're going to spend the time and money, then make sure it's a tale worth telling.'

J. C. Calciano, Webdance Festival organizer

Online festivals are diverse, with some specializing in films which just happen to be shown online, such as the *iflicks* festival, in which 16 mm films are sometimes more common that digital. Others show films which have been made specifically with the web in mind, including Flash animations. Don't confuse these with digital film festivals, however, which showcase films made on this format but in a conventional theatre setting, such as the Digidance Digital Cinema Festival or the RESFEST Digital Film Festival. Clearly, the opportunities for buyers to make contact with you are greater in a more conventional environment, as opposed to a virtual one which cannot cater for filmmakers to meet and network. Yet these online festivals are popular with filmmakers because of the potentially global catchment area of their viewing public and the lower entrance costs. These festivals should not be seen as focusing purely on a film's mode of production; most are run by filmmakers sympathetic to the independent ideal and more interested in the content of a movie than its format.[17]

<u>Go to:</u> Chapter 7:3, 'Shooting for the web', for a guide to making web movies.

[16] www.webdancefilmfestival.com/ Webdance site.
[17] www.digidanceonline.com/ Digidance site.
     www.resfest.com/ Digital online festival site.

Interview

'In RESFEST, we look for new innovators, those who push the envelope of what one can do graphically or how one can tell/show a story. Comedies and those films that tug the emotions are more successful, but again, those filmmakers showing us something new or showing how to look at something in a new way, that's success in my opinion.'

Sid Goto, curator, RESFEST online festival

The Crunch

- Film festivals help get your film noticed.
- Go to film markets: hang out and take in the atmosphere.
- Put together a press or distributor's pack for market screenings.
- Look for specialist festivals.
- Investigate online festivals.
- Festivals are about more than just watching and selling films. Go there to meet other filmmakers and exchange ideas.

9 | Understanding film

1. Introduction

Now that you are working within the medium of film, it seems like a good point to look around and see what the rest of the world is doing. But this is no idle detour; a knowledge of what has gone before, what is happening now and what is on the horizon is what will sustain you in making relevant films.

Many filmmakers refer to films of the past as a kind of collective memory, a shared pool which all new filmmakers attempt to make themselves a part of. Within this pool are the many ideas that have shaped the way filmmakers work and the way critics have assessed their work, as well as the numerous films that have sustained individual filmmakers and inspired them to make greater and better works. As soon as you make a movie you are a part of that pool, adding to it for better or worse, but it also exists as a repository which can be tapped into, a reservoir of memory and history which you need to be versed in so that you can start to take from it as much as you add to it. In practice, this means finding out what ideas are central to filmmaking and what kinds of ways there are of looking at films. It also means getting an angle on where you stand, whether you agree or disagree with certain methods, techniques or concepts. In terms of artistic development, looking at films in detail and understanding the mechanisms behind them and the industry that builds them leads to a better understanding of the shortcomings in one's own work.

The aim of this chapter is give an outline of film ideas and history and help to set these in context to what is relevant to you as an independent filmmaker, making films in the twenty-first century.

2. Key ideas in film

Basic debates

People argue about film and they argue about films. This stretches beyond having an opinion about whether a particular film is good; it is more about the bigger picture, about where film as an art form – if it is one (and even that is one such debate) – is heading, where it has come from and who is leading it. These arguments and beliefs are deeply held by filmmakers and critics, and reflect the need of this very young art form to establish its credentials as one that ranks alongside art, literature or music, despite it being a synthesis of all these art forms. It suffers from its close connection to its less revered cousin, television, and from its immense success as an industry, and has a hard time trying to convince viewers that films are deeper than they seem, that they contain all sorts of ideas threaded in by the director.

An even harder time is had by those trying to point out how social and cultural issues can affect the way we view films. As if it wasn't complicated enough, the viewer is now as much a part of the equation as the filmmaker when it comes to working out what a film is about. And before you head for the shelf marked 'action movies' at the video store, even those films are part of this debate and, in terms of social considerations, even more so than the arthouse films.

Did you know?
Arthouse, or art cinema, refers to a specific kind of experimental European cinema. Usually, this cinema is found in the low- or mid-budget range and tends to exist outside of the main funding systems of television or film studios.

Is film art or commodity?

Over the first hundred years of its existence, film has made such enormous technical and artistic strides, largely due to the fact that it has been wholly part of a profit-driven industry. The income generated by movies has led to greater and faster developments than in other art forms. But there lies one of the main debates surrounding film: is it an art form or a commodity, is it something that can be discussed or just consumed? Although it has not been around for as long as painting or literature, we need to ask whether a form of expression needs to earn its spurs over centuries or whether a hundred years or so of frenetic activity is enough.

Cahiers du Cinéma

Much of the argument surrounding this question was put forward by a group of French critics who have shaped film theory, for better or worse, articulating their ideas on the nature of film in an influential journal, *Cahiers du Cinéma*, in the 1950s. They argued that film could not yet be a true art form because it lacked the ability to challenge the governing norms of culture and a capitalist state; that it was, in fact, furthering those norms by its perpetuating the ideas held by the governing ideology. Movies needed to make money so that the studios could make more movies, so they were unlikely to challenge society if this was their aim. To subscribe to this, of course, you have to first believe that the norms of society needed challenging and in this there is a geographical division between America and Europe, with the more radical views being aimed at Hollywood from Europe. It has long been the stereotype that Hollywood bosses eschew anything that seeks to incorporate artistic above financial motivations, and it is from this point that the division has developed between the two camps. But it may also be argued that this argument is too simplistic. Can any art form exist outside of financial support? Certainly an art form so dependent on high production costs as film needs vast sums to sustain it and inevitably is then tainted by the hand that feeds it. A kind of bargain is struck whereby films get made and make money, but only a limited amount of innovation is sanctioned, enough innovation to keep the viewing public returning to the cinema, but not too much to alienate them.[1]

Film vs other art forms

The question of whether film is an art form is easier to answer if we consider a much less contentious form, such as painting. Here, the case for painting as an art form is not in doubt, the only question is about which particular paintings can be called art. Film, on the other hand, has to justify its place in its entirety alongside other arts, purely because it is so closely allied to the market economy. However, it is often commerce and business that confer artistic status on a form, as might be said of the strong presence of patrons in the early development of painting in renaissance Italy. In that period, in the fifteenth and sixteenth centuries, financial support spurred on great equivalent technological advances, such as the development of oil paint, helped by wealthy patrons such as the Medici family, the modern version of which could be said to be the great studios of Hollywood.

So, what is the answer: art form or commodity? There is no final end to this debate, but you are more likely to win an argument on this question by suggesting that we acknowledge that all art has to muddy its hands in commerce and that for cinema it is the price paid for reaching such vast numbers of people. Ultimately, it is filmmakers that answer the question by treating the form as art, as an expression of their own ideas and as a creative act. A more pertinent question is perhaps not whether it is an art form at all, but what criteria the industry uses to determine what represents this art form. These criteria are largely based on business concerns at the top end of the studio system, but there are many areas, such as the independent sector and many indigenous industries around the world, in which artistic concerns are woven into business concerns.

The auteur

Leading on from the debate of film versus art, a related idea evolved of how to distinguish the artistic film from the purely business-minded one. At the core of an argument by the same French critics was the idea that film could only achieve – some would say return to – its status as an art form if directors made groups of films within which there were certain ideas and intentions running. Over time, an oeuvre would be developed whereby a director could be recognized by the kinds of individualized ideas they put into their films, whether this is personal hang-ups, social beliefs or particular styles of working. Crucially, this had to be the result of one person, an author, or as the theorists termed them, the *auteur*. The model for this route was to be found in literature, where a writer might develop a certain set of values and means of conveying them which were entirely his or her own. But before any wider connection with literature is suggested, it must be noted that these theorists positioned themselves against literature within the cinema, rejecting the script as the arbiter of a film's meaning.[2]

---

[1] www.cahiersducinema.com/   Site related to influential journal.
[2] www.gc.cc.fl.us/eng2111/auteurtheory/sld001.htm   Good slide presentation on auteur theory.

The auteur in a collaborative industry

However, the problem for filmmakers is that the industry was essentially working against this route. As a filmmaker, you would be working alongside a large number of other people, each with their own ideas, but all of whom are working for the studio. The studio, therefore, restricted the progress of film as an art form, so the theorists held. This system of dominance by the studio reflected only society's prevailing ideology and rejected that of the individual, maverick director. Few directors could hope to achieve any sense of artistic freedom, but those who did (or more precisely, those who were seen to have a unique package of content and method) became classed as auteurs. A roster of 'great directors' developed and these became seen as the only arbiters of artistic film.

Did you know?
The *Cahiers* group identified as auteurs Alfred Hitchcock, Jean Renoir, John Ford, Orson Welles and, latterly, David Lynch and Wim Wenders.

What makes an auteur?

The criteria for a director to be described as an auteur, today, have shifted only slightly from the position of the 1950s.

An auteur:

- Must rise above a mediocre script and impose their own vision on it, transforming it into art.
- Must make films that have subjective and personalized ideas about the subject matter.
- Must show consistency of style and theme in their work. Hence the idea that an auteur simply makes the same film over and over.
- Will reveal their style and theme through the analysis of shot, known to the French critics as '*mise-en-shot*'.
- Will hold that the appearance of a film is more important than the script. The method and the means which the director employs to carry the film are where the true meaning to the film lies, rather than in the script.

Weaknesses in auteur theory

This theory is persuasive but it tends to concentrate on those directors whose work is seen by a large number of theatre-goers. Art forms such as painting or literature are not defined as such by looking solely at their successful practitioners, and in fact within these art forms there is the view that great art is not necessarily acknowledged during its time. Similarly, many filmmakers have indeed followed a personal path throughout their careers but have failed to reach a wider public, including the attention of critics.

Auteur helps marketing

The studio and the wider industry have benefited from the idea of the auteur, since a film can be sold to an audience on a wider basis than simply the stars who act in it. The directors can have star billing and their individual style is used to sell the film, propelling the auteur right into the heart of the commercial filmmaking system. For some critics, recognizing the 'marks of greatness' is now part of marketing a film, in that the film will 'attract audiences by offering the possibility of using their specialist knowledge'. Some audiences are now almost as keen as critics to interpret film as art and do so by getting to know the common threads present in a director's work.

The history of auteur theory overlaps with the debate regarding film as an art form or commodity. The auteur confirms film's status as an art form and at the same time the struggles which the director has to go through to repel interference from the studio demonstrate that it is a commodity. The bitter conflicts with studios of auteurs such as Hitchcock, Welles and Fritz Lang became seen as proof of their artistic individuality.

Challenges to the auteur

Challenges to auteur theory have been put forward ever since, with the main arguments centring on the idea that traditional auteur theory ignored many ideas that are now seen as important, such as the role of the spectator, the context within which they watch the movie and our own point of view when we interpret films. Most critics agree that auteurs are now found within the traditional Hollywood system, but differ about whom it considers auteur material. The opposing type of director, according to *Cahiers du Cinéma*, was the '*metteur-en-scène*', a mere technician bringing scripts to the screen with no real artistic value.

The problem with this idea is that many directors move between the two positions, between great films and bad films. This is not explained purely by the fact that a director may have to take any job at the start of a career, but because some directors make mediocre films and good ones *throughout*. It is almost one of the hallmarks of the artist that great films are followed by inexplicable diversions down what seem to the rest of us like a dead end. Few artists can maintain a flawless career, unless they reject experimentation and follow a well-defined path that they know sells well. Francis Ford Coppola was heralded as an auteur when he made films such as *Apocalypse Now* (1979), but several years later many critics felt he suffered a loss of form with films such as *Jack* (1996). A further challenge to the perhaps narrow theory of the auteur has been made from the increase in filmmakers imbuing their movies with feminism and psychoanalysis. Filmmaking itself became seen by some as a political act. Added to this, the emergence of video on the Internet and the ease with which the unknown filmmaker can gain attention may lead to the idea of a select band of directors being eroded.

Ultimately, though, we can talk about both the idea of art versus commodity and that of the place for the auteur as being part of the same question: the auteur and the commodity-led industry defined each other through their opposition, yet were bound together by overlapping needs.

Structuralism

Structuralism acquired huge importance throughout film theory because it offered a new way of understanding a film's meaning and how that meaning is affected by the total system of values which makes up our culture. It is a way of looking at films, or more precisely, looking *into* them, and was one of the most dominant movements in the way critics and academics looked at film in the 1970s. In context, it is just another in a long line of disciplines to enter film debate, including psychoanalysis and philosophy in the 1970s and history in the 1980s. However, 'it is doubtless this work which has legitimized film studies as a discipline and brought cinema firmly into the academic arena' (Susan Hayward, *Key Concepts in Film and Cinema Studies*, p. 351, Routledge, 1996).[3]

Problematic for filmmakers

It attracts film scholars because it allows for the analysis of film as a whole art form but for filmmakers, however, this approach can be less than helpful because it tries to look at all films in the same way. Patrick Phillips (*Genre, Star and Auteur, Introduction to Film Studies*, p. 160, Routledge) describes it in a way which might cause filmmakers to run riot: 'It [a structuralist approach] allows for containment of all the surface variables that make every film different from every other for a study of a film text or a group of film texts to become manageable.' Needless to say, problems arise with this way of looking at films, but it has gained some influence over the years and has led directly to more contemporary ideas.

Where it began

It is a school of thought that gained prominence as a result of the ideas of a Swiss linguist, Ferdinand de Saussure (1857–1913). Saussure's achievement was to change the way that language was analysed, suggesting that a society's language actually carries with it ideology about that society, enabling us to study the way society works and what we think and feel by studying the structures of the ways we communicate. Since then, these ideas have been applied to anthropology, sociology, art and literature. In film theory, structuralism quickly gained currency as part of the general movement to forge a rigorous academic approach to film, to match that applied to other art forms.

How structuralists look at film

When structuralists looked at a film, they were not solely concerned with meaning within the film itself, or how the director has imparted his or her ideas, but by the mechanisms – the structures – by which we read the film. They see it as a language, consisting of the 'signified', or the concept that is being imparted, and the 'signifier', or the physical manifestation of that sign.

[3] www.brocku.ca/english/courses/4F70/struct.html   Informative articles on structuralism.
www.classics.cam.ac.uk/Faculty/structuralism.html   Guide to relevent publications on structuralism.
http://members.tripod.com/~afronord/theory.html   Bad web design but clear and helpful notes on structuralism in film.

Metz's theories

Christian Metz attempted to place structuralist theories more clearly within film studies. A French theorist, he was ideally placed to apply structuralism to film from his background as a linguist. Metz set about trying to classify film language, to find out what makes up the set of signs that are used throughout cinema. Since a story is told through agreed conventions, he argued, film could indeed be said to be a 'language'.[4]

Grand Syntagmatique

But Metz qualified this by arguing that film language lacked the rigour of spoken language and could not therefore be analysed by looking at the individual shot, but by looking at a group of shots and the meanings that evolve within these. His theory, named the '*Grand Syntagmatique*', aimed to look at a film through sequences, or segments of narrative, called 'syntagmas'. Metz thought that by doing so he would see the recurrence of these segments throughout film in general and start to evolve a sense of film syntax. It's a long-winded approach, kind of like working out what the English language is by seeing how often certain phrases come up.

Go to: Chapter 6:5, 'Montage editing', for more details about montage in filmmaking.

Inevitably, Metz's ideas have run into criticism for being too restrictive. Film is, after all, full of opportunities for connotation, with symbols, alluded meanings and so on, which are, by their nature, so open to interpretation that it is impossible to decipher absolutely what certain parts of films mean. And, as filmmakers are all too ready to testify, meaning is what you make it, based on who you are and what you believe. Some (for example, Quentin Tarantino) would go further and state that to force an audience into one particular reading of a film is not what they want to do. It could also be argued that the question of whether film is an art form, to return to the earlier problem, is answered by the fact that its potential is revealed only by recognizing the wide range of connotations which arise in its products. In creative activity, the human mind naturally alludes to experiences and ideas on the fringes of the actual creative task, and it is this which lends it its artistic depth.

Film debate has moved on

The result of structuralism as a whole was to energize debate about film, particularly in the 1970s. Since then, film theory has moved on. Post-structuralism tried to answer some of the problems with the original theory by centring debate more on the audience, and looking at what it is that motivates and informs the audience, at how they decode what they see. For filmmakers, this approach is less fraught, since it accepts that there are many readings of a film and allows for cultural differences.

Post-modernism

This theory has been much more useful for filmmakers, partly because it lets them have much more fun with filmmaking and make their movies far more unpredictable. The prominence of this theory in

[4] www.courses.rochester.edu/rodowick/FS255/Contemporary/MetzImaginary/
Another excellent Rochester College page: how to understand Metz's theories.

films is less to do with filmmakers reading scholarly works about it and more to do with the fact that it has completely penetrated so many art forms, especially in popular culture. It is, therefore, hard to avoid and anyone making films in this kind of climate, surrounded by post-modern pop music, television programme advertising and art, inevitably finds that it filters into their movies.[5]

In films, it manifests itself in exciting ways, often called bricolage, allowing for the borrowing of styles from the past, from other cultures, and enabling the filmmaker to make stylistic leaps in one film. One of the most obvious tools in doing this is in the mixing of genres. Genres are types of films, grouped together by their use of the same ways of telling a story, such as the western, the musical, the gangster movie and so on. Genres shift and evolve over time and this provides even more possible combinations. The filmmaker can then pick and mix styles taken from different genres and from different periods in film history.

Good and not so good

Sometimes this is done in an obvious and overt way, as in *From Dusk Till Dawn* (Robert Rodriguez, 1995), in which the vampire movie collides clumsily with the gangster movie, but elsewhere it is done with more panache, as in the films of the Coen brothers, who have skilfully played with our expectations of genres from the start of their careers. In *O Brother, Where Art Thou?* (2000), for example, what seems like a re-run of the classic 1940s road movie/buddy movie, three escaped convicts embark on an odyssey of epic proportions, bringing in elements of mythology, Homer and American history. None of these meaningful, political elements should normally find themselves within this genre and, in fact, this genre was all but dead and buried until this film, but the Coen brothers clearly relish the chance to re-enter a genre that has a place in film history and subvert it to produce a captivating, fantastical journey.

In another example, David Lynch parodies other films and styles in some of his later movies, including *Blue Velvet* (1986). In this film, Lynch refers to genres such as film noir, the teen movie and the detective film. For Lynch and other directors, this free use of styles and genres is yet another way of adding meaning and depth to a film. For instance, at the film's opening we see an oddly naive image of a local fire truck ambling by, the occupants waving like something from a child's book. This is then followed by an unsettling close-up image of beetles crawling among the undergrowth in a nearby garden, as if from a completely different genre. Elsewhere in the film, Lynch displays other characteristics of the post-modern film, such as nostalgia, pastiche of movies, excessive sexual and violent scenes played out in a disturbingly amoral way, and the inclusion of cars and costumes from previous periods of history.

Effects of style change

In the hands of some directors this might be no more than playing with styles, but for Lynch it offers a way of saying something about the underside of contemporary life. But it is also the very jarring

[5] www.colorado.edu/English/ENGL2012Klages/pomo.html   Clear introduction to post-modernism from University of Chicago Professor Mary Klages.

effect of this kind of sudden stylistic change that makes it so useful to the director. Film audiences have become accustomed to the ingredients of every kind of film, whether it is gangster, musical or war film, and appear to need this kind of fusion of elements to renew their enjoyment of movies. The director is helped in this task by having an array of elements to incorporate into the film which have a separate life outside of it. For example, music can refer to one set of values recognized by the audience, while the corresponding images reflect a very different set. Or a style of dress with one set of connotations can be used to subvert a character, as with the young victims of the two hitmen at the start of *Pulp Fiction* (1994) – we expect to see streetwise, menacing smugglers, but instead see characters completely unlikely to be found within such a scene.

Post-modernism in Hollywood

Post-modernism has, to a great extent, become part of the Hollywood mainstream, with genres such as horror only able to survive as viable movie-making forms thanks to self-conscious parodies in films such as *Scary Movie* (1999) or *Scream* (1996). But it remains the case that in order to parody and pillage from the past, a filmmaker must first have wide knowledge of that past; post-modernism will only lose its power when audiences no longer have the kind of sophisticated knowledge of film that they now possess.[6]

The Crunch

- Build opinions on the great debates in the study of film. You owe it to your films.
- Is film art? Just because money oils the wheels of the industry doesn't mean it's not.
- Auteur directors: they need the Hollywood industry; it needs them.
- Structuralism and post-structuralism: most filmmakers don't respond well to this stuff.
- Post-modernism: filmmakers like this because it offers freedom and experimentation.
- Hollywood likes post-modernism: they can repackage genres and film styles for better marketing.

3. How films work

The filmmaker as artist

At the heart of understanding film in general is the ability to read and understand film in particular, the detail of it. A film is composed of many elements, the most important of which are hidden from obvious view and require not so much the trained eye as the alert and observant eye. All the evidence needed to fully understand a film is contained within the screen and all it takes to allow the film to reveal itself is to have some idea of what to look for, of what could be significant.

---

[6] www.basilisk.com   Site devoted to post-modern film, architecture, philosophy, literature, music and perception.
www.hydra.umn.edu/fobo/index.html   Collection of articles on all things post-modern.
www.notbored.com   Site inspired by situationist ideas.
www.anxst.com/postmodern   Post-modern comic books by Greg Beda.

But why do we need to understand a film? Isn't it enough simply to watch the film and take from it whatever we like? For viewers, the answer is that although films are certainly more rewarding if you get the whole picture – implicit and explicit – that the director is conveying, some pleasure or insight is possible whatever level of understanding you bring to bear. For filmmakers, on the other hand, it is imperative that there is an insider's understanding of what makes a film effective, how it manages to put across certain ideas or emotions. If you have looked at films from the inside, seeing how they are structured, what shape they are and how they juggle all the elements that compose them, then you have far more chance of finding that your own films, too, stand up to such rigorous analysis. In the grand tradition of spy thrillers, the one who triumphs is the one who manages to get the blueprints of the device that conquers the world. This section looks at how to get to the blueprint of a film.

Looking at art

To begin this process, it would again be useful to look at art. How exactly should works of art be viewed? We consume art in different ways depending on the form it takes. Film makes this process a little more convoluted since it involves the synthesis of other art forms: design, music, theatre, literature. But it remains primarily a visual form and, arguably, its best exponents have perceived it this way. In other forms of visual art, there are lessons to be learnt from the way works of art are received by the public and this can tell us something about the way films work.

Ahead of its time

Art at its most forward thinking tends to produce extreme reactions in viewers. When Picasso painted 'Les Demoiselles D'Avignon' in 1907, it was clear to the artist that this painting was not to be exhibited – perhaps until the viewing public had caught up with the giant step forward which Picasso had taken. This epoch-making painting is now seen as the most conscious and successful attempt to free the artist from the need to portray according to natural appearances. Twenty years later, when exhibited for the first time, it still provoked outrage. This case shows how art depends on the right climate to be viewed in; it needs the public to be in step with the artist in order for it to gain approval. The trick for the artist is to remain within the bounds of what art is considered to be while at the same time shifting these boundaries outward. Films, too, present us with problems in that we are more likely to watch, and perhaps emulate, movies that stand firmly within the current view of what is 'good' filmmaking.

To a certain extent, art gets around this problem by having a well-established system of state patronage, whereby works of art are produced and artists sustained regardless of the breadth of their popular success. Filmmakers, on the other hand, have to rely almost solely on a profit-driven system in order to carry on doing what they do.

Negative reactions to change

Those at the forefront of change tend to provoke more negative reactions than those who follow an established trend and yet it is often these innovative works that help to push forward art and film to greater depths of meaning and greater heights of technical achievement. In the earliest days of cinema, Georges Melies was concerned solely with finding more innovative ways of telling fantastical stories, in the process inventing many special camera effects that remained a staple of filmmaking for decades. Throughout cinema history, challenging films have helped define what cinema is. But it remains the case that as a filmmaker you are more likely to encounter opposition if you try something new. Todd Solondz is now a successful director of independent movies, including *Happiness* (1998) and *Welcome to the Dollhouse* (1995), but his unique way of looking at modern society was rejected at the start of his career. 'After [completing my first movie], I left the business, or it left me.'[7]

The artist's vision

The cause of this negative feeling towards a work of art is partly the sense that a set of unwritten codes have been violated. An art form relies on a shared method of communicating, between author and viewer, and demonstrates an awareness of these conventions while at the same time seeking to bend them. As time goes by, code is agreed and then broken by the next generation of artists, then new code is agreed and that too is broken. These ways of communicating vary over time and are the reason why any practitioner of the arts needs to have one ear close to the ground to hear how art is being received. But the other ear must be resolutely turned inward, at the individual concerns and vision of the filmmaker. The degree to which the filmmaker hears with one or the other and the balance between the two may determine the manner in which a film is received. Upsetting this balance too far can, on the one hand, push a film so far from convention as to be unwatchable and, at the other end of the scale, so conformist as to be dull and cliché-ridden. The artistic vision of the filmmaker is, in the most successful works, tempered with a sense of what the viewer is used to seeing.

Watching through someone else's eyes

As film viewers and makers, we need to try to understand what the filmmaker is saying and see it from their point of view; we need to approach a film on his or her terms, as well as bringing our own experiences to it. This means accepting that a director may present ideas or a story in a way which breaks the code, but if we make an effort to look into the film to see what the director is trying to say – through the eyes of its creator – we then stand to gain most from it and learn the most. Give the filmmaker a break; try not to apply too many expectations and rely instead on letting the film have its say. In practice, this means being alert to the tools which the director is using and the codes which we expect to see.

When we look at a film, then, we must bring to bear one part of what the viewer knows as an individual, one part of what the filmmaker knows and one part of what society 'knows' (what you could call the 'zeitgeist'). This triangle is broadly equal on all sides and may lead to a clear view of what a film means and how it stands in comparison to other works.

---

[7] www.nwlink.com/~erick/silentera/Melies/melies.html   Information on Georges Melies, early filmmaker and visual effects pioneer.

> **Did you know?**
> The term 'zeitgeist' is a German word meaning, literally, time ghost, or spirit of the times. It refers to the social, political, moral and cultural flavour of a period.

Film form

As we saw in the section on structure in Chapter 4:4, every film has a shape, an inner structure hidden to the viewer. This shape is referred to as the 'form' of a film and tells us much about the way the director's mind is working, and what we are to take from the film.

What is form?

Watching a film is a two-way business; the film is only a collection of images and sounds, and it moves at a bewildering rate, compressing time and space. But it can only do this because, as viewers, we have ways of perceiving them. Our minds are predetermined to assemble what we see and we try constantly to make connections, to round off what we see into narratives, to add it all up. This applies not only to when we listen to stories, but to any aspect of our interaction with the world. This is partly a survival instinct, originally enabling us to sense danger, ordering the range of signals hitting our senses and arranging them into some structure. It is the reason why we like stories structured the way they are, with a beginning, middle, an end, and a reason and purpose to each part of the story. The concept of form is about responding to this ordering mentality in the viewer and using it to give the process of telling a story more impact. Therefore, film is about using the spectator as a participant by utilizing the in-built devices with which the viewer takes in information.

Form is composed of two elements:

1 The style of the film, determining the surface manner in which the story is told, such as editing technique, use of sound and music, lighting design and so on.
2 The structure of the film, determining the arrangement of the pieces that make up the story and the speed at which they are delivered.

In looking at these elements it is important to link form and content together. Form is the shape that the film takes, while content is what it is saying. Good filmmaking rests on the careful dovetailing of these two elements, so that the shape of a film is directly a result of what the film is about. When we say 'about' here, we actually need to be more precise and define it as the total meaning of the film, rather than just the surface sequence of events in the story. So, if we look at a film with unusual content, such as *Eraserhead* (David Lynch, 1976), we see that the very strange nature of the story is reflected well in the unusual shape of the film; it doesn't function like other films, in that it rejects the traditional way of telling stories, using dreamlike sequences, sections that deviate from the so-called story and an ending that does not seek to resolve the story. Furthermore, in terms of style, the lighting, soundtrack and dialogue all confirm this form. This feels right, since the shape of the film reflects the strange illogical workings of the story. The film works because form and content match.

Symbolism

A symbol is a sign, a carrier of meaning in typically visual form, and is one of the most effective ways for depth of meaning to manifest itself. Its visual nature means that what it represents is not always easily translated into words, and its reception by the viewer may vary, according to culture and experience. This does not undermine the symbol, but may actually lend it longevity.

Being able to notice a symbol is less easy than defining it. In films there is such a wealth of visual material contained in every shot that we have to exercise some criteria if we are to distinguish a visual element which alludes to something else from that which is merely functional.

Symbols and subject matter

The key to doing this is in having some understanding of what a film's content is – often invoked in the film's first passages, but further clarified in the title, or in advance publicity. In Mike Leigh's *Secrets and Lies* (1995), the title gives us a clear idea of the theme that resides within the plot. From the outset, it is clear that plot is going to be subservient to theme, that meaning will result from entertaining ideas that arise from the film, rather then restricting our view to implications of the events on those particular characters in the plot. *Independence Day* (1996) also tries to do this, with a title describing more than the simple events of the plot, but fails to deliver in presenting further symbolism to satisfy its claims, hurriedly progressing the theme at the end with words in a scene of Bill Pullman's speech as President of the triumphant United States.

Know about the director

As well as the title, we can look to other examples by the same director, or other films within the same genre. When watching Alfred Hitchcock's *The Birds* (1963), for example, we see broken crockery hanging on the dresser before we see the horror of the victim of a bird attack, and earlier on the floor during and after a bird attack, the camera lingering on it so that we take note of this visual element. Hitchcock has said that, for him, this represented disruption in a domestic setting, so we recognize allusions to his own experiences of family life, and in turn our own. This symbol stretches beyond the original intention of creating suspense and preparing us for the appearance of the victim; it reaches out to the audience's own experiences in an outward ripple. But we do not necessarily need to have prior knowledge of Hitchcock's own hang-ups here; by presenting this symbol repeatedly, we can start to look for it and it becomes a signifier of more than it would elsewhere. We add it to our canon of symbols and take it to our next Hitchcock experience.

Symbolism rests on more than just props. It can exist in any tangible object or set of objects within the film, and even as an unseen object. In Kubrick's *The Shining*, for example, the maze into which the deranged Jack enters parallels the labyrinthine layout of the hotel, and through careful presentation of this element of the set, we are led towards seeing it as a parallel of Jack's mind (for example, in a scene in which Jack looks at a model of the maze, or when we see him encounter different incidents in the hotel that his wife cannot be a part of). When we later see him lose his way within the maze, the dramatic effect is magnified many times. The symbolism, quietly generated throughout the film, of these places and their resemblance to Jack's mind moves the scene of Jack physically losing his way in the maze to one on a much higher plane, of losing his way psychologically, of being imprisoned within his own mind and suffering as a result.

Symbols evolve

Symbols reflect the concerns of the director, but also tell us as much about those of society and, since symbols change over time, help a film become something of a historical document in revealing the then prevailing zeitgeist. If we look at the two versions of *Cape Fear*, there are conflicting ways symbols are used. In the first version, made by J. Lee Thompson in 1961, a lawyer's family is subjected to a terrifying ordeal at the hands of an ex-convict whose case he performed badly with. In this version, Robert Mitchum plays the stalker and fulfils the kind of symbolism one would expect: of a shadowy threat of evil against the inherent integrity of he who makes and keeps the laws.

By the time Martin Scorsese took it on, exactly 30 years later, the moral and social climate in America had changed significantly, and the astute Scorsese made changes to the story that reflected this. In his version, symbols are dramatically different. The lawyer's family is now dysfunctional and consumed with betrayals and in-fighting, while the stalker (played by Robert De Niro) believes them in need of redemption. To a certain extent, the roles of lawyer and stalker are reversed, and to cap the subversion of the symbols in the original film, Scorsese has Robert Mitchum appear as an attorney for the stalker.

Examples such as this show that symbolism has become more sophisticated as directors now have the opportunity to play with our expectations of a symbol and subvert it.

Motif

A further vehicle for the meanings in a film is the motif. A motif, according to a dictionary definition, is a dominating theme, but also a recurring design. In textile design, a motif would be a shape or design element which recurs throughout the whole design, carrying more of what the design is about than other parts, and its recurrence would confirm this. This is true of film and helps us to understand how it is applied in the moving image. In film, a motif is a recurring element which carries meaning and can include a colour, object or place.

It must be a tangible part of a film, in other words, something which we can see, and may often be a central part of the plot. It will become a bearer of a film's underlying theme and, with skill on the part of the director, will be both specific enough to relate to the film's purpose, but broad enough to have some relation to wider experience.

Motif in Hollywood

In Hollywood films, motif is perhaps less concerned with broadening a theme than with making it more explicit for the audience. There is a subtle difference between, for instance, the eye motif in *Don't Look Now* (Nic Roeg, 1973) and the mountain motif in *Close Encounters of the Third Kind* (Steven Spielberg, 1977).

In *Close Encounters*, a recurring image of a flat-peak mountain is seen throughout the movie, serving to heighten the moment when Richard Dreyfuss finally sees it for real. But at no point is the motif claimed to be anything greater than what it is – a plot device – and any further investigation is self-serving. With Roeg's example, however, the result of our delving further into the motif is rewarding and reveals much more about the film, but also stretches outside its filmic boundaries to offer a more reflective consideration of the issues raised by the film. Let's take one of those examples in more detail.

Example: motif in Don't Look Now

In *Don't Look Now*, we are primed to look for and reflect upon images outside of the immediate action. Roeg's skilful and systematic use of montage breaks down our reliance on the script and our need to maintain a chronological flow to the story. We start to decipher images which appear almost without reason and, together with our need to construct meaning out of what we see, we start to make connections. In other words, we infuse meaning into objects or images that normally would pass us by. Roeg makes sure, however, that this is no wild goose chase, but is actually pertinent to the scenes we see unfolding.

In many parts of *Don't Look Now*, vision is a part of the action. In the extraordinary opening montage, we see Donald Sutherland and Julie Christie enjoying a Sunday afternoon, oblivious (they can't *see*) to the danger of their small daughter at the edge of a nearby river. Sutherland then runs out of the house as if he has heard something within (now he sees, but with perhaps second sight), but is too late to save the child. At the film's terrifying closing montage, his implied or partial second sight and his curiosity in terms of physical sight – to see the strange figure he glimpses throughout the film – leads him to disaster.

Theme and motif

Between these two points, various elements reinforce the eye motif: the medium who claims to have seen the dead girl is herself physically blind and we get occasional shots of her eyes when Sutherland is in danger. The overwhelming sense in the film is of seeing and not seeing, both metaphorically and physically. Inserted shots that seem to momentarily throw our understanding of the plot in fact serve to clarify the film's ultimate meaning. The net result of these tangential moments is only achieved, however, by Roeg setting about breaking the rules of temporal and spatial reality, enabling us to see everything within the film as potentially important, rather than doggedly following the plot.

Symbolism and motif for the filmmaker

Where does all this leave the filmmaker? Without doubt, symbolism and motif can elevate a film when deployed sensitively. They can help make it more than just the sum of its separate clips, lending the film an inner life and helping to convey far more profound ideas than can be contained within a story. Nor is it restricted to any particular genre; a film that is not necessarily setting out to be insightful or deep can benefit from the placing of elements within the film which hint at bigger ideas.

Film style

Moving away now from the areas of a film that need some interpretation, we can look at the way the film as a whole appears, the surface style. These surface elements include camera composition, sound, lighting, location, editing and acting. Directors will display their style, the individual way they make a movie, through the way they use these elements, a process involving almost infinite variables of approach. We can talk collectively about the fundamental way a director arranges what the camera sees by using the term '*mise-en-scène*', a French term meaning 'staging an action'. *Mise-en-scène* is a useful way of being able to group these stylistic choices together and discuss the style of a director according to what system they use. There is no pre-set system of staging, suitable for certain genres; directors can shoot a scene in any way they like but, ultimately, they need to have established a pattern of staging for a movie, broken only when it is appropriate. *Mise-en-scène* is essentially centred on what the camera sees, not the choices involved in how the camera records it.

Style evolves gradually

The choices a director makes in staging the action usually emanate from the content of the movie, and should be subservient to this and the form of the film. This hierarchy is essential since movies developed from style alone flounder when it comes to establishing a core to their purpose and theme. Throughout the planning stages, a sense of overall style is developed and the central theme is exhibited through the way each aspect of the staging is managed. In film noir, for example, the use of lighting was deliberately dark and high contrast, reflecting the essentially dark nature of the subject matter.

Mise-en-scène as a concept may be said to be more useful for the film scholar than the filmmaker, because it artificially separates the staging of the action from other stylistic choices, whereas the reality of filmmaking is that these stylistic choices are interacting more freely. So, camera composition is a result of what has been staged and staging is a result of what the director wants the camera to tell us. It is unrealistically optimistic to hope that decisions of setting will remain unchanged when shooting; it is more likely that unforeseen opportunities in setting subtly alter the way you choose to point the camera.

Mise-en-scène is only part of the choices available to the director when setting a scene. Further variables arise when you start to consider the way the set is lit, what sounds are placed with it and how the shots are edited. Although filmmaking involves a more organic resolution of the issues of style, it is without doubt a less exhausting process to place these choices in some sort of order: so that the setting informs the lighting, which informs the cinematography, which in turn determines the shot duration. But be prepared for reversals in this hierarchy on set, as you find better ways to make the movie you want.

Style changes within a movie

To complicate matters further, film style is no longer constant throughout a film, with various styles mixed together. In today's post-modern world, filmmakers freely use style as a tool by which they can make a film more complex. In *Pulp Fiction* (1994), for example, Tarantino stages some scenes in direct homage to French New Wave of the 1960s, such as those including the boxer and his girlfriend, whose dialogue borders on the pastiche of these movies. Style is now a more self-conscious element of a movie, with the power to radically alter the original meaning of it, as seen in cinematic reworkings of Shakespeare plays. *Richard III* (Richard Loncraine, 1995) included fascist overtones, setting the action in the inter-war years, and as such managed to say as much about our period as it does of that of the King. In *Tempest* (Paul Mazursky, 1982), the play is transposed into modern-day Manhattan, highlighting insecurities and mid-life crises.

The Crunch

- Give the filmmaker a break; understand what they are trying to say.
- You are an artist: don't expect people to like what you do – yet.
- Film form is about style and structure.
- Symbols and motifs strengthen the film's theme.
- Symbols and motifs help make the audience see the theme.

4. Film history

This section is going to take a brief look at what kinds of movies will have most effect on the way you make your own. The context you work in is going to provide a backdrop to your films whether you want it or not; what has gone before will colour the way the film-going public and critics perceive what you make. Film and video as media are pervasive in global culture and take many forms, from the feature film, television programmes, Internet movies to video art and experimental work. Look around and see what other people are making, what has been made in the past and how all this helps define the kind of filmmaker you are today.

Independent cinema

Independent cinema in America provides a fascinating resource for the filmmaker. If it is possible to learn everything you need to know about filmmaking by looking at films, then independent film offers more than enough to go around. Independent filmmaking remains by default the place where you start, the economic bottom of the ladder.

It's about money and method

Strictly speaking, independent film as a term refers to a financial position. It tells you that the movie was made without the aid of the large studio system. Independent movies are often made by a complex network of finance, although larger ones can, and often do, get involved in later stages with studio assistance in finishing costs and distribution. But this definition is only half the story; it is also a term, similar to 'low budget', which has come to denote a certain approach to film with shared values regarding innovation, artistic rigour and integrity. Although many directors in this sector of the industry do not fulfil this expectation, many have proved to be some of the most fascinating of modern filmmakers, making films which prove that film can be art, but at the same time can be commercially successful.

Pioneers

The pioneer of independent film is often said to be John Cassavetes, with his 1960 film, *Shadows*. Martin Scorsese's enthusiasm for Cassavetes has helped cement his reputation as the pioneer of films in which the director is in complete artistic control and possesses the vision and drive to see his work through to conclusion:[8]

> 'Cassavetes embodied the emergence of a new school of guerrilla filmmaking in New York. John was fearless – a true renegade setting up one psychodrama after another with the complicity of a close group of actor friends.'
>
> *Martin Scorsese (A Personal Journey Through American Movies, p. 162,*
> *Faber & Faber, 1997)*

However, the iron grip of major distributors kept non-Hollywood movies from widespread theatrical release, until the emergence of mostly east coast distributors such as New Line, who saw that there was demand for these new, cult films from a wider audience.

Filmmakers themselves were becoming galvanized into action by the successes of directors such as Jim Jarmusch with *Stranger Than Paradise* (1984) in the early 1980s, seen as the film which opened the flood gates for the independent sector. The same year also saw the release of *Blood Simple* by the Coen brothers, *Paris, Texas* by Wim Wenders and Jonathan Demme's *Stop Making Sense*, and all grossed more than $2 million dollars, making it a new golden age for independent films.

Minority groups get a voice

Independent film also opened up filmmaking to previously sidelined groups of society. Gay experience was portrayed sympathetically for the first time in 1982 with Robert Towne's *Personal*

---

[8] www.filmref.com/   Updated articles on independent films.
www.ifctv.com/   Excellent articles and news in independent films.
www.inetfilm.com/   Independent film news.

Best and John Sayles' *Lianna*. Spike Lee brought his unique style to bear in films such as *She's Gotta Have It* (1986) and showed black experience far removed from the ghettoized roles of earlier Hollywood. In Lee's case, it was the film's commercial success that proved to distributors and financiers alike that independent film had struck a seam previously unmined.

Crossover: commercial success

Commercial success is a thread that runs throughout the 1980s, when independent cinema was fast evolving. Independent films had previously accounted for only a small part of overall film-going in the United States and as such was seen as no threat to the major film-producing factories such as Universal, Disney and Warner. But the turning point came at the end of the 1980s, when independent films started to account for 15 per cent of all box office revenue in the United States.

The Hollywood studios soon took notice and what caught their eyes were the profits that were generated by films shot on such low budgets. If a film costs $5 million and makes a return of $10 million, it is less profitable than a film which cost $50 000 and also makes $10 million. The nascent home video market contributed to the success of independent movies. The ground-breaking film *The Thin Blue Line* (1988), which effectively re-invented the non-fiction film, sold over 35 000 video cassettes, improving profit margins even further above the $1.2 million that it took in theatrical release in the first year. The cost of the film illustrates the vast potential for higher cost : profit ratios, as an advance of $40 000 from Miramax was felt to be enough to cover costs and see profit for its director.

The next big leap forward came in 1989, with the arrival of Steven Soderbergh's *Sex, Lies and Videotape*. This film was the first to show the enormous 'crossover' potential of an independent film as it grossed over $30 million domestically, from an advance of $1 million.

> *'Sex, Lies and Videotape* . . .showed just how far a first feature, released by an independent no less, could go all over the world. By using videotape both in the title and in the film itself, Soderbergh almost literally ushered in the new era of the video-educated filmmaker.'
>
> *John Pierson (Spike, Mike, Slackers and Dykes, Faber & Faber, 1995)*

Following this, in the 1990s, independent film has taken bigger steps into the market with hits such as *Pulp Fiction*. The decade started with *Slacker* (1991), a $23 000 film with no particular plot detailing the lives of various 'slackers' in Austin, Texas, in which director Richard Linklater gave a face to what was termed generation X. It eventually grossed over $500 000, mostly in video rental. More than many films, the apparent ease with which the film was constructed inspired many young filmmakers to follow suit, but this belied Linklater's careful approach and in-depth knowledge of film history.

Quentin Tarantino made the most sustained push at the gates of Hollywood with *Reservoir Dogs* (1991) and *Pulp Fiction* (1994), both independent films and making huge profits, though once again, video rental and sale was prominent in eventual total receipts.

Independent films today

Far from burning out, the independent model is as bright as it was, though its distributors have moved away from the kind of controversial, ground-breaking films seen in the early development of the sector. The success of Todd Solondz with *Welcome to the Dollhouse* in 1996 proved that directors could still appear from nowhere with a low-budget film, go on to win prizes at Sundance and break through into wider release. His second feature, *Happiness* (1998), pushed the boundaries of acceptability for some viewers, but in 2001 was voted the most popular and inspiring independent film (imdb.com database).

Despite its success, or perhaps due to it, the independent tag remains as much a signal of a certain type of film as a description of its economic roots. Independent has come to denote artistic freedom and a reliance (albeit forced) on creativity rather than effects, art rather than spectacle.

Classic Hollywood cinema

It is worth considering sometimes, in an age dominated by one enormously successful sector of the industry, that the codes within which most filmmakers work, and which have been adopted as the 'right' way to work, are simply a certain set of conventions, whose dominance has risen and is assured through the economic clout of the Hollywood industry. There are many other ways to make movies, but the Hollywood model has become by far the most predominant – to the extent that all other modes are judged by how much they deviate from this norm. We talk about the chasm between 'alternative' or 'independent' film and the rest of the Hollywood-led industry, implying that Hollywood is the standard and others' approaches are 'alternative' to the standard, or 'independent' from it economically.

However, our awareness of global culture should tell us that one approach is not necessarily any greater than another, despite economic dominance of one sort. To the thriving and energetic Indian film industry, Hollywood has proved to be a great influence, but it has resolutely maintained its own particular approach. European, Australian and Asian filmmaking have each demonstrated unique properties, participating in some of the Hollywood conventions but doing so with essential cultural differences.

So, if we look at what constitutes Hollywood film in its classical sense, we do so with the knowledge that it occupies a decisive role in film history, but that its greatest period was some half a century ago, and it is now only part of an international cultural diversity in filmmaking.

Hollywood storytelling

Within the study of film, however, Hollywood still provides some key texts and provides a useful interface between popular culture and academic study. It also gives us a framework to see how the development of this method of storytelling has become so pervasive and so effective. If our ability to enjoy a film is based on losing our sense of it as an artificial experience, in other words, to suspend disbelief, Hollywood has moved towards that ideal more than any player in film history. Virtually the whole notion of narrative film, continuity editing and genre all owe their existence to early Hollywood.

Early cinema

The early dominance of European centres of filmmaking, in Denmark, Berlin and London, was eclipsed by the greater economic capacity of the emerging studios in Hollywood between 1910 and 1935. Small filmmaking firms merged with others to form major concerns, such as that formed by Metro, Goldwyn and Mayer (MGM), and at this point narrative film quickly became the established mode. Although the principles of narrative and continuity were by no means an invention of Hollywood, it was here that the frenetic pace of film production, in response to massive public demand, enabled great strides to be made towards film as a spectacular and absorbing experience. Narrative film depends wholly on being able to tell a story that moves across vast amounts of time and space without any disruption of the flow of the film. Techniques that help in doing this proved to be successful in attracting audiences, thereby enabling this one mode to dominate. As Bordwell and Thomson demonstrate (*Film Art: An Introduction*, McGraw-Hill, 1993), between 1907 and 1917, in particular, shots and methods of editing evolved which are still common currency, such as the shot/reverse shot (see *The Cheat*, 1915), the establishing shot (see *Are Parents People?*, 1925) and the eyeline match (*The Americano*, 1916).

Genre

The need to market movies led to the development of genre, in which they were categorized by common elements such as props, characters and story. Each genre had different ways of conveying stories, and these conventions were rigorously adhered to. When you watched a musical, it did not seem in the least bit strange that the actors broke into song, nor that they danced in massive formation. But place this code within a gangster drama and the film would have been impossible to sell. Genre is at once an economic necessity and a way of making the viewing experience for an audience more controllable, such that nothing too unexpected would occur. Narrative film in this era of classic Hollywood developed into a way of reaffirming common values (*The Wizard of Oz*) and offering escape from daily drudgery for depression-hit America.

Changes

Post-war Hollywood lacked the success of the pre-war years, due in part to the arrival of television, but also due to the arrival of sound in the 1920s and 1930s, which had presented a major challenge to the way films were made, but had also created the genre of the musical. In addition, the dominance of the studio system was overturned in the late 1950s, when a lawsuit was settled in which the eight major filmmaking studios were blocked from continuing their tight control of the nation's theatres. Independent production began to gather pace, the result of new income tax laws, enabling freelance filmmakers to make movies and get their films seen in theatres.

New Hollywood

Hollywood film underwent changes in the 1970s, and it is often referred to as New Hollywood. The concept of whether there was, indeed, anything new about films produced in this period is hotly debated. For some critics, films such as *Taxi Driver* (Martin Scorsese, 1976), *Easy Rider* (Dennis Hopper, 1969) and *Apocalypse Now* (Francis Ford Coppola, 1979) all pointed to the emergence of a new filmmaker actively challenging society and the way it viewed war, crime and sub-culture. For others, New Hollywood was no more than a perpetuation of the same. Definitions are debated, but it is the merging of classic Hollywood means of filmmaking with European art film that characterized its progress. Many of its key players were admirers of French New Wave (Scorsese of Godard) and saw within it a chance to remake American film. Coppola had ambitions to create a new studio, on the model of the great studios of the inter-war years, but his Zoetrope Studio, based in San Fransisco – basing it there was itself a major statement about rejecting Hollywood – led him to financial ruin. But the ease with which these filmmakers quickly asserted their stamp over Hollywood changed the way the studios made films. For example, Coppola's decision to use subtitles in his *Godfather II* (1974) was considered daring for a mainstream film, but did nothing to dent its success.

High concept

Since the 1970s, an idea dominated Hollywood which was to lead to dramatic economic ascendancy. The top 10 highest-grossing films have all been made since 1975 and testify to its success. The release of *Jaws* in that year kicked off the idea known as 'high concept', initiating the summer blockbuster as an economic bulwark. Merchandising became crucial to the selling of a film, and pre-release advertising became a way of ensuring success. The point about high concept is that it became possible to conceive of films that were guaranteed to be hits, by virtue of television saturation advertising, a strong star presence, and a tried and tested plot.

Film arguably became more of a commodity than at any previous time, but the industry held that high concept merely gave people what they wanted. In Robert Altman's satire on Hollywood, *The Player* (1992), this is demonstrated starkly and comically when the bored film executive (Tim Robbins) listens to a constant stream of 'pitches' from scriptwriters, each of which involves the combining of various high-concept winning elements. In this context, *Alien* (1979) becomes '*Jaws* in space', a merging of two familiar merchandising gold-mines.

For many critics, then, the new golden age of Hollywood was in the 1970s, before the arrival of mass marketing and focus groups. But as a profit-driven industry, it has never made any claims to its being an artistic powerhouse. Its longevity lies in its ability to repeat formulae, to understand what makes cinema a spectacle and make it sell.[9]

[9] http://classicfilm.miningco.com/   Classic movies site.
www.hollywoodreporter.com/   Get to know Hollywood daily.
www.hcdonline.com/   Hollywood Creative Directory – who's who in film production.

Video art

As video has penetrated the consumer market and made potential filmmakers out of everyone, so it has also been picked up by visual artists. Video is now an established discipline in fine art courses, alongside painting and sculpture, and for many artists makes these more conventional pursuits redundant. While video art is fast gaining ground among artists who see it as yet another expressive tool, it is also having an impact on mainstream fields of the film and television industry. Video artists are going on to make feature films, music videos and commercials; advertisers are borrowing ideas from art gallery video shows and, to return the compliment, artists freely take from film history as inspiration for video work. It's a relationship which sees very different areas of film and video feeding off each other, with video artists coming up with the most unusual uses of the medium.[10]

How will I know it when I see it?

Video art covers a broad spectrum of work. It differs from cinema mainly in its rejection of narrative and its particular total pursuit of finding more original, innovative ways of using the medium. It tends to include some of the following:

- Non-narrative, based on an idea rather than a story.
- Shown in art galleries rather than cinemas or television.
- Has more in common with abstract movies than any other part of film history.
- Makes use of large, multiple projection screens.
- Is almost always shot with video.
- Makes use of the latest technology.
- Much longer than other uses of the medium.
- Does not fit into any aspect of current marketing in the film world: either too long, too weird or too shocking.
- Ideas tend to have originated from the art world or literature rather than traditional film genres.

Bill Viola is one of the pioneers of video art as it struggled to attain a serious status. His work rejected the technical, gimmick-based vignettes of the early stage of development, in favour of something that looked at all aspects of human experience.[11]

Tip   A high point in Viola's work is his 'Nantes Triptych', commissioned for exhibition in the French town. In this work, three cinema-scale screens depict three different images. The first is a long, continuous edit of a woman in the latter stages of labour through to birth. The centre panel shows a dark suspension tank, in which a figure, fully clothed, is submerged. He moves only occasionally and again there are no cuts between the start and end of the piece. The final panel on the right is a long, poignant image of the artist's mother as she lies dying in a hospital bed.

---

[10]   www.vdb.org/   Comprehensive view of video art; a database representing over 300 artists.
www.videoculture.org/   Examples of video art.
[11]   www.cnca.gob.mx/viola/   Viola's back catalogue displayed.

In Britain, the growth of video art has been fast. The nation's most coveted prize for young, contemporary artists – the Turner – has twice been won by video artists, with video art nominated several other times. One of those winners is Gillian Wearing, whose innovative use of the medium has led to some fascinating works. One of her most controversial shows a mother beating her daughter, but the film is played backwards so the mother seems to be rescuing rather than abusing the daughter. This simple 'trick' gives the film enormous emotional weight and yet is a simple and inexpensive idea.

Even if you haven't previously considered using video in this unusual way, the benefits can help your other movies: its creativity is astonishing, and its best exponents are able to forge images and scenes no less poetic than in cinema. The degree to which artists bend the medium and devise unusual ways to exploit it is something filmmakers share.

Tip Many artists start working in filmmaking and cope well with the budgetary restrictions, making feature films with a great amount of creativity, such as John Maybury with *Love is the Devil* (1998). An earlier painter-turned-filmmaker, David Lynch, achieved this as he developed from an artist who wanted his paintings 'to move a little', to a filmmaker whose films resemble paintings: non-linear in structure and theme, symbolic and highly visually inventive.

The Crunch

- Independent films: harder to get made but better to watch.
- Hollywood likes cheap indie films; it likes cheap directors even more.
- Classic Hollywood films deserve investigation.
- New Hollywood directors grew up in the independent arena.
- High concept: steer clear of it if you want your friends to still speak to you. However, you will become very rich.
- Video art: filmmakers and artists share common ground.

10 100 films for filmmakers

During the centennial buzz around the 100th anniversary of cinema, there were numerous lists published of the top 100 films from just about every angle: the top 100 movies of all time, the top independent movies, the top viewers choices and so on. For the most part, these have attempted to compile lists from the point of view of what makes great film art, those which have contributed in raising the status of cinema to the level of a serious art form. But for filmmakers, there are other criteria which may be followed; some movies advance the path of filmmaking but are not in the pantheon of great movies. Looking at films for their inspirational qualities, technical innovation or creative ingenuity will lead to a very different list.

This list is no more than a roll call of the films that help filmmakers. The history of independent film has a running theme in which the filmmaker has a road to Damascus experience after seeing a movie and is forever affected by it. For some, it can be the decisive moment when movies become a career path not a pastime.

> 'I was twelve years old when I saw *On the Waterfront*. It was a breakthrough for me. Kazan was forging a new acting style. It had the appearance of realism but actually it revealed something in the natural behaviour of people that I hadn't seen before.'
>
> *Martin Scorsese (A Personal Journey Through American Movies,*
> *by Martin Scorsese and Michael Henry Wilson, Faber & Faber, 1997)*

The films are listed in alphabetical order.

The Adventures of Priscilla, Queen of the Desert (1994) Stephan Elliot, Australia, 98 min
A new take on the road movie, with extravagant visuals and poignant plot.

Alphaville (1965) Jean-Luc Godard, France/Italy, 98 min
A precursor of *Blade Runner* and other visions of a paranoid future. Watch this film to see how ingenious camerawork can transform Paris into a futurist city with no props.

Annie Hall (1977) Woody Allen, USA, 93 min

Badlands (1974) Terrence Malick, USA, 94 min
Watch this movie for the strange, sensitive camerawork of Tak Fujimoto and the unusual depiction of a young, isolated, murderous couple on the run.

Being John Malkovich (2000) Spike Jonze, USA, 112 min

Being There (1979) Hal Ashby, UK/USA, 123 min

La Belle et la Bete (Beauty and the Beast) (1946) Jean Cocteau, France, 92 min
A classic of fantasy, watch this film for its painting-like composition.

Betty Blue (1986) Jean-Jacques Beineix, France, 121 min

The Birds (1963) Alfred Hitchcock, USA, 119 min
The Birds is not considered by most to be Hitchcock's best, eclipsed by *Vertigo* or *Psycho*, but it remains one of the most illuminating. Once again, Hitchcock's obsessive pre-production work in storyboards pushes the film's visuals forward, towards silence, telling its most rewarding story non-verbally, through signs and symbols. Try watching it without dialogue, focusing on the precise and purposeful use of symbolism.

Blackmail (1929) Alfred Hitchcock, UK, 85 min

Blade Runner: The Director's Cut (1982/1991) Ridley Scott, USA, 112 min
This version of *Blade Runner* restores the images as the main focus of the film, removing the last-minute voice-over imposed by a nervous studio. For the filmmaker, it demonstrates how ingenuity and production design can evoke a convincing futuristic world without vast special effects. Try also watching *Dark Star* (John Carpenter, 1974) for proof that science fiction is possible on small budgets.

The Blair Witch Project (1999) Dan Myrick, USA, 77 min
One of a clutch of lower-than-low-budget movies which have shown that it is still possible to strike major distribution deals for home-made, independent movies.

Blood Simple (1983) Joel Coen, USA, 99 min

Blue (1993) Derek Jarman, UK, 78 min
A film composed entirely of sounds, against a constant blue screen, this is a daring use of the medium and a lesson in using sound.

Blue Velvet (1986) David Lynch, USA, 120 min

Brazil (1985) Terry Gilliam, UK, 142 min

Breaking the Waves (1996) Lars von Trier, Denmark/Netherlands/Sweden, 159 min
A film made mostly using the Dogme rules, this offers a chance to see a completely natural (bar the ending) film made without artificial light or camera support, with captivating results.

Breathless (A Bout de Souffle) (1959) Jean-Luc Godard, France, 90 min

The Cabinet of Dr Caligari (1919) Robert Wiene, Germany, 5587 ft, 48 min
A unique film made with dark, twisted sets and painted light, this film remains one of the most effective horror films.

Caravaggio (1986) Derek Jarman, UK, 93 min

The Cars That Ate Paris (1974) Peter Weir, Australia, 91 min
A low-budget science fiction comedy-thriller by the director of *The Truman Show*.

Cat People (1942) Jacques Tourneur, USA, 73 min
Martin Scorsese believes that this horror classic proves the importance of creative images over lavish effects. 'Tourneur had practically no budget and of course none of today's technologies. But he knew that dark [shadow] has a life of its own.' (*A Personal Journey Through Film*, p. 95, Faber & Faber, 1997.)

Un Chien Andalou (1929) Luis Buñuel/Salvador Dali, Spain/France, 17 min
Watch this movie for its pioneering use of surrealist symbolism in film.

Chinatown (1974) Roman Polanski, USA, 131 min

Clerks (1993) Kevin Smith, USA, 90 min

The Cook, The Thief, His Wife and Her Lover (1989) Peter Greenaway, UK/France, 124 min

Crazy Love (1987) Dominique Deruddere, Belgium, 87 min

The Crowd (1927) King Vidor, USA, 90 min
A masterpiece of silent cinema which proves that images say more than words, as Vidor's use of symbolism describes the life of an immigrant to depression-hit America.

Dancer in the Dark (2000) Lars von Trier, Denmark
Any film produced under the auspices of the Dogme conditions is going to question whether the artificiality of the way we usually shoot is necessary. With no artificial lights, no ambient soundtrack to smooth over the continuity cracks and no crane shots or smooth dollies, this is the antithesis of the Hollywood norm. Yet this musical has the power to take the audience back to the emotional highs of the great age of the Hollywood spectacle musical. At Cannes, half the audience cheered, the other booed. It walked off with the top prize for its director.

Days of Heaven (1978) Terrence Malick, USA, 94 min
Nestor Almendros's cinematography is at the perfect pitch for the elusive storytelling of Malick's second movie. Artificial light is never used, in favour of the 'magic hour' of light, just before sunset. Each frame is a painting, showing the great Almendros at his best.

The Decalogue (1988) Krzysztof Kieslowski, Poland, 10 hr (in 10 parts)
An extraordinary work, each film is a meditation on the 10 commandments. Unexpectedly uplifting, moral and tautly filmed.

Delicatessen (1990) Jean-Pierre Jeunet/Marc Caro, France, 99 min

Dr Strangelove, or How I Learned to Stop Worrying and Love the Bomb (1963) Stanley Kubrick, UK, 94 min
Possibly the best of Kubrick's movies, mixing styles and displaying the director's use of lighting and composition.

La Dolce Vita (1960) Federico Fellini, France/Italy, 176 min
A story of moral decay in fashionable Rome, the tone set by the opening shot of a stone Christ carried across the skyline by helicopter, the film takes us through the life of a dispirited journalist, a witness to the banal, spiritless life of the socialites. Look at it for the astonishing cinematography.

Don't Look Now (1973) Nicolas Roeg, UK, 110 min
This movie is a chilling example of the power of montage. Look at the opening and closing montage sequences, a mode of assembly that relies on intuition rather than forethought. Or look at the way connections are made between scenes, disrupting what we think we know about the film's world. This is filmmaking that says it's OK to rely on your creative, chaotic urges, pitted as they are against the needs of the industry. The trick in this film is that the method neatly dovetails into the theme, of intuition versus logic, as Donald Sutherland treads a line between the two. Unlike Roeg, he courts disaster.

Double Indemnity (1944) Billy Wilder, USA, 106–min
This film helped to set the tone – resolutely dark – for a decade or more of thrillers. Watch it for the way it uses lighting, dominating it with shadow to expressive effect.

The Elephant Man (1980) David Lynch, USA, 124 min
A depiction of Victorian London as steamy hell, stunningly photographed in black and white by Freddie Francis.

Eraserhead (1976) David Lynch, USA, 89 min
A low-budget classic that uses sound in new and unique ways, and demonstrates that you can make a great film over several years while holding down a day job.

Fargo (1995) Joel Coen, USA, 98 min

Freaks (1932) Tod Browning, USA, 64 min
A unique film detailing the solidarity of the physically malformed against the cruel disregard of the physically perfect in a travelling circus, it is now recognized as a masterpiece of cinema.

The Garden (1990) Derek Jarman, UK, 92 min
An array of dreams from the director's mind shot with a budget that belies the quality and intensity of the images, this film inspires the low-budget filmmaker with big ideas.

Gas, Food, Lodging (1991) Allison Anders, USA, 101 min

Goodfellas (1990) Martin Scorsese, USA, 145 min

The Grandmother (1970) David Lynch, USA, 35 min
An emotionally strong film that blends a brief narrative with abstract scenes and animation, this is a low-budget film unlike any other.

La Haine (1995) Mathieu Kassovitz, France, 98 min
Gritty black and white images depicting 24 hours in the life of three frustrated and angry Parisian boys.

The Hairdresser's Husband (1990) Patrice Leconte, France, 80 min
Exquisite photography and an underlying, understated eroticism told with lingering edits and poignant tracking shots.

Happiness (1999) Todd Solondz, USA, 139 min

The Haunting (1963) Robert Wise, UK, 112 min

Hearts of Darkness: A Filmmaker's Apocalypse (1991) Fax Bahr/George Hickenlooper, USA, 96 min
A fascinating and cautionary documentary of the making of Francis Ford Coppola's *Apocalypse Now* (1979).

The Ice Storm (1997) Ang Lee, USA, 113 min

I Walked with a Zombie (1943) Jacques Tourneur, USA, 69 min

Kes (1969) Ken Loach, UK, 113 min
A sparse, taut film that sits within the social realist stream of European movies, this is the tale of a young boy who escapes for a while the grim life of a coal mining community, told with simple, documentary-style camerawork, long edits and no softened storytelling. Notable also for Chris Menges's photography, director of *A World Apart* (1987).

M (1931) Fritz Lang, Germany, 118 min

The Magnificent Ambersons (1942) Orson Welles, USA, 88 min

Manhattan (1979) Woody Allen, USA, 96 min
The first sequence of images of New York is among the most evocative opening scenes in which the photography of Gordon Willis pushes to the limits the effect of light on film. Willis uses film and light as a northern Renaissance painter, picking out enough form and detail to reveal the subject but always presenting the idea of the city in a new way.

The Man Who Fell to Earth (1976) Nicolas Roeg, UK, 140 min

A Matter of Life and Death (1946) Emeric Pressburger/Michael Powell, UK, 104 min

Memento (2000) USA, 115 min
A remarkable film that takes us through a narrative in reverse. Look at it for ideas on how to make ideas and script do all the work, if you are on a tight budget.

My Life as a Dog (1985) Lasse Hallstrom, Sweden, 101 min

Naked (1993) Mike Leigh, UK, 131 min

The Night of the Hunter (1955) Charles Laughton, USA, 93 min

Night of the Living Dead (1969) George A. Romero, USA, 96 min
A low-budget classic, filmed whenever the actors and crew could get away from their day jobs, over a period of time that defies its smooth continuity.

North by Northwest (1959) Alfred Hitchcock, USA, 136 min
For the Hitchcock fan this paranoid thriller is one of the high points of the director's career. For the filmmaker, the use of long, non-verbal sequences, not always during action, shows to startling effect how far removed from the stage or literature is film. Meaning is visual in this movie, as in so many of his, with Hitchcock's schooling in silent film coming to the fore.

Nosferatu, The Vampire (1922) F. W. Murnau, Germany, 6453 ft, 74 min
An expressionist version of the Dracula tale, this film uses light and dark more effectively than any other horror film since, using suggestion rather than explicit thrills to evoke menace from the strange Count Orlock.

O Brother, Where Art Thou? (2000) Joel Coen, USA
A deceptively loose tale of three convicts on the run across 1930s America, this is a staggering series of tableaux, infused with mythology. Its images are strange and captivating, its style comic but reflective, this is a film like no other. And yet it makes connections with the Golden Age of Hollywood

with an unexpectedly moral conclusion, biblical in its scale but never high-handed. Watch it for striking images and use of colour.

Once Upon a Time in America (1983) Sergio Leone, USA, 229 min

On the Waterfront (1954) Elia Kazan, USA, 108 min

Passionless Moments (1984) Jane Campion, Australia

Paths of Glory (1957) Stanley Kubrick, USA, 86 min

Performance (1970) Nicolas Roeg/Donald Cammell, UK, 105 min

The Piano (1993) Jane Campion, Australia, 120 min

The Player (1992) Robert Altman, USA, 124 min
Watch this one for its damning look inside Hollywood.

Psycho (1960) Alfred Hitchcock, USA, 109 min

Pulp Fiction (1994) Quentin Tarantino, USA, 154 min
Watch this film for an insider's view of post-modern filmmaking, and for the extraordinary structure of the narrative.

Rear Window (1954) Alfred Hitchcock, USA, 112 min

The Red Shoes (1948) Emeric Pressburger/Michael Powell, UK, 133 min

Reservoir Dogs (1991) Quentin Tarantino, USA, 99 min

Secrets and Lies (1995) Mike Leigh, UK, 141 min

Sex, Lies and Videotape (1989) Steven Soderbergh, USA, 100 min

Shadows (1959) John Cassavetes, USA, 89 min

She's Gotta Have It (1986) Spike Lee, USA, 85 min

The Shining (1980) Stanley Kubrick, UK, 146 min

Stranger Than Paradise (1984) Jim Jarmusch, USA/Germany, 89 min
A stepping stone in the history of independent film, this is a unique study in character, as two friends find themselves travelling through the usual road movie backdrop, but with considerably more style and emotional impact.

The Tales of Hoffmann (1951) Michael Powell/Emeric Pressburger, UK, 127 min
It is useful to watch a key Scorsese movie such as *Goodfellas* after seeing *The Tales of Hoffmann*, as the director has talked about the influence of this film on his work. Intense music and sharp compositions leave nothing to chance – high theatrical cinema at its most lavish.

Taxi Driver (1976) Martin Scorsese, USA, 114 min

The Terence Davies Trilogy (1974–1983) Terence Davies, UK, 85 min
Watch this movie, in fact three short movies put together, for the beautiful images and lingering editing.

The Thin Blue Line (1988) Errol Morris, USA, 101 min
The film that marked a turning point for the documentary form, this film is one of the most important independent films of the 1980s, not least because it overturned the wrongful conviction of its subject, but also for the poetic way it presents elusive fact. Using reconstructions, like returning memories, and interspersed with interviews, it has the feel of narrative fiction and was indeed presented as a non-fiction film rather than documentary, but it retains a zest for truth.

The Thing (1982) John Carpenter, USA, 109 min

The Third Man (1949) Carol Reed, UK, 104 min
Robert Krasker's noir camerawork makes this a classic of cinematography.

Three Colours: Blue (Trois Couleurs: Bleu) (1993) Krzysztof Kieslowski, France, 98 min
Remarkable cinematography and a belief in the symbolism and power of colour.

Trainspotting (1995) Danny Boyle, UK, 93 min

True Stories (1986) David Byrne, USA, 89 min

TwentyFourSeven (1997) Shane Meadows, UK, 96 min
Characterization, images and jaunty editing are paramount in Meadows' second, low-budget feature.

The Vanishing (Spoorloos) (1988) George Sluizer, Netherlands/France, 106 min

Vertigo (1958) Alfred Hitchcock, USA 128 min

Walkabout (1970) Nicolas Roeg, Australia, 100 min

Wings of Desire (Der Himmel uber Berlin) (1987) Wim Wenders, Germany/France, 128 min

Wisconsin Death Trip (1999) James Marsh, UK, 60 min

A non-fiction film with some of the most extraordinary cinematography, it recounts from newspaper stories the lives and deaths of the occupants of a small American town.

The Wizard of Oz (1939) Victor Fleming, USA, 101 min

The Yards (2001), James Gray, USA, 113 min
The atmosphere generated here is compelling, the result dense and dramatic, accomplished within the scope of the low-budget filmmaker.

Glossary of film and video terms

4:1:1 A way of measuring the ratio between brightness signal and colour signals. This ratio is the smallest and is roughly 50 per cent of the value of 4:2:2 in terms of horizontal colour resolution (vertical colour resolution remains the same). Panasonic's DVC Pro uses this ratio.

4:2:0 This sampling ratio is very similar to 4:1:1, except that it is the vertical colour resolution values which are reduced by 50 per cent, while the horizontal remains the same.

4:2:2 This is a higher quality resolution used by many high-end cameras, including Digital Betacam and Sony's DVC Pro 50. Resolution is about twice the value of 4:1:1 or 4:2:0.

4:4:4:4 This sampling rate is as high as 4:2:2 but has an additional Key signal.

A

A/D conversion This is another way of saying analog-to-digital conversion. Data coming from an analog device such as a VHS camera or a VCR will need to be translated into digital information before editing software can read them. It looks at the curved electrical waves present in analog information and reduces them to jagged shapes able to be described in numbers.

AES/EBU These refer to the Audio Engineering Society and the European Broadcasting Union, and relate to standards that have been agreed for transmission of audio data.

Aliasing Aliasing refers to the degrading of video pictures by high-frequency video information. This results in jagged edges or lines, strobing effects on sharp horizontal lines and on rotating objects such as wheels.

Alpha channel Alpha channel is used for placing transparent elements over your picture, such as text. When you type in a line of credits, for example, they will need to be seen with the text opaque and the background transparent. This transparency is the alpha channel function.

Alternative cinema   A loose term ascribed to any group of films defined by common characteristics, which is in opposition to the dominant, narrative, mainstream film.

Ambient sound   Also referred to as 'presence', this is the natural background sound of a set or location. It needs to be maintained throughout a scene to ensure continuity.

Analog   This is the method of storing information that was dominant until digital arrived. It involves the recording of information using variable waves, as opposed to digital, which operates only in terms of yes or no, one or zero. Analog data is transferred by the recorder copying the electrical information, but it will lose some of this information each time it copies, leading to an increasing loss of quality in each subsequent copy.

Angle   The point of view of the camera.

Animatic   A simple animated sequence made from a storyboard, mostly used for television commercials.

Anti-aliasing   This is a way of getting smoother pictures in video and graphics. It works by blurring the edges slightly on curved or tilted objects.

Aperture   The round hole, the iris, at the front of the lens through which light enters the camera. It is measured in f-stops, with a smaller f-stop number referring to a larger opening, which allows more light to pass through. Each stop admits 100 per cent more light than the last. F-stops also affect depth of field, smaller iris holes allowing more objects to remain in focus.

Art cinema   A term loosely applied to any film which rejects the dominant mode of filmmaking and is characterized by a high degree of personal expression. For example: Ingmar Bergman, Peter Greenaway.

Artefact   This refers to interference that occurs on video images due to technical limitations or due to excessive data compression.

ASC   American Institute of Cinematographers.

Aspect ratio   This is the relative lengths of the horizontal and vertical sides of the video image. Television tends to use a ratio of 4:3, with 16:9 becoming more prevalent.

Audio mixer   A device or software program for mixing sounds from various sources, such as microphone, CD, tape.

Auteur   A term ascribed to a particular kind of director whose control over their films is such that they can be said to be the 'author', despite the large number of people involved in the movie. Auteurs develop a body of work through repeating, or developing, certain key concerns in their films.

B

Back light   Any light that comes from behind the subject, lighting up the background and reverse of the subject.

Bandwidth   This describes the rate at which certain amounts of data can be transmitted over a given period of time, usually a second. Modems are graded by how many bits of information they can accept per second, while the level of connection to the telephone network also affects the data rate.

Batch digitizing   Batch digitizing is the process of recording data consisting of video clips onto the hard drive, from a DV tape or other format. Only when it has been digitized onto the hard drive can it be edited. When a movie is being cut on digital equipment, a great amount of footage may require a high compression rate, resulting in less data taking up space on the hard disk. However, as the movie gets cut together, space is left over from the redundant footage and the remaining clips used in the film can be re-digitized at a lower compression rate, resulting in a much higher quality image.

Betacam   Until digital, this was the highest analog video format available. Recent years have seen the development of Betacam SX, a digital version using MPEG–2 high compression rates.

Bidirectional mic   A microphone which picks up sound on two sides of the mic.

Bit   A binary digit, the most basic unit in digital technology, not to be confused with a byte.

Boom   A microphone attached to an extension arm which is held above or below the action, out of view of the camera.

Breakout box   An attachment to a computer commonly bought as part of a capture card set-up, which allows the user to plug-in and digitize analog signals.

Bricolage   The combination of different styles and genres of cinema, it reflects the use of post-modernism in film.

Broadcast quality   This is a standard which all television licensees are required to adhere to, maintaining the highest possible picture resolution. Betacam SP is often regarded as the benchmark and those DV systems which match it are seen as broadcast quality. In technical terms, a compression rate of 1:2 (which is as low as possible) or a data rate of 50 Mbits per second are correct.

Browser   A piece of software which allows the user to view Internet contents.

Byte   One byte is equal to 8 bits of digital information.

C

Call sheet   A daily list of who is needed for that day's shooting, what parts of the script will be covered and where this will be.

Capture   The means of digitizing analog material or recording digital material onto a computer. Specific software is available to accomplish this, but it is also a part of editing software.

Capture card   Also known as a digitizer, this is a board that connects to the computer and enables video digital signals to be read. Some also allow analog to be read by first converting them into digital signal, hence the name digitizer.

Cardioid mic   A type of microphone which has a range spreading in a heart shape on both sides of the mic.

Charge-Coupled Device   A chip situated near the camera lens which converts images into digital information.

Chrominance   This is the colour part of the video signal referring to hue and saturation, the other being the luminance, or brightness, of the signal.

Clip   A single sequence of video footage.

Close-up (CU)   A shot of a subject which usually shows the head from the neck up.

Codec   Compressor/decompressor. A piece of technology which enables the compression of video. In order to be able to view (to decompress) the compressed movie, the viewer must have a copy of the same codec as the sender.

Colour temperature   A term describing the colour value of certain light sources. Light sources which are blue/white, such as winter sunlight, have a high colour temperature, while candlelight, which emits an orange cast on the subject, is very low.

Compression   Since so many data are generated by video files, methods have been developed for reducing the sizes of these files and making editing more feasible for smaller systems. There are many methods of compression, differing in what parts of the video signal they economize on and what information is excluded. Compression often results in a loss of visible picture quality, but in some cases, notably MPEG–2, quality is visibly equal to the original uncompressed version.

Contact mic   A microphone which is attached to a surface, for recording musical instruments.

Continuity   The means of maintaining the smooth flow of events within narrative film.

Continuity editing   A method of editing, dominant in Hollywood cinema, which determines that the style of editing must be as invisible as possible and that the viewer can become immersed in the plot and characters.

Contrast   The degree to which the brightness (luminance) of the video image contains light and shadow. A high-contrast picture has few middle tones and mostly bright light and deep shadow.

Crane   A piece of camera equipment which can move in any direction. Video cranes now also have the facility to be remotely operated, obtaining greater varieties of shot.

Cross-cutting   A way of editing a simple dialogue sequence in which the two actors are shot symmetrically, cutting between the two.

Cut   The transition from one scene to another in editing.

Cutaway   A shot away from the main action.

D

D1, D2, D3, D5, D6, D7, D9   Video formats for recording, developed by different companies to provide varying levels of sound and vision resolution. D1 is the most expensive form of recording, used in high-end work. Sony's D2 has all but been discontinued, as the rival to this format, Panasonic's D3, has gained ground. D5 is the favourite for post-production work because it works without data reduction. D6 allows for 12 audio channels, developed by Philips, while D7 is the standard for Panasonic's DVC Pro. D9 was developed by JVC and marketed as Digital S.

DAT   Digital Audio Tape offers 3 hours of digital sound on a tape half the size of an analog audio cassette tape. DAT is the only consumer recording standard that does not compress audio data, meaning that the whole signal is held on the tape. DAT is easy to use on location; indexing of the tape and rewinding are extremely fast (50 seconds for a 120-minute tape) so you can quickly access any place on the DAT tape.

Data rate   The amount of data that can be transmitted in a set period of time.

Depth of field   The area within which objects are in focus. It varies according to the aperture (size of the iris).

Diagetic   This refers to the parts of a shot that directly relate to the narrative. Diagetic sound, for example, would refer to sounds emanating from the scene itself and not added later in post-production.

Digital   In video terms, a system of recording which records images in binary language, representing a mathematical model of the original signal. They do not degrade when copied, but are prone to other problems from the system that plays or stores the digital information.

Digital 8   A format for recording digital signals on Hi–8 tapes instead of the smaller DV tapes.

Digital S   See D9.

Digitize   The method of translating analog information into digital information.

Distribution   A term referring to the marketing of a movie between the production studio or filmmaker and theatres and broadcasters.

Documentary   A form of film which uses real events, either recorded or retold, as part of a thesis or narrative.

Dolby Digital   A multi-channel sound format in which five channels are stored as well as the additional woofer effect channel. Dolby is a trademark of Dolby Laboratories and is used in DVD and cinema projection.

Dolly   A camera support on wheels that can be moved in any direction.

DP   Director of Photography, a person responsible for overseeing how the camera is used on a movie and how the set is lit. To the DP, lighting is as crucial as camera angle.

Drop-frame timecode   A form of timecode which caters for the odd frame rate of 29.9 fps in NTSC television standard. It works by removing 108 frames – from the timecode *not* the film – per hour, but does *not* drop a frame every tenth minute. The result is accurate timecode in a whole number.

Dropped frames   A common problem of many edit software capture facilities. When capturing, a clip may lose several frames and this can lead to problems if the amount of these frames is sufficient to lead to jumps within the edit. Designated capture software, rather than editing software, is less likely to drop frames.

DV   A format for recording sound and vision on 6.35 mm wide tape. It compresses data at a rate of 5:1, sampling the image at 4:2:0 for PAL and 4:1:1 for NTSC. It functions at a rate of 25 megabits per second.

DVCAM   A format for recording sound and vision, developed by Sony. The difference with DV is that it runs on wider tape track (15 mm) and the tape speed is higher, resulting in shorter playing times for cassettes.

DVC Pro   A format for recording video and sound developed by Panasonic. It is similar in quality to DV, but uses wider tape (18 mm) and has a slightly higher chrominance level.

DVC Pro 50   A tape format similar to DVC Pro, but using a higher sampling rate of 4:2:2 and double (50) the megabits per second to that of DV.

DVD   Digital Verstaile Disc. A method of storing large amounts of video material on small, CD-sized discs (12 cm diameter).

E

Edit Decision List (EDL)   The EDL is a list of shots that are to compose a final cut for a movie, listed in the form of the timecode at the start and end of the appropriate clips on the footage tape.

ENG   Electronic News Gathering. This refers mainly to the use of light, mobile equipment for news reports in situ.

Establishing shot   A shot, usually at the start of a scene, which informs the audience of the basic elements of the scene: who is present, what period in history, what time of day and so on.

Extreme close-up (ECU)   A camera angle which, when on a face, focuses only on the eyes or mouth.

F

Fill light   After a key light has set the main focus of light on a subject, a fill light softens the effect.

Filter   In non-linear video editing, a filter refers to a special visual effect, such as cropping, stretching or re-colouring an image.

FireWire   See IEEE 1394.

Focal length   A measurement of the magnification of a lens indicated in millimetres. A zoom lens allows the camera to film closer or farther from the subject, without moving either, because it has a variable focal length.

Focus   A point at which the rays of light from a subject converge after passing through a lens, resulting in maximum sharpness of vision.

Frame   The smallest unit of video footage, In each second of video there are, in the PAL standard, 25 frames per second (fps). NTSC uses 29.9 fps.

Framing   The process of arranging the elements of a scene within the camera viewfinder.

G

Gaffer   A crew member responsible for the placing and rigging of lighting equipment.

Generation loss   In video reproductions, this refers to any loss of picture or sound quality resulting from the copying of information. In DV editing, it is rare to encounter losses, but successive compression and decompression of a clip will result in losses occurring.

Genre   A way of categorizing movies in which a group of films share characteristics such as story, style, setting and so on. Genre is increasingly being fragmented in recent years, with movies fusing different genres together in bricolage.

Gigabyte   One gigabyte equals 1024 megabytes.

Grip   Crew member responsible for handling props, scenery and equipment.

H

Hard disk   A magnetic storage component of a computer for recording large quantities of data. A hard disk is measured not just by the amount of data it can store, but by the speed at which it revolves, enhancing performance.

Hi 8   An analog video format geared towards the consumer market.

HMI lamps   Very powerful lamps which replaced arc lamps on sets.

Hollywood cinema   A term ascribed to a collection of conventions of filmmaking, including continuity editing, character identification and certain moral codes, which gained its peak in the Hollywood of the 1920s.

Hypercardioid mic   A type of microphone which has an extremely narrow pick-up but which works well in picking up sounds at long distances.

I

IEEE 1394 (FireWire, iLink)   A standard method of transmitting data, connecting a peripheral (camera or VCR) to a computer. It is far superior to any other cable used in video and transmits at a rate of 400 Mb per second, four times faster than the main consumer connection, USB.

Independent film   Strictly speaking, an independent film is one which has not been financed by a major production studio, but with independent production houses being bought up by larger companies, it has also come to denote a certain approach to filmmaking based on challenging movie convention, either in terms of subject matter or style.

Insert   A cut which is inserted into the action as a cutaway. It also refers to a method of analog editing in which clips can be inserted into a programme without disturbing the control track.

Interlace   A term used in video referring to the way picture information is split up. A first field contains all the uneven lines of the picture, while the second field contains all the even lines, so in the PAL standard, 50 fields are transmitted, leading to 25 frames – the human eye cannot distinguish between the two sets of fields, reading them as one image.

Iris   The opening at the front of the lens which allows light to enter the camera.

ITU   International Telecommunications Union, a body which oversees technical standards in broadcasting.

J

JPEG   A method of compressing data for still images, standardized by the Joint Photographic Experts Group.

Jump cut   A tool used by some directors to introduce disturbance into a scene, produced by cutting between two shots of the same subject but from slightly different angles, within the 30-degree rule.

K

Key frame   A way of determining how a clip is altered, by the use of filters, transitions or fades. A key frame is marked at the start, middle and end of the clip, with appropriate settings given for each part.

Key light   A main dominant lamp which focuses on the subject.

L

Lavalier mic   A type of microphone which is clipped to the actor or attached to a section of a set, with limited pick-up range, but discreet and flexible.

Layers   A term referring to the layers of video which are composited together to form a final cut, including superimposed images or text.

LCD display   A small monitor attached to consumer camcorders which enables better quality viewing of an image.

Levels   Commonly used in association with sound, this refers to the relative volume of different audio tracks. In compression, the term is used to describe the quality steps in MPEG.

Linear editing   A term referring to analog editing systems in which two or more VCRs are connected and clips are recorded from one to another in the correct sequence.

Logging   A term referring to the searching and noting of takes on a tape of footage. If timecode is used, this will determine more easily where tracks are located.

Longitudinal timecode (LTC)   A way of recording timecode in which the signal holding the code is recorded onto a sound track or separate longitudinal track.

Long shot   A wide image showing a panorama or landscape.

M

Match shot   A way of setting up two shots so that the camera cuts between them with no loss of continuity. Movements of the subject, lighting and camera angle are all arranged so that the matched shots blend seamlessly with each other.

Medium shot   A shot that shows the subject from the waist up.

Modem   A device for decoding data sent across the Internet via telephone cables. The speed of the modem determines the amount of data that can be received per second, measured in bits. Most consumer modems operate at a speed of 56 kb per second.

Monitor   A television screen attached to a camera while shooting so that a clearer view of the shot can be seen. It is useful for ensuring that colour, contrast and light values are kept at the same level throughout shooting. In digital editing, it is used to refer to the window in which clips are cut down to a more exact size before placing on the timeline.

Monopod   A one-legged camera support.

Montage   An approach to editing in which seemingly unlikely shots are placed together. Two shots can be made to create or suggest a third meaning. There are many variations of montage editing, including parallel montage, in which simultaneous events are told in parallel, and involuted montage, in which a narrative is told without regard for chronology.

MPEG   A standard for compressing video data. The difference between MPEG and other forms of compression is that MPEG is more sophisticated, analysing data from groups of frames and making decisions about what data can be excluded. MPEG–1 and MPEG–4 work with relatively low amounts of data and are suited to telecommunications. MPEG–2 is one of the most important versions, used in consumer DVD compression, and results in high-quality images.

Multimedia   A much misunderstood term used to refer to any interactive medium. Strictly speaking, it refers to the combining of more than one means of communication in one medium.

N

New Hollywood   A term referring to the development of a new kind of Hollywood movie in the 1970s, including such directors as Scorsese and Coppola.

Noise   A term referring to the variations in picture signal which produce unwelcome disturbances in quality. It refers most often to vision, despite its connotations with sound.

Non-linear editing   Also known as digital editing, this term is the more accurate one, since it refers to the ability of the editor to access and rearrange any part of the movie, without having to re-edit the rest of it, as was the case with linear, analog editing.

NTSC   National Television Standards Committee, a body which set standards for television transmission adopted in many territories, including the USA.

O

Off-line editing   When editing a movie, this refers to the process in which clips are edited on lower cost systems first and then passed on to an on-line editor for final cutting on more expensive systems. Since digital editing allows for high quality at very little cost, this practice is becoming obsolete.

Omnidirectional mic   A type of microphone which picks up sound from all around the mic.

On-line editing   This refers to the practice of compiling a final edit of a movie as a second stage cut, derived from the earlier, off-line edit.

P

PAL   Phase Alternating Line, a broadcasting standard used in the UK, Australia and other territories, which is based on a lower frame rate than NTSC, at 24 fps. But PAL also uses a greater number of lines on the screen, at 625, leading to a slightly higher resolution.

PALplus   A new system derived from PAL, but which uses a slightly different aspect ratio, 16:9, and which produces a higher quality of picture through pre-filtering of the video signal.

Pan   A horizontal movement of the camera at a fixed position to show several aspects of a setting, or following a subject in movement.

Parabolic mic   Not a mic as such, but a dish-like attachment to a mic which greatly enhances the pinpoint range of the mic, used with cardioid mics.

Pixel   A picture element or picture point, the smallest dot in the television screen. Video pictures are measured in pixels with PAL at 720×576 pixels.

Plan sequence   A French term referring to a single, uncut shot involving several camera movements to make a whole scene.

Plug-in   An extension to software which serves to extend the capacity of the software in some way. For example, many editing programs promote plug-ins capable of enhancing the range of special effects available in the program.

Point of view shot (POV)   A shot which aims to show the viewpoint of a subject, typically with a hand-held camera.

Post-modern   A term referring to a cultural development in the late twentieth century which still affects cinema. It is characterized by the borrowing and fusing of different elements from global and historical culture to forge provocative and interesting new combinations.

Post-production   The stage in filmmaking in which shots are edited, soundtrack is added and any further effects or modifications are made.

Post-structuralist   The movement away from the academic confines of the structuralist approach to analysing movies, gathering pace in the 1990s. It sought to move attention in film studies away from the movie itself and look at the spectator and the context within which the film is viewed.

Pre-production   In filmmaking, the stage in which the film is planned in terms of the script, visuals, budget, schedule and other demands, prior to the start of shooting (production).

Production   In filmmaking, the shooting stage of the process in which all clips and sounds are gathered.

Progressive download   In video streaming, this refers to a method of sending video data on the Internet that enables a movie to start playing before the whole file has downloaded. Picture quality is greater than with real-time downloading, though there is a slight wait to start playing the film, the length of which depends on the speed of your connection. A calculation is made as to how long it will take for the whole movie to download and the film starts playing only when there is enough video to sustain uninterrupted playback.

PZM   A pressure zone microphone, a small sensitive mic often fixed on the camcorder.

Q

QuickTime   A trademark of Apple Computers, this is one of the most popular video formats, enabling high-quality video data to be used on all types of computer.

R

RAM   Random Access Memory, the temporary data section of a computer which the processor is currently using at any given point, erased when it is switched off, when the data must be saved and transferred elsewhere.

Real-time downloading   A term used on the Internet to refer to video which is sent to the viewer without waiting for it to download. Picture quality is sacrificed for speed and it is mostly used for news clips and interviews, where resolution is less of an issue.

Real-time editing   A version of editing programs which offers reduced rendering ability, enabling the user to see effects and transitions on clips as soon as they are placed on the timeline, without having to wait for the program to render, or build, the files into a complete film.

Redhead   A type of lamp which has become a generic term for a strong, usually 800 W, tungsten halogen lamp made by the Ianiro company. It is versatile and can be used as much for main, key light as for other softer lights, using barn doors and reflectors to bounce the light.

Rendering   The process by which editing software builds video files and effects as one complete sequence. When editing, it is not possible to watch the film as it develops because each clip, and any effects placed on them, do not exist as one complete file and must first be rendered to see the movie. Certain programs offer real-time editing but these are often limited in their reduction of rendering.

Resolution   The clarity of the video picture, often another word for sharpness. In technical terms, resolution is measured in lines on the screen, pixels or megahertz. Although the screen may accept a certain level of resolution, each stage of production, including the kind of camera used, through to post-production, including the standard of editing equipment, can affect final picture resolution.

Rushes   Rushes are your footage, usually called this because you are looking at them soon after shooting in order to check how the film is progressing.

S

Sampling ratio   The amount of data displayed in terms of brightness and colour, or luminance and chrominance. Luminance is often sampled at a much higher rate than colours, often double the amount. Quantities such as 4:2:2, for example, refer to luminance and colour sampling, and vary according to the camera.

SECAM   Sequential Couleur Avec Memoire, a television broadcasting standard developed in France and used in many Eastern European nations. It is most similar to, and compatible with, PAL.

Server   A piece of central equipment which acts as a conduit for a user to access the Internet.

Shotgun mic   A type of microphone which has a narrow range and is pointed at the subject.

SMPTE/EBU timecode   The current standard timecode used in professional video. It consists of four pairs of digits – hours:minutes:seconds:frame – the last pair differs depending on what broadcasting standard is being used (maximum of 24 for PAL or 29 for NTSC).

Structuralism   A movement in academic circles in the 1970s which sought to understand the structures by which a film is made, but ignoring the variables inherent in the spectator's viewing of it. It was later superseded by post-structuralism.

Studio system   A term referring to the dominance of major studios in Hollywood in the classic period of Hollywood production from the 1920s until the 1950s, when a lawsuit broke the majors' stranglehold on film production and opened the doors to independent production.

Supercardioid mic   A type of microphone with a limited width of range, but which can pick up sounds up to 4 metres away.

T

Timecode   See SMPTE timecode.

Timeline   A window in digital editing programs on which the film is built clip by clip. Layers of images or text are placed on separate tracks on the timeline and the final arrangement is rendered to produce a movie.

Tracking shot   A movement of the camera alongside a moving subject.

Transition   A visual effect in editing programs, in which one clip merges into the next, for example by a dissolve, or by a wipe across the screen or other effect.

Trimming   The process of reducing the size of clips in editing programs, to the exact length required.

Tripod   A three-legged camera support.

U

Unidirectional mic   A versatile type of microphone which picks up sound in front of the mic.

V

VHS   Video Home System, the most common consumer analog format, developed by JVC, using 12.7 mm tape. VHS is not suitable for professional use because of its poor resolution.

Viewfinder   A part of the camera through which the image being recorded can be seen.

W

White balance   A feature of consumer camcorders which assesses the correct balance of light to ensure accurate colour representation.

Wide-angle lens   A lens with a short focal distance but which can focus on a wide range of objects in a frame.

Wild sound   Also referred to as non-synchronous sound, this encompasses all sounds not recorded on location or set, and not related to the action, but which add realism or effect.

X

XLR   In audio technology, the XLR–3 is a cable connection able to transmit high-quality audio signals.

Y

Y/C   A video signal connection in which luminance (Y) and chrominance (C) are transmitted separately, leading to higher picture quality, better than that achieved with composite signals. This connection is often referred to as S-Video.

Z

Zoom lens   A lens with a variable focus, enabling the camera to focus on subjects in the distance.

Bibliography

Books

Careers in Film and Video – Ricki Ostrov and Alison King. Kogan Page, 1992.

The Cinema Book – eds Cook and Bernick. BFI Publishing, 1999.

Dealmaking in the Film and Television Industry – Mark Litwak. Silman-James Press, 1994.

Digital Video A–Z. Fast Electronic, FAST, 1999.

Dogme 95 – Richard Kelly. Faber & Faber, 2000.

Don't Look Now – Mark Sanderson. BFI Publishing, 1996.

Film Art: An Introduction – Bordwell and Thompson. McGraw-Hill, 1993.

The Filmmaker's Art – Haig P. Manoogian. Basic Books, New York, 1966.

Film Production, The Complete Uncensored Guide – Greg Merritt. Lone Eagle, 1998.

Film Studies – eds John Hill and Pamela Church Gibson. OUP, 2000.

Genre, Star and Auteur, Introduction to Film Studies – Patrick Phillips. Routledge.

Hitchcock on Hitchcock – ed. Sidney Gottleib. Faber & Faber, 1995.

How to Read a Film (3rd edition) – James Monaco. OUP, 2000.

Independent Feature Film Production – Gregory Goodell. St Martin's Griffin, New York, 1998.

An Introduction to Film Studies – ed. Jill Neames. Routledge, 1996.

Key Concepts in Film and Cinema Studies – Susan Hayward. Routledge, 1996.

A Man with a Camera – Nestor Almendros. Faber & Faber, 1982.

A Personal Journey with Martin Scorsese Through American Movies – Martin Scorsese and Michael Henry Wilson. Faber & Faber, 1997.

Postmodernist Culture – Steven Connor. Blackwell, 1989.

Premiere Quick Start Guide – Antony Bolante. Peachpit Press, 1999.

Spike, Mike, Slackers and Dykes – John Pierson. Faber & Faber, 1995.

Time Out Film Guide – ed. John Pym. Penguin, 1999.

Techniques of the Selling Writer – Dwight Swain. University of Oklahoma Press, 1981.

The Videomaker Handbook – ed. Jim Stinson. Focal Press, 1996.

Video Production Handbook, Third Edition – Gerald Millerson. Focal Press, 2001.

Articles

Chapter 1:1

Interview with Grant Millar – www.netribution.co.uk.

Chapter 3:1

'Is it broadcast quality?' – Clark Brown. © Oak Tree Press, 1997, reproduced on www.videouniversity.com website, 2001.

Chapter 4:4

'Screenwriting' – article by Marilyn Ellsworth, www.screentalk.com, 2000.

Chapter 5

Quote from Next Wave Films founder, Peter Broderick – *Guardian* article by Chris Lakeman Fraser, 19 October 2000.

Chapter 5:7

'Better sound recording' – Fred Ginsburg. Equipment Emporium website, 1999.

Chapter 6:4

'Ambient sound – the silent killer' – article by Thomas Koch, Digital idiots website, 2001.

Chapter 7:2

'Power tips: Cleaner 5' – article by Martin Gisbourne and Joseph Linaschke, *DVWorld*, March 2001.

Chapter 7:4

'Users guide to webfilm' – Kate Stables, *Guardian Unlimited* (www.guardianunlimited.co.uk), 30 September 2000.

Chapter 8:1

Interview with Roseann S. Cherenson – www.indienetwork.com, May 2001–09–01.

Index

⨍ Focal Press

www.focalpress.com

Join Focal Press on-line

As a member you will enjoy the following benefits:

- an email bulletin with **information on new books**
- a regular **Focal Press Newsletter**:
    - o   featuring a selection of new titles
    - o   keeps you informed of **special offers, discounts and freebies**
    - o   alerts you to **Focal Press news and events** such as author signings and seminars
- complete access to **free content** and reference material on the focalpress site, such as the focalXtra articles and commentary from our authors
- a **Sneak Preview** of selected titles (sample chapters) *before* they publish
- a chance to have your say on our **discussion boards** and **review books** for other Focal readers

Focal Club Members are invited to give us feedback on our products and services.
Email: worldmarketing@focalpress.com – we want to hear your views!

Membership is **FREE**. To join, visit our website and register. If you require any further information regarding the on-line club please contact:

> Lucy Lomas-Walker
> Email: lucy.lomas-walker@repp.co.uk
> Tel: +44 (0) 1865 314438
> Fax: +44 (0)1865 314572
> Address: Focal Press, Linacre House,
> Jordan Hill, Oxford, UK, OX2 8DP

Catalogue

For information on all Focal Press titles, our full catalogue is available online at www.focalpress.com and all titles can be purchased here via secure online ordering, or contact us for a free printed version:

USA
Email: christine.degon@bhusa.com
Tel: +1 781 904 2607

Europe and rest of world
Email: jo.coleman@repp.co.uk
Tel: +44 (0)1865 314220

Potential authors

If you have an idea for a book, please get in touch:

USA
editors@focalpress.com

Europe and rest of world
focal.press@repp.co.uk